Penguin Education

Political Sociology

Edited by Alessandro Pizzorno

KU-570-636

Penguin Modern Sociology Readings

General Editor
Tom Burns

Political Sociology

Selected Readings

Edited by Alessandro Pizzorno

Penguin Books

Penguin Books Ltd, Harmondsworth,
Middlesex, England
Penguin Books Inc., 7110 Ambassador Road,
Baltimore, Md 21207, U.S.A.
Penguin Books Australia Ltd,
Ringwood, Victoria, Australia

First published 1971
This selection copyright © Alessandro Pizzorno, 1971
Introduction and notes copyright © Alessandro Pizzorno, 1971

Made and printed in Great Britain by
Cox & Wyman Ltd,
London, Reading and Fakenham
Set in Intertype Times

Contents

Introduction

In his book, *Social Science and Political Theory*, Runciman assigns the birth of political sociology to that moment in the history of political thought when the distinction between the social and the political was established. The new concept of 'civil society' emerged in opposition to the concept of state. Runciman fixes the 1840s, when Marx wrote his criticism of Hegel's *Philosophy of Law* and Von Stein his history of nineteenth-century social movements, as the moment of the first empirical delineation of this distinction. The concept of society was, indeed, a new one, but it was also the fruit of a long process of intellectual elaboration. Hobbes, Locke, Ferguson and finally Hegel had all added new dimensions and clarity to it. By the middle of the nineteenth century, it had come to denote the system of social exchange relationships, or more concretely, the domain of the capitalist economy. In fact, the emergence of this concept had coincided with the emergence of the bourgeoisie as an autonomous and dominant class. Control through exchange seemed on the verge of taking the place of the traditional forms of authority. As a consequence, political phenomena were considered to be dependent on social structure. Sociologists, political theorists and even historians, of both the right and the left – Comte as well as Marx, De Bonald as well as Guizot – were all in agreement on this point.

In a certain sense, the concepts of 'civil' society, social structure and social system provided intellectuals with the theoretical weapon with which to challenge the politicians. In effect, they said: 'We know the laws which govern social events; you politicians don't really amount to much since what you do can never change these laws. Your reforms are mere illusions, and your power is mere pretence; neither can affect the course of history.' Perhaps this was the intellectuals' revenge after the bitter disappointment of the French Revolution. Their hopes of collaboration with the new political class in the total reform of man and society had ended miserably. By mocking the 'ideologues', Napoleon had driven students of society and politics to work out the laws of social reality at a deeper level, at which they would be invulnerable to the control and understanding, as well as the ridicule, of the politicians.

This distinction between state and society has had, furthermore, a strange history of its own. It has prospered in continental Europe, never really disappearing from the political culture, although it achieved somewhat less prominence in British social thought. In the United States, on the other hand, it has been almost unknown. When modern political science developed there, it left out the concept of state. Thanks mainly to the work of Bentley, 'power' became the central object in the study of politics. Political groups, struggling with one another to increase their power, were seen as the protagonists of the political process. The distinction between state and society was contradicted by the reality of the American social system. And it became clear that this was only an extreme case of a process which had also taken place in Europe, the merging of the bourgeoisie and the state apparatus.

When the state, in industrially advanced societies, developed new forms of autonomous activity, it became necessary to devise new conceptual tools. The concept of political group began to appear insufficient. The 'systems' approach, which is represented in this volume by Easton, is one of the major responses to this theoretical challenge. It has the merit of pointing to the wholeness and interdependence of the political world, but lacks the capacity to grasp the specificity of modern politics. As a result, the categories of state and society have reappeared, but this time they derive their intellectual impact from two different theoretical traditions. On the one hand, the distinction has been developed by what we may call the historical or comparative or Weberian school of political sociology. According to Collins (in his article, 'A comparative approach to political sociology'): 'In the sphere of "society", groups are formed as "constellations of interests", in which the parties act together voluntarily for what they feel is their mutual benefit. ... In the sphere of the "state", coordination is based on dominance, in which one individual or group is placed in a position to enforce his will on others.' Collins's article is part of a reader with the 'polemical' title *State and Society*, a representative collection of the major examples of work employing this approach. Historical and comparative analysis dominate, and the concepts of interest and of the struggle for the defence of interests replace those of function and of the integration of the social system.

On the other hand, the refusal to employ functional categories and the utilization of the state–society distinction also characterizes a wing of neo-Marxist thought, which, at least in part, is an outgrowth of the work of Gramsci. For writers in this tradition the theoretical problem, and for some the practical problem as well, is to distinguish between political activity which challenges power in the societal sphere and political activity which does so in the sphere of the state alone.

Mention of this latter problem introduces another criterion which I have used in the selection of the texts for Part One and which seems to me to be as important as the distinction between state and society even though it is generally obscured or entirely ignored. It is the distinction between two possible meanings of the term 'political' and thus also between two types of political action. When the social thinkers of the nineteenth century interpreted the 'political' to be merely an outgrowth of social structural phenomena, they meant by 'politics' the working of state institutions, administrative activity, the promotion or defence of private interests according to the rules of the system. But at the same time, the French Revolution had already given political action a new and more fundamental content. Tocqueville was the first to grasp this new phenomenon. In the Reading which opens this collection, he shows how political activity during the revolution had assumed many of the characteristics which had formerly been associated with religious life. It was not, however, the same phenomenon which had been evident in previous civil wars motivated by religious differences, such as the English civil wars of the seventeenth century. In those, the religious motivation had been conscious and explicit, while political activity was, at least nominally, nothing more than the expression of one's religion. In the French Revolution the opposite had been true; political activity had no religious motivation, but had acquired the qualities of total commitment to universal goals which previously had been confined to religious movements. And Tocqueville, in admirable fashion, traces out the roots of this phenomenon in the political system which had preceded the Revolution. The administrative centralization of the absolute monarchy had made the idea of '*l'homme en général*' the object of political activity. If every man was considered the equal of any other in the eyes of the political authority, then every act of that authority, every political act, necessarily acquired universal significance. In such a situation, neither the abstract politics of the '*philosophes*' seeking to establish a spiritual power of their own, nor, thereafter, the practical politics of the revolutionaries, could avoid assuming religious characteristics.

Marx himself, in one of his first published works, 'On the Jewish question', recognized this new relationship between politics and religion. He attributed its early causes to the split between political society and religious society during the Reformation; and later, to the separation between the state and civil society as a result of the development of the bourgeoisie. While the state remained the seat of politics in its daily, technico-administrative sense, civil society became the battleground for man's total emancipation, that is, for the class struggle which was, by nature, altogether different from the political conflicts which took place within the sphere of the state.

Let me briefly review the preceding discussion: our contemporary conception of politics is the consequence of two strands of social and intellectual development. The first led to the distinction between the society and the state, between the social and the political, and to the conclusion that the latter was determined by the former.

The second pointed to the dual nature of politics itself: that of politics as administration, and as the clash between groups and individuals pursuing their interests within the rules of a particular institutional system, in other words, as the pursuit of negotiable ends; the other, as the politics of total commitment, as the effort to transform society as a whole, as the pursuit of non-negotiable ends. Revolutionary 'praxis' as defined by Marx, and the politics of the class struggle in general, are examples of this second type. Since the French Revolution, both these components, though in varying proportions, have been present in every political commitment, in every political situation. And they are present as well in contemporary political discourse. When we say that politics is a 'dirty game' we can nevertheless imagine other political activity pursuing higher goals; when we believe we are committed to changing the world, we nevertheless keep open, more or less consciously, the possibility of negotiation.

In attacking ideologues and 'abstract' intellectuals, latter-day political scientists have often insisted that politics is essentially the art of compromise and negotiation. Their arguments are justified if they are meant as a critique of naïve idealism in the analysis of politics. But it becomes mere wishful thinking when one refuses to recognize that political actions are also oriented toward non-negotiable ends, and do not always conform to the rules of the existing institutional systems. Too much of politics escapes our comprehension and comes to be considered merely the expression of irrational impulses if one declines to consider *both* of its possible forms.

It is, therefore, this broad conception of politics which has guided the general selection of Readings for this anthology. The themes for the individual parts have been selected with a preference for the controversial over the resolved. That is, I have preferred those pieces of sociological work which, though their methodology may not always meet modern professional standards, are relevant to the contemporary political debate. Unfortunately, for reasons of space, I have had to omit work on politics in the Third World from this volume.

In the first part, as we have noted above, the theme is that of the limits of politics, of the ambiguity of the ends which guide political action. The theme of Part Two is the structure of power in states which have experienced the industrial and bourgeois revolutions. How can one describe the structure of power in the contemporary state? Who governs? How do they govern? For whom do they govern? The simplest response to these questions is found in Marxist thought where government, it is claimed, is nothing more than the administrative board of the bourgeoisie. The expression is forceful but generic, and brings us no closer to a model adequate for the analysis of concrete situations. When Marx examines specific historical events, his conclusions vary markedly from this formula. In the text of the *Eighteenth Brumaire*, which is included below, his analysis of the autonomous development of the administrative machinery of the state during a series of diverse political regimes could have easily been endorsed by Tocqueville. The state and the various social classes are judged to have a complex relationship, rather than a uni-directional one. The class most directly represented in the organs of state is that of the small landholders, not the grand bourgeoisie, even though the latter was just in that period consolidating its economic power. And the state is perceived as maintaining a certain degree of freedom from the bourgeoisie. It is seen, that is, as an actor with its own interests, not simply as the direct representative of a single social class (even though, of course, it can never be 'above' the conflict of classes). Marx, in short, considers the analysis of the social relationships of production a necessary, but not sufficient, condition for understanding the specific phenomenon of political power.

A similar observation can be made about the theory of elites which, since the work of Mosca, has always enjoyed some degree of favour. That a few command while the many obey is so obvious as to be banal. Its success can only be explained by observing that a particular culture exchanged the doctrine of popular sovereignty for a theory which described reality. Mosca, however, goes beyond that assertion: the few who command are also those who live at the expense of the many who obey and produce. Furthermore, the 'political formula' by which a regime establishes its legitimacy is always an outgrowth of relationships grounded in force. First, a social group imposes itself on another through the use of force; then it legitimizes its dominion with a 'political formula' around which it organizes a consensus. And if one remains at this level of generality, Marx and Mosca, and even, in part, Weber agree on certain fundamental principles. But more acute instruments of analysis are needed if one wishes to study the exercise of political power in contemporary societies. Without this effort to develop more specific models, as the Reading of Marx on the state and that of Dahl on elites included in this volume show, we can never go beyond the general indications furnished by the classics. Who are these few who govern? That is to say, on the basis of what other characteristics can they be identified? How are they subdivided, what groups do they form? What interests do they explicitly, or *implicitly*, represent? How are the agreements reached by which the equilibrium of power is maintained? By what process is power accumulated, that is, how does power become concentrated in such a way that the government can operate? The texts I have included represent examples of possible responses to these questions. Even if they do not succeed in constructing a model of the organization of political power, they do underline certain central points.

First, both Mills and Kaysen, beginning from very different premises, show that the importance of large economic enterprises in the political systems of the economically advanced countries is constantly increasing. These enterprises not only represent a large concentration of power which they can use to exert pressure on the government when it is in their interests to do so, but they also enjoy a great deal of *indirect* power. This resides, first, in the fact that the decisions that these enterprises can make may affect the destiny of a substantial portion of a population in the same way as those made by officials or heads of state. To give such types of decisions a different name than 'political' amounts to playing with words. Second, it resides in the fact that the decisions taken by political authorities are deeply conditioned by the very existence of these large organizations, that is, their interests need not *explicitly* be present in the Cabinet chamber or the Minister's office. This observation will explain why I have not included in this anthology any examples of the numerous studies, especially of local politics, which tend to measure the power of political actors by the frequency of their presence at times when decisions are made. Despite the utility and interest of these studies, they are not of direct relevance to the problem I have chosen to illustrate here, which is: in what way does the presence of a particular kind of organization influence the orientation of a political system, even when it does not intervene directly in the process of administrative decision-making?

In addition to those organizations directly involved in the productive process, there are other institutions capable of concentrating a great deal of power. Mills points to the army in a country like the United States, particularly when it is fighting overseas. In other circumstances the same form of analysis could be applied to the state bureaucracy. In other words, the structure of political relationships is characterized by organizations or institutions capable of transforming a concentration of productive, financial, military or other types of resources into political power. The key to power, then, is to be found in those structures where the resources which can be utilized to promote certain interests are concentrated. This is not yet a full answer to the question about who is in power, but it is an important step toward it.

The large organizations cannot help but be actors in the political process. Their mere existence dictates such a role. Pressure groups, on the other hand, openly seek to influence the political authorities in order to assure particular decisions. As such, they are more elements of the system through which particular interests battle over scarce resources, than of the structure of power in its more global sense. Beer shows that the system of pressure groups corresponds to an oligopolistic market. The large groups are the focus of most of the power and, through a process of negotiation with one another, make all the decisions in which they have an interest. The specific characteristic of this type of negotiation is that each negotiating unit is considerably dependent on all the others, since each has some sector in which it enjoys a monopoly. In such a system of partial monopolies, even the political parties become merely large groups like the others, exercising monopoly control in specific, and restricted, spheres: for example, the organization of consensus, or the assignment of public offices not controlled by the bureaucracy.

Political parties are probably the institution which best characterizes the contemporary political system, and Part Three is devoted both to them and to pressure groups. The debate about their changing nature has not been confined to professional political science, but has spread to more practical political discussion as well. It has, in fact, become clear that the traditional model of the political party is no longer sufficient if we wish to understand its mode of operation and the role it plays in contemporary society. The work of Duverger provided the focus, at the beginning of the 1950s, for a most important controversy on the developmental trends in the organizations of modern parties. The French scholar, using a Weberian scheme of classification, distinguishes between mass parties and cadre parties. The former are stably organized, both at the centre and in local sections, participation is continuous, and the interests of the party take precedence over electoral exigencies; the latter are organized to fulfil an electoral and parliamentary function, and participation is scarce and discontinuous. Duverger argues that the mass parties will become an increasing part of modern politics while the cadre parties are destined to disappear. At first, American scholars repeated this classification, while at the same time emphasizing the differences between 'responsible' parties, like the British, which had a programme and could discipline the government in order to secure its enactment, and, unorganized, decentralized parties, like those in the United States, which were unable to give direction to the government. More recent studies have shown that, if there is a trend at all, what is emerging is a mixed type of party which, while it has local organizations like those of the mass parties, is characterized by the very weak participation and by the sporadic, merely electoral, activity of the cadre parties. In other words, one can detect a pattern of convergence among previously different types of parties operating in the parliamentary democracies. American and European parties will be something different for a certain time to come, but less different than they were. This pattern of convergence, however, does not appear to mark an irreversible historical trend, linked, for example, to the technological and economic developments of modern society. Rather, the phenomenon which can probably best explain why this or that type of party is dominant at a particular time is what Deutsch and Germani have called 'social mobilization'. Pronounced social mobilization occurs during periods of rapid industrialization, or intense urbanization, or after a war, or during a change of regime, or other similar social and political events, and it is at such times that mass parties are likely to appear. In periods of relative calm, of political routine, the parties tend to adapt themselves to the parliamentary game and to dealing with the administrative bureaucracy, while mass participation diminishes.

With respect to the studies of political participation, two points attract our attention. A great deal of research has demonstrated that the curve of participation has a rather precise profile: the higher the social status (income, education, professional position) of an individual, the greater the probability of his political participation. This rule, however, is subject to an important exception: the relationship between status and participation disappears or is even reversed in the presence of political parties organized on the basis of class. The Reading of Rokkan and Campbell is one of the most interesting in a series of reports of various studies which have shown that, in capitalist political systems, the base organizations of class-oriented political parties and the subcultures linked to those parties have been able to maintain a high level of political participation among low status social strata.

The problem of social change is central to any sociological perspective. In the field of politics it is something more than a simple theoretical issue. Traditionally, those who studied society did so in order to discover how to change it. Even the sociologists of 'order', like Saint-Simon, Comte and Durkheim, wanted to discover how to create order out of the disorder they saw around them. It is only in the past few decades that sociological reflection has been oriented more toward the mechanisms which maintain the social order, than toward the forces which can change it. Hence, contemporary academic sociology has made little contribution to the theory of social or political change.

The difficulty lies, of course, in the very definition of change. Since everything in society can be seen as continually changing, we need to stand on a fixed point from which to perceive when change is occuring. This cannot be provided by some conventional definition, agreed upon by the community of scholars. Inevitably we must have recourse to some subjective criteria. Generally we find them in the political or ideological discourse of our time. By saying that no real change had happened in French society with the revolution of 1789, Tocqueville shifted the criteria by which political change was defined, and linked it to the theme of administrative centralization and its social consequences, which was to become one of the most important political issues of the last hundred years. The same could be said of the Marxian idea that political change only occurs with the transformation of the type of ownership of the means of production.

In other words, an ideological referent, or some kind of 'point of view', is a logical necessity in the analysis of political change, because a conventional definition of this concept is futile. As a consequence, excessively sophisticated attempts to elaborate a general theory are less fruitful than an approach that tries to identify the 'social forces' capable of provoking, carrying out, or giving direction to, change.

Marxism was the first theory to link systematically an analysis of social change to the emergence of a new class as a revolutionary agent; and for a long time, the working class was at the centre of the debate about the possibilities of revolution and the creation of a new society. Before the spreading of the socialist movement to southern and eastern European countries, toward the end of the last century, a Marxist who believed that the peasantry represented a revolutionary force, rather than an essentially conservative or static one, was held to be a heretic. The granting of the formal rights of citizenship to the working class, the institutionalization of class struggle, even though never complete, has cast doubt on the revolutionary potentialities of the industrial proletariat. In recent years peasants, marginal groups (economic and cultural) and even technicians, have all been suggested as the potential agents of transformations of society. The assumptions about the sources of this potential are, of course, different in each case; we find some examples in the writings of Fanon and Touraine in Part Four.

Along with 'when has change occurred?' and 'who are the carriers of change?' a third question has traditionally been part of sociological reflection and political debate: 'how does change happen?' The responses to this demand have traditionally been of two types: either, change occurs gradually, by successive reforms, that is, peacefully and with consensus; or, change occurs by revolution, with violence and division. In order to clarify these alternatives, we return to our first question and again examine how we can know when a change has been significant. Revolutionary violence, in fact, does seem to have been assumed to be a sort of 'guarantee' that radical changes had occurred; and this idea is not only a part of Marxist tradition, but also is inherent in Durkheim's concept of 'collective enthusiasm', which he considered a preliminary phase in the creation of the values of a new society.

Furthermore, the reform–revolution dilemma relates as well to the two conceptions of politics I distinguished in the first part of this Introduction. A revolutionary conception of change is linked to a religious conception of politics, to a view of politics as the pursuit of absolute, non-negotiable ends. A reformist conception, on the other hand, is based on a view of politics as the effort to gain limited ends through negotiation among various interests within the rules of an established system.

ei. radical v. moderate
physical force v. constitutional.

— symbiosis between the
two is ignored.

Part One On the Nature of Politics

De Tocqueville is the first to suggest that the French Revolution gave a new meaning to political action, close to what traditionally had been reserved to the religious sphere. Parsons prefers to stress, in an evolutionary perspective, that process of differentiation from religion which defines the modern secular conception of politics.

If at one end of the spectrum it seems difficult to distinguish politics from religion, at the other extreme political practice seems merely to amount to a series of technical decisions concerned with means rather than ends. Habermas critically discusses both the Weberian and the technocratic models for discriminating between political and technical realms of action. He introduces a third model in which the degree of 'publicity' accompanying any decision is crucial in drawing this distinction.

Another traditional question related to the nature of politics concerns the force–concensus debate regarding the basis of political power. In the following excerpt, which is to some extent a synthesis of his scattered reflections on politics, Weber emphasizes the element of force. Indeed, the monopoly of force specifically characterizes the institution of the state. Power founded upon force is then legitimized. For Weber the three sources of legitimacy are tradition, charisma and the legal order.

The cybernetic approach to the study of politics, illustrated in the seminal Reading by Easton, does not explicitly provide an interpretation of the nature of politics. Yet it implicitly assumes that politics is understandable only insofar as the actors follow certain rules and avoid ends not 'processable' by the existing institutional system.

1 Alexis de Tocqueville

Parties

Excerpt from Alexis de Tocqueville, *Democracy in America*, vol. 1,
edited by J. P. Mayer and Max Lerner, translated by George Lawrence,
Fontana, 1968, pp. 214–16. First published in French in 1835.

I must first define an important distinction between parties.

There are some countries so huge that the different populations inhabiting them, although united under the same sovereignty, have contradictory interests resulting in permanent opposition between them. In such cases the various factions of the same people do not, strictly speaking, form parties, but distinct nations; were civil war to break out, it would be a conflict between rival peoples rather than between factions.

But when there are differences between the citizens concerning matters of equal importance to all parts of the country, such for instance as the general principles of government, then what I really call parties take shape.

Parties are an evil inherent in free governments, but they do not always have the same character and the same instincts.

There are times when nations are tormented by such great ills that the idea of a total change in their political constitution comes into their minds. There are other times when the disease is deeper still and the whole social fabric is compromised. That is the time of great revolutions and of great parties.

Between these centuries of disorder and of misery there are others in which societies rest and the human race seems to take breath. That is in truth only apparently so: time does not halt its progress for peoples any more than for men; both men and peoples are daily advancing into an unknown future, and when we think that they are stationary, that is because we do not see their movements. Men may be walking and seem stationary to those who are running.

However that may be, there are times when the changes taking place in the political constitution and social structure of peoples are so slow and imperceptible that men think they have reached a final state; then the human spirit believes itself firmly settled on certain fundamentals and does not seek to look beyond a fixed horizon.

That is the time for intrigues and small parties.

What I call great political parties are those more attached to principles than to consequences, to generalities rather than to particular cases, to ideas rather than to personalities. Such parties generally have nobler features, more generous passions, more real convictions, and a bolder and more open look than others. Private interest, which always plays the greatest part in political passions, is there more skilfully concealed beneath the veil of public interest; sometimes it even passes unobserved by those whom it prompts and stirs to action.

On the other hand, small parties are generally without political faith. As they are not elevated and sustained by lofty purposes, the selfishness of their character is openly displayed in all their actions. They glow with a factitious zeal; their language is violent, but their progress is timid and uncertain. The means they employ are as disreputable as the aim sought. That is why, when a time of calm succeeds a great revolution, great men seem to disappear suddenly and minds withdraw into themselves.

Great parties convulse society; small ones agitate it; the former rend and the latter corrupt it; the first may sometimes save it by overthrowing it, but the second always create unprofitable trouble.

America has had great parties; now they no longer exist. This has been a great gain in happiness but not in morality.

2 Alexis de Tocqueville

The French Revolution

Excerpt from Alexis de Tocqueville, *The Ancien Régime and the French Revolution*, translated by Stuart Gilbert, Fontana, 1966, pp. 41–4. First published in French in 1856.

Whereas all social and political revolutions had so far been confined to the countries in which they took their rise, the French Revolution aspired to be world-wide and its effect was to erase all the old national frontiers from the map. We find it uniting or dividing men throughout the world, without regard to national traditions, temperaments, laws and mother tongues, sometimes leading them to regard compatriots as foes and foreigners as their kinsmen. Or, perhaps, it would be truer to say that it created a common intellectual fatherland whose citizenship was open to men of every nationality and in which racial distinctions were obliterated.

In all the annals of recorded history we find no mention of any *political* revolution that took this form; its only parallel is to be found in certain *religious* revolutions. Thus when we seek to study the French Revolution in the light of similar movements in other countries and at other periods, it is to the great religious revolutions we should turn.

Schiller rightly points out in his *History of the Thirty Years War* that one of the most striking effects of the reformation that took place in the sixteenth century was the bringing together of races which knew next to nothing of each other and the creation of a novel sense of fellow feeing between them. So it was that when Frenchmen were fighting against Frenchmen, the English intervened, while men hailing from remote Baltic hinterlands advanced into the heart of Germany to defend the cause of Germans of whose very existence they had until then been almost unaware. Foreign wars tended to assume the nature of civil wars, while in civil wars foreigners came to take a hand. Former interests were superseded by new interests, territorial disputes by conflicts over moral issues, and all the old notions of diplomacy were thrown into the melting pot – much to the horror and dismay of the professional politicians of the age. Precisely the same thing happened in Europe after 1789.

Thus the French Revolution, though ostensibly political in origin, functioned on the lines, and assumed many of the aspects, of a religious revolution. Not only did it have repercussions far beyond French territory, but like all great religious movements it resorted to propaganda and broadcast a gospel. This was something quite unprecedented: a political revolution that sought proselytes all the world over and applied itself as ardently to converting foreigners as compatriots. Of all the surprises that the French Revolution launched on a startled world, this surely was the most astounding. But there was more to it than that; let us try to carry our analysis a stage further and to discover if this similarity of effects may not have stemmed, in fact, from an underlying similarity of causes.

Common to all religions is an interest in the human personality, the man-in-himself irrespective of the trappings foisted on him by local traditions, laws and customs. The chief aim of a religion is to regulate both the relations of the individual man with his Maker and his rights and duties towards his fellow men on a universal plane, independently, that is to say, of the views and habits of the social group of which he is a member. The rules of conduct thus enjoined apply less to the man of any given nation or period than to man in his capacity of son, father, master, servant, neighbour. Since these rules are based on human nature, pure and simple, they hold good for men in general all the world over. To this is due the fact that religious revolutions have often ranged so far afield and seldom been confined, like political revolutions, to their country of origin or even to a single race. Moreover, when we look more deeply into the matter, we find that the more a religion has the universal, abstract qualities described above, the vaster is its sphere of influence and the less account it takes of differences of laws, local conditions and temperaments.

The pagan religions of antiquity were always more or less linked up with the political institutions and the social order of their environment, and their dogmas were conditioned to some extent by the interests of the nations, or even the cities, where they flourished. A pagan religion functioned within the limits of a given country and rarely spread beyond its frontiers. It sometimes sponsored intolerance and persecutions, but very seldom embarked on missionary enterprises. This is why there were no great religious revolutions in the Western World before the Christian era. Christianity, however, made light of all the barriers which had prevented the pagan religions from spreading, and very soon won to itself a large part of the human race. I trust I shall not be regarded as lacking in respect for this inspired religion if I say it partly owed its triumph to the fact that, far more than any other religion, it was catholic in the exact sense, having no links with any specific form of government, social order, period or nation.

The French Revolution's approach to the problems of man's existence here on earth was exactly similar to that of the religious revolutions as regards his afterlife. It viewed the 'citizen' from an abstract angle, that is to say as an entity independent of any particular social order, just as religions view the individual, without regard to nationality or the age he lives in. It did not aim merely at defining the rights of the French citizen, but sought also to determine the rights and duties of men in general towards each other and as members of a body politic.

It was because the Revolution always harked back to universal, not particular, values and to what was the most 'natural' form of government and the most 'natural' social system that it had so wide an appeal and could be imitated in so many places simultaneously.

No previous political upheaval, however violent, had aroused such passionate enthusiasm, for the ideal the French Revolution set before it was not merely a change in the French social system but nothing short of a regeneration of the whole human race. It created an atmosphere of missionary fervour and, indeed, assumed all the aspects of a religious revival – much to the consternation of contemporary observers. It would perhaps be truer to say that it developed into a species of religion, if a singularly imperfect one, since it was without a God, without a ritual or promise of a future life. Nevertheless, this strange religion has, like Islam, overrun the whole world with its apostles, militants and martyrs.

It must not be thought, however, that the methods employed by the Revolution had no precedents or that the ideas it propagated were wholly new. In all periods, even in the Middle Ages, there had been leaders of revolt who, with a view to effecting certain changes in the established order, appealed to the universal laws governing all communities, and championed the natural rights of man against the State. But none of these ventures was successful; the firebrand which set all Europe ablaze in the eighteenth century had been easily extinguished in the fifteenth. For doctrines of this kind to lead to revolutions, certain changes must already have taken place in the living conditions, customs and manners of a nation and prepared men's minds for the reception of new ideas.

There are periods in a nation's life when men differ from each other so profoundly that any notion of 'the same law for all' seems to them preposterous. But there are other periods when it is enough to dangle before their eyes a picture, however indistinct and remote, of such a law and they promptly grasp its meaning and hasten to acclaim it. In fact, the most extraordinary thing about the Revolution is not that it employed the methods which led to its success or that certain men should have conceived the ideas which supplied its driving force. What was wholly novel was that so many nations should have simultaneously reached a stage in their development which enabled those methods to be successfully employed and that ideology to be so readily accepted.

3 Max Weber

Politics as a Vocation

Excerpt from Max Weber, 'Politics as a vocation', in *From Max Weber: Essays in Sociology*, edited and translated by H. H. Gerth and C. Wright Mills, Oxford University Press, 1946, pp. 77–87. First published in German in 1919.

This lecture, which I give at your request, will necessarily disappoint you in a number of ways. You will naturally expect me to take a position on actual problems of the day. But that will be the case only in a purely formal way and toward the end, when I shall raise certain questions concerning the significance of political action in the whole way of life. In today's lecture, all questions that refer to what policy and what content one should give one's political activity must be eliminated. For such questions have nothing to do with the general question of what politics as a vocation means and what it can mean. Now to our subject matter.

What do we understand by politics? The concept is extremely broad and comprises any kind of *independent* leadership in action. One speaks of the currency policy of the banks, of the discounting policy of the Reichsbank, of the strike policy of a trade union; one may speak of the educational policy of a municipality or a township, of the policy of the president of a voluntary association, and, finally, even of the policy of a prudent wife who seeks to guide her husband. Tonight, our reflections are, of course, not based upon such a broad concept. We wish to understand by politics only the leadership, or the influencing of the leadership, of a *political* association, hence today, of a *state*.

But what is a 'political' association from the sociological point of view? What is a 'state'? Sociologically, the state cannot be defined in terms of its ends. There is scarcely any task that some political association has not taken in hand, and there is no task that one could say has always been exclusive and peculiar to those associations which are designated as political ones:

today the state, or historically, those associations which have been the predecessors of the modern state. Ultimately, one can define the modern state sociologically only in terms of the specific *means* peculiar to it, as to every political association, namely, the use of physical force.

'Every state is founded on force', said Trotsky at Brest-Litovsk. That is indeed right. If no social institutions existed which knew the use of violence, then the concept of 'state' would be eliminated, and a condition would emerge that could be designated as 'anarchy', in the specific sense of this word. Of course, force is certainly not the normal or the only means of the state – nobody says that – but force is a means specific to the state. Today the relation between the state and violence is an especially intimate one. In the past, the most varied institutions – beginning with the sib – have known the use of physical force as quite normal. Today, however, we have to say that a state is a human community that (successfully) claims the *monopoly of the legitimate use of physical force* within a given territory. Note that 'territory' is one of the characteristics of the state. Specifically, at the present time, the right to use physical force is ascribed to other institutions or to individuals only to the extent to which the state permits it. The state is considered the sole source of the 'right' to use violence. Hence, 'politics' for us means striving to share power or striving to influence the distribution of power, either among states or among groups within a state.

This corresponds essentially to ordinary usage. When a question is said to be a 'political' question, when a cabinet minister or an official is said to be a 'political' official, or when a decision is said to be 'politically' determined, what is always meant is that interests in the distribution, maintenance or transfer of power are decisive for answering the questions and determining the decision or the official's sphere of activity. He who is active in politics strives for power either as a means in serving other aims, ideal or egoistic, or as 'power for power's sake', that is, in order to enjoy the prestige-feeling that power gives.

Like the political institutions historically preceding it, the state is a relation of men dominating men, a relation supported by means of legitimate (i.e. considered to be legitimate) violence. If the state is to exist, the dominated must obey the authority claimed by the powers that be. When and why do men obey? Upon what inner justifications and upon what external means does this domination rest?

To begin with, in principle, there are three inner justifications, hence basic *legitimations* of domination.

First, the authority of the 'eternal yesterday', i.e. of the mores sanctified through the unimaginably ancient recognition and habitual orientation to conform. This is 'traditional' domination exercised by the patriarch and the patrimonial prince of yore.

There is the authority of the extraordinary and personal *gift of grace* (charisma), the absolutely personal devotion and personal confidence in revelation, heroism, or other qualities of individual leadership. This is 'charismatic' domination, as exercised by the prophet or – in the field of politics – by the elected war lord, the plebiscitarian ruler, the great demagogue or the political party leader.

Finally, there is domination by virtue of 'legality', by virtue of the belief in the validity of legal statute and functional 'competence' based on rationally created *rules*. In this case, obedience is expected in discharging statutory obligations. This is domination as exercised by the modern 'servant of the state' and by all those bearers of power who in this respect resemble him.

It is understood that, in reality, obedience is determined by highly robust motives of fear and hope – fear of the vengeance of magical powers or of the power-holder, hope for reward in this world or in the beyond – and besides all this, by interests of the most varied sort. Of this we shall speak presently. However, in asking for the 'legitimations' of this obedience, one meets with these three 'pure' types: 'traditional', 'charismatic' and 'legal'.

These conceptions of legitimacy and their inner justifications are of very great significance for the structure of domination. To be sure, the pure types are rarely found in reality. But today we cannot deal with the highly complex variants, transitions and combinations of these pure types, which problems belong to 'political science'. Here we are interested above all in the second of these types: domination by virtue of the devotion of those who obey the purely personal 'charisma' of the 'leader'. For this is the root of the idea of a *calling* in its highest expression.

Devotion to the charisma of the prophet, or the leader in war, or to the great demagogue in the *ecclesia* or in parliament, means that the leader is personally recognized as the innerly 'called' leader of men. Men do not obey him by virtue of tradition or statute, but because they believe in him. If he is more than a narrow and vain upstart of the moment, the leader lives for his cause and 'strives for his work'. The devotion of his disciples, his followers, his personal party friends is oriented to his person and to its qualities.

Charismatic leadership has emerged in all places and in all historical epochs. Most importantly in the past, it has emerged in the two figures of the magician and the prophet on the one hand, and in the elected war lord, the gang leader and *condottiere* on the other hand. *Political* leadership in the form of the free 'demagogue' who grew from the soil of the city state is of greater concern to us; like the city state, the demagogue is peculiar to the Occident and especially to Mediterranean culture. Furthermore, political leadership in the form of the parliamentary 'party leader' has grown on the soil of the constitutional state, which is also indigenous only to the Occident.

These politicians by virtue of a 'calling', in the most genuine sense of the word, are of course nowhere the only decisive figures in the cross-currents of the political struggle for power. The sort of auxiliary means that are at their disposal is also highly decisive. How do the politically dominant powers manage to maintain their domination? The question pertains to any kind of domination, hence also to political domination in all its forms, traditional as well as legal and charismatic.

Organized domination, which calls for continuous administration, requires that human conduct be conditioned to obedience towards those masters who claim to be the bearers of legitimate power. On the other hand, by virtue of this obedience, organized domination requires the control of those material goods which in a given case are necessary for the use of physical violence. Thus, organized domination requires control of the personal executive staff and the material implements of administration.

The administrative staff, which externally represents the organization of political domination, is, of course, like any other organization, bound by obedience to the power-holder and not alone by the concept of legitimacy, of which we have just spoken. There are two other means, both of which appeal to personal interests: material reward and social honor. The fiefs of vassals, the prebends of patrimonial officials, the salaries of modern civil servants, the honor of knights, the privileges of estate and the honor of the civil servant comprise their respective wages. The fear of losing them is the final and decisive basis for solidarity between the executive staff and the power-holder. There is honor and booty for the followers in war; for the demagogue's following, there are 'spoils' – that is, exploitation of the dominated through the monopolization of office – and there are politically determined profits and premiums of vanity. All of these rewards are also derived from the domination exercised by a charismatic leader.

To maintain a dominion by force, certain material goods are required, just as with an economic organization. All states may be classified according to whether they rest on the principle that the staff of men themselves *own* the administrative means, or whether the staff is 'separated' from these means of administration. This distinction holds in the same sense in which today we say that the salaried employee and the proletarian in the capitalistic enterprise are 'separated' from the material means of production. The power-holder must be able to count on the obedience of the staff members, officials or whoever else they may be. The administrative means may consist of money, building, war material, vehicles, horses or whatnot. The question is whether or not the power-holder himself directs and organizes the administration while delegating executive power to personal servants, hired officials or personal favorites and confidants, who are non-owners, i.e. who do not use the material means of administration in their own right but are directed by the lord. The distinction runs through all administrative organizations of the past.

These political associations in which the material means of administration are autonomously controlled, wholly or partly, by the dependent administrative staff may be called associations organized in 'estates'. The vassal in the feudal association, for instance, paid out of his own pocket for the administration and judicature of the district enfeoffed to him. He supplied his own equipment and provisions for war, and his subvassals did likewise. Of course, this had consequences for the lord's position of power, which only rested upon a relation of personal faith and upon the fact that the legitimacy of his possession of the fief and the social honor of the vassal were derived from the overlord.

However, everywhere, reaching back to the earliest political formations, we also find the lord himself directing the administration. He seeks to take the administration into his own hands by having men personally dependent upon him: slaves, household officials, attendants, personal 'favorites' and prebendaries enfeoffed in kind or in money from his magazines. He seeks to defray the expenses from his own pocket, from the revenues of his patrimonium; and he seeks to create an army which is dependent upon him personally because it is equipped and provisioned out of his granaries, magazines and armories. In the association of 'estates', the lord rules with the aid of an autonomous 'aristocracy' and hence shares his domination with it; the lord who personally administers is supported either by members of his household or by plebeians. These are propertyless strata having no social honor of their own; materially, they are completely chained to him and are not backed up by any competing power of their own. All forms of patriarchal and patrimonial domination, Sultanist despotism and bureaucratic states belong to this latter type. The bureaucratic state order is especially important; in its most rational development, it is precisely characteristic of the modern state.

Everywhere the development of the modern state is initiated through the action of the prince. He paves the way for the expropriation of the autonomous and 'private' bearers of executive power who stand beside him, of those who in their own right possess the means of administration, warfare and financial organization, as well as politically usable goods of all sorts. The whole process is a complete parallel to the development of the capitalist enterprise through gradual expropriation of the independent producers. In the end, the modern state controls the total means of political organization, which actually come together under a single head. No single official personally owns the money he pays out, or the buildings, stores, tools and war machines he controls. In the contemporary 'state' – and this is essential for the concept of state – the 'separation' of the administrative staff, of the administrative officials, and of the workers from the material means of administrative organization is completed. Here the most modern development begins, and we see with our own eyes the attempt to inaugurate the expropriation of this expropriator of the political means, and therewith of political power.

The revolution (of Germany, 1918) has accomplished, at least in so far as leaders have taken the place of the statutory authorities, this much: the leaders, through usurpation or election, have attained control over the political staff and the apparatus of material goods; and they deduce their legitimacy – no matter with what right – from the will of the governed. Whether the leaders, on the basis of this at least apparent success, can rightfully entertain the hope of also carrying through the expropriation within the capitalist enterprises is a different question. The direction of capitalist enterprises, despite far-reaching analogies, follows quite different laws than those of political administration.

Today we do not take a stand on this question. I state only the purely *conceptual* aspect for our consideration: the modern state is a compulsory association which organizes domination. It has been successful in seeking to monopolize the legitimate use of physical force as a means of domination within a territory. To this end the state has combined the material means of organization in the hands of its leaders, and it has expropriated all autonomous functionaries of estates who formerly controlled these means in their own right. The state has taken their positions and now stands in the top place.

During this process of political expropriation, which has occurred with varying success in all countries on earth, 'professional politicians' in another sense have emerged. They arose

Max Weber 33

first in the service of a prince. They have been men who, unlike the charismatic leader, have not wished to be lords themselves, but who have entered the *service* of political lords. In the struggle of expropriation, they placed themselves at the princes' disposal and by managing the princes' politics they earned, on the one hand, a living and, on the other hand, an ideal content of life. Again, it is *only* in the Occident that we find this kind of professional politician in the service of powers other than the princes. In the past, they have been the most important power instrument of the prince and his instrument of political expropriation.

Before discussing 'professional politicians' in detail, let us clarify in all its aspects the state of affairs their existence presents. Politics, just as economic pursuits, may be a man's avocation or his vocation. One may engage in politics, and hence seek to influence the distribution of power within and between political structures, as an 'occasional' politician. We are all 'occasional' politicians when we cast our ballot or consummate a similar expression of intention, such as applauding or protesting in a 'political' meeting, or delivering a 'political' speech, etc. The whole relation of many people to politics is restricted to this. Politics as an avocation is today practised by all those party agents and heads of voluntary political associations who, as a rule, are politically active only in case of need and for whom politics is, neither materially nor ideally, 'their life' in the first place. The same holds for those members of state counsels and similar deliberative bodies that function only when summoned. It also holds for rather broad strata of our members of parliament who are politically active only during sessions. In the past, such strata were found especially among the estates. Proprietors of military implements in their own right, or proprietors of goods important for the administration, or proprietors of personal prerogatives may be called 'estates'. A large portion of them were far from giving their lives wholly, or merely preferentially, or more than occasionally, to the service of politics. Rather, they exploited their prerogatives in the interest of gaining rent or even profits; and they became active in the service of political associations only when the overlord of their status-equals especially demanded it. It was not different in the case of some of the auxiliary forces which the prince drew into the struggle for the creation of a political organization to be exclusively at his disposal. This was the nature of the *Räte von Haus aus* (councilors) and, still further back, of a considerable part of the councilors assembling in the 'Curia' and other deliberating bodies of the princes. But these merely occasional auxiliary forces engaging in politics on the side were naturally not sufficient for the prince. Of necessity, the prince sought to create a staff of helpers dedicated wholly and exclusively to serving him, hence making this their major vocation. The structure of the emerging dynastic political organization, and not only this but the whole articulation of the culture, depended to a considerable degree upon the question of where the prince recruited agents.

A staff was also necessary for those political associations whose members constituted themselves politically as (so-called) 'free' communes under the complete abolition or the far-going restriction of princely power.

They were 'free' not in the sense of freedom from domination by force, but in the sense that princely power legitimized by tradition (mostly religiously sanctified) as the exclusive source of all authority was absent. These communities have their historical home in the Occident. Their nucleus was the city as a body politic, the form in which the city first emerged in the Mediterranean culture area. In all these cases, what did the politicians who made politics their major vocation look like?

There are two ways of making politics one's vocation: Either one lives 'for' politics or one lives 'off' politics. By no means is this contrast an exclusive one. The rule is, rather, that man does both, at least in thought, and certainly he also does both in practice. He who lives 'for' politics makes politics his life, in an internal sense. Either he enjoys the naked possession of the power he exerts, or he nourishes his inner balance and self-feeling by the consciousness that his life has *meaning* in the service of a 'cause'. In this internal sense, every sincere man who lives for a cause also lives off this cause. The distinction hence refers to a much more substantial aspect of the matter, namely, to the economic. He who strives to make politics a permanent *source of income* lives 'off' politics as a vocation, whereas he who does not do this lives 'for' politics. Under the dominance of the private property order, some – if you wish – very trivial preconditions must exist in order for a person to be able to live 'for' politics in this economic sense. Under normal conditions, the politician must be economically independent of the income politics can bring him. This means, quite simply, that the politician must be wealthy or must have a personal position in life which yields a sufficient income.

This is the case, at least in normal circumstances. The war lord's following is just as little concerned about the conditions of a normal economy as is the street crowd following of the revolutionary hero. Both live off booty, plunder, confiscations, contributions and the imposition of worthless and compulsory means of tender, which in essence amounts to the same thing. But necessarily, these are extraordinary phenomena. In every-day economic life, only some wealth serves the purpose of making a man economically independent. Yet this alone does not suffice. The professional politician must also be econ-omically 'dispensable', that is, his income must not depend upon the fact that he constantly and personally places his ability and thinking entirely, or at least by far predominantly, in the service of economic acquisition. In the most unconditional way, the rentier is dispensable in this sense. Hence, he is a man who receives completely unearned income. He may be the territorial lord of the past or the large landowner and aristocrat of the present who receives ground rent. In Antiquity and the Middle Ages they who received slave or serf rents or in modern times rents from shares or bonds or similar sources – these are rent-iers.

Neither the worker nor – and this has to be noted well – the entrepreneur, especially the modern, large-scale entrepreneur, is economically dispensable in this sense. For it is precisely the entrepreneur who is tied to his enterprise and is therefore *not* dispensable. This holds for the entrepreneur in industry far more than for the entrepreneur in agriculture, considering the seasonal character of agriculture. In the main, it is very difficult for the entrepreneur to be represented in his enterprise by some-one else, even temporarily. He is as little dispensable as is the medical doctor, and the more eminent and busy he is the less dispensable he is. For purely organizational reasons, it is easier for the lawyer to be dispensable; and therefore the lawyer has played an incomparably greater, and often even a dominant, role as a professional politician. We shall not continue in this classification; rather let us clarify some of its ramifications.

The leadership of a state or of a party by men who (in the economic sense of the word) live exclusively for politics and not off politics means necessarily a 'plutocratic' recruitment of the leading political strata. To be sure, this does not mean that such plutocratic leadership signifies at the same time that the politically dominant strata will not also seek to live 'off' politics, and hence that the dominant stratum will not usually exploit their political domination in their own economic interest. All that is unquestionable, of course. There has never been such a stratum that has not somehow lived 'off' politics. Only this is meant: that the professional politician need not seek remuneration directly for his political work, whereas every politician without means must absolutely claim this. On the other hand, we do not mean to say that the propertyless politician will pursue private economic advantages through politics, exclusively, or even predominantly. Nor do we mean that he will not think, in the first place, of 'the subject matter'. Nothing would be more incorrect. According to all experience, a care for the economic 'security' of his existence is consciously or unconsciously a cardinal point in the whole life orientation of the wealthy man. A quite reckless and unreserved political idealism is found if not exclusively at least predominantly among those strata who by virtue of their propertylessness stand entirely outside of the strata who are interested in maintaining the economic order of a given society. This holds especially for extraordinary and hence revolutionary epochs. A non-plutocratic recruitment of interested politicians, of leadership and following, is geared to the self-understood precondition that regular and reliable income will accrue to those who manage politics.

Either politics can be conducted 'honorifically' and then, as one usually says, by 'independent', that is, by wealthy, men, and especially by rentiers. Or, political leadership is made accessible to propertyless men who must then be rewarded. The professional politician who lives 'off' politics may be a pure 'prebendary' or a salaried 'official'. Then the politician receives either income from fees and perquisites for specific services – tips and bribes are only an irregular and formally illegal variant of this category of income – or a fixed income in kind, a money salary, or both. He may assume the character of an 'entrepreneur', like the *condottiere* or the holder of a farmed-out or purchased office, or like the American boss who considers his costs a capital investment which he brings to fruition through exploitation of his influence. Again, he may receive a fixed wage, like a journalist, a party secretary, a modern cabinet minister or a political official. Feudal fiefs, land grants and prebends of all sorts have been typical, in the past. With the development of the money economy, perquisites and prebends especially are the typical rewards for the following of princes, victorious conquerors or successful party chiefs. For loyal services today, party leaders give offices of all sorts – in parties, newspapers, cooperative societies, health insurance, municipalities, as well as in the state. *All* party struggles are struggles for the patronage of office, as well as struggles for objective goals.

4 David Easton

The Analysis of Political Systems

Excerpts from David Easton, 'An approach to the analysis of political systems', *World Politics*, vol. 9, 1957, no. 3, pp. 383–400.

Some attributes of political systems

In an earlier work I have argued for the need to develop general, empirically oriented theory as the most economical way in the long run to understand political life. Here I propose to indicate a point of view that, at the least, might serve as a springboard for discussion of alternative approaches and, at most, as a small step in the direction of a general political theory. I wish to stress that what I have to say is a mere orientation to the problem of theory; outside of economics and perhaps psychology, it would be presumptuous to call very much in social science 'theory', in the strict sense of the term.

Furthermore, I shall offer only a Gestalt of my point of view, so that it will be possible to evaluate, in the light of the whole, those parts that I do stress. In doing this, I know I run the definite risk that the meaning and implications of this point of view may be only superficially communicated; but it is a risk I shall have to undertake since I do not know how to avoid it sensibly.

The study of politics is concerned with understanding how authoritative decisions are made and executed for a society. We can try to understand political life by viewing each of its aspects piecemeal. We can examine the operation of such institutions as political parties, interest groups, government and voting; we can study the nature and consequences of such political practices as manipulation, propaganda and violence; we can seek to reveal the structure within which these practices occur. By combining the results we can obtain a rough picture of what happens in any self-contained political unit.

In combining these results, however, there is already implicit the notion that each part of the larger political canvas does not stand alone but is related to each other part; or, to put it positively, that the operation of no one part can be fully understood without reference to the way in which the whole itself operates. I have suggested in my book (1953) that it is valuable to adopt this implicit assumption as an articulate premise for research and to view political life as a system of interrelated activities. These activities derive their relatedness or systemic ties from the fact that they all more or less influence the way in which authoritative decisions are formulated and executed for a society.

Once we begin to speak of political life as a system of activity, certain consequences follow for the way in which we can undertake to analyse the working of a system. The very idea of a system suggests that we can separate political life from the rest of social activity, at least for analytical purposes, and examine it as though for the moment it were a self-contained entity surrounded by, but clearly distinguishable from, the environment or setting in which it operates. In much the same way, astronomers consider the solar system a complex of events isolated for certain purposes from the rest of the universe.

Furthermore, if we hold the system of political actions as a unit before our mind's eye, as it were, we can see that what keeps the system going are inputs of various kinds. These inputs are converted by the processes of the system into outputs and these, in turn, have consequences both for the system and for the environment in which the system exists. The formula here is very simple but, as I hope to show, also very illuminating: inputs – political system or processes – outputs. These relationships are shown diagrammatically in Figure 1. This diagram represents a very primitive 'model' – to dignify it with a fashionable name – for approaching the study of political life.

Political systems have certain properties because they are systems. To present an overall view of the whole approach, let me identify the major attributes, say a little about each, and then treat one of these properties at somewhat greater length, even though still inadequately.

Properties of identification. To distinguish a political system from other social systems, we must be able to identify it by describing its fundamental units and establishing the boundaries that demarcate it from units outside the system.

(a) Units of a political system. The units are the elements of which we say a system is composed. In the case of a political system, they are political actions. Normally it is useful to look at these as they structure themselves in political roles and political groups.

(b) Boundaries. Some of the most significant questions with regard to the operation of political systems can be answered only if we bear in mind the obvious fact that a system does not exist in a vacuum. It is always immersed in a specific setting or environment. The way in which a system works will be in part a function of its response to the total social, biological and physical environment.

The special problem with which we are confronted is how to distinguish systematically between a political system and its setting. Does it even make sense to say that a political system has a boundary dividing it from its setting? If so, how are we to identify the line of demarcation?

Without pausing to argue the matter, I would suggest that it is useful to conceive a political system as having a boundary in the same sense as a physical system. The boundary of a political system is defined by all those actions more or less directly related to the making of binding decisions for a society; every social action that does not partake of this characteristic will be excluded from the system and thereby will automatically be viewed as an external variable in the environment.

Inputs and outputs. Presumably, if we select political systems for special study, we do so because we believe that they have characteristically important consequences for society, namely, authoritative decisions. These consequences I shall call the outputs. If we judged that political systems did not have important outputs for society, we would probably not be interested in them.

Unless a system is approaching a state of entropy – and we can assume that this is not true of most political systems – it must have continuing inputs to keep it going. Without inputs the system can do no work; without outputs we cannot identify the work done by the system. The specific research tasks in this connection would be to identify the inputs and the forces that shape and change them, to trace the processes through which they are transformed into outputs, to describe the general conditions under which such processes can be maintained, and to establish the relationship between outputs and succeeding inputs of the system.

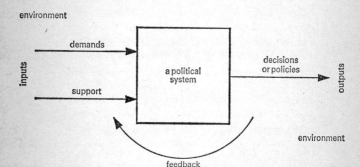

Figure 1

From this point of view, much light can be shed on the working of a political system if we take into account the fact that much of what happens within a system has its birth in the efforts of the members of the system to cope with the changing environment. We can appreciate this point if we consider a familiar biological system such as the human organism. It is subject to constant stress from its surroundings to which it must adapt in one way or another if it is not to be completely destroyed. In part, of course, the way in which the body works represents responses to needs that are generated by the very organization of its anatomy and functions; but in large part, in order to understand both the structure and the working of the body, we must also be very sensitive to the inputs from the environment.

In the same way, the behavior of every political system is to some degree imposed upon it by the kind of system it is, that is, by its own structure and internal needs. But its behavior also reflects the strains occasioned by the specific setting within which the system operates. It may be argued that most of the significant changes within a political system have their origin in shifts among the external variables. Since I shall be devoting the bulk of this article to examining some of the problems related to the exchange between political systems and their environments, I shall move on to a rapid description of other properties of political systems.

Differentiation within a system. As we shall see in a moment, from the environment come both energy to activate a system and information with regard to which the system uses this energy. In this way a system is able to do work. It has some sort of output that is different from the input that enters from the environment. We can take it as a useful hypothesis that if a political system is to perform some work for anything but a limited interval of time, a minimal amount of differentiation in its structure must occur. In fact, empirically it is impossible to find a significant political system in which the same units all perform the same activities at the same time. The members of a system engage in at least some minimal division of labor that provides a structure within which action takes place.

Integration of a system. This fact of differentiation opens up a major area of inquiry with regard to political systems. Structural differentiation sets in motion forces that are potentially disintegrative in their results for the system. If two or more units are performing different kinds of activity at the same time, how are these activities to be brought into the minimal degree of articulation necessary if the members of the system are not to end up in utter disorganization with regard to the production of the outputs of interest to us? We can hypothesize that if a structured system is to maintain itself, it must provide mechanisms whereby its members are integrated or induced to cooperate in some minimal degree so that they make authoritative decisions.

Inputs: demands

Now that I have mentioned some major attributes of political systems that I suggest require special attention if we are to develop a generalized approach, I want to consider in greater detail the way in which an examination of inputs and outputs will shed some light on the working of these systems.

Among inputs of a political system there are two basic kinds: demands and support. These inputs give a political system its dynamic character. They furnish it both with the raw material or information that the system is called upon to process and with the energy to keep it going.

The reason why a political system emerges in a society at all – that is, why men engage in political activity – is that demands are being made by persons or groups in the society that cannot all be fully satisfied. In all societies one fact dominates political life: scarcity prevails with regard to most of the valued things. Some of the claims for these relatively scarce things never find their way into the political system but are satisfied through the private negotiations of or settlements by the persons involved. Demands for prestige may find satisfaction through the status relations of society; claims for wealth are met in part through the economic system; aspirations for power find expression in educational, fraternal, labor and similar private organizations. Only where wants require some special organized effort on the part of society to settle them authoritatively may we say that they have become inputs of the political system.

Systematic research would require us to address ourselves to several key questions with regard to these demands.

1. How do demands arise and assume their particular character in a society? In answer to this question, we can point out that demands have their birth in two sectors of experience: either in the environment of a system or within the system itself. We shall call these the external and internal demands, respectively.

Let us look at the external demands first. I find it useful to see the environment not as an undifferentiated mass of events but rather as systems clearly distinguishable from one another and from the political system. In the environment we have such systems as the ecology, economy, culture, personality, social structure and demography. Each of these constitutes a major set of variables in the setting that helps to shape the kind of demands entering a political system. For purposes of illustrating what I mean, I shall say a few words about culture.

The members of every society act within the framework of an ongoing culture that shapes their general goals, specific objectives and the procedures that the members feel ought to be used. Every culture derives part of its unique quality from the fact that it emphasizes one or more special aspects of behavior and this strategic emphasis serves to differentiate it from other cultures with respect to the demands that it generates. As far as the mass of the people is concerned, some cultures, such as our own, are weighted heavily on the side of economic wants, success, privacy, leisure activity and rational efficiency. Others, such as that of the Fox Indians, strive toward the maintenance of harmony, even if in the process the goals of efficiency and rationality may be sacrificed. Still others, such as the Kachins of highland Burma, stress the pursuit of power and prestige. The culture embodies the standards of value in a society and thereby marks out areas of potential conflict, if the valued things are in short supply relative to demand. The typical demands that will find their way into the political process will concern the matters in conflict that are labeled important by the culture. For this reason we cannot hope to understand the nature of the demands presenting themselves for political settlement unless we are ready to explore systematically and intensively their connection with the culture. And what I have said about culture applies, with suitable modifications, to other parts of the setting of a political system.

But not all demands originate or have their major locus in the environment. Important types stem from situations occurring within a political system itself. Typically, in every ongoing system, demands may emerge for alterations in the political relationships of the members themselves, as the result of dissatisfaction stemming from these relationships. For example, in a political system based upon representation, in which equal representation is an important political norm, demands may arise for equalizing representation between urban and rural voting districts. Similarly, demands for changes in the process of re-cruitment of formal political leaders, for modifications of the way in which constitutions are amended, and the like may all be internally inspired demands.

I find it useful and necessary to distinguish these from exter-nal demands because they are, strictly speaking, not inputs of the system but something that we can call 'withinputs', if we can tolerate a cumbersome neologism, and because their conse-quences for the character of a political system are more direct than in the case of external demands. Furthermore, if we were not aware of this difference in classes of demands, we might search in vain for an explanation of the emergence of a given set of internal demands if we turned only to the environment.

2. How are demands transformed into issues? What deter-mines whether a demand becomes a matter for serious political discussion or remains something to be resolved privately among the members of society? The occurrence of a demand, whether internal or external, does not thereby automatically convert it into a political *issue*. Many demands die at birth or linger on with the support of an insignificant fraction of the society and are never raised to the level of possible political decision. Others become issues, an issue being a demand that the members of a political system are prepared to deal with as a significant item for discussion through the recognized channels in the system.

The distinction between demands and issues raises a number of questions about which we need data if we are to understand the processes through which claims typically become trans-formed into issues. For example, we would need to know some-thing about the relationship between a demand and the location of its initiators or supporters in the power structures of the society, the importance of secrecy as compared with publicity in presenting demands, the matter of timing of demands, the possession of political skills or know-how, access to channels of communication, the attitudes and states of mind of possible publics, and the images held by the initiators of demands with regard to the way in which things get done in the particular political system. Answers to matters such as these would possibly yield a conversion index reflecting the probability of a set of demands being converted into live political issues.

If we assume that political science is primarily concerned with the way in which authoritative decisions are made for a society, demands require special attention as a major type of input of political systems. I have suggested that demands influence the behaviour of a system in a number of ways. They constitute a significant part of the material upon which the system operates. They are also one of the sources of change in political systems, since as the environment fluctuates it generates new types of demand-inputs for the system. Accordingly, without this attention to the origin and determinants of demands we would be at a loss to be able to treat rigorously not only the operation of a system at a moment of time but also its change over a specified interval. Both the statics and historical dynamics of a political system depend upon a detailed understanding of demands, particularly of the impact of the setting on them.

Inputs: support

Inputs of demands alone are not enough to keep a political system operating. They are only the raw material out of which finished products called decisions are manufactured. Energy in the form of actions or orientations promoting and resisting a political system, the demands arising in it, and the decisions issuing from it must also be put into the system to keep it running. This input I shall call support. Without support, demands could not be satisfied or conflicts in goals composed. If demands are to be acted upon, the members of a system undertaking to pilot the demands through to their transformation into binding decisions and those who seek to influence the relevant processes in any way must be able to count on support from others in the system. Just how much support, from how many and which members of a political system, are separate and important questions that I shall touch on shortly.

What do we mean by support? We can say that A supports B either when A acts on behalf of or when he orients himself favorably toward B's goals, interests and actions. Supportive behavior may thus be of two kinds. It may consist of actions promoting the goals, interests and actions of another person. We may vote for a political candidate, or defend a decision by the highest court of the land. In these cases, support manifests itself through overt action.

On the other hand, supportive behavior may involve not external observable acts, but those internal forms of behavior we call orientations or states of mind. As I use the phrase, a supportive state of mind is a deep-seated set of attitudes or predispositions, or a readiness to act on behalf of some other person. It exists when we say that a man is loyal to his party, attached to democracy, or infused with patriotism. What such phrases as these have in common is the fact that they refer to a state of feelings on the part of a person. No overt action is involved at this level of description, although the implication is that the individual will pursue a course of action consistent with his attitudes. Where the anticipated action does not flow from our perception of the state of mind, we assume that we have not penetrated deeply enough into the true feelings of the person but have merely skimmed off his surface attitudes.

Supportive states of mind are vital inputs for the operation and maintenance of a political system. For example, it is often said that the struggle in the international sphere concerns mastery over men's minds. To a certain extent this is true. If the members of a political system are deeply attached to a system or its ideals the likelihood of their participating in either domestic or foreign politics in such a way as to undermine the system is reduced by a large factor. Presumably, even in the face of considerable provocation, ingrained supportive feelings of loyalty may be expected to prevail.

We shall need to identify the typical mechanisms through which supportive attitudes are inculcated and continuously reinforced within a political system. But our prior task is to specify and examine the political objects in relation to which support is extended.

The domain of support

Support is fed into the political system in relation to three objects: the community, the regime and the government. There must be convergence of attitude and opinion as well as some willingness to act with regard to each of these objects. Let us examine each in turn.

The political community. No political system can continue to operate unless its members are willing to support the existence of a group that seeks to settle differences or promote decisions through peaceful action in common. The point is so obvious – being dealt with usually under the heading of the growth of national unity – that it may well be overlooked; and yet it is a premise upon which the continuation of any political system depends. To refer to this phenomenon we can speak of the political community. At this level of support we are not concerned with whether a government exists or whether there is loyalty to a constitutional order. For the moment we only ask whether the members of the group that we are examining are sufficiently oriented toward each other to want to contribute their collective energies toward pacific settlement of their varying demands. . . .

The regime. Support for a second major part of a political system helps to supply the energy to keep the system running. This aspect of the system I shall call the regime. It consists of all those arrangements that regulate the way in which the demands put into the system are settled and the way in which decisions are put into effect. They are the so-called rules of the game, in the light of which actions by members of the system are legitimated and accepted by the bulk of the members as authoritative. Unless there is a minimum convergence of attitudes in support of these fundamental rules – the constitutional principles, as we call them in Western society – there would be insufficient harmony in the actions of the members of a system to meet the problems generated by their support of a political community. The fact of trying to settle demands in common means that there must be known principles governing the way in which resolutions of differences of claims are to take place.

The government. If a political system is going to be able to handle the conflicting demands put into it, not only must the members of the system be prepared to support the settlement of these conflicts in common and possess some consensus with regard to the rules governing the mode of settlement; they must also be ready to support a government as it undertakes the concrete tasks involved in negotiating such settlements. When we come to the outputs of a system, we shall see the rewards that are available to a government for mobilizing support. At this point, I just wish to draw attention to this need on the part of a government for support if it is going to be able to make decisions with regard to demands. Of course, a government may elicit support in many ways: through persuasion, consent or manipulation. It may also impose unsupported settlements of demands through threats of force. But it is a familiar axiom of political science that a government based upon force alone is not long for this world; it must buttress its position by inducing a favorable state of mind in its subjects through fair or foul means.

The fact that support directed to a political system can be broken down conceptually into three elements – support for the community, regime and government – does not mean, of course, that in the concrete case support for each of these three objects is independent. In fact we might and normally do find all three kinds of support very closely intertwined, so that the presence of one is a function of the presence of one or both of the other types. . . .

Quantity and scope of support

How much support needs to be put into a system and how many of its members need to contribute such support if the system is to be able to do the job of converting demands to decisions? No ready answer can be offered. The actual situation in each case would determine the amount and scope required. We can, however, visualize a number of situations that will be helpful in directing our attention to possible generalizations.

Under certain circumstances very few members need to support a system at any level. The members might be dull and apathetic, indifferent to the general operations of the system, its progress or decisions. In a loosely connected system such as India has had, this might well be the state of mind of by far the largest segment of the membership. Either in fact they have not been affected by national decisions or they have not perceived that they were so affected. They may have little sense of identification with the present regime and government and yet, with regard to the input of demands, the system may be able to act on the basis of the support offered by the known 3 per cent of the Western-oriented politicians and intellectuals who are politically active. In other words, we can have a small minority putting in quantitatively sufficient supportive energy to keep the system going. However, we can venture the hypothesis that where members of a system are putting in numerous demands, there is a strong probability that they will actively offer support or hostility at one of the three levels of the system, depending upon the degree to which these demands are being met through appropriate decisions.

Alternatively, we may find that all the members of a system are putting in support, but the amount may be so low as to place one or all aspects of the system in jeopardy. Modern France is perhaps a classic illustration. The input of support at the level of the political community is probably adequate for the maintenance of France as a national political unit. But for a variety of historical and contemporary reasons, there is considerable doubt as to whether the members of the French political system are putting in anything but a low order of support to the regime or any particular government. This low amount of support, even though spread over a relatively large segment of the population, leaves the French political system on somewhat less secure foundations than is the case with India. There support is less widespread but more active – that is, quantitatively greater – on the part of a minority. As this illustration indicates, the amount of support is not necessarily proportional to its scope.

It may seem from the above discussion as though the members of a political system either put in support or withhold it – that is, demonstrate hostility or apathy. In fact, members may and normally do simultaneously engage in supportive and hostile behavior. What we must be interested in is the net balance of support.

Mechanisms of support

To this point I have suggested that no political system can yield the important outputs we call authoritative decisions unless, in addition to demands, support finds it way into the system. I have discussed the possible object to which support may be directed, and some problems with regard to the domain, quantity, and scope of support. We are now ready to turn to the main question raised by our attention to support as a crucial input: how do systems typically manage to maintain a steady flow of support? Without it a system will not absorb sufficient energy from its members to be able to convert demands to decisions.

In theory, there might be an infinite variety of means through which members could be induced to support a system; in practice, certain well-established classes of mechanisms are used. Research in this area needs to be directed to exploring the precise way in which a particular system utilizes these mechanisms and to refining our understanding of the way in which they contribute to the making of authoritative policy.

A society generates support for a political system in two ways: through outputs that meet the demands of the members of society; and through the processes of politicization. Let us look at outputs first.

Outputs as a mechanism of support

An output of a political system, it will be recalled, is a political decision or policy. One of the major ways of strengthening the ties of the members to their system is through providing decisions that tend to satisfy the day-to-day demands of these members. Fundamentally this is the truth that lies in the aphorism that one can fool some of the people some of the time but not all of them all of the time. Without some minimal satisfaction of demands, the ardor of all but the most fanatical patriot is sure to cool. The outputs, consisting of political decisions, constitute a body of specific inducements for the members of a system to support that system.

Inducements of this kind may be positive or negative. Where negative, they threaten the members of the system with various kinds of sanctions ranging from a small monetary fine to physical detention, ostracism or loss of life, as in our own system with regard to the case of legally defined treason. In every system support stems in part from fear of sanctions or compulsion; in autocratic systems the proportion of coerced support is at a maximum. For want of space I shall confine myself to those cases where positive incentives loom largest.

Since the specific outputs of a system are policy decisions, it is upon the government that the final responsibility falls for matching or balancing outputs of decisions against input of demand. But it is clear that to obtain the support of the members of a system through positive incentives, a government need not meet all the demands of even its most influential and ardent supporters. Most governments, or groups such as political parties that seek to control governments, succeed in building up a reserve of support. This reserve will carry the government along even though it offends its followers, so long as over the extended short run these followers perceive the particular government as one that is in general favorable to their interests. One form that this reserve support takes in Western society is that of party loyalty, since the party is the typical instrument in a mass industrialized society for mobilizing and maintaining support for a government. However, continuous lack of specific rewards through policy decisions ultimately leads to the danger that even the deepest party loyalty may be shaken. . . .

Thus a system need not meet *all the demands* of its members so long as it has stored up a reserve of support over the years. Nor need it satisfy even *some of the demands* of all its members. Just whose demands a system must seek to meet, how much of their demands, at what time, and under what conditions are questions for special research. We can say in advance that at least the demands of the most influential members require satisfaction. But this tells us little unless we know how to discover the influentials in a political system and how new sets of members rise to positions of influence.

The critical significance of the decisions of governments for the support of the other two aspects of a system – namely, the political community and the regime – is clear from what I have said above. Not all withdrawal of support from a government has consequences for the success or failure of a regime or community. But persistent inability of a government to produce satisfactory outputs for the members of a system may well lead to demands for changing of the regime or for dissolution of the political community. It is for this reason that the input–output balance is a vital mechanism in the life of a political system.

Politicization as a mechanism of support

It would be wrong to consider that the level of support available to a system is a function exclusively of the outputs in the form of either sanctions or rewards. If we did so conclude, we could scarcely account for the maintenance of numerous political systems in which satisfaction of demands has been manifestly low, in which public coercion is limited, and yet which have endured for epochs. Alternatively, it might be difficult to explain how political systems could endure and yet manage to flout or thwart urgent demands, failing thereby to render sufficient *quid pro quo* for the input of support. The fact is that whatever reserve of support has been accumulated through past decisions is increased and reinforced by a complicated method for steadily manufacturing support through what I shall call the process of politicization. It is an awkward term, but nevertheless an appropriately descriptive one.

As each person grows up in a society, through a network of rewards and punishments the other members of society communicate to and instill in him the various institutionalized goals and norms of that society. This is well known in social research as the process of socialization. Through its operation a person learns to play his various social roles. Part of these goals and norms relate to what the society considers desirable in political life. The ways in which these political patterns are learned by the members of society constitute what I call the process of politicization. Through it a person learns to play his political roles, which include the absorption of the proper political attitudes.

Let us examine a little more closely something of what happens during the process of politicization. As members of a society mature, they must absorb the various orientations toward political matters that one is expected to have in that society. If the expectations of the members of society with regard to the way each should behave in specific political situations diverged beyond a certain range, it would be impossible to get common action with regard to the making of binding decisions. It is essential for the viability of an orderly political system that the members of the system have some common basic expectations with regard to the standards that are to be used in making political evaluations, to the way people will feel about various political matters, and to the way members of the system will perceive and interpret political phenomena.

The mechanism through which this learning takes place is of considerable significance in understanding how a political system generates and accumulates a strong reserve of support. Although we cannot pursue the details, we can mention a few of the relevant dimensions. In the first place, of course, the learning or politicization process does not stop at any particular period for the individual; it starts with the child and, in the light of our knowledge of learning, may have its deepest impact through the teen age. . . .

In the second place, the actual process of politicization at its most general level brings into operation a complex network of rewards and punishments. For adopting the correct political attitudes and performing the right political acts, for conforming to the generally accepted interpretations of political goals, and for undertaking the institutionalized obligations of a member of the given system, we are variously rewarded or punished. For conforming we are made to feel worthy, wanted and respected and often obtain material advantages such as wealth, influence, improved opportunities. For deviating beyond the permissible range, we are made to feel unworthy, rejected, dishonored and often suffer material losses. . . .

In the third place, the means used for communicating the goals and norms to others tend to be repetitive in all societies. The various political myths, doctrines and philosophies transmit to each generation a particular interpretation of the goals and norms. The decisive links in this chain of transmission are parents, siblings, peers, teachers, organizations and social leaders, as well as physical symbols such as flags or totems, ceremonies and rituals freighted with political meaning.

These processes through which attachments to a political system become built into the maturing member of a society I have lumped together under the rubric of politicization. . . .

When the basic political attachments become deeply rooted

or institutionalized, we say that the system has become accepted as legitimate. Politicization therefore effectively sums up the way in which legitimacy is created and transmitted in a political system. And it is an empirical observation that in those instances where political systems have survived the longest, support has been nourished by an ingrained belief in the legitimacy of the relevant governments and regimes.

What I am suggesting here is that support resting on a sense of the legitimacy of a government and regime provides a necessary reserve if the system is to weather those frequent storms when the more obvious outputs of the system seem to impose greater hardships than rewards. Answers to questions concerning the formation, maintenance, transmission and change of standards of legitimacy will contribute generously to an understanding of the way in which support is sufficiently institutionalized so that a system may regularly and without excessive expenditure of effort transform inputs of demand into outputs of decision.

That there is a need for general theory in the study of political life is apparent. The only question is how best to proceed. There is no one royal road that can be said to be either the correct one or the best. It is only a matter of what appears at the given level of available knowledge to be the most useful. At this stage it appears that system theory, with its sensitivity to the input–output exchange between a system and its setting offers a fruitful approach. It is an economical way of organizing presently disconnected political data and promises interesting dividends.

Reference

EASTON, D. (1953), *The Political System*, Kropt.

5 Talcott Parsons

Political Systems and Bureaucracy

Excerpt from Talcott Parsons, Introduction to Part Two of Talcott
Parsons, Edward Shils. Kaspar D. Naegele and Jesse R. Pitts (eds.),
Theories of Society, Free Press 1961, pp. 246–9.

The keynote of the preceding discussion has been that political
and economic functions, in the earlier stages of structural social
evolution, are embedded in the three-fold matrix of ascriptive
solidarities (notably of kinship and ethnic group, but also of
relative territorial fixity), of religion and of stratification with
its introduction of hierarchically differentiated ascriptions. The
political functions tend to be more specialized in upper groups
and more closely associated with society-wide religious leadership; and economic functions tend to be more segmented and
distributed among the masses of the population organized in
largely ascriptive units.

Political foci of further differentiation
Bureaucracy

In general, two types of sources provide the impetus to further
differentiation. The more obvious and more frequently considered centers in the political sphere and is primarily concerned (with respect to one main subtype) with the extension of
various types of bureaucratic organization, both military and
civil. The second is the development of modes of religious organization and orientation that are autonomous in relation
to the more general social structure, particularly its upper
echelons.

The essential point about bureaucratization is that it frees the
necessary resources from ascriptive ties, which would prevent
their disposability, for collective goals according to the exigencies which arise. The most obvious of these ascriptive ties
are extended kinship and the kinds of decentralized territorial
jurisdiction associated, for example, with feudal systems. The

crucial resource in this case is the services of persons, organized in such a way that their loyalty to the implementing political organization takes precedence over other loyalties.

Though top political authority usually remains embedded in the lineage structures of kinship, in and below ministerial and high-command levels there may be more or less free disposability of personnel for the goals of higher authority. This process is, however, subject to a series of complex exigencies. The most important such contingency is probably the 'internal' problem of the patterning of the organizational structure itself. Others are the problems of economic provision; of integration with other structures, with special reference to the bases on which personnel in the bureaucratic structure are given 'security' in relation to conflicting claims on their loyalty; and of the basis of making legitimate such extensive claims on the societal resources.

Different sorts of organizational tasks vary widely. The military looms large in many societies, and usually the line between defense and offense is a thin one. But the great, economically significant public works of earlier eras belong mainly in this category – e.g. the irrigation and canal works of the river valley civilizations. Such projects may also be oriented to goals concerned with religion and/or integrative symbolization. Two cases of this are the enormous mobilization of resources for building temples and other religio-political monuments, like the pyramids of Egypt; and building palaces, which are both utilitarian facilities and symbols of the regimes' greatness and contributions to the society.

Necessarily qualified, Weber's dictum that bureaucracy is the most effective administrative instrument ever developed may be adopted as our point of reference. Internally, bureaucracy's principal characteristics as an ideal type consist in an adequate balance between competence and responsibility on the part of its various units. The requisite standards of competence vary with the nature of the task, and are connected with the related evolution of culture in the instrumental fields, the various technologies, etc. It is only very late that full-fledged science becomes an important component of competence. Responsibility concerns primarily the effectiveness with which units can be coordinated in the service of any organization task. Responsibility is associated especially with the nature of the authority and leadership operating within the organization. The fundamental problem is balancing the two essentially independent elements of competence and authority.

The effectiveness of internal organization is dependent on the external relations of a bureaucratic organization, in proportion to the large-scale and formidable character of the task. The factors of economic provision and security come to a head in the problem of the degrees of approximation to the institutionalization of occupational roles. The crucial problem is that of the ways in which and the degrees to which the performance of service can be made independent of involvement in relational contexts external to the organization, when organizational interests conflict potentially with the external interest. As Weber has made clear, the optimum arrangement is full money remuneration, so that neither the operative organization nor any of its subunits need have any claim or stake in the *sources* of economic provision; conversely, the structures constituting these sources need not have control over the organization's operation. This involves complex conditions, two of the most important being the extent of market systems and the feasibility of money taxation. Anything approximating a full system of money remuneration for a large-scale bureaucratic apparatus is found only in a few historical cases. Anything less than a full system, however, imposes severe constraints on the independence of the bureaucratic organization; even more important, where subunits are independently provided for through fiefs, benefices, etc., a powerful centrifugal force tends to arise that easily threatens the internal authority structure of the organization.

The problem of security is closely related to this. The fortunes of the organization may be subject to severe and unexpected vicissitudes; and the status of the individual or subunit within the organization may be seriously insecure. The specialization of bureaucratic roles *ipso facto* means that other, more particularistic bases of security must be sacrificed; because, in general, these involve a diffuse fusion with non-bureaucratic bases of status. Only through the very wide extension of occupational organization through the society as a whole can a close and stable approximation to Weber's ideal type of bureaucracy be achieved.

The famous Chinese Mandarin bureaucracy is an illuminating example of a 'compromise' formation. In the society as a whole, this stood virtually alone. The individual had no alternative 'occupational' career. Yet there was considerable risk in the process of qualification for office through the examination system, in part as a direct consequence of its universalistic rigor. Furthermore, once qualified, the individual's career chances were still uncertain. This situation influenced strongly the coexistence, over so many centuries, of the bureaucratic system and the social predominance of a landed gentry with full political control at the local levels. The gentry lineage was the security base from which it was possible to take the risks of an official career, and to which were fed back the proceeds of success. This was a mutually profitable symbiosis; but the functional necessity of the security base was a fundamental barrier to the further rationalization of Chinese bureaucracy.

Extreme predominance of the security base over organizational obligations is demonstrated in the military organization of Western feudalism. The leadership of military contingents was so strongly based in their own local feudal nexus that a central command could be sure of commanding their loyalty only within very narrow limits. A truly national level of military organization was not possible without structurally segregating military roles from the feudal network.

For present purposes, the most significant aspect of the problem of the legitimation of bureaucratic organizations and their operations is the relation of bureaucratic organization to any generalized system of law existing in the society. In other words, under certain circumstances groups who are somehow recognized as authorities on what is 'normatively correct' in the society tend to become dominant in directing and operating bureaucracies. Another aspect of the Chinese case demonstrates this: the famous Confucian literati were essentially 'lawyers'; they were trained in the 'proprieties'; they knew what conduct was right and proper for the superior man. Their expert status took in this respect precedence over any standards of technical competence or even organizational effectiveness, thus providing another very severe set of limitations on the rationalization of the bureaucracy.

Another example is the prominent role played by legally trained personnel in the civil bureaucracies of Continental Europe in modern times, particularly in Germany. In general, emancipation from the restrictive aspects of 'legalism' while not yet having attained adequate legitimation presents a serious set of problems. Often, the alternative to such legalistic restriction has been a Machiavellian power-orientation by the bureaucracy that has led to severe problems of integration in another direction.[1]

Political democracy

There is a second mode of differentiating the political components of social structure from their diffuse matrices. Bureaucratic organization concerns the *implementation* of goal-orientated decisions and leadership. The other case concerns the mechanism for arriving at such decisions and for structuring the support for leadership. The development of 'political democracy' in classical antiquity is the great example of emancipation from ascription. In the bureaucratic empires, political allegiance remained, as in primitive societies, in virtually all respects ascribed to the 'legitimate' authority structure – generally including a generous component of prescription by force. But in Greece and Rome, the institutionalization of the role of citizenship, though restricted to privileged minorities of the total population, included the right to participate in collective decision- and policy-making, and hence the right to allocate support between alternative leadership elements rather than restriction to the one legitimate authority. It is obvious that

1. The same essential sociological principles apply to the cases of economic and of political bureaucracy; the firm, though oriented to economic production, has a prominent 'political' (in the analytical sense) component in its organization. In this context, the association of the family firm with a kinship lineage has had functions similar to those of the gentry lineages in Chinese bureaucracy. The market is, like the official career, a field of serious risk-taking; and family property and the continuity of kinship status in the community have provided an important cushion underlying the risk. Only with the development of a very extensive occupational system in recent times could stable economic and political bureaucracy exist without some such cushion.

the stability of such a system would be precarious; it is not surprising that this pattern appeared only under special circumstances and in small-scale units. However, its importance as the basic model for modern political enfranchisement is clear.

It is important that the differentiation of the political from other elements was still incomplete in classical Greece and Rome. In the Greek *polis* and the Roman *urbs*, no clear differentiation between political and religious functions developed. The *polis* was both church and state, though, through certain types of secularization, its political aspect tended to become predominant. For present purposes, the essential point is that a considerable proportion of the population were enfranchised, that is, they were freed from specific ascriptive allegiances *within* (not *to*) the *polis*. It is significant that this development did not occur originally in societies which developed complex bureaucratic structures, and that, in Rome, as the *urbs* increased in scale, the incidence of the development became greatly attenuated. This set of circumstances, because of Rome's historical background as a city-state, probably played an important part in the acuteness of the problem of legitimacy in later Rome.

Law

The same general social complex – classical antiquity – is the most important source of development of an *independent* system of law. As noted, the legal element was central in the Chinese development but it took a form which did not readily become differentiated from either the political or the religious – on the contrary, it formed the focus of a special kind of codification of the religio-political fusion. There was thus essentially no pattern of institutionalization of legal rights *against* the state or religion.

The Greek legal system was similar, except that the all-important democratic element institutionalized rights, within the state, to participate in decision-making. In Greece, the legal system did not become generalized on an independent basis. In Rome, whose political dominion grew while internally the democratic element declined in importance, relations to the populations of the Empire became structured in dual form:

the extension of the privileges of Roman citizenship to larger and larger circles throughout the Empire; and the development of the *jus gentium* as a legal system applicable to all under Roman jurisdiction. Though administered by political authority and backed by religious sanctions, the system of Roman Law became an independent entity in a unique sense. Roman Law, in addition to classical culture, was clearly one of the most important legacies from antiquity to the modern Western world.

This aspect of law should be distinguished from the types of religious law, to be discussed briefly below, institutionalized in Judaism and Islam. The most important achievement of Roman Law was its type of differentiation of law from religion and from political leadership. In Judaism and Islam, religious sanction was lent to detailed prescriptions of conduct – this made the Roman type of differentiation impossible. To this day, this is a central problem in Islamic societies.

6 Jürgen Habermas

The Scientization of Politics and Public Opinion

Jürgen Habermas, 'The scientization of politics and public opinion', *Toward a Rational Society*, translated by Jeremy J. Schapiro, Heinemann, 1971, pp. 62–80. First published in German in 1964.

The scientization of politics is not yet a reality, but it is a real tendency for which there is evidence: the scope of research under government contract and the extent of scientific consultation to public services are primary examples. From the beginning the modern state, which arose from the need for central financial administration in connection with the market patterns of an emerging national and territorial economy, was dependent on the expertise of officials trained in the law. However, their technical knowledge did not differ fundamentally in form from professional knowledge of the sort possessed by the military. Just as the latter had to organize standing armies, so the officials had to organize a permanent administration. Both were practicing an art more than applying a science. It is only recently that bureaucrats, the military and politicians have been orienting themselves to strictly scientific recommendations in the exercise of their public functions – indeed, this practice has only existed on a large scale since the Second World War. This marks a new or second stage of that 'rationalization' which Max Weber had already comprehended as the basis for the development of bureaucratic domination. It is not as though scientists had seized state power; but the exercise of power domestically and its assertion against external enemies are no longer rationalized only through the mediation of administrative activity organized through the division of labor, regulated according to differentiated responsibilities, and linked to instituted norms. Instead they have been structurally transformed by the objective exigencies of new technologies and strategies.

Following a tradition that goes back to Hobbes, Weber found clear definitions for the relation of expertise and political practice. His famous confrontation of administration by officials versus political leadership served to separate strictly the functions of the expert from those of the politician (Weber, 1958). The latter makes use of technical knowledge, but the practice of self-assertion and domination requires in addition that a person or group with specific interests make decisions and carry them out. In the last analysis political action cannot rationally justify its own premises. Instead a decision is made between competing value orders and convictions, which escape compelling arguments and remain inaccessible to cogent discussion. As much as the objective knowledge of the expert may determine the techniques of rational administration and military security and thereby subject the means of political practice to scientific rules, practical decision in concrete situations cannot be *sufficiently* legitimated through reason. Rationality in the choice of means accompanies avowed irrationality in orientation to values, goals and needs. According to Weber only complete division of labor between the objectively informed and technically schooled general staffs of the bureaucracy and the military on the one hand and leaders with a power instinct and intense will on the other will make possible the scientization of politics.

Today we are confronted with the question whether this *decisionistic model* is valid for the second stage of the rationalization of domination. Systems analysis and especially decision theory do not merely make new technologies available, thus improving traditional instruments; they also rationalize choice as such by means of calculated strategies and automatic decision procedures. To this extent the objective necessity disclosed by the specialists seems to assert itself over the leaders' decisions.

Following a tradition that extends back through Saint-Simon to Bacon, the decisionistic definition of the relation of expertise to political practice is being abandoned by many in favor of a *technocratic model* (Ellul, 1967; Schelsky, 1961). The dependence of the professional on the politician appears to have reversed itself. The latter becomes the mere agent of a scientific intelligentsia, which, in concrete circumstances, elaborates the objective implications and requirements of available techniques and resources as well as of optional strategies and rules of control. If it is possible to rationalize decisions about practical questions, as a choice in situations of uncertainty, to the point where the 'symmetry of uncertainty' (Rittel) and thus the problems of decision in general are reduced step by step, then the politician in the technical state is left with nothing but a fictitious decision-making power. The politician would then be at best something like a stopgap in a still imperfect rationalization of power, in which the initiative has in any case passed to scientific analysis and technical planning. The state seems forced to abandon the substance of power in favor of an efficient way of applying available techniques in the framework of strategies that are objectively called for. It appears to be no longer an apparatus for the forcible realization of interests that have no foundation in principle and can only be answered for decisionistically. It becomes instead the organ of thoroughly rational administration.

But the weaknesses of this technocratic model are evident. On the one hand, it assumes an immanent necessity of technical progress, which owes its appearance of being an independent, self-regulating process only to the way in which social interests operate in it – namely through continuity with unreflected, unplanned, passively adaptive natural history (Krauch, 1961). On the other hand, this model presupposes a continuum of rationality in the treatment of technical and practical problems, which cannot in fact exist (Bahrdt, 1961; Habermas, 1963). For the new methods that characterize the rationalization of power in its second stage do not bring about the disappearance of the problem-complex connected with the decision of practical issues. Within the framework of research operations that expand our power of technical control we can make no cogent statements about 'value systems', that is, about social needs and objective states of consciousness, about the directions of emancipation and regression. Either there are still other forms of decision than the theoretical-technical for the rational clarification of practical issues that cannot be completely answered by technologies and strategies, or no reasons can be given for decisions in such issues. In that case we would have to return to the decisionistic model.

This conclusion has been drawn by Hermann Lübbe:

Whereas the politician once was respected more than the expert because the latter merely knew and planned what the former knew how to carry out, the situation has now been reversed. For the expert knows how to understand what is prescribed by the logic of real conditions, while the politician takes positions in conflict situations for which there is no court of earthly reason (1962b).

Lübbe incorporates the new stage of rationalization into the decisionistic model. But he maintains the antithesis between technical knowledge and the exercise of political power as defined by Weber and Carl Schmitt. He reproaches the technocratic self-understanding of the new experts with camouflaging what is really as political as ever with the 'logic of reality'. True, the scope of pure decision has been restricted to the degree that the politician disposes of an augmented and more refined arsenal of technical means and can make use of aids to strategic decision. But within this confined area what decisionism always presupposed has now become true for the first time. Only now has the problem-complex of political decisions been reduced to a core that simply cannot be rationalized any further. Calculation by decision procedures, when carried to extremes, reduces the decision itself to its pure form, purging it of every element that could be made accessible in any way to cogent analysis.

In this respect, however, the *expanded decisionistic model* has lost none of its original dubiousness. To be sure, it has descriptive value for the practice of scientifically informed decisions as they are made today in the centers of command in the mass democracies, prototypically in the United States. But this does not mean that there are logical reasons why this type of decision must be withdrawn from further reflection. Rationalization may in fact be discontinued at the gaps in politically directed technological-strategic research and replaced by decisions. If so, it is a noteworthy social fact explicable on the basis of objective constellations of interests. But it is not something that necessarily follows from the nature of the real problems, unless scientific discussion or any disciplined consideration going beyond the bounds of the positivistically approved mode of discourse is to be excluded from the very beginning. Since this is not the case, we can observe that the decisionistic model, however much it approximates the actual procedures of scientized politics, is inadequate according to its own theoretical claims. For there is obviously an interdependence between values that proceed from interest situations and techniques that can be utilized for the satisfaction of value-oriented needs. If so-called values in the long run lose their connection with the technically appropriate satisfaction of real needs, they become functionless and die out as ideologies. Inversely, new values can develop from new techniques in changed interest situations. In both cases, the decisionistic separation of questions of value and life from those of objective necessity remains abstract. The possibility that the introduction of continually augmented and improved techniques does not merely remain bound to undiscussed value orientations but also subjects traditional values to a sort of pragmatic corroboration was discussed some time ago by Dewey. Ultimately, in this view, value convictions are supposed to persist only to the extent that they can be controllably connected to available and imaginable techniques, that is, to the possible realization of value by producing goods or changing situations. True, Dewey did not take into account the difference between the control of technical recommendations by means of their results and the practical confirmation of techniques in the hermeneutically clarified context of concrete situations. Nevertheless, he insisted on the pragmatic examination and consequently the rational discussion of the relation between available techniques and practical decisions. This relation is ignored by the decisionists' viewpoint.

In the *pragmatistic model* the strict separation between the function of the expert and the politician is replaced by a critical interaction. This interaction not only strips the ideologically supported exercise of power of an unreliable basis of legitimation but makes it accessible *as a whole* to scientifically informed discussion, thereby substantially changing it. Despite the technocratic view, experts have not become sovereign over politicians subjected to the demands of the facts and left with a purely fictitious power of decision. Nor, despite the implications of the decisionistic model, does the politician retain a preserve outside of the necessarily rationalized areas of practice in which practical problems are decided upon as ever by acts of the will. Rather, reciprocal communication seems possible and necessary, through which scientific experts advise the decision-makers and politicians consult scientists in accordance with practical needs. Thus, on the one hand the development of new techniques is governed by a horizon of needs and historically determined interpretations of these needs, in other words, of value systems. This horizon has to be made explicit. On the other hand, these social interests, as reflected in the value systems, are regulated by being tested with regard to the technical possibilities and strategic means for their gratification. In this manner they are partly confirmed, partly rejected, articulated, and reformulated, or denuded of their ideologically transfigured and compelling character.

So far we have considered the three models of the relation of expertise and politics without reference to the structure of modern mass democracy. Only one of them, the pragmatistic, is necessarily related to democracy. If the division of power and responsibility between experts and leaders is carried out according to the decisionistic pattern, then the politically functioning public realm of the citizenry can serve only to legitimate the ruling group. The election and confirmation of governing individuals, or those capable of governing, are as a rule plebiscitary acts. The reason that democratic choice takes the form of acclamation rather than public discussion is that choice applies only to those who occupy positions with decision-making power and not to the guidelines of future decisions themselves. At best these decision-makers legitimate themselves before the public. Decisions themselves, according to the decisionistic view, must remain basically beyond public discussion. The scientization of politics then automatically accords with the theory developed by Weber, extended by Schumpeter, and now unquestioned by modern political sociology, a theory that in the last analysis reduces the process of democratic decision-making to a regulated acclamation procedure for elites alternately appointed to exercise power. In this way power, untouched in its irrational substance, can be legitimated but not rationalized.

The claim to rationalization, in contrast, is upheld by the technocratic model of scientized politics. Of course, the reduction of political power to rational administration can be conceived here only at the expense of democracy itself. If politicians were strictly subjected to objective necessity, a politically functioning public could at best legitimate the administrative personnel and judge the professional qualifications of salaried officials. But if the latter were of comparable qualifications it would in principle be a matter of indifference which competing elite group obtained power. A technocratic administration of industrial society would deprive any democratic decision-making process of its object. This conclusion has been drawn by Helmut Schelsky: '. . . the people's political will is supplanted by the objective exigencies that man produces as science and labor' (1961).

In contrast, the successful transposition of technical and strategic recommendations into practice is, according to the pragmatistic model, increasingly dependent on mediation by the public as a political institution. Comunication between experts and the agencies of political decision determines the direction of technical progress on the basis of the tradition-bound self-understanding of practical needs. Inversely it measures and criticizes this self-understanding in the light of the possibilities for gratification created by technology. Such communication must therefore necessarily be rooted in social interests and in the value-orientations of a given social life-world. In both directions the feedback-monitored communication process is grounded in what Dewey called 'value beliefs'. That is, it is based on a historically determined preunderstanding, governed by social norms, of what is practically necessary in a concrete situation. This preunderstanding is a consciousness that can only be enlightened hermeneutically, through articulation in the discourse of citizens in a community. Therefore the communication provided for in the pragmatistic model, which is supposed to render political practice scientific, cannot occur independently of the communication that is always already in process on the prescientific level. The latter type of communication, however, can be institutionalized in the democratic form of public discussions among the citizen body. The relation of the *sciences* to *public opinion* is constitutive for the scientization of politics.

It is true that this relation has never been made explicit in the tradition of pragmatistic thought. For Dewey it seemed self-evident that the relation of reciprocal guidance and enlightenment between the production of techniques and strategies on the one hand and the value-orientations of interested groups on the other could be realized within the unquestionable horizon of common sense and an uncomplicated public realm. But the *structural change in the bourgeois public realm* would have demonstrated the naïvete of this view even if it were not already invalidated by the internal development of the sciences. For the latter have made a basically unsolved problem out of the appropriate translation of technical information even between individual disciplines, let alone between the sciences and the public at large. Anyone who adheres to the notion of permanent communication between the sciences, considered in terms of their political relevance, and informed public opinion becomes suspect of wanting to put scientific discussion on a mass basis and thus to misuse it ideologically. This position in turn provokes a critique of ideology that opposes the simplified and overextended interpretation of scientific results in accordance with a weltanschauung, and instead firmly insists upon the positivistic separation of theory and practice. Weber's thesis of the neutrality of the sciences with regard to preexisting practical valuations can be convincingly employed against illusionary rationalizations of political problems, against *short-circuiting* the connection between technical expertise and a public that can be influenced by manipulation, and against the distorted response which scientific information meets with in a deformed public realm (Lübbe, 1962a).

Nevertheless, as soon as this critique calls into question a more extensive rationalization of the power structure as such, it succumbs to the limitations of positivism and to an ideology that makes science impervious to self-reflection. For then it confuses the actual difficulty of effecting permanent communication between science and public opinion with the violation of logical and methodological rules. True, as it stands the pragmatistic model cannot be applied to political decision-making in modern mass democracies. However, this is not because discussing practical questions both with reference to available techniques and strategies and within the horizon of the explicated self-understanding of a social life-world would require the illusory rationalization of unfounded acts of will. The reason is rather that this model neglects the specific logical characteristics and the social preconditions for the reliable translation of scientific information into the ordinary language of practice and inversely for a translation from the context of practical questions back into the specialized language of technical and strategic recommendations (Krauch, 1963). The example of the United States, the country in which the scientization of political practice has progressed the furthest, shows how such hermeneutic tasks arise in the discussion between scientists and politicians and how they are solved without their becoming conscious as such. This tacit hermeneutic is not explicitly subjected to scientific discipline, and only therefore does it seem, both externally and in the self-understanding of those involved, that there is a logically necessary division of labor between technical consultation and enlightened decision.

Communication between politically authorized contracting agencies and objectively knowledgeable and competent scientists at major research and consulting organizations marks the critical zone of the translation of practical questions into scientifically formulated questions and the translation of scientific information back into answers to practical questions. Of course this statement does not really capture the dialectic of the process. The Heidelberg Research Project in Systems Analysis has reported a revealing example. The headquarters of the US Air Force using experienced contact men presents a roughly outlined problem of military technology or organization to the program department of a research and consulting organization. The starting point is a vaguely formulated need. A more rigorous version of the problem first arises during the course of protracted communication between officers, themselves scientifically trained, and the project director. But contact is not broken off once the real problem is identified and successfully defined, for this suffices only to conclude a detailed contract. During the research itself, information is exchanged at all levels, from the president of the research organization down to the technician, with the corresponding personnel at the contracting institution. Communication may not end until the solution of the problem has basically been found, for only when the solution can be foreseen in principle is the goal of the project ultimately defined. The preunderstanding of the problem – the practical need of the contracting agency – is articulated in the measure that theoretical solutions, and consequently techniques of execution, crystallize in rigorously constructed models. The communication between the two partners is like a net of rational discussion stretching between practice and science. It must not break if during the development of specific technologies or strategies the originally vague, preunderstood interest in the elimination of a problematic situation is not to be frustrated – if instead its intention is to be preserved in formalized scientific models.

Inversely, practical needs, corresponding goals and value systems themselves also become specific and determinate only in relation to their technically possible realization. The understanding that social groups engaged in political action have of their situation is so dependent on the techniques available for the realization of interests that research projects are often not motivated by practical problems but instead brought to the attention of politicians by scientists. Given knowledge of the state of research, techniques can be projected for which connections with practical needs then have to be sought or for which connections with newly articulated needs have to be created. However, up to this point in problem-solving and the articulation of needs, only one-half of the process of translation has been covered. The technically appropriate solution of a problematic situation that has been brought to consciousness in a precise manner must in turn be translated back into the totality of the historical situation in which it has practical consequences. Ultimately, the evaluation of completed systems and evolved strategies requires the same form of interpreting a concrete situation with which the translation process began in the preunderstanding of the initial practical situation.

The process of translation that has become customary between political authorities that grant contracts and the consultants has also been institutionalized on a large scale. At the governmental level bureaucracies to direct research and development and scientific consulting agencies have been set up. Their function again reflects the singular dialectic of the transposition of science into political practice. In the framework of these agencies permanent communication between science and politics is established. Otherwise it could only arise *ad hoc* with the granting of special research commissions. The first government committee for scientists, founded by President Roosevelt in 1940, shortly before America entered the war, assumed the two functions now fulfilled by a large consulting apparatus. Political consultation has two tasks. The first is to interpret the results of research within the horizon of guiding interests that determine the political actors' understanding of their situation. The second is to evaluate projects and to stimulate and choose programs that orient the process of research in the direction of practical issues.

As soon as this task is taken out of the context of individual problems and the development of research as a whole is considered, the real problem of the dialogue between science and politics reveals itself to be the formulation of a long-term research policy. This would be the attempt to bring under control the traditional, fortuitous unplanned relations between technical progress and the social life-world. The direction of technical progress today is still largely determined by social interests that arise spontaneously from the compulsion to reproduce social life; they are not reflected as such and confronted with the declared political self-understanding of social groups. Consequently new technical potentials intrude unprepared into existing forms of life conduct. They only make more evident the disproportion between the results of the most intensive rationality and unreflected goals, petrified value systems and obsolete ideologies. The advisory bodies concerned with research policy give rise to a new type of interdisciplinary, future-oriented research, which ought to clarify the immanent developmental state and social preconditions of technical progress in connection with the cultural and educational level of society as a whole. They would thus offer a viewpoint different from that bounded by preexisting, unreflected social interests. These investigations, too, obey a hermeneutic interest in knowledge. For they make it possible to confront given social institutions and their self-understanding with the technology that is actually used and potentially available. Inversely, as part of this projected clarification by means of the critique of ideology, they make it possible to reorient social needs and declared goals. The formulation of a long-term research policy, the preparation of new industries that utilize future scientific information and the planning of an educational system for a qualified younger generation whose jobs are yet to be created are part of an endeavor to direct consciously what has previously taken place spontaneously and without planning: the mediation of technological progress with the conduct of life in large industrial societies. This endeavor embodies the dialectic of enlightened will and self-conscious potential.

The communication between experts at major research and consulting organizations and political authorities about individual projects takes place within an objectively delimited problem area, and discussion between consulting scientists and the government remains bound to the constellation of given situations and available potentials. But for this third task of programming social development as a whole, the dialogue between scientists and politicians is freed from the influence of *specific* problems. It must of course link up to a concrete situation, namely to a historical phase of tradition and to concrete social interests on the one hand, and to a given level of technical knowledge and industrial utilization on the other. Beyond this, however, the attempt at a long-term research and education policy oriented to immanent possibilities and objective consequences must be left up to the dialectic which we have become acquainted with in its earlier phases. It must enlighten those who take political action about their tradition-bound self-understanding of their interests and goals in relation to socially potential technical knowledge and capacity. At the same time it must put them in a position to judge practically, in the light of these articulated and newly interpreted needs, in what direction they want to develop their technical knowledge and capacity in the future. This discussion necessarily moves within a circle. For only to the extent that, knowing the technical potential of our historically determined will, we orient ourselves to the given situation, can we know in turn what specifically orientated expansion of our technical potential we want for the future.

In the last analysis the process of translation between science and politics is related to public opinion. This relation is not external to it, as though it were a question of taking prevailing constitutional norms into account. Rather it follows immanently and necessarily from the requirements of the confrontation of *technical knowledge and capacity* with *tradition-bound self-understanding*. The latter forms the horizon within which needs are interpreted as goals and goals are hypostatized as values. An element of anticipation is always contained in the integration of technical knowledge and the hermeneutical process of arriving at self-understanding. For it is set in motion by discussion among scientists isolated from the citizenry. The enlightenment of a scientifically instrumented political will according to standards of rationally binding discussion can proceed only from the horizon of communicating citizens themselves and must lead back to it. The consultants who would like to find out what will is expressed by political organizations are equally subject to the hermeneutic constraint of participating in the historical self-understanding of a social group – in the last analysis, in the conversations of citizens. Such an explication is, of course, bound to the methods of the hermeneutic sciences. But the latter do not destroy the dogmatic core of traditional, historically generated interpretations, they only clarify them. The two additional steps of employing the social sciences to analyse this self-understanding in connection with social interests on the one hand, and of ascertaining available techniques and strategies on the other lead beyond this area of public discourse. But the result of these steps, as the enlightenment of political will, can become effective only within the communication of citizens. For the articulation of needs in accordance with technical knowledge can be ratified exclusively *in the consciousness of the political actors themselves*. Experts cannot delegate to themselves this act of confirmation from those who have to account with their life histories for new interpretations of social needs and for accepted means of mastering problematic situations. With this reservation, however, the experts must anticipate the act of confirmation. Insofar as they assume this representative role, the experts necessarily think within the context of the philosophy of history, but in an experimental way and without being able to share the teleology and dogma of the tradition.

While integrating technology into the hermeneutically explicated self-understanding of a given situation, the process of the scientization of politics could be realized only if we had the guarantee that political will had obtained the enlightenment it wanted and simultaneously that enlightenment had permeated existing political will as much as it could under given, desired, and controllable circumstances. This could be guaranteed only by the ideal conditions of general communication extending to the entire public and free from domination. These considerations of principle must not, however, disguise the fact that the empirical conditions for the application of the pragmatistic model are lacking. The depoliticization of the mass of the population and the decline of the public realm as a political institution are components of a system of domination that tends to exclude practical questions from public discussion. The bureaucratized exercise of power has its counterpart in a public realm confined to spectacles and acclamation. This takes care of the approval of a mediatized population (Habermas, 1968). But even if we disregard the limits established by the existing system and assume that a social basis could be found today for public discussion among a broad public, the provision of relevant scientific information would still not be simple.

Leaving aside the public's ability to respond, the very results of research that are of the greatest practical consequence are the most inaccessible. While earlier industrially utilizable information was sometimes kept secret or protected for reasons of economic competition, today the free flow of information is blocked primarily by regulations of military secrecy. The interval between discovery and public disclosure for strategically relevant findings is at least three years and in many cases more than a decade.

There is an additional barrier between science and public knowledge that disturbs the flow of communication on the most basic level: the bureaucratic encapsulation that arises from the organization of the modern research process. Along with the forms of individual scholarship and an unproblematic unity of research and teaching, the unconstrained and formerly automatic contact of the individual scientist with the larger public, whether of students or of educated laymen, has disappeared. The concrete, objective interest of the scientist integrated into a large organization, aimed at the solution of narrowly circumscribed problems, no longer needs to be coupled from the beginning with a teacher's or publicist's concern with the transmission of knowledge to a public of auditors or readers. For the client at the gates of organized research, to whom scientific information is addressed, is now no longer (at least immediately) a public engaged in learning or discussion. It is instead a contracting agency interested in the outcome of the research process for the sake of its technical application. Formerly the task of literary presentation belonged to scientific reflection itself. In the system of large-scale research it is replaced by the memorandum formulated in relation to the contract and the research report aimed at technical recommendations.

Of course, there has grown up an esoteric scientific public in which experts exchange knowledge through professional journals or at conferences. But one would scarcely have expected to see contacts established between it and the literary, let alone political public, even if a singular difficulty had not necessitated a new form of communication. It has been calculated that the differentiation of research during the past one hundred years has doubled the number of professional and technical journals every fifteen years. Today, fifty thousand scientific journals are put out around the globe (Price, 1961; 1963; Dreitzel, 1963). With the rising flood of information that the scientific community has to deal with, attempts multiply to summarize the material, which is increasingly difficult to survey, and to order and process it to make an overview possible.

Journals of abstracts and reports are the first step in the direction of a process of translation that transforms and refines the raw material of original information. A number of journals serve the same purpose of communication between scientists of different disciplines who need an interpreter to be able to employ important information in neighboring fields for their own work. The more specialized research becomes, the greater the distances that important information must traverse in order to enter into the work of another expert. Physicists may even use *Time Magazine* to inform themselves about new developments in technology and chemistry. Helmut Krauch is undoubtedly right in suspecting that in Germany, too, interchange among scientists is already dependent on scientific journalism extending from elaborately written reports to the scientific columns of the daily press (Krauch, 1963). Cybernetics, which has developed its models on the basis of processes in physiology and communications technology, neuropsychology and economics, thus connecting findings of the most remote disciplines, is a good example of how important it is to keep communication channels open even if information from one specialist to another has to take the long route of ordinary language and the everyday understanding of the layman. Given a high degree of division of labor, the lay public often provides the shortest path of internal understanding between mutually estranged specialists. But this necessity for the translation of scientific information, which grows out of the needs of the research process itself, also benefits the endangered communication between scientists and the general public in the political sphere.

An additional tendency that counters the communication block between the two areas results from the international pressure for the peaceful coexistence of competing social systems. As Oskar Morgenstern has shown, military secrecy regulations, which inhibit the free flow of information in the public realm, become increasingly less compatible with the conditions of armament control, which becomes ever more urgent (1962). The growing risks of a precarious balance of deterrence necessitate reciprocally controlled disarmament. And the comprehensive inspection system that this presupposes can work effectively only if the principle of public accessibility is extended rigorously to international relations, strategic plans, and, above all, to militarily employable potentials. The core of this potential is strategically utilizable research itself. The program of an Open World thus demands in the first instance the free exchange of scientific information. Under the aegis of a general arms race, state monopolization of the technologically productive sciences is around the corner. Given the needs of information exchange, there is some evidence that this monopolization may be regarded as a transitional phase on the way to the collective utilization of information on the basis of unrestricted communication between science and the public realm.

However, neither the inner scientific requirement of translation nor the external requirement of free exchange of research information would actually suffice to set in motion a discussion of the practical consequences of scientific results among a responsible public, if the responsible scientists themselves did not ultimately take the initiative. The third tendency that we should like to adduce in favor of such discussion arises from the role conflict in which representative scientists become involved as scientists on the one hand and citizens on the other. To the extent that the sciences are really taken into the service of political practice, scientists are objectively compelled to go beyond the technical recommendations that they produce and reflect upon their practical consequences. This was especially and dramatically true for the atomic physicists involved in the production of the atomic and hydrogen bombs.

Since then there have been discussions in which leading scientists have argued about the political ramifications of their research practice, such as the damages that radioactive fallout have caused to the present health of the population and to the genetic substance of the human species. But the examples are few and far between. They show at least that responsible scientists, disregarding their professional or official roles, cross the boundaries of their inner scientific world and address themselves directly to public opinion when they want either to avert practical consequences connected with the choice of specific technologies or to criticize specific research investments in terms of their social effects.

Nevertheless, one would scarcely know from these small beginnings that the discussion that has begun in the offices of scientific consultants to government agencies basically has to be transferred to the broader political forum of the general public. The same holds for the dialogue now going on between scientists and politicians about the formulation of a long-term research policy.

As we have seen, the preconditions are unfavorable on both sides. On the one hand we can no longer reckon with functioning institutions for public discussion among the general public. On the other, the specialization of large-scale research and a bureaucratized apparatus of power reinforce each other only too well while the public is excluded as a political force. The choice that interests us is not between one elite that effectively exploits vital resources of knowledge over the heads of a mediatized population and another that is isolated from inputs of scientific information, so that technical knowledge flows inadequately into the process of political decision-making. The question is rather whether a productive body of knowledge is merely transmitted to men engaged in technical manipulation for purposes of control or is simultaneously appropriated as the linguistic possession of communicating individuals. A scientized society could constitute itself as a rational one only to the extent that science and technology are mediated with the conduct of life through the minds of its citizens.

There is a special dimension in which the controlled translation of technical into practical knowledge and thus the scientifically guided rationalization of political power is possible. Political rationalization occurs through the enlightenment of political will, correlated with instruction about its technical potential. This dimension is evaded when such enlightenment is considered either impossible because of the need for authoritative decisions or superfluous because of technocracy. In both cases, the objective consequences would be the same: a premature halt to possible rationalization. And the illusory attempts of the technocrats to have political decisions be directed only by the logic of objective exigency would justify the decisionists by leaving sheerly arbitrary what remains an irreducible remnant of practice on the periphery of technological rationality.

References

BAHRDT, H. P. (1961), 'Helmut Schelskys technischer Staat', *Atomzeitalter*, no. 9, p. 195.

DREITZEL, H. P. (1963), 'Wachstum und Fortschritt der Wissenschaft', *Atomzeitalter*, no. 11, p. 289.

ELLUL, J. (1967), *The Technological Society*, Random House.

HABERMAS, J. (1963), 'Von sozialen Wandel akademischer Bildung' in *Universitätstage 1963*, Berlin.

HABERMAS, J. (1968), *Strukturwandel der Offentlichkeit*, Neuwied, 3rd edn.

KRAUCH, H. (1961), 'Wider den technischen Staat', *Atomzeitalter*, no. 9, p. 201.

KRAUCH, H. (1963), 'Technische Information und offentliches Bewusstsein', *Atomzeitalter*, no. 9, p. 235.

LÜBBE, H. (1962a), 'Die Freiheit der Theorie', *Archiv fur Rechts- und Sozialphilosophie*.

LÜBBE, H. (1962b), 'Zur Politischen Theorie der Technokratie', *Der Staat*, vol. 1, no. 7, p. 21.

MORGENSTERN, O. (1962), *Strategie heute*, Frankfurt.

PRICE, D. J. de S. (1961), *Science since Babylon*, Yale University Press.

PRICE, D. J. de S. (1963), *Little Science, Big Science*, Columbia University Press.

SCHELSKY, H. (1961), *Der Mensch in der wissenschaftlichen Zivilisation*, Cologne-Opladen.

WEBER, M. (1958), *Gesammelte Politischen Schriften*, Tübingen, 2nd edn.

Part Two **The Operation of Power**

The question 'who governs?' has recently been at the centre of the debate in political sociology and political science. Very much in line with current trends in the social sciences in general, attention has been concentrated upon measuring the power of some given political actor. But even if we are able to measure some phenomena which we label 'power', we lack criteria with which to identify, other than physically, the holders of power,

The Marxist tradition is unconcerned with the question 'who governs?'. For Marx the analysis had to be devoted to the working of a given system in order to describe and explain the operations which secure the distribution of values. But Marx generally avoided the problem of the reciprocal impact of the economic system and the public administrative system, or state. Only in the *Eighteenth Brumaire* from which the following text is taken, he comes close to a consideration of the state as an autonomous object of analysis.

Mosca was the first to put the ruling class as such at the centre of the scientific study of politics. In this way, he opened one of the richer fields of political research. Much of it deals with local politics; it is not included here, with the exception of the reading by Banfield and Wilson, for the reason already given in the introduction. Mills's work on national power elites might be seen as a less rigorous extension of methods applied to the study of local politics. In fact, I think that it is more to be seen as an effort to describe the component part of a structure, than to identify an elite. The Dahl Reading must be understood within the same polemic between elitists and pluralists. This Reading and his later volume *Who Governs?* are among the best examples of the pluralist conception. But the argument in the Reading reaches a point, it seems to me, beyond this polemic, showing implicitly how any attempt to measure power is self-defeating if the problem of the definition of the subjects of power is not first solved. The Reading of the economist Kaysen strengthens such a conviction, suggesting how much escapes the sociologist's observation if he limits himself to the decision-making process and does not analyse the structural conditions of power.

Starting from the analysis of some local cases, Banfield and Wilson propose a sort of 'brokerage' theory of power: since power in a democracy is institutionally dispersed, and at the same time can be put to operation only by someone who controls a large amount of it, some 'broker' is needed who buys power from the many and sells it to the few. If this offers a penetrating analysis of power in western democracy, in socialist societies the crucial element in the power structure has to be seen in the party. This may concentrate power and/or distribute it. The Wiatr and Przeworski Reading indicates how a party may balance the concentration of power by participation and transmission of criticism. The Reading from the Schurmann study on Communist China points to a crucial function performed by the official ideology, seen as a communication system, in concentrating power and, at the same time, diffusing consensus.

7 Karl Marx

State Power and Society

Excerpt from Karl Marx, *Eighteenth Brumaire of Louis Bonaparte*, reprinted in L. S. Feuer (ed.), *Marx and Engels: Basic Writings*, Collins, 1959, pp. 334–45. First published in 1852.

The French bourgeoisie balked at the domination of the working proletariat; it has brought the *lumpenproletariat* to domination, with the chief of the Society of 10 December at the head. The bourgeoisie kept France in breathless fear of the future terrors of red anarchy; Bonaparte discounted this future for it when, on 4 December, he had the eminent bourgeois of the Boulevard Montmartre and the Boulevard des Italiens shot down at their windows by the liquor-inspired army of order. It apotheosized the sword; the sword rules it. It destroyed the revolutionary press; its own press has been destroyed. It placed popular meetings under police supervision; its salons are under the supervision of the police. It disbanded the democratic National Guards; its own National Guard is disbanded. It imposed a state of siege; a state of siege is imposed upon it. It supplanted the juries by military commissions; its juries are supplanted by military commissions. It subjected public education to the sway of the priests; the priests subject it to their own education. It transported people without trial; it is being transported without trial. It repressed every stirring in society by means of the state power; every stirring in its society is suppressed by means of the state power. Out of enthusiasm for its purse it rebelled against its own politicians and men of letters; its politicians and men of letters are swept aside, but its purse is being plundered now that its mouth has been gagged and its pen broken. The bourgeoisie never wearied of crying out to the revolution what St Arsenius cried out to the Christians: '*Fuge, tace, quiesce* (Flee, be silent, keep still)!' Bonaparte cries to the bourgeoisie: '*Fuge, tace, quiesce* (Flee, be silent, keep still)!'

The French bourgeoisie had long ago found the solution to

Napoleon's dilemma: *'Dans cinquante ans l'Europe sera républicaine ou cosaque* [In fifty years Europe will be either republican or Cossack].' It had found the solution to it in the *'république cosaque'*. No Circe, by means of black magic, has distorted that work of art, the bourgeois republic, into a monstrous shape. That republic has lost nothing but the semblance of respectability. Present-day France was contained in a finished state within the parliamentary republic. It required only a bayonet thrust for the bubble to burst and the monster to spring forth before our eyes.

Why did the Paris proletariat not rise in revolt after 2 December?

The overthrow of the bourgeoisie had as yet been only decreed; the decree had not been carried out. Any serious insurrection of the proletariat would at once have put fresh life into the bourgeoisie, would have reconciled it with the army and ensured a second June defeat for the workers.

On 4 December the proletariat was incited by bourgeois and *épicier* to fight. On the evening of that day several legions of the National Guard promised to appear, armed and uniformed, on the scene of battle. For the bourgeois and the *épicier* had got wind of the fact that in one of his decrees of 2 December, Bonaparte abolished the secret ballot and enjoined them to record their 'yes' or 'no' in the official registers after their names. The resistance of 4 December intimidated Bonaparte. During the night he caused placards to be posted on all the street corners of Paris, announcing the restoration of the secret ballot. The bourgeois and the *épicier* believed that they had gained their end. Those who failed to appear next morning were the bourgeois and the *épicier*.

By a *coup de main* during the night of 1 to 2 December, Bonaparte had robbed the Paris proletariat of its leaders, the barricade commanders. An army without officers, averse to fighting under the banner of the *Montagnards* because of the memories of June 1848 and 1849 and May 1850, it left to its vanguard, the secret societies, the task of saving the insurrectionary honor of Paris, which the bourgeoisie had so unresistingly surrendered to the soldiery that, later on, Bonaparte could sneeringly give as his motive for disarming the National

Guard – his fear that its arms would be turned against it itself by the anarchists!

'*C'est le triomphe complet et définitif du socialisme* [This is the complete and definitive triumph of socialism]!' Thus Guizot characterized 2 December. But if the overthrow of the parliamentary republic contains within itself the germ of the triumph of the proletarian revolution, its immediate and palpable result was *the victory of Bonaparte over parliament, of the executive power over the legislative power, of force without phrases over the force of phrases.* In parliament the nation made its general will the law, that is, it made the law of the ruling class its general will. Before the executive power it renounces all will of its own and submits to the superior command of an alien will, to authority. The executive power, in contrast to the legislative power, expresses the heteronomy of a nation, in contrast to its autonomy. France, therefore, seems to have escaped the despotism of a class only to fall back beneath the despotism of an individual, and, what is more, beneath the authority of an individual without authority. The struggle seems to be settled in such a way that all classes, equally impotent and equally mute, fall on their knees before the rifle butt.

But the revolution is thoroughgoing. It is still journeying through purgatory. It does its work methodically. By 2 December 1851, it had completed one half of its preparatory work; it is now completing the other half. First it perfected the parliamentary power, in order to be able to overthrow it. Now that it has attained this it perfects the *executive power*, reduces it to its purest expression, isolates it, sets it up against itself as the sole target, in order to concentrate all its forces of destruction against it. And when it has done this second half of its preliminary work, Europe will leap from its seat and exultantly exclaim: 'Well grubbed, old mole!'

This executive power, with its enormous bureaucratic and military organization, with its ingenious state machinery, embracing wide strata, with a host of officials numbering a half million, besides an army of another half million, this appalling parasitic body, which enmeshes the body of French society like a net and chokes all its pores, sprang up in the days of the absolute monarchy, with the decay of the feudal system, which it helped to hasten. The seignorial privileges of the landowners and towns became transformed into so many attributes of the state power, the feudal dignitaries into paid officials and the motley pattern of conflicting medieval plenary powers into the regulated plan of a state authority whose work is divided and centralized as in a factory. The first French Revolution, with its task of breaking all separate local, territorial, urban and provincial powers in order to create the civil unity of the nation, was bound to develop what the absolute monarchy had begun, centralization, but at the same time the extent, the attributes and the agents of governmental power. Napoleon perfected this state machinery. The Legitimist monarchy and the July monarchy added nothing but a greater division of labor, growing in the same measure as the division of labor within bourgeois society created new groups of interests, and, therefore, new material for state administration. Every *common* interest was straightaway severed from society, counterposed to it as a higher, *general* interest, snatched from the activity of society's members themselves, and made an object of government activity, from a bridge, a schoolhouse and the communal property of a village community to the railways, the national wealth and the national university of France. Finally, in its struggle against the revolution, the parliamentary republic found itself compelled to strengthen, along with the repressive measures, the resources and centralization of governmental power. All revolutions perfected this machine instead of smashing it. The parties that contended in turn for domination regarded the possession of this huge state edifice as the principal spoils of the victor.

But under the absolute monarchy, during the first revolution, under Napoleon bureaucracy was only the means of preparing the class rule of the bourgeoisie. Under the Restoration, under Louis Philippe, under the parliamentary republic it was the instrument of the ruling class, however much it strove for power of its own.

Only under the second Bonaparte does the state seem to have made itself completely independent. As against civil society, the state machine has consolidated its position so thoroughly that the chief of the Society of 10 December suffices for its head, an adventurer blown in from abroad, raised on the shield by a drunken soldiery, which he has bought with liquor and sausages, and which he must continually ply with sausage anew. Hence the downcast despair, the feeling of most dreadful humiliation and degradation that oppresses the breast of France and makes her catch her breath. She feels dishonored.

And yet the state power is not suspended in mid-air. Bonaparte represents a class, and the most numerous class of French society at that, the *small-holding* [*Parzellen*] *peasants.*

Just as the Bourbons were the dynasty of big landed property and just as the Orleans were the dynasty of money, so the Bonapartes are the dynasty of the peasants, that is, the mass of the French people. Not the Bonaparte who submitted to the bourgeois parliament, but the Bonaparte who dispersed the bourgeois parliament is the chosen of the peasantry. For three years the towns had succeeded in falsifying the meaning of the election of 10 December, and in cheating the peasants out of the restoration of the empire. The election of 10 December 1848 has been consummated only by the *coup d'état* of 2 December 1851.

The small-holding peasants form a vast mass, the members of which live in similar conditions but without entering into manifold relations with one another. Their mode of production isolates them from one another instead of bringing them into mutual intercourse. The isolation is increased by France's bad means of communication and by the poverty of the peasants. Their field of production, the small holding, admits of no division of labor in its cultivation, no application of science, and, therefore, no diversity of development, no variety of talent, no wealth of social relationships. Each individual peasant family is almost self-sufficient; it itself directly produces the major part of its consumption, and thus acquires its means of life more through exchange with nature than in intercourse with society. A small holding, a peasant and his family; alongside them another small holding, another peasant and another family. A few score of these make up a village, and a few score of villages make up a department. In this way the great mass of the French nation is formed by simple addition of homologous magnitudes, much as potatoes in a sack form a sack of potatoes. In so far as millions of families live under economic conditions of existence that separate their mode of life, their interests and their culture from those of the other classes and put them in hostile opposition to the latter, they form a class. In so far as there is merely a local interconnection among these small-holding peasants and the identity of their interests begets no community, no national bond and no political organization among them, they do not form a class. They are consequently incapable of enforcing their class interest in their own name, whether through a parliament or through a convention. They cannot represent themselves, they must be represented. Their representative must at the same time appear as their master, as an authority over them, as an unlimited government power that protects them against the other classes and sends them rain and sunshine from above. The political influence of the small-holding peasants, therefore, finds its final expression in the executive power subordinating society to itself.

Historical tradition gave rise to the belief of the French peasants in the miracle that a man named Napoleon would bring all the glory back to them. And an individual turns up who gives himself out as the man because he bears the name of Napoleon, in consequence of the Code Napoleon, which lays down that *la recherche de la paternité est interdite*. [Research into paternity is forbidden.] After a vagabondage of twenty years and after a series of grotesque adventures the legend finds fulfilment and the man becomes Emperor of the French. The fixed idea of the nephew was realized because it coincided with the fixed idea of the most numerous class of the French people.

But, it may be objected, what about the peasant risings in half of France, the raids on the peasants by the army, the mass incarceration and transportation of peasants?

Since Louis XIV, France has experienced no similar persecution of the peasants 'on account of demagogic practices'.

But let there be no misunderstanding. The Bonaparte dynasty represents not the revolutionary, but the conservative peasant; not the peasant that strikes out beyond the condition of his social existence, the small holding, but rather the peasant who wants to consolidate this holding, not the country folk who, linked up with the towns, want to overthrow the old order through their own energies, but on the contrary, those who, in stupefied seclusion within this old order, want to see themselves and their small holdings saved and favored by the ghost of the empire. It represents not the enlightenment, but the super-stition of the peasant; not his judgement, but his prejudice; not his future, but his past; not his modern Cevennes, but his modern Vendée.

The three-year rigorous rule of the parliamentary republic had freed a part of the French peasants from the Napoleonic illusion and had revolutionized them, even if only superficially; but the bourgeoisie violently repressed them as often as they set themselves in motion. Under the parliamentary republic the modern and the traditional consciousness of the French peasant contended for mastery. This progress took the form of an in-cessant struggle between the schoolmasters and the priests. The bourgeoisie struck down the schoolmasters. For the first time the peasants made efforts to behave independently in the face of the activity of the government. This was shown in the continual conflict between the *maires* and the prefects. The bourgeoisie deposed the *maires*. Finally, during the period of the par-liamentary republic, the peasants of different localities rose against their own offspring, the army. The bourgeoisie punished them with states of siege and punitive expeditions. And this same bourgeoisie now cries out about the stupidity of the masses, the vile multitude, that has betrayed it to Bonaparte. It has itself forcibly strengthened the empire sentiments [*Imperi-alismus*] of the peasant class, it conserved the conditions that form the birthplace of this peasant religion. The bourgeoisie, to be sure, is bound to fear the stupidity of the masses as long as they remain conservative and the insight of the masses as soon as they become revolutionary.

In the rising after the *coup d'état* a part of the French peasants protested, arms in hand, against their own vote of 10 December 1848. The school they had gone through since 1848 had sharpened their wits. But they had made themselves over to the underworld of history; history held them to their word, and the majority was still so prejudiced that in precisely the red-dest Departments the peasant population voted openly for Bonaparte. In its view, the National Assembly had hindered his progress. He had now merely broken the fetters that the towns had imposed on the will of the countryside. In some parts the peasants even entertained the grotesque notion of a convention side by side with Napoleon.

After the first revolution had transformed the peasants from semi-villeins into freeholders, Napoleon confirmed and regulated the conditions on which they could exploit undisturbed the soil of France which had only just fallen to their lot and slake their youthful passion for property. But what is now causing the ruin of the French peasant is his small holding itself, the division of the land, the form of property which Napoleon consolidated in France. It is precisely the material conditions which made the feudal peasant a small-holding peasant and Napoleon an emperor. Two generations have sufficed to produce the inevitable result: progressive deterioration of agriculture, progressive indebtedness of the agriculturist. The 'Napoleonic' form of property, which at the beginning of the nineteenth century was the condition for the liberation and enrichment of the French country folk, has developed in the course of this century into the law of their enslavement and pauperization. And precisely this law is the first of the *idées napoléoniennes* which the second Bonaparte has to uphold. If he still shares with the peasants the illusion that the cause of their ruin is to be sought not in this small-holding property itself but outside it, in the influence of secondary circumstances, his experiments will burst like soap bubbles when they come in contact with the relations of production.

The economic development of small-holding property has radically changed the relation of the peasants to the other classes of society. Under Napoleon the fragmentation of the land in the countryside supplemented free competition and the beginning of big industry in the towns. The peasant class was the ubiquitous protest against the landed aristocracy, which had just been overthrown. The roots that small-holding property struck in French soil deprived feudalism of all nutriment. Its landmarks formed the natural fortifications of the bourgeoisie against any surprise attack on the part of its old overlords. But in the course of the nineteenth century the feudal lords were replaced by urban usurers; the feudal obligation that went with the land was replaced by the mortgage; aristocratic landed property was replaced by bourgeois capital. The small holding of the peasant is now only the pretext that allows the capitalist to draw profits, interest and rent from the soil, while leaving it to the tiller of the soil himself to see how he can extract his wages. The mortgage debt burdening the soil of France imposes on the French peasantry payment of an amount of interest equal to the annual interest on the entire British national debt. Small-holding property, in this enslavement by capital to which its development inevitably pushes forward, has transformed the mass of the French nation into troglodytes. Sixteen million peasants (including women and children) dwell in hovels, a large number of which have but one opening, others only two, and the most favored only three. And windows are to a house what the five senses are to the head. The bourgeois order, which at the beginning of the century set the state to stand guard over the newly arisen small holding and manured it with laurels, has become a vampire that sucks out its blood and brains and throws them into the alchemistic cauldron of capital. The Code Napoleon is now nothing but a *codex* of distraints, forced sales and compulsory auctions. To the four million (including children, etc.) officially recognized paupers, vagabonds, criminals and prostitutes in France must be added five million who hover on the margin of existence and either have their haunts in the countryside itself, or, with their rags and their children, continually desert the countryside for the towns and the towns for the countryside. The interests of the peasants, therefore, are no longer, as under Napoleon, in accord with, but in opposition to the interests of the bourgeoisie, to capital. Hence the peasants find their natural ally and leader in the *urban proletariat*, whose task is the overthrow of the bourgeois order. But *strong and unlimited government* – and this is the second '*idée napoléonienne*' which the second Napoleon has to carry out – is called upon to defend this 'material' order by force. This '*ordre matériel*' also serves as the catchword in all of Bonaparte's proclamations against the rebellious peasants.

Besides the mortgage which capital imposes on it, the small holding is burdened by *taxes*. Taxes are the source of life for the bureaucracy, the army, the priests and the court, in short, for the whole apparatus of the executive power. Strong government and heavy taxes are identical. By its very nature smallholding property forms a suitable basis for an all-powerful and innumerable bureaucracy. It creates a uniform level of relationships and persons over the whole surface of the land. Hence it also permits of uniform action from a supreme center on all points of this uniform mass. It annihilates the aristocratic intermediate grades between the mass of the people and the state power. On all sides, therefore, it calls forth the direct interference of this state power and the interposition of its immediate organs. Finally, it produces an unemployed surplus population for which there is no place either on the land or in the towns, and which accordingly reaches out for state offices as a sort of respectable alms and provokes the creation of the state posts. By the new markets which he opened at the point of the bayonet, by the plundering of the Continent, Napoleon repaid the compulsory taxes with interest. These taxes were a spur to the industry of the peasant, whereas now they rob his industry of its last resources and complete his inability to resist pauperism. And an enormous bureaucracy, well gallooned and well fed, is the 'idée napoléonienne' which is most congenial of all to the second Bonaparte. How could it be otherwise, seeing that alongside the actual classes of society he is forced to create an artificial caste, for which the maintenance of his regime becomes a bread-and-butter question? Accordingly, one of his first financial operations was the raising of officials' salaries to their old level and the creation of new sinecures.

Another 'idée napoléonienne' is the domination of the *priests* as an instrument of government. But while in its accord with society, in its dependence on natural forces and its submission to the authority which protected it from above the small holding that had newly come into being was naturally religious, the small holding that is ruined by debts, at odds with society and authority, and driven beyond its own limitations naturally becomes irreligious. Heaven was quite a pleasing accession to the narrow strip of land just won, more particularly as it makes the weather; it becomes an insult as soon as it is thrust forward as substitute for the small holding. The priest then appears as only the anointed bloodhound of the earthly police – another '*idée napoléonienne*'. On the next occasion, the expedition against Rome will take place in France itself, but in a sense opposite to that of M. de Montalembert.

Lastly, the culminating point of the '*idées napoléoniennes*' is the preponderance of the *army*. The army was the *point d'honneur* of the small-holding peasants; it was they themselves transformed into heroes, defending their new possessions against the outer world, glorifying their recently won nationhood, plundering and revolutionizing the world. The uniform was their own state dress; war was their poetry; the small holding, extended and rounded off in imagination, was their fatherland, and patriotism the ideal form of the sense of property. But the enemies against whom the French peasant has now to defend his property are not the Cossacks; they are the *huissiers* and the tax collectors. The small holding lies no longer in the so-called fatherland, but in the register of mortgages. The army itself is no longer the flower of the peasant youth; it is the swamp flower of the peasant *lumpenproletariat*. It consists in large measure of *remplaçants*, of substitutes, just as the second Bonaparte is himself only a *remplaçant*, the substitute for Napoleon. It now performs its deeds of valor by hounding the peasants in masses like chamois, by doing *gendarme* duty, and if the internal contradictions of his system chase the chief of the Society of 10 December over the French border, his army, after some acts of brigandage, will reap not laurels, but thrashings.

One sees *all 'idées napoléoniennes' are ideas of the undeveloped small holding in the freshness of its youth*; for the small holding that has outlived its day, they are an absurdity. They are only the hallucinations of its death struggle, words that are transformed into phrases, spirits transformed into ghosts. But the parody of the empire [*das Imperialismus*] was necessary to free the mass of the French nation from the weight of tradition and to work out in pure form the opposition between the state power and society. With the progressive undermining of small-holding property, the state structure erected upon it collapses. The centralization of the state that modern society requires arises only on the ruins of the military bureaucratic government machinery which was forged in opposition to feudalism.

8 Gaetano Mosca

The Political Class

Excerpts from Gaetano Mosca, *The Ruling Class*, translated by
Hannah D. Kahn, McGraw-Hill, 1939, pp. 50–65. First published in
Italian in 1896.

Among the constant facts and tendencies that are to be found in
all political organisms, one is so obvious that it is apparent to
the most casual eye. In all societies – from societies that are very
meagerly developed and have barely attained the dawnings of
civilization, down to the most advanced and powerful societies
– two classes of people appear – a class that rules and a class
that is ruled. The first class, always the less numerous, performs all political functions, monopolizes power and enjoys the
advantages that power brings, whereas the second, the more
numerous class, is directed and controlled by the first, in a
manner that is now more or less legal, now more or less arbitrary and violent, and supplies the first, in appearance at least,
with material means of subsistence and with the instrumentalities that are essential to the vitality of the political organism.

In practical life we all recognize the existence of this ruling
class (or political class,[1] as we have elsewhere chosen to define it).[2] We all know that, in our own country, whichever
it may be, the management of public affairs is in the hands
of a minority of influential persons, to which management, wil-
lingly or unwillingly, the majority defer. We know that the
same thing goes on in neighboring countries, and in fact we
should be put to it to conceive of a real world otherwise organized – a world in which all men would be directly subject to a
single person without relationships of superiority or subordination, or in which all men would share equally in the
direction of political affairs. If we reason otherwise in theory,

1. A definition which I have preferred to retain for this volume. [Ed.]
2. *Teorica dei governi e governo parlamentare*, ch. 1.

that is due partly to inveterate habits that we follow in our thinking and partly to the exaggerated importance that we attach to two political facts that loom far larger in appearance than they are in reality.

The first of these facts – and one has only to open one's eyes to see it – is that in every political organism there is one individual who is chief among the leaders of the ruling class as a whole and stands, as we say, at the helm of the state. That person is not always the person who holds supreme power according to law. At times alongside of the hereditary king or emperor there is a prime minister or a major-domo who wields an actual power that is greater than the sovereign's. At other times, in place of the elected president the influential politician who has procured the president's election will govern. Under special circumstances there may be, instead of a single person, two or three who discharge the functions of supreme control.

The second fact, too, is readily discernible. Whatever the type of political organization, pressures arising from the discontent of the masses who are governed, from the passions by which they are swayed, exert a certain amount of influence on the policies of the ruling, the political, class.

But the man who is at the head of the state would certainly not be able to govern without the support of a numerous class to enforce respect for his orders and to have them carried out; and granting that he can make one individual, or indeed many individuals, in the ruling class feel the weight of his power, he certainly cannot be at odds with the class as a whole or do away with it. Even if that were possible, he would at once be forced to create another class, without the support of which action on his part would be completely paralysed. On the other hand, granting that the discontent of the masses might succeed in deposing a ruling class, inevitably, as we shall later show, there would have to be another organized minority within the masses themselves to discharge the functions of a ruling class. Otherwise all organization, and the whole social structure, would be destroyed.

From the point of view of scientific research the real superiority of the concept of the political class lies in the fact that the varying structure of classes has a preponderant importance in determining the political type, and also the level of civilization, of the different peoples. According to a manner of classifying forms of government that is still in vogue, Turkey and Russia were both, up to a few years ago, absolute monarchies, England and Italy were constitutional, or limited, monarchies, and France and the United States were classed as republics. The classification was based on the fact that, in the first two countries mentioned, headship in the state was hereditary and the chief was nominally omnipotent; in the second two, his office is hereditary but his powers and prerogatives are limited; in the last two, he is elected.

That classification is obviously superficial. Absolutisms though they were, there was little in common between the manners in which Russia and Turkey were managed politically, the levels of civilization in the two countries and the organization of their ruling classes being vastly different. On the same basis, the regime in Italy, a monarchy, is much more similar to the regime in France, a republic, than it is to the regime in England, also a monarchy; and there are important differences between the political organizations of the United States and France, though both countries are republics.

As we have already suggested, ingrained habits of thinking have long stood, as they still stand, in the way of scientific progress in this matter. The classification mentioned above, which divides governments into absolute monarchies, limited monarchies and republics, was devised by Montesquieu and was intended to replace the classical categories of Aristotle, who divided governments into monarchies, aristocracies and democracies. What Aristotle called a democracy was simply an aristocracy of fairly broad membership. Aristotle himself was in a position to observe that in every Greek state, whether aristocratic or democratic, there was always one person or more who had a preponderant influence. Between the day of Polybius and the day of Montesquieu, many writers perfected Aristotle's classification by introducing into it the concept of 'mixed' governments. Later on the modern democratic theory, which had its source in Rousseau, took its stand upon the concept that the majority of the citizens in any state can participate, and in fact *ought* to participate, in its political life, and the doctrine of popular sovereignty still holds sway over many minds in spite of the fact that modern scholarship is making it increasingly clear that democratic, monarchical and aristocratic principles function side by side in every political organism. We shall not stop to refute this democratic theory here, since that is the task of this work as a whole. Besides, it would be hard to destroy in a few pages a whole system of ideas that has become firmly rooted in the human mind. As Las Casas aptly wrote in his life of Christopher Columbus, it is often much harder to unlearn than to learn.

We think it may be desirable, nevertheless, to reply at this point to an objection which might very readily be made to our point of view. If it is easy to understand that a single individual cannot command a group without finding within the group a minority to support him, it is rather difficult to grant, as a constant and natural fact, that minorities rule majorities, rather than majorities minorities. But that is one of the points – so numerous in all the other sciences – where the first impression one has of things is contrary to what they are in reality. In reality the dominion of an organized minority, obeying a single impulse, over the unorganized majority is inevitable. The power of any minority is irresistible as against each single individual in the majority, who stands alone before the totality of the organized minority. At the same time, the minority is organized for the very reason that it is a minority. A hundred men acting uniformly in concert, with a common understanding, will triumph over a thousand men who are not in accord and can therefore be dealt with one by one. Meanwhile it will be easier for the former to act in concert and have a mutual understanding simply because they are a hundred and not a thousand. It follows that the larger the political community, the smaller will the proportion of the governing minority to the governed majority be, and the more difficult will it be for the majority to organize for reaction against the minority.

However, in addition to the great advantage accruing to them from the fact of being organized, ruling minorities are usually so constituted that the individuals who make them up are distinguished from the mass of the governed by qualities that give them a certain material, intellectual or even moral superiority; or else they are the heirs of individuals who possessed such qualities. In other words, members of a ruling minority regularly have some attribute, real or apparent, which is highly esteemed and very influential in the society in which they live.

In primitive societies that are still in the early stages of organization, military valor is the quality that most readily opens access to the political class. In societies of advanced civilization, war is the exceptional condition. It may be regarded as virtually normal in societies that are in the initial stages of their development; and the individuals who show the greatest ability in war easily gain supremacy over their fellows – the bravest become chiefs. The fact is constant, but the forms it may assume, in one set of circumstances or another, vary considerably.

As a rule the dominance of a warrior class over a peaceful multitude is attributed to a superposition of races, to the conquest of a relatively unwarlike group by an aggressive one. Sometimes that is actually the case – we have examples in India after the Aryan invasions, in the Roman Empire after the Germanic invasions and in Mexico after the Aztec conquest. But more often, under certain social conditions, we note the rise of a warlike ruling class in places where there is absolutely no trace of a foreign conquest. As long as a horde lives exclusively by the chase, all individuals can easily become warriors. There will of course be leaders who will rule over the tribe, but we will not find a warrior class rising to exploit, and at the same time to protect, another class that is devoted to peaceful pursuits. As the tribe emerges from the hunting stage and enters the agricultural and pastoral stage, then, along with an enormous increase in population and a greater stability in the means of exerting social influence, a more or less clean-cut division into two classes will take place, one class being devoted exclusively to agriculture, the other class to war. In this event, it is inevitable that the warrior class should little by little acquire such ascendancy over the other as to be able to oppress it with impunity.

Poland offers a characteristic example of the gradual metamorphosis of a warrior class into an absolutely dominant class. Originally the Poles had the same organization by rural villages as prevailed among all the Slavic peoples. There was no distinction between fighters and farmers – in other words, between nobles and peasants. But after the Poles came to settle on the broad plains that are watered by the Vistula and the Niemen, agriculture began to develop among them. However, the necessity of fighting with warlike neighbors continued, so that the tribal chiefs, or *voivodes*, gathered about themselves a certain number of picked men whose special occupation was the bearing of arms. These warriors were distributed among the various rural communities. They were exempt from agricultural duties, yet they received their share of the produce of the soil, along with the other members of the community. In early days their position was not considered very desirable, and country dwellers sometimes waived exemption from agricultural labor in order to avoid going to war. But gradually as this order of things grew stabilized, as one class became habituated to the practice of arms and military organization while the other hardened to the use of the plow and the spade, the warriors became nobles and masters, and the peasants, once companions and brothers, became villeins and serfs. Little by little the warrior lords increased their demands to the point where the share they took as members of the community came to include the community's whole produce minus what was absolutely necessary for subsistence on the part of the cultivators; and when the latter tried to escape such abuses they were constrained by force to stay bound to the soil, their situation taking on all the characteristics of serfdom pure and simple.

In the course of this evolution, around the year 1333, King Casimir the Great tried vainly to curb the overbearing insolence of the warriors. When peasants came to complain of the nobles, he contented himself with asking whether they had no sticks and stones. Some generations later, in 1537, the nobility forced all tradesmen in the cities to sell such real estate as they owned, and landed property became a prerogative of nobles only. At the same time the nobility exerted pressure upon the king to open negotiations with Rome, to the end that thenceforward only nobles should be admitted to holy orders in Poland. That barred townsmen and peasants almost completely from honorific positions and stripped them of any social importance whatever.[3]

We find a parallel development in Russia. There the warriors who formed the druzhina, or escort, of the old knezes (princes descended from Rurik) also received a share in the produce of the mirs (rural peasant communities) for their livelihood. Little by little this share was increased. Since land abounded and workers were scarce, the peasants often had an eye to their advantage and moved about. At the end of the sixteenth century, accordingly, the Czar Boris Godunov empowered the nobles to hold peasants to their lands by force, so establishing serfdom. However, armed forces in Russia were never composed exclusively of nobles. The muzhiks, or peasants, went to war as common soldiers under the druzhina. As early as the sixteenth century, Ivan the Terrible established the order strelitzes which amounted practically to a standing army, and which lasted until Peter the Great replaced it with regiments organized along western European lines. In those regiments members of the old druzhina, with an intermixture of foreigners, became officers, while the muzhiks provided the entire contingent of privates.[4]

Among peoples that have recently entered the agricultural stage and are relatively civilized, it is the unvarying fact that the strictly military class is the political class. Sometimes the bearing of arms is reserved exclusively to that class, as happened in India and Poland. More often the members of the governed class are on occasion enrolled – always, however, as common soldiers and in the less respected divisions. So in Greece, during the war with the Medes, the citizens belonging to the richer and more influential classes formed the picked corps (the cavalry and the hoplites), the less wealthy fought as peltasts or as slingers, while the slaves, that is the laboring masses, were almost entirely barred from military service. We find analogous arrangements in republican Rome, down to the period of the Punic Wars and even as late as the day of Marius;

3. Mickiewicz, 1875, *Les Slaves*, vol. 1, ch. 24, pp. 376–80; *Histoire populaire de Pologne*, chs. 1, 2.

4. Leroy-Beaulieu, 1881–2, *L'Empire des tzars et les Russes*, vol. 1, p. 338.

in Latin and Germanic Europe during the Middle Ages; in Russia, as just explained, and among many other peoples. Caesar notes repeatedly that in his time the backbone of the Gallic armies was formed by cavalrymen recruited from the nobility. The Aedui, for example, could not hold out against Ariovistus after the flower of their cavalry had been killed in battle.

Everywhere – in Russia and Poland, in India and medieval Europe – the ruling warrior classes acquire almost exclusive ownership of the land. Land, as we have seen, is the chief source of production and wealth in countries that are not very far advanced in civilization. But as civilization progresses, revenue from land increases proportionately. With the growth of population there is, at least in certain periods, an increase in rent, in the Ricardian sense of the term, largely because great centers of consumption arise – such at all times have been the great capitals and other large cities, ancient and modern. Eventually, if other circumstances permit, a very important social transformation occurs. Wealth rather than military valor comes to be the characteristic feature of the dominant class: the people who rule are the rich rather than the brave.

The condition that in the main is required for this transformation is that social organization shall have concentrated and become perfected to such an extent that the protection offered by public authority is considerably more effective than the protection offered by private force. In other words, private property must be so well protected by the practical and real efficacy of the laws as to render the power of the proprietor himself superfluous. This comes about through a series of gradual alterations in the social structure whereby a type of political organization, which we shall call the 'feudal state', is transformed into an essentially different type, which we shall term the 'bureaucratic state'. We are to discuss these types at some length hereafter, but we may say at once that the evolution here referred to is as a rule greatly facilitated by progress in pacific manners and customs and by certain moral habits which societies contract as civilization advances.

Once this transformation has taken place, wealth produces

political power just as political power has been producing wealth. In a society already somewhat mature – where, therefore, individual power is curbed by the collective power – if the powerful are as a rule the rich, to be rich is to become powerful. And, in truth, when fighting with the mailed fist is prohibited whereas fighting with pounds and pence is sanctioned, the better posts are inevitably won by those who are better supplied with pounds and pence.

There are, to be sure, states of a very high level of civilization which in theory are organized on the basis of moral principles of such a character that they seem to preclude this overbearing assertiveness on the part of wealth. But this is a case – and there are many such – where theoretical principles can have no more than a limited application in real life. In the United States all powers flow directly or indirectly from popular elections, and suffrage is equal for all men and women in all the states of the Union. What is more, democracy prevails not only in institutions but to a certain extent also in morals. The rich ordinarily feel a certain aversion to entering public life, and the poor a certain aversion to choosing the rich for elective office. But that does not prevent a rich man from being more influential than a poor man, since he can use pressure upon the politicians who control public administration. It does not prevent elections from being carried on to the music of clinking dollars. It does not prevent whole legislatures and considerable numbers of national congressmen from feeling the influence of powerful corporations and great financiers.[5]

In China, too, down to a few years ago, though the government had not accepted the principle of popular elections, it was organized on an essentially equalitarian basis. Academic degrees gave access to public office, and degrees were conferred by examination without any apparent regard for family or wealth. According to some writers, only barbers and certain classes of boatmen, together with their children, were barred from competing for the various grades of the mandarinate.[6] But though the moneyed class in China was less numerous, less

5. Jannet, *Le istituzioni politiche e sociali degli Stati Uniti d'America*, pt 2, ch. 10.
6. Rousset, 1878, *À travers la Chine*.

wealthy, less powerful than the moneyed class in the United States is at present, it was none the less able to modify the scrupulous application of this system to a very considerable extent. Not only was the indulgence of examiners often bought with money. The government itself sometimes sold the various academic degrees and allowed ignorant persons, often from the lowest social strata, to hold public office.[7]

In all countries of the world those other agencies for exerting social influence – personal publicity, good education, specialized training, high rank in church, public administration and army – are always readier of access to the rich than to the poor. The rich invariably have a considerably shorter road to travel than the poor, to say nothing of the fact that the stretch of road that the rich are spared is often the roughest and most difficult. . . .

In some countries we find hereditary castes. In such cases the governing class is explicitly restricted to a given number of families, and birth is the one criterion that determines entry into the class or exclusion from it. Examples are exceedingly common. There is practically no country of long-standing civilization that has not had a hereditary aristocracy at one period or another in its history. We find hereditary nobilities during certain periods in China and ancient Egypt, in India, in Greece before the wars with the Medes, in ancient Rome, among the Slavs, among the Latins and Germans of the Middle Ages, in Mexico at the time of the Discovery and in Japan down to a few years ago.

In this connection two preliminary observations are in point. In the first place, all political classes tend to become hereditary in fact if not in law. All political forces seem to possess a quality that in physics used to be called the force of inertia. They have a tendency, that is, to remain at the point and in the state in which they find themselves. Wealth and military valor are easily maintained in certain families by moral tradition and by heredity. Qualification for important office – the habit of, and to an extent the capacity for, dealing with affairs of consequence –

7. Siribaldo de Mas, *La Chine et les puissances chrétiennes*, vol. 2, pp. 332-4; Huc, *L'Empire chinois*.

is much more readily acquired when one has had a certain familiarity with them from childhood. Even when academic degrees, scientific training, special aptitudes as tested by examinations and competitions, open the way to public office, there is no eliminating that special advantage in favor of certain individuals which the French call the advantage of *positions déjà prises*. In actual fact, though examinations and competitions may theoretically be open to all, the majority never have the resources for meeting the expense of long preparation, and many others are without the connections and kinships that set an individual promptly on the right road, enabling him to avoid the gropings and blunders that are inevitable when one enters an unfamiliar environment without any guidance or support.

The democratic principle of election by broad-based suffrage would seem at first glance to be in conflict with the tendency toward stability which, according to our theory, ruling classes show. But it must be noted that candidates who are successful in democratic elections are almost always the ones who possess the political forces above enumerated, which are very often hereditary. In the English, French and Italian parliaments we frequently see the sons, grandsons, brothers, nephews and sons-in-law of members and deputies, ex-members and ex-deputies.

In the second place, when we see a hereditary caste established in a country and monopolizing political power, we may be sure that such a status *de jure* was preceded by a similar status *de facto*. Before proclaiming their exclusive and hereditary right to power the families or castes in question must have held the scepter of command in a firm grasp, completely monopolizing all the political forces of that country at that period. Otherwise such a claim on their part would only have aroused the bitterest protests and provoked the bitterest struggles.

Hereditary aristocracies often come to vaunt supernatural origins, or at least origins different from, and superior to, those of the governed classes. Such claims are explained by a highly significant social fact, namely that every governing class tends to justify its actual exercise of power by resting it on some universal moral principle. This same sort of claim has come forward in our time in scientific trappings. A number of writers, developing and amplifying Darwin's theories, contend that upper classes represent a higher level in social evolution and are therefore superior to lower classes by organic structure. Gumplowicz we have already quoted. That writer goes to the point of maintaining that the divisions of populations into trade groups and professional classes in modern civilized countries are based on ethnological heterogeneousness.[8]

Now history very definitely shows the special abilities as well as the special defects – both very marked – which have been displayed by aristocracies that have either remained absolutely closed or have made entry into their circles difficult. The ancient Roman patriciate and the English and German nobilities of modern times give a ready idea of the type we refer to. Yet in dealing with this fact, and with the theories that tend to exaggerate its significance, we can always raise the same objection – that the individuals who belong to the aristocracies in question owe their special qualities not so much to the blood that flows in their veins as to their very particular upbringing, which has brought out certain intellectual and moral tendencies in them in preference to others.

Among all the factors that figure in social superiority, intellectual superiority is the one with which heredity has least to do. The children of men of highest mentality often have very mediocre talents. That is why hereditary aristocracies have never defended their rule on the basis of intellectual superiority alone, but rather on the basis of their superiorities in character and wealth.

It is argued, in rebuttal, that education and environment may serve to explain superiorities in strictly intellectual capacities but not differences of a moral order – will power, courage, pride, energy. The truth is that social position, family tradition, the habits of the class in which we live, contribute more than is commonly supposed to the greater or lesser development of the qualities mentioned. If we carefully observe individuals who have changed their social status, whether for better or for worse, and who consequently find themselves in environments different from the ones they have been accustomed to, it is apparent that their intellectual capacities are much less sensibly affected than their moral ones. Apart from a greater breadth of

8. Gumplowicz, *Der Rassenkampf*, book 2, ch. 33.

view that education and experience bring to anyone who is not altogether stupid, every individual, whether he remains a mere clerk or becomes a minister of state, whether he reaches the rank of sergeant or the rank of general, whether he is a millionaire or a beggar, abides inevitably on the intellectual level on which nature has placed him. And yet with changes of social status and wealth the proud man often becomes humble, servility changes to arrogance, an honest nature learns to lie, or at least to dissemble, under pressure of need, while the man who has an ingrained habit of lying and bluffing makes himself over and puts on an outward semblance at least of honesty and firmness of character. It is true, of course, that a man fallen from high estate often acquires powers of resignation, self-denial and resourcefulness, just as one who rises in the world sometimes gains in sentiments of justice and fairness. In short, whether a man change for the better or for the worse, he has to be exceptionally level-headed if he is to change his social status very appreciably and still keep his character unaltered. Mirabeau remarked that, for any man, any great climb on the social ladder produces a crisis that cures the ills he has and creates new ones that he never had before.[9]

Courage in battle, impetuousness in attack, endurance in resistance – such are the qualities that have long and often been vaunted as a monopoly of the higher classes. Certainly there may be vast natural and – if we may say so – innate differences between one individual and another in these respects; but more than anything else traditions and environmental influences are the things that keep them high, low or just average, in any large group of human beings. We generally become indifferent to danger or, perhaps better, to a given type of danger, when the persons with whom we daily live speak of it with indifference and remain cool and imperturbable before it. Many mountaineers or sailors are by nature timid men, yet they face unmoved, the ones the dangers of the precipice, the others the perils of the storm at sea. So peoples and classes that are accustomed to warfare maintain military virtues at the highest pitch.

9. *Correspondance entre le comte de Mirabeau et le comte de La Marck*, vol. 2, p. 228.

So true is this that even peoples and social classes which are ordinarily unaccustomed to arms acquire the military virtues rapidly when the individuals who compose them are made members of organizations in which courage and daring are traditional, when – if one may venture the metaphor – they are cast into human crucibles that are heavily charged with the sentiments that are to be infused into their fiber. Mohammed II recruited his terrible Janizaries in the main from boys who had been kidnapped among the degenerate Greeks of Byzantium. The much despised Egyptian fellah, unused for long centuries to war and accustomed to remaining meek and helpless under the lash of the oppressor, became a good soldier when Mehemet Ali placed him in Turkish or Albanian regiments. The French nobility has always enjoyed a reputation for brilliant valor, but down to the end of the eighteenth century that quality was not credited in anything like the same degree to the French bourgeoisie. However, the wars of the Republic and the Empire amply proved that nature had been uniformly lavish in her endowments of courage upon all the inhabitants of France. Proletariat and bourgeoisie both furnished good soldiers and, what is more, excellent officers, though talent for command had been considered an exclusive prerogative of the nobility. Gumplowicz's theory that differentiation in social classes depends very largely on ethnological antecedents requires proof at the very least. Many facts to the contrary readily occur to one – among others the obvious fact that branches of the same family often belong to widely different social classes.

9 C. Wright Mills

The Structure of Power in American Society

C. Wright Mills, 'The structure of power in American society', *British Journal of Sociology*, vol. 9, 1958, no. 1, pp. 29–41.

Power has to do with whatever decisions men make about the arrangements under which they live, and about the events which make up the history of their times. Events that are beyond human decision do happen; social arrangements do change without benefit of explicit decision. But in so far as such decisions are made, the problem of who is involved in making them is the basic problem of power. In so far as they could be made but are not, the problem becomes who fails to make them?

We cannot today merely assume that in the last resort men must always be governed by their own consent. For among the means of power which now prevail is the power to manage and to manipulate the consent of men. That we do not know the limits of such power, and that we hope it does have limits, does not remove the fact that much power today is successfully employed without the sanction of the reason or the conscience of the obedient.

Surely nowadays we need not argue that, in the last resort, coercion is the 'final' form of power. But then, we are by no means constantly at the last resort. Authority (power that is justified by the beliefs of the voluntarily obedient) and manipulation (power that is wielded unbeknown to the powerless) – must also be considered, along with coercion. In fact, the three types must be sorted out whenever we think about power.

In the modern world, we must bear in mind, power is often not so authoritative as it seemed to be in the medieval epoch: ideas which justify rulers no longer seem so necessary to their exercise of power. At least for many of the great decisions of our time – especially those of an international sort – mass 'persuasion' has not been 'necessary'; the fact is simply accomplished. Furthermore, such ideas as are available to the powerful are often neither taken up nor used by them. Such ideologies usually arise as a response to an effective debunking of power; in the United States such opposition has not been effective enough recently to create the felt need for new ideologies of rule.

There has, in fact, come about a situation in which many who have lost faith in prevailing loyalties have not acquired new ones, and so pay no attention to politics of any kind. They are not radical, not liberal, not conservative, not reactionary. They are inactionary. They are out of it. If we accept the Greek's definition of the idiot as an altogether private man, then we must conclude that many American citizens are now idiots. And I should not be surprised, although I do not know, if there were not some such idiots even in Germany. This – and I use the word with care – this spiritual condition seems to me the key to many modern troubles of political intellectuals, as well as the key to much political bewilderment in modern society. Intellectual 'conviction' and moral 'belief' are not necessary, in either the rulers or the ruled, for a ruling power to persist and even to flourish. So far as the role of ideologies is concerned, their frequent absences and the prevalence of mass indifference are surely two of the major political facts about the western societies today.

How large a role any explicit decisions do play in the making of history is itself an historical problem. For how large that role may be depends very much upon the means of power that are available at any given time in any given society. In some societies, the innumerable actions of innumerable men modify their milieux, and so gradually modify the structure itself. These modifications – the course of history – go on behind the backs of men. History is drift, although in total 'men make it'. Thus, innumerable entrepreneurs and innumerable consumers by ten-thousand decisions per minute may shape and re-shape the free-market economy. Perhaps this was the chief kind of limitation Marx had in mind when he wrote, in *The Eighteenth Brumaire*: that 'Men make their own history, but they do not make it just as they please; they do not make it under circumstances chosen by themselves. . . .'

But in other societies – certainly in the United States and in the Soviet Union today – a few men may be so placed within the structure that by their decisions they modify the milieux of many other men, and in fact nowadays the structural conditions under which most men live. Such elites of power also make history under circumstances not chosen altogether by themselves, yet compared with other men, and compared with other periods of world history, these circumstances do indeed seem less limiting.

I should contend that 'men are free to make history', but that some men are indeed much freer than others. For such freedom requires access to the means of decision and of power by which history can now be made. It has not always been so made; but in the later phases of the modern epoch it is. It is with reference to this epoch that I am contending that if men do not make history, they tend increasingly to become the utensils of history-makers as well as the mere objects of history.

The history of modern society may readily be understood as the story of the enlargement and the centralization of the means of power – in economic, in political and in military institutions. The rise of industrial society has involved these developments in the means of economic production. The rise of the nation-state has involved similar developments in the means of violence and in those of political administration.

In the western societies, such transformations have generally occurred gradually, and many cultural traditions have restrained and shaped them. In most of the Soviet societies, they are happening very rapidly indeed and without the great discourse of western civilization, without the Renaissance and without the Reformation, which so greatly strengthened and gave political focus to the idea of freedom. In those societies, the enlargement and the coordination of all the means of power has occurred more brutally, and from the beginning under tightly centralized authority. But in both types, the means of power have now become international in scope and similar in form. To be sure, each of them has its own ups and downs; neither is as yet absolute; how they are run differs quite sharply.

Yet so great is the reach of the means of violence, and so great the economy required to produce and support them, that we have in the immediate past witnessed the consolidation of these two world centres, either of which dwarfs the power of Ancient Rome. As we pay attention to the awesome means of power now available to quite small groups of men we come to realize that Caesar could do less with Rome than Napoleon with France; Napoleon less with France than Lenin with Russia. But what was Caesar's power at its height compared with the power of the changing inner circles of Soviet Russia and the temporary administrations of the United States? We come to realize – indeed they continually remind us – how a few men have access to the means by which in a few days continents can be turned into thermonuclear wastelands. That the facilities of power are so enormously enlarged and so decisively centralized surely means that the powers of quite small groups of men, which we may call elites, are now of literally inhuman consequence.

My concern here is not with the international scene but with the United States in the middle of the twentieth century. I must emphasize 'in the middle of the twentieth century' because in our attempt to understand any society we come upon images which have been drawn from its past and which often confuse our attempt to confront its present reality. That is one minor reason why history is the shank of any social science: we must study it if only to rid ourselves of it. In the United States, there are indeed many such images and usually they have to do with the first half of the nineteenth century. At that time the economic facilities of the United States were very widely dispersed and subject to little or to no central authority.

The state watched in the night but was without decisive voice in the day.

One man meant one rifle and the militia were without centralized orders.

Any American as old-fashioned as I can only agree with R. H. Tawney that

Whatever the future may contain, the past has shown no more excellent social order than that in which the mass of the people were the masters of the holdings which they ploughed and the tools with which they worked, and could boast. . . . It is a quietness to a man's mind to live upon his own and to know his heir certain.

But then we must immediately add: all that is of the past and of little relevance to our understanding of the United States today. Within this society three broad levels of power may now be distinguished. I shall begin at the top and move downward.

The power to make decisions of national and international consequence is now so clearly seated in political, military and economic institutions that other areas of society seem off to the side and, on occasion, readily subordinated to these. The scattered institutions of religion, education and family are increasingly shaped by the big three, in which history-making decisions now regularly occur. Behind this fact there is all the push and drive of a fabulous technology; for these three institutional orders have incorporated this technology and now guide it, even as it shapes and paces their development.

As each has assumed its modern shape, its effects upon the other two have become greater, and the traffic between the three has increased. There is no longer, on the one hand, an economy, and, on the other, a political order, containing a military establishment unimportant to politics and to money-making. There is a political economy numerously linked with military order and decision. This triangle of power is now a structural fact, and it is the key to any understanding of the higher circles in America today. For as each of these domains has coincided with the others, as decisions in each have become broader, the leading men of each – the higher military, the corporation executives, the political directorate – have tended to come together to form the power elite of America.

The political order, once composed of several dozen states with a weak federal-centre, has become an executive apparatus which has taken up into itself many powers previously scattered, legislative as well as administrative, and which now reaches into all parts of the social structure. The long-time tendency of business and government to become more closely connected has since the Second World War reached a new point of explicitness. Neither can now be seen clearly as a distinct world. The growth of executive government does not mean merely the 'enlargement of government' as some kind of autonomous bureaucracy: under American conditions, it has meant the ascendency of the corporation man into political eminence. Already during the New Deal, such men had joined the political directorate; as of the Second World War they came to dominate it. Long involved with government, now they have moved into quite full direction of the economy of the war effort and of the post-war era.

The economy, once a great scatter of small productive units in somewhat automatic balance, has become internally dominated by a few hundred corporations, administratively and politically interrelated, which together hold the keys to economic decision. This economy is at once a permanent-war economy and a private-corporation economy. The most important relations of the corporation to the state now rest on the coincidence between military and corporate interests, as defined by the military and the corporate rich, and accepted by politicians and public. Within the elite as a whole, this coincidence of military domain and corporate realm strengthens both of them and further subordinates the merely political man. Not the party politician, but the corporation executive, is now more likely to sit with the military to answer the question: what is to be done?

The military order, once a slim establishment in a context of civilian distrust, has become the largest and most expensive feature of government; behind smiling public relations, it has all the grim and clumsy efficiency of a great and sprawling bureaucracy. The high military have gained decisive political and economic relevance. The seemingly permanent military threat places a premium upon them and virtually all political and economic actions are now judged in terms of military definitions of reality: the higher military have ascended to a firm position within the power elite of our time.

In part at least this is a result of an historical fact, pivotal for the years since 1939: the attention of the elite has shifted from domestic problems – centred in the 1930s around slump – to international problems – centred in the 1940s and 1950s around war. By long historical usage, the government of the United States has been shaped by domestic clash and balance; it does not have suitable agencies and traditions for the democratic handling of international affairs. In considerable part, it is in this vacuum that the power elite has grown.

1. To understand the unity of this power elite, we must pay attention to the psychology of its several members in their respective milieux. In so far as the power elite is composed of men of similar origin and education, of similar career and style of life, their unity may be said to rest upon the fact that they are of similar social type, and to lead to the fact of their easy intermingling. This kind of unity reaches its frothier apex in the sharing of that prestige which is to be had in the world of the celebrity. It achieves a more solid culmination in the fact of the interchangeability of positions between the three dominant institutional orders. It is revealed by considerable traffic of personnel within and between these three, as well as by the rise of specialized go-betweens as in the new style high-level lobbying.

2. Behind such psychological and social unity are the structure and the mechanics of those institutional hierarchies over which the political directorate, the corporate rich and the high military now preside. How each of these hierarchies is shaped and what relations it has with the others determine in large part the relations of their rulers. Were these hierarchies scattered and disjointed, then their respective elites might tend to be scattered and disjointed; but if they have many interconnections and points of coinciding interest, then their elites tend to form a coherent kind of grouping. The unity of the elite is not a simple reflection of the unity of institutions, but men and institutions are always related; that is why we must understand the elite today in connection with such institutional trends as the development of a permanent-war establishment, alongside a privately incorporated economy, inside a virtual political vacuum. For the men at the top have been selected and formed by such institutional trends.

3. Their unity, however, does not rest solely upon psychological similarity and social intermingling, nor entirely upon the

structural blending of commanding positions and common interests. At times it is the unity of a more explicit coordination.

To say that these higher circles are increasingly coordinated, that this is *one* basis of their unity, and that at times – as during open war – such coordination is quite wilful, is not to say that the coordination is total or continuous, or even that it is very surefooted. Much less is it to say that the power elite has emerged as the realization of a plot. Its rise cannot be adequately explained in any psychological terms.

Yet we must remember that institutional trends may be defined as opportunities by those who occupy the command posts. Once such opportunities are recognized, men may avail themselves of them. Certain types of men from each of these three areas, more far-sighted than others, have actively promoted the liaison even before it took its truly modern shape. Now more have come to see that their several interests can more easily be realized if they work together, in informal as well as in formal ways, and accordingly they have done so.

The idea of the power elite is of course an interpretation. It rests upon and it enables us to make sense of major institutional trends, the social similarities and psychological affinities of the men at the top. But the idea is also based upon what has been happening on the middle and lower levels of power, to which I now turn.

There are of course other interpretations of the American system of power. The most usual is that it is a moving balance of many competing interests. The image of balance, at least in America, is derived from the idea of the economic market: in the nineteenth century, the balance was thought to occur between a great scatter of individuals and enterprises; in the twentieth century, it is thought to occur between great interest blocs. In both views, the politician is the key man of power because he is the broker of many conflicting powers.

I believe that the balance and the compromise in American society – the 'countervailing powers' and the 'veto groups', of parties and associations, of strata and unions – must now be seen as having mainly to do with the middle levels of power.

It is these middle levels that the political journalist and the scholar of politics are most likely to understand and to write about – if only because, being mainly middle class themselves, they are closer to them. Moreover these levels provide the noisy content of most 'political' news and gossip; the images of these levels are more or less in accord with the folklore of how democracy works; and, if the master-image of balance is accepted, many intellectuals, especially in their current patrioteering, are readily able to satisfy such political optimism as they wish to feel. Accordingly, liberal interpretations of what is happening in the United States are now virtually the only interpretations that are widely distributed.

But to believe that the power system reflects a balancing society is, I think, to confuse the present era with earlier times, and to confuse its top and bottom with its middle levels.

By the top levels, as distinguished from the middle, I intend to refer, first of all, to the scope of the decisions that are made. At the top today, these decisions have to do with all the issues of war and peace. They have also to do with slump and poverty which are now so very much problems of international scope. I intend also to refer to whether or not the groups that struggle politically have a chance to gain the positions from which such top decisions are made, and indeed whether their members do usually hope for such top national command. Most of the competing interests which make up the clang and clash of American politics are strictly concerned with their slice of the existing pie. Labour unions, for example, certainly have no policies of an international sort other than those which given unions adopt for the strict economic protection of their members. Neither do farm organizations. The actions of such middle-level powers may indeed have consequence for top-level policy; certainly at times they hamper these policies. But they are not truly concerned with them, which means of course that their influence tends to be quite irresponsible.

The facts of the middle levels may in part be understood in terms of the rise of the power elite. The expanded and centralized and interlocked hierarchies over which the power elite presides have encroached upon the old balance and relegated it to the middle level. But there are also independent developments of the middle levels. These, it seems to me, are better understood as an affair of intrenched and provincial demands than as a centre of national decision. As such, the middle level often seems much more of a stalemate than a moving balance.

1. The middle level of politics is not a forum in which there are debated the big decisions of national and international life. Such debate is not carried on by nationally responsible parties representing and clarifying alternative policies. There are no such parties in the United States. More and more, fundamental issues never come to any point or decision before the Congress, much less before the electorate in party campaigns. In the case of Formosa, in the spring of 1955, the Congress abdicated all debate concerning events and decisions which surely bordered on war. The same is largely true of the 1957 crisis in the Middle East. Such decisions now regularly by-pass the Congress, and are never clearly focused issues for public decision.

The American political campaign distracts attention from national and international issues, but that is not to say that there are no issues in these campaigns. In each district and state, issues are set up and watched by organized interests of sovereign local importance. The professional politician is of course a party politician, and the two parties are semi-feudal organizations: they trade patronage and other favours for votes and for protection. The differences between them, so far as national issues are concerned, are very narrow and very mixed up. Often each seems to be forty-eight parties, one to each state; and accordingly, the politician as campaigner and as Congressman is not concerned with national party lines, if any are discernible. Often he is not subject to any effective national party discipline. He speaks for the interests of his own constituency, and he is concerned with national issues only in so far as they affect the interests effectively organized there, and hence his chances of re-election. That is why, when he does speak of national matters, the result is so often such an empty rhetoric. Seated in his sovereign locality, the politician is not at the national summit. He is on and of the middle levels of power.

2. Politics is not an arena in which free and independent

organizations truly connect the lower and middle levels of society with the top levels of decision. Such organizations are not an effective and major part of American life today. As more people are drawn into the political arena, their associations become mass in scale, and the power of the individual becomes dependent upon them; to the extent that they are effective, they have become larger, and to that extent they have become less accessible to the influence of the individual. This is a central fact about associations in any mass society: it is of most consequence for political parties and for trade unions.

In the 1930s it often seemed that labour would become an insurgent power independent of corporation and state. Organized labour was then emerging for the first time on an American scale, and the only political sense of direction it needed was the slogan, 'organize the unorganized'. Now without the mandate of the slump, labour remains without political direction. Instead of economic and political struggles it has become deeply entangled in administrative routines with both corporation and state. One of its major functions, as a vested interest of the new society, is the regulation of such irregular tendencies as may occur among the rank and file.

There is nothing, it seems to me, in the make-up of the current labour leadership to allow us to expect that it can or that it will lead, rather than merely react. In so far as it fights at all it fights over a share of the goods of a single way of life and not over that way of life itself. The typical labour leader in the USA today is better understood as an adaptive creature of the main business drift than as an independent actor in a truly national context.

3. The idea that this society is a balance of powers requires us to assume that the units in balance are of more or less equal power and that they are truly independent of one another. These assumptions have rested, it seems clear, upon the historical importance of a large and independent middle class. In the latter nineteenth century and during the Progressive Era, such a class of farmers and small businessmen fought politically – and lost – their last struggle for a paramount role in national decision. Even then, their aspirations seemed bound to their own imagined past.

This old, independent middle class has of course declined. On the most generous count, it is now 40 per cent of the total middle class (at most 20 per cent of the total labour force). Moreover, it has become politically as well as economically dependent upon the state, most notably in the case of the sub-sidized farmer.

The *new* middle class of white-collar employees is certainly not the political pivot of any balancing society. It is in no way politically unified. Its unions, such as they are, often serve merely to incorporate it as hanger-on of the labour interest. For a considerable period, the old middle class *was* an independent base of power; the new middle class cannot be. Political freedom and economic security *were* anchored in small and independent properties; they are not anchored in the worlds of the white-collar job. Scattered property holders were economically united by more or less free markets; the jobs of the new middle class are integrated by corporate authority. Economically, the white-collar classes are in the same condition as wage workers; politically, they are in a worse condition, for they are not organized. They are no vanguard of historic change; they are at best a rear-guard of the welfare state.

The agrarian revolt of the 1890s, the small-business revolt that has been more or less continuous since the 1880s, the labour revolt of the 1930s – each of these has failed as an independent movement which could countervail against the powers that be; they have failed as politically autonomous third parties. But they have succeeded, in varying degree, as interests vested in the expanded corporation and state; they have succeeded as parochial interests seated in particular districts, in local divisions of the two parties and in the Congress. What they would become, in short, are well-established features of the *middle* levels of balancing power, on which we may now observe all those strata and interests which in the course of American history have been defeated in their bids for top power or which have never made such bids.

Fifty years ago many observers thought of the American state as a mask behind which an invisible government operated. But nowadays, much of what was called the old lobby, visible or invisible, is part of the quite visible government. The 'governmentalization of the lobby' has proceeded in both the legislative and the executive domain, as well as between them. The executive bureaucracy becomes not only the centre of decision but also the arena within which major conflicts of power are resolved or denied resolution. 'Administration' replaces electoral politics; the manoeuvring of cliques (which include leading Senators as well as civil servants) replaces the open clash of parties.

The shift of corporation men into the political directorate has accelerated the decline of the politicians in the Congress to the middle levels of power; the formation of the power elite rests in part upon this relegation. It rests also upon the semi-organized stalemate of the interests of sovereign localities, into which the legislative function has so largely fallen; upon the virtually complete absence of a civil service that is a politically neutral but politically relevant depository of brain-power and executive skill; and it rests upon the increased official secrecy behind which great decisions are made without benefit of public or even of Congressional debate.

There is one last belief upon which liberal observers everywhere base their interpretations and rest their hopes. That is the idea of the public and the associated idea of public opinion. Conservative thinkers, since the French Revolution, have of course Viewed With Alarm the rise of the public which they have usually called the masses, or something to that effect. 'The populace is sovereign,' wrote Gustave Le Bon, 'and the tide of barbarism mounts.' But surely those who have supposed the masses to be well on their way to triumph are mistaken. In our time, the influence of publics or of masses within political life is in fact decreasing, and such influence as on occasion they do have tends, to an unknown but increasing degree, to be guided by the means of mass communication.

In a society of publics, discussion is the ascendant means of communication, and the mass media, if they exist, simply enlarge and animate this discussion, linking one face-to-face public with the discussions of another. In a mass society, the dominant type of communication is the formal media, and publics become mere markets for these media: the 'public' of a radio programme consists of all those exposed to it. When we try to look upon the United States today as a society of publics, we realize that it has moved a considerable distance along the road to the mass society.

In official circles, the very term, 'the public', has come to have a phantom meaning, which dramatically reveals its eclipse. The deciding elite can identify some of those who clamour publicly as 'Labour', others as 'Business', still others as 'Farmer'. But these are not the public. 'The public' consists of the unidentified and the non-partisan in a world of defined and partisan interests. In this faint echo of the classic notion, the public is composed of these remnants of the old and new middle classes whose interests are not explicitly defined, organized or clamorous. In a curious adaptation, 'the public' often becomes, in administrative fact, 'the disengaged expert', who, although ever so well informed, has never taken a clear-cut and public stand on controversial issues. He is the 'public' member of the board, the commission, the committee. What 'the public' stands for, accordingly, is often a vagueness of policy (called 'open-mindedness'), a lack of involvement in public affairs (known as 'reasonableness'), and a professional disinterest (known as 'tolerance').

All this is indeed far removed from the eighteenth-century idea of the public of public opinion. That idea parallels the economic idea of the magical market. Here is the market composed of freely competing entrepreneurs; there is the public composed of circles of people in discussion. As price is the result of anonymous, equally weighted, bargaining individuals, so public opinion is the result of each man's having thought things out for himself and then contributing his voice to the great chorus. To be sure, some may have more influence on the state of opinion than others, but no one group monopolizes the discussion, or by itself determines the opinions that prevail.

In this classic image, the people are presented with problems. They discuss them. They formulate viewpoints. These viewpoints are organized, and they compete. One viewpoint 'wins out'. Then the people act on this view, or their representatives are instructed to act it out, and this they promptly do.

Such are the images of democracy which are still used as working justifications of power in America. We must now recognize this description as more a fairy tale than a useful approximation. The issues that now shape man's fate are neither raised nor decided by any public at large. The idea of a society that is at bottom composed of publics is not a matter of fact; it is the proclamation of an ideal, and as well the assertion of a legitimation masquerading as fact.

I cannot here describe the several great forces within American society as well as elsewhere which have been at work in the debilitation of the public. I want only to remind you that publics, like free associations, can be deliberately and suddenly smashed, or they can more slowly wither away. But whether smashed in a week or withered in a generation, the demise of the public must be seen in connection with the rise of centralized organizations, with all their new means of power, including those of the mass media of distraction. These, we now know, often seem to expropriate the rationality and the will of the terrorized or – as the case may be – the voluntarily indifferent society of masses. In the more democratic process of indifference the remnants of such publics as remain may only occasionally be intimidated by fanatics in search of 'disloyalty'. But regardless of that, they lose their will for decision because they do not possess the instruments for decision; they lose their sense of political belonging because they do not belong; they lose their political will because they see no way to realize it.

The political structure of a modern democratic state requires that such a public as is projected by democratic theorists not only exist but that it be the very forum within which a politics of real issues is enacted.

It requires a civil service that is firmly linked with the world of knowledge and sensibility, and which is composed of skilled men who, in their careers and in their aspirations, are truly independent of any private, which is to say, corporation, interests.

It requires nationally responsible parties which debate openly and clearly the issues which the nation, and indeed the world, now so rigidly confronts.

It requires an intelligentsia, inside as well as outside the universities, who carry on the big discourse of the western world, and whose work is relevant to and influential among parties and movements and publics.

And it certainly requires, as a fact of power, that there be free associations standing between families and smaller communities and publics, on the one hand, and the state, the military, the corporation, on the other. For unless these do exist, there are no vehicles for reasoned opinion, no instruments for the rational exertion of public will.

Such democratic formations are not now ascendant in the power structure of the United States, and accordingly the men of decision are not men selected and formed by careers within such associations and by their performance before such publics. The top of modern American society is increasingly unified, and often seems wilfully coordinated; at the top there has emerged an elite whose power probably exceeds that of any small group of men in world history. The middle levels are often a drifting set of stalemated forces: the middle does not link the bottom with the top. The bottom of this society is politically fragmented, and even as a passive fact, increasingly powerless: at the bottom there is emerging a mass society.

These developments, I believe, can be correctly understood neither in terms of the liberal nor the Marxian interpretation of politics and history. Both these ways of thought arose as guidelines to reflection about a type of society which does not now exist in the United States. We confront there a new kind of social structure, which embodies elements and tendencies of all modern society, but in which they have assumed a more naked and flamboyant prominence.

That does not mean that we must give up the ideals of these classic political expectations. I believe that both have been concerned with the problem of rationality and of freedom: liberalism, with freedom and rationality as supreme facts about the individual; Marxism, as supreme facts about man's role in the political making of history. What I have said here, I suppose, may be taken as an attempt to make evident why the ideas of freedom and of rationality now so often seem so ambiguous in the new society of the United States of America.

10 Robert A. Dahl

A Critique of the Ruling Elite Model

Robert A. Dahl, 'A critique of the ruling elite model',
American Political Science Review, vol. 52, 1958, pp. 463-9.

A great many people seem to believe that 'they' run things: the old families, the bankers, the City Hall machine or the party boss behind the scene. This kind of view evidently has a powerful and many-sided appeal. It is simple, compelling, dramatic, 'realistic'. It gives one standing as an inside-dopester. For individuals with a strong strain of frustrated idealism, it has just the right touch of hard-boiled cynicism. Finally, the hypothesis has one very great advantage over many alternative explanations: It can be cast in a form that makes it virtually impossible to disprove.

Consider the last point for a moment. There is a type of quasi-metaphysical theory made up of what might be called an infinite regress of explanations. The ruling elite model *can* be interpreted in this way. If the overt leaders of a community do not appear to constitute a ruling elite, then the theory can be saved by arguing that behind the overt leaders there is a set of covert leaders who do. If subsequent evidence shows that this covert group does not make a ruling elite, then the theory can be saved by arguing that behind the first covert group there is another, and so on.

Now whatever else it may be, a theory that cannot even in principle be controverted by empirical evidence is not a scientific theory. The least that we can demand of any ruling elite theory that purports to be more than a metaphysical or polemical doctrine is, first, that the burden of proof be on the proponents of the theory and not on its critics; and, second, that there be clear criteria according to which the theory could be disproved.

With these points in mind, I shall proceed in two stages. First,

I shall try to clarify the meaning of the concept 'ruling elite' by describing a very simple form of what I conceive to be a ruling elite system. Second, I shall indicate what would be required in principle as a simple but satisfactory test of any hypothesis asserting that a particular political system is, in fact, a ruling elite system. Finally, I shall deal with some objections.

A simple ruling elite system

If a ruling elite hypothesis says anything, surely it asserts that within some specific political system there exists a group of people who to some degree exercise power or influence over other actors in the system. I shall make the following assumptions about power (Dahl, 1957).

1. In order to compare the relative influence of two actors (these may be individuals, groups, classes, parties or what not), it is necessary to state the scope of the responses upon which the actors have an effect. The statement, 'A has more power than B', is so ambiguous as to verge on the meaningless, since it does not specify the scope.

2. One cannot compare the relative influence of two actors who always perform identical actions with respect to the group influenced. What this means as a practical matter is that ordinarily one can test for differences in influence only where there are cases of differences in initial preferences. At one extreme, the difference may mean that one group prefers alternative A and another group prefers B, A and B being mutually exclusive. At the other extreme, it may mean that one group prefers alternative A to other alternatives, and another group is indifferent. If a political system displayed complete consensus at all times, we should find it impossible to construct a satisfactory direct test of the hypothesis that it was a ruling elite system, although indirect and rather unsatisfactory tests might be devised.

Consequently, to know whether or not we have a ruling elite, we must have a political system in which there is a difference in preferences, from time to time, among the individual human beings in the system. Suppose, now, that among these individuals there is a set whose preferences regularly prevail in all cases of disagreement, or at least in all cases of disagreement over key political issues (a term I propose to leave undefined here). Let me call such a set of individuals a 'controlling group'. In a full-fledged democracy operating strictly according to majority rule, the majority would constitute a controlling group, even though the individual members of the majority might change from one issue to the next. But since our model is to represent a ruling elite system, we require that the set be *less than a majority in size*.

However, in any representative system with single member voting districts where more than two candidates receive votes, a candidate *could* win with less than a majority of votes; and it is possible, therefore, to imagine a truly sovereign legislature elected under the strictest 'democratic' rules that was none the less governed by a legislative majority representing the first preferences of a minority of voters. Yet I do not think we would want to call such a political system a ruling elite system. Because of this kind of difficulty, I propose that we exclude from our definition of a ruling elite any controlling group that is a product of rules that are actually followed (that is, 'real' rules) under which a majority of individuals could dominate if they took certain actions permissible under the 'real' rules. In short, to constitute a ruling elite a controlling group must not be *a pure artifact of democratic rules*.

A ruling elite, then, is a controlling group less than a majority in size that is not a pure artifact of democratic rules. It is a minority of individuals whose preferences regularly prevail in cases of differences in preference on key political issues. If we are to avoid an infinite regress of explanations, the composition of the ruling elite must be more or less definitely specified.

Some bad tests

The hypothesis we are dealing with would run along these lines: 'Such and such a political system (the US, the USSR, New Haven or the like) is a ruling elite system in which the ruling elite has the following membership.' Membership would then be specified by name, position, socio-economic class, socio-economic roles or what not.

Let me now turn to the problem of testing a hypothesis of this sort, and begin by indicating a few tests that are sometimes mistakenly taken as adequate.

The first improper test confuses a ruling elite with a group that has a high *potential for control*. Let me explain. Suppose a set of individuals in a political system has the following property: there is a very high probability that if they agree on a key political alternative, and if they all act in some specified way, then that alternative will be chosen. We may say of such a group that it has a *high potential for control*. In a large and complex society like ours, there may be many such groups. For example, the bureaucratic triumvirate of Professor Mills would appear to have a high potential for control (Mills, 1956). In the City of New Haven, with which I have some acquaintance, I do not doubt that the leading business figures together with the leaders of both political parties have a high potential for control. But a potential for control is not, except in a peculiarly Hobbesian world, equivalent to actual control. If the military leaders of this country and their subordinates agreed that it was desirable, they could most assuredly establish a military dictatorship of the most overt sort; nor would they need the aid of leaders of business corporations or the executive branch of our government. But they have not set up such a dictatorship. For what is lacking are the premises I mentioned earlier, namely agreement on a key political alternative and some set of specific implementing actions. That is to say, a group may have a high potential for control and a *low potential for unity*. The actual *political effectiveness* of a group is a function of its potential for control *and* its potential for unity. Thus a group with a relatively low potential for control but a high potential for unity may be more politically effective than a group with a high potential for control but a low potential for unity.

The second improper test confuses a ruling elite with a group of individuals who have more influence than any others in the system. I take it for granted that in every human organization some individuals have more influence over key decisions than do others. Political equality may well be among the most Utopian of all human goals. But it is fallacious to assume that the absence of political equality proves the existence of a ruling elite.

The third improper test, which is closely related to the preceding one, is to generalize from a single scope of influence. Neither logically nor empirically does it follow that a group with a high degree of influence over one scope will necessarily have a high degree of influence over another scope within the same system. This is a matter to be determined empirically. Any investigation that does not take into account the possibility that different elite groups have different scopes is suspect. By means of sloppy questions one could easily seem to discover that there exists a unified ruling elite in New Haven; for there is no doubt that small groups of people make many key decisions. It appears to be the case, however, that the small group that runs urban redevelopment is not the same as the small group that runs public education, and neither is quite the same as the two small groups that run the two parties. Moreover the small group that runs urban redevelopment with a high degree of unity would almost certainly disintegrate if its activities were extended to either education or the two political parties.

A proposed test

If tests like these are not valid, what can we properly require?

Let us take the simplest possible situation. Assume that there have been some number – I will not say how many – of cases where there has been disagreement within the political system on key political choices. Assume further that the hypothetical ruling elite prefers one alternative and other actors in the system prefer other alternatives. Then unless it is true that in all or very nearly all of these cases the alternative preferred by the ruling elite is actually adopted, the hypothesis (that the system is dominated by the specified ruling elite) is clearly false.

I do not want to pretend either that the research necessary to such a test is at all easy to carry out or that community life lends itself conveniently to strict interpretation according to the requirements of the test. *But I do not see how anyone can suppose that he has established the dominance of a specific group in a community or a nation without basing his analysis on the careful examination of a series of concrete decisions.* And these decisions must either constitute the universe or a fair sample from the universe of key political decisions taken in the political system.

Now it is a remarkable and indeed astounding fact that neither Professor Mills (1956) nor Professor Hunter (1953) has seriously attempted to examine any array of specific cases to test his major hypothesis. Yet I suppose these two works more than any others in the social sciences of the last few years have sought to interpret complex political systems essentially as instances of a ruling elite.

To sum up: The hypothesis of the existence of a ruling elite can be strictly tested only if:

1. The hypothetical ruling elite is a well-defined group.

2. There is a fair sample of cases involving key political decisions in which the preferences of the hypothetical ruling elite run counter to those of any other likely group that might be suggested.

3. In such cases, the preferences of the elite regularly prevail.

Difficulties and objections

Several objections might be raised against the test I propose.

First, one might argue that the test is *too weak*. The argument would run as follows: If a ruling elite *doesn't* exist in a community, then the rest is satisfactory; that is, if every hypothetical ruling elite is compared with alternative control groups, and in fact no ruling elite exists, then the test will indeed show that there is no minority whose preferences regularly prevail on key political alternatives. But – it might be said – suppose a ruling elite *does* exist. The test will not *necessarily* demonstrate its existence, since we may not have selected the right group as our hypothetical ruling elite. Now this objection is valid; but it suggests the point I made at the outset about the possibility of an infinite regress of explanations. Unless we use the test on every possible combination of individuals in the community, we cannot be certain that there is not some combination that constitutes a ruling elite. But since there is no more *a priori* reason to assume that a ruling elite does exist than to assume that one does not exist, the burden of proof does not rest upon the critic of the hypothesis, but upon its proponent. And a proponent must specify what group he has in mind as his ruling elite. Once the group is specified, then the test I have suggested is, at least in principle, valid.

Second, one could object that the test is *too strong*. For suppose that the members of the 'ruled' groups are indifferent as to the outcome of various political alternatives. Surely (one could argue) if there is another group that regularly gets its way in the face of this indifference, it is in fact the ruling group in the society. Now my reasons for wishing to discriminate this case from the other involve more than a mere question of the propriety of using the term 'ruling elite', which is only a term of convenience. There is, I think, a difference of some theoretical significance between a system in which a small group dominates over another that is opposed to it, and one in which a group dominates over an indifferent mass. In the second case, the alternatives at stake can hardly be regarded as 'key political issues' if we assume the point of view of the indifferent mass; whereas in the first case it is reasonable to say that the alternatives involve a key political issue from the standpoint of both groups. Earlier I refrained from defining the concept 'key political issues'. If we were to do so at this point, it would seem reasonable to require as a necessary although possibly not a sufficient condition that the issue should involve actual disagreement in preferences among two or more groups. In short, the case of 'indifference *v* preference' would be ruled out.

However, I do not mean to dispose of the problem simply by definition. The point is to make sure that the two systems are distinguished. The test for the second, weaker system of elite rule would then be merely a modification of the test proposed for the first and more stringent case. It would again require an examination of a series of cases showing uniformly that when 'the word' was authoritatively passed down from the designated elite, the hitherto indifferent majority fell into ready compliance with an alternative that had nothing else to recommend it intrinsically.

Third, one might argue that the test will not discriminate between a true ruling elite and a ruling elite together with its satellites. This objection is in one sense true and in one sense false. It is true that on a series of key political questions, an apparently unified group might prevail who would, according to our test, thereby constitute a ruling elite. Yet an inner core might actually make the decisions for the whole group.

However, one of two possibilities must be true. Either the inner core and the front men always agree at all times in the decision process, or they do not. But if they always agree, then it follows from one of our two assumptions about influence that the distinction between an 'inner core' and 'front men' has no operational meaning; that is, there is no conceivable way to distinguish between them. And if they do not always agree, then the test simply requires a comparison at those points in time when they disagree. Here again, the advantages of concrete cases are palpable, for these enable one to discover who initiates or vetoes and who merely complies.

Fourth, it might be said that the test is either too demanding or else it is too arbitrary. If it requires that the hypothetical elite prevails in *every single case*, then it demands too much. But if it does not require this much, then at what point can a ruling elite be said to exist? When it prevails in seven cases out of ten? Eight out of ten? Nine out of ten? Or what? There are two answers to this objection. On the one hand, it would be quite reasonable to argue, I think, that since we are considering only key political choices and not trivial decisions, if the elite does not prevail in *every* case in which it disagrees with a contrary group, it cannot properly be called a ruling elite. But since I have not supplied an independent definition of the term 'key political choices', I must admit that this answer is not wholly satisfactory. On the other hand, I would be inclined to suggest that in this instance as in many others we ought not to assume that political reality will be as discrete and discontinuous as the concepts we find convenient to employ. We can say that a system approximates a true ruling elite system, to a greater or lesser degree, without insisting that it exemplify the extreme and limiting case.

Fifth, it might be objected that the test I have proposed would not work in the most obvious of all cases of ruling elites, namely in the totalitarian dictatorships. For the control of the elite over the expression of opinion is so great that overtly there is no disagreement; hence no cases on which to base a judgement arise. This objection is a fair one. But we are not concerned here with totalitarian systems. We are concerned with the application of the techniques of modern investigation to American communities, where, except in very rare cases, terror is not so pervasive that the investigator is barred from discovering the preferences of citizens. Even in Little Rock, for example, newspaper men seemed to have had little difficulty in finding diverse opinions; and a northern political scientist of my acquaintance has managed to complete a large number of productive interviews with White and Negro Southerners on the touchy subject of integration.

Finally one could argue that even in a society like ours a ruling elite might be so influential over ideas, attitudes and opinions that a kind of false consensus will exist – not the phony consensus of a terroristic totalitarian dictatorship but the manipulated and superficially self-imposed adherence to the norms and goals of the elite by broad sections of a community. A good deal of Professor Mills's argument can be interpreted in this way, although it is not clear to me whether this is what he means to rest his case on.

Even more than the others this objection points to the need to be circumspect in interpreting the evidence. Yet here, too, it seems to me that the hypothesis cannot be satisfactorily confirmed without something equivalent to the test I have proposed. For once again either the consensus is perpetual and unbreakable, in which case there is no conceivable way of determining who is ruler and who is ruled. Or it is not. But if it is not, then there is some point in the process of forming opinions at which the one group will be seen to initiate and veto, while the rest merely respond. And we can only discover these points *by examination of a series of concrete cases where key decisions are made*: decisions on taxation and expenditures, subsidies, welfare programs, military policy and so on.

It would be interesting to know, for example, whether the initiation and veto of alternatives having to do with our missile program would confirm Professor Mills's hypothesis, or indeed any reasonable hypothesis about the existence of a ruling elite. To the superficial observer it would scarcely appear that the military itself is a homogeneous group, to say nothing of their supposed coalition with corporate and political executives. If the military alone or the coalition together is a ruling elite, it is either incredibly incompetent in administering its own fundamental affairs or else it is unconcerned with the success of its policies to a degree that I find astounding.

However I do not mean to examine the evidence here. For the whole point of this paper is that the evidence for a ruling elite, either in the United States or in any specific community, has not yet been properly examined so far as I know. And the evidence has not been properly examined, I have tried to argue, because the examination has not employed satisfactory criteria to determine what constitutes a fair test of the basic hypothesis.

References

DAHL, R. A. (1957), 'The concept of power', *Behav. Sci.*, vol. 2, pp. 201–15.
HUNTER, F. (1953), *Community Power Structure*, University of North Carolina Press.
MILLS, C. W. (1956), *The Power Elite*, Oxford University Press.

11 Carl Kaysen

The Corporation: How Much Power? What Scope?

Excerpts from Carl Kaysen, 'The corporation: how much power? what scope?', in Edward S. Mason (ed.), *The Corporation in Modern Society*, Harvard University Press, 1960, pp. 85–105.

The proposition that a group of giant business corporations, few in number but awesome in aggregate size, embodies a significant and troublesome concentration of power is the cliché which serves this volume as a foundation stone. I propose here to analyse this proposition, both to trace out what I consider its valid content to be, and to reflect briefly on its possible implications for social action. Let me anticipate my conclusion on the first point by saying that its familiarity is no argument against its truth.

The power of any actor on the social stage I define as the scope of significant choice open to him. Accordingly, his power over others is the scope of his choices which affect them significantly. Our fundamental proposition thus asserts that a few large corporations exert significant power over others; indeed, as we shall see, over the whole of society with respect to others. It is worth noting that this sense of 'power' is not that in which we speak of the 'power' of a waterfall or a fusion reaction, or any other transformation in a fully deterministic system; rather it is appropriate to a social system in which we see human actors, individually or in organized groups, as facing alternative courses of action, the choice among which is not fully determined without reference to the actors themselves.

We usually demonstrate the concentration of power in a small number of large corporate enterprises by showing what part of various total magnitudes for the whole economy the largest enterprises account for. The statistics are indeed impressive: I shall list a few of the more striking.[1]

1. The sources for the figures quoted are listed in order below:
Total business population: 1956, 4·3 million; 1954, 4·2 million, whence my current estimate: US Department of Commerce (1957, p. 482).

1. There are currently some 4·5 million business enterprises in the United States. More than half of these are small, unincorporated firms in retail trade and service. Corporations formed only 13 per cent of the total number; 95 per cent of the unincorporated firms had fewer than twenty employees.

2. A recent census survey covered all the firms in manufacturing, mining, retail and wholesale trade, and certain service industries; in total some 2·8 million. These firms employed just thirty million persons. The twenty-eight giant firms with 50,000 or more employees – just 0·001 per cent of the total number – accounted for about 10 per cent of the total employment. The 438 firms with 5000 or more employees (including the twenty-eight giants) accounted for 28 per cent of the total. In manufacturing, where large corporations are characteristically more important than in the other sectors covered, 263,000 firms reported just over seventeen million employees: twenty-three giants with 50,000 or more employees reported 15 per cent of the total, 361 with 5000 or more, just under 40 per cent.

3. The most recent compilation of the corporation income-tax returns showed 525,000 active non-financial corporations reporting a total of $413 billion of assets. The 202 corporations in the largest size class – each with assets of $250 million or more – owned 40 per cent of this total.

4. The last survey of the National Science Foundation reported some 15,500 firms having research and development laboratories. The largest seven among them employed 20 per cent of the total number of technical and scientific personnel in the whole group, and accounted for 26 per cent of the total ex-

Corporate share and size distribution: US Department of Commerce (1955); figures refer to 1 January 1952, for share, and 1 January 1947, for size distribution. If anything, the figures understate the numerical preponderance of small unincorporated enterprises today.

The census figures refer to 1954: US Department of Commerce (1958).

Asset holding of large corporations: US Treasury (1958, Table 5, p. 41).

Research and development expenditures: US National Science Foundation (1956).

Defense contracts: US Department of Defense (1957).

For a fuller but slightly dated discussion see Adelman (1951).

penditures on research and development. The largest forty-four, all those with 25,000 or more employees in total, accounted for 45 per cent of the total number of technicians and scientists, and more than 50 per cent of the total expenditures.

5. The one hundred companies that received the largest defense contracts over the period July 1950–June 1956 received nearly two thirds of the total value of all defense contracts during the period. The largest ten contractors accounted for just short of one third of the total value of all contracts. These were General Motors, General Electric, American Telephone and Telegraph, and seven large aircraft manufacturers.

Large corporations are not of the same importance in all sectors of the economy.[2] In agriculture they are of no importance; in service, trade and construction, proprietorships and partnerships and small corporations that are essentially similar in all but legal form predominate. Conversely, activity in the utility, transportation, mining, manufacturing and financial sectors is overwhelmingly the activity of corporations, and predominantly that of corporate giants. The share of total business accounted for by corporations in these sectors ranged from 85 per cent for finance to 100 per cent of utilities; by contrast it was between 50 and 60 per cent for trade and construction, less than 30 per cent in service, and less than 10 per cent in agriculture. The five sectors in which large corporations predominate produced 51 per cent of the total national income, and 57 per cent of the privately-produced national income. Moreover, the strategic importance of these sectors as compared with trade and service – the largest part of the small-business part of the economy – is greater than their contribution to national income would indicate. The relative share of giant corporations in these sectors was larger than in the economy as a whole. The cor-

2. The figures on the relative importance of corporations come from Gordon (1946, p. 14, Appendix A). These figures refer to 1939; no more recent ones are available and they almost certainly understate the relative importance of corporations. The shares of the sectors in national income are calculated from the figures for national income by industrial origin for 1956 given in US Department of Commerce (1957, p. 300). The share of large corporations in asset holdings of all corporations are from US Treasury (1958, Table 5, p. 41).

porate income-tax returns of 1955 showed the relative importance of the largest corporations, as in the accompanying table.

Table 1 The Relative Share of Giant Corporations in Various Sectors of the United States Economy

Sector	All corporations		Corporations with assets of $250 million or more	
	Number (thousands)	Assets (billions of dollars)	Number	Proportion of assets of all corporations (percentage)
Manufacturing	124·2	201·4	97	42
Mining*	9·7	13·3	5(19)	17(32)
Public utilities	4·8	62·9	56	72
Transportation	21·9	43·5	30	61
Finance	214·6	474·9	218	46

* The figures in parentheses show the number and share of corporations with assets of $100 million or more, since the number of mining corporations in the largest size class is so small.

Many more figures similar to these could be added to the list. They show clearly that a few large corporations are of overwhelmingly disproportionate importance in our economy, and especially in certain key sectors of it. Whatever aspect of their economic activity we measure – employment, investment, research and development, military supply – we see the same situation. Moreover, it is one which has been stable over a period of time. The best evidence – though far from complete – is that the degree of concentration has varied little for the three or four decades before 1947; more recent material has not yet been analysed. Further, the group of leading firms has had a fairly stable membership, and turnover within it is, if anything, declining (Adelman, 1951; Friedland, 1957; Weston, 1953). We are thus examining a persistent situation, rather than a rapidly changing one, and one which we can expect to continue into the future.

Carl Kaysen 139

Disproportionate share alone, however, is not a valid basis for inferring power as I have defined it. In addition, we must consider the range of choice with respect to significant decisions open to the managers of the large corporation. The disproportionate share of the sun in the total mass of our solar system would not justify the ascription to it of 'power' over the planets, since in the fully-determinate gravitational system the sun has no choice among alternative paths of motion which would change the configuration of the whole system. Though the relative weight of the sun is great, its range of choice is nil, and it is the product of the two, so to speak, which measures 'power'. It is to an examination of the managers' range of choice that we now turn.

Our economy is organized on a decentralized, competitive basis. Each business firm, seeking higher profit by providing more efficiently what consumers want, is faced by the competition of others, seeking the same goal through the same means. Coordination and guidance of these activities is the function of the system of markets and prices. These form the information network that tells each manager what is and what is not currently profitable, and, in turn, registers the effects of each business decision, of changes in consumers' tastes, and the availability and efficiency of productive factors. Ideally, in a system of competitive markets, the signals would indicate only one possible course for any particular manager consistent with profitability. Nor would this depend on the degree to which the manager was committed to the goal of profit-maximization; margins between costs and prices would be so narrow as to make bankruptcy the alternative to 'correct' choices. In practice, of course, no real firm functions in markets operating with the sureness, swiftness and freedom from frictions that would eliminate the discretion of management entirely and make the firm merely an instrument which registered the forces of the market. But firms operating in highly competitive markets are closely constrained by market pressures, and the range of economic decision consistent with survival and success that is open to them is narrow.

By contrast, there exist much less competitive markets in which firms are insulated from these compulsions and the range of discretionary choice in management decisions is correspondingly widened. There is a wide variety of situations which can confer such market power on firms. In practice, the most important is large size relative to the market: the situation in which a few large firms account for all or nearly all of the supply. Large size relative to the market is associated with large absolute size of firm. Other reasons, including barriers to the entry of new firms into the market provided by product differentiation and advertising, by patents, by control over scarce raw materials, or by collusive action of existing firms, or by government limitation of competition, are also significant, but they are of less importance than the oligopolistic market structure common in those sectors of the economy that are dominated by large firms.

In manufacturing, nearly two-thirds of the identifiable markets, accounting for about 60 per cent of the value of manufacturing output, showed significant elements of oligopoly; they were especially important in the durable goods and capital equipment fields. In mining, the proportion of identifiable markets with oligopolistic structures was much higher, but since the largest mining industry – bituminous coal – is unconcentrated, these accounted for less than 25 per cent of total mineral output. Public utilities, transportation and finance are all subject to more or less direct government regulation, of more or less effectiveness. But the underlying market structures in these areas are either monopolistic, as in electric and gas utilities and telephone communication, or oligopolistic, as in transportation and finance.[3] Thus, typically, the large corporation in which we are interested operates in a situation in which the constraints imposed by market forces are loose, and the scope for managerial choice is considerable. It is this scope combined with the large relative weight of the giant corporation that defines its economic power; it is substantially on its economic power that other kinds of power depend.

The powerful firm can use its power primarily to increase its profit over what it could earn in a competitive market: the

3. These estimates are taken from Kaysen and Turner (1959). See ch. 2 and the appendices. The figures are based on data for 1954 for manufacturing, and on scattered years for other industries.

traditional economic view of the drawback of market power has been the achievement of monopoly profit by the restriction of supply. But it need not do so. While the firm in the highly competitive market is constrained to seek after maximum profits, because the alternative is insufficient profit to insure survival, the firm in the less competitive market can choose whether to seek maximum profit or to be satisfied with some 'acceptable' return and to seek other goals. Further, the firm in a competitive market must attend more closely to immediate problems, and leave the long future to take care of itself; while the firm with considerable market power necessarily has a longer time-horizon, and takes into account consequences of its decisions reaching further into the future. This in turn increases the range of choice open to it, for the future is uncertain, and no single 'correct' reading of it is possible. Many courses of action may be consistent with reasonable expectations of the future course of events. The more dominant the position of any particular firm in a single market, the further into the future will it see the consequences of its own choices as significant, and correspondingly, the wider will be its range of significant choice. The width of choice and the uncertainty of consequences combine to rob the notion of maximum profit of its simplicity; at the minimum of complexity, the firm must be viewed as seeking some combination of anticipated return and possible variation, at the same time perhaps safeguarding itself against too much variation. But even this is too simple. In the absence of the constraints of a competitive market, the firm may seek a variety of goals: 'satisfactory' profits, an 'adequate' rate of growth, a 'safe' share of the market, 'good' labor relations, 'good' public relations, and so forth, and no particular combination need adequately describe the behavior of all large firms with significant market power.

The large corporations with which we are here concerned characteristically operate many plants and sell and buy in many markets. Their power in some markets can be used to reinforce their power in others; their large absolute size, and the pool of capital at their command, adds something to their power in any particular market which is not explained simply by the structure of that market. In the extreme, the operations of the firm in a particular market can be completely or almost completely insensitive to its economic fortunes in that market, and thus the range of choice of decisions with respect to it may be widened far beyond that possible to any firm confined within its boundaries. Absolute size has to a certain extent the same effect in respect to the operations of any particular short time-period: the impact of likely short-period losses or failures may bulk insufficiently large to form a significant constraint on action.

We have spoken so far of the powers of choice of the corporation and the management interchangeably. By and large, this is justified. Corporate management is typically – in the reaches of business we are examining – an autonomous center of decision, organizing the affairs of the corporation and choosing its own successors. While stockholders are significant as part of the environment in which management operates, they exercise little or no power of choice themselves. The views of stockholders, as reflected in their willingness to hold or their desire to dispose of the corporation's stock, are certainly taken into account by management, but only as one of a number of elements which condition their decisions. The ideology of corporate management which describes them as one among a number of client groups whose interests are the concern of management – labor, consumers and the 'public' forming the others – is in this particular realistic.

How does the giant corporation manifest its power? Most directly, in economic terms, the noteworthy dimensions of choice open to it include prices and price-cost relations, investment, location, research and innovation, and product character and selling effort. Management choice in each of these dimensions has significance for the particular markets in which the firm operates, and with respect to some of them, may have broader significance for the economy as a whole.

Prices and price-cost relations, in turn, show at least four important aspects. First is the classic question of the general level of prices in relation to costs: are profits excessive? Second, and perhaps more important, is the effect of margins on the level of costs themselves. Where the pressure of competition does not force prices down to costs, costs themselves have a tendency to rise: internal managerial checks alone cannot overcome the tendency to be satisfied with costs when the overall level of profit is satisfactory. Third, there is the problem of interrelations among margins on related products: does the price of a Chevrolet bear the same relation to its costs as the price of a Cadillac, or is there a tendency to earn more in the long run on resources converted into the one than into the other? This form of distortion of price-cost relations is common in the multiproduct firm, and can coexist with a modest average profit margin. Finally, there are the interrelations, both directly within a single firm and indirectly through labor and product markets, of prices and wages. Where price increases are the response to wage increases which in turn respond to price increases, the pricing policy of a firm or group of firms can be an inflationary factor of some importance. This has been the case in the steel industry in the postwar period (Eckstein, 1958). A related problem is the behavior of prices in the face of declining demand. When a group of firms can raise prices relative to wages although unused capacity is large and increasing, they make a contribution to aggregate instability, in this case in a deflationary rather than an inflationary direction. There again the steel industry provides a recent example.

The investment decisions of large firms are of primary importance in determining the rates of growth of particular industries, and where the role of these industries in the economy is a strategic one, their impact may be much wider. Again we may point to the steel industry. Overpessimism about expansion in the early postwar period contributed to the continuing bottleneck in steel that was apparent until the 1957 recession. In the twenties, the slowness with which aluminum capacity was expanded led to recurrent shortages in that market. The speed, or slowness, with which investment in nuclear-fueled electric power generation is now going forward, even with the aid of considerable government subsidy, is again the product of the decisions of a relatively small number of major power producers. This is not to argue that the pace chosen is the wrong one, but simply to indicate a choice of possibly broad significance, lying in large part in the hands of a few corporate managements.

A particular kind of investment decision, the consequences of which may reach far into the future and beyond the specific firm or industry involved, is the decision about location. Where new plants are placed both in regional terms and in relation to existing centers of population affects the balance of regional development and the character of urban and suburban growth. Characteristically, it is the large multiplant enterprise which has the widest set of alternatives from among which to choose in making this decision; smaller firms are tied closely to their existing geographic centers.

Even more far reaching are the choices of large enterprises in respect to innovation. Decisions as to the technical areas which will be systematically explored by research and development divisions and decisions as to what scientific and technical novelties will be translated into new products and new processes and tried out for economic viability have very deep effects. Ultimately, the whole material fabric of society, the structure of occupations, the geographic distribution of economic activity and population are all profoundly affected by the pattern of technical change. Not all significant technical change springs from the activities of organized research and development departments, but they do appear to be of increasing importance. And the disproportionate share of a few large corporations in this sphere is greater than in any other. Here again, I am not arguing that the decisions now taken on these matters are necessarily inferior to those which would result from some different distribution of decision-making power, but only pointing to the locus of an important power of choice. [. . .]

Any discussion of equity moves rapidly from an economic to what is essentially a political view, since equity is ultimately a value problem whose social resolution is of the essence of politics. When we make this move, a new order of equity problems connected with the power of the large firm appears. This is the problem of the relation between the large enterprise and the host of small satellite enterprises which become its dependents. These may be customers bound to it by a variety of contractual relations, such as the service stations bound to the major oil companies who are their suppliers (and frequently their landlords and bankers as well), or the automobile dealers connected with the manufacturers by franchise arrangements. Or they may be customers without explicit contractual ties, yet none the less dependent on the maintenance of 'customary' relations with large suppliers of their essential raw material, as has been the case with small fabricators of aluminum and steel products, whose business destinies have been controlled by the informal rationing schemes of the primary producers in the frequent shortage periods of the postwar decade. Or they may be small suppliers of large firms: canners packing for the private brands of the large chain grocers, furniture or clothing manufacturers producing for the chain department stores and mail-order houses, subcontractors producing for the major military suppliers. In any case, these small firms are typically wholly dependent on their larger partners. It is worth noting that this dependence may be consistent with a fairly competitive situation in the major product market of the large purchaser, or even the overall selling market of the large supplier, provided the particular submarket in which the transactions between large and small firm occur is segmented enough to make it costly and risky for the small firm to seek new sources or outlets.

All these relations present a double problem. First, is the treatment which the dependent firms experience 'fair' in the concrete: Have there been cancellations of dealers' franchises by major automobile manufacturers for no cause, or, worse, in order to transfer them to firms in which company executives had an interest? Have aluminum companies 'favored' their own fabricating operations at the expense of independent fabricators during periods of short supply?[4] Second, and more fundamental, is what might be called the procedural aspect of the problem. Whether unfair treatment by large firms of their small clients abounds, or is so rare as to be written off as the vagary of a few executives, the question of whether it is appropriate for the large firm to possess what amount to life-and-death powers over other business remains.

4. See, on automobiles, the *Hearings* on Automobile Marketing Practices before the Interstate and Foreign Commerce Committee of the Senate, 84 Cong., 2 Sess. On aluminum, see the *Hearings* before Subcommittee no. 3 of the Select Committee on Small Business, House of Representatives, 84 Cong., 1 Sess. (1956) and the *Hearings* before the same Subcommittee, 85 Cong., 1 and 2 Sess. (1958).

And the same question arises more broadly than in respect to the patron-client relations of large firms and their dependent small suppliers and customers. All of the areas of decision in which powerful managements have wide scope for choice, with effects reaching far into the economy, that we discussed above raise the same question. Not the concrete consequences of choice measured against the economic standards of efficiency, stability, progressiveness and equity, but the power and scope of choice itself is the problem. This view of the problem may appear somewhat abstract, and even be dismissed as a piece of academic fussiness: if the outcomes are in themselves not objectionable, why should we concern ourselves with the process of decision which led to them; and, if they are, why not address ourselves to improving them directly? But so to argue ignores the point that choice of economic goals is itself a value choice, and thus a political one; and that direct concern with the loci of power and constraints on its use may legitimately rank in importance as political goals with the attainment of desired economic values. If the regime of competition and the arguments of *laissez-faire* ever commended themselves widely, it has been primarily on political rather than economic grounds. The replacement of the all-too-visible hand of the state by the invisible hand of the marketplace, which guided each to act for the common good while pursuing his own interests and aims without an overt show of constraint, was what attracted general ideological support to the liberal cause. The elegance of the optimum allocation of resources which Walras and Pareto saw in the ideal competitive economy by contrast has remained a concept of importance only to the most academic economist. When the invisible hand of the competitive market is, in turn, displaced to a significant extent by the increasingly visible hand of powerful corporate management, the question '*Quo warranto?*' is bound to arise, whatever decisions are in fact made. And the fact is that the power of corporate management is, in the political sense, irresponsible power, answerable ultimately only to itself. No matter how earnestly management strives to 'balance' interests in making its decisions – interests of stockholders, of employees, of customers, of the 'general public', as well as the institutional interests of the enterprise – it is ultimately its own conception of these interests and their desirable relations that rules. When the exercise of choice is strongly constrained by competitive forces, and the power of decision of any particular management is narrow and proportioned to the immediate economic needs of the enterprise, the political question of the warrant of management authority and its proper scope does not arise. When, as we have argued, the scope of choice is great and the consequences reach widely into the economy and far into the future, the problem of the authority and responsibility of the choosers is bound to become pressing.

The market power which large absolute and relative size gives to the giant corporation is the basis not only of economic power but also of considerable political and social power of a broader sort. Some of the political power of large business is of course the product of group action to defend group interests and, in this sense, presents no problems peculiar to large business, except perhaps the problem of the large availability of funds and certain non-purchasable resources of specialized talent and prestige in support of its interest. That we pay, in the form of percentage depletion, an outrageous subsidy to the oil and gas business (which goes to many small producers as well as to the giant integrated oil firms) is a phenomenon of no different order than that we pay nearly equally outrageous ones to farmers. On the other hand, it is money rather than votes which supports the one, and votes rather than money which support the other; and the latter situation is, as the former is not, in accord with our professed political morality. More special to the position of the large firm is the power in both domestic and foreign affairs which the large oil companies have by virtue of their special positions as concessionaires – frequently on a monopoly basis in a particular country – in exploiting the oil of the Middle East and the Caribbean. Here the large firms exercise quasi-sovereign powers, have large influence on certain aspects of the foreign policy of the United States and the Atlantic Alliance, and operate in a way which is neither that of public government nor that of private business. While the oil companies are the most spectacular examples of the involvement of strong American companies with weak foreign governments in areas which are important to national policy, they are not the only ones, and other examples could be cited.

Perhaps the most pervasive influence of big business on national politics lies in the tone of the mass media. Both because of the influence of advertising – itself heavily concentrated in the largest firms, and the big-business character of many publishing and broadcasting enterprises, the political tone of the media is far from reflecting even approximately the distribution of attitudes and opinions in the society as a whole. But an influence may be pervasive without thereby being powerful, and the importance of this state of affairs is open to argument.

It is when we step down from the level of national politics to the state and local levels that the political power of the large corporation is seen in truer perspective. The large national-market firm has available to it the promise of locating in a particular area or expanding its operations there, the threat of moving or contracting its operations as potent bargaining points in its dealings with local and even state political leaders. The branch manager of the company whose plant is the largest employer in a town or the vice-president of the firm proposing to build a plant which will become the largest employer in a small state treats with local government not as a citizen but as a quasi-sovereign power. Taxes, zoning laws, roads and the like become matters of negotiation as much as matters of legislation. Even large industrial states and metropolitan cities may face similar problems: the largest three employers in Michigan account for probably a quarter of the state's industrial employment; in Detroit the proportion is more nearly a third. At this level, the corporation's scope of choice, its financial staying power, its independence of significant local forces are all sources of strength in dealing with the characteristically weak governments at the local and often at the state levels.

The broader social power which the high executives of large corporations exercise – in part in their own positions, in part in their representative capacity as 'business leaders' – is more difficult to define and certainly less definite than the kind of political power and economic power discussed above. Yet it is no less important, and to the extent that it is linked to the economic power of the large firm – a point to which I return immediately below – no less relevant to our discussion. One aspect of this broad power to which we have already referred is the position that corporate management occupies as taste setter or style leader for the society as a whole. Business influence on taste ranges from the direct effects through the design of material goods to the indirect and more subtle effects of the style of language and thought purveyed through the mass media – the school of style at which all of us are in attendance every day. Further, these same business leaders are dominant social models in our society: their achievements and their values are to a large extent the type of the excellent, especially for those strata of society from which leaders in most endeavors are drawn. This, more shortly stated, is the familiar proposition that we are a business society, and that the giant corporation is the 'characteristic', if not the statistically typical, institution of our society, and, in turn, the social role of high executives is that appropriate to leading men in the leading institution.

How much is this kind of social power, as well as the political power discussed above, connected with the market power of giant firms? Is it simply a consequence of their economic power, or does it depend on deeper elements in our social structure? These are questions to which any firm answer is difficult, in part because they can be interpreted to mean many different things. To assert that any diminution in the underlying power of large firms in the markets in which they operate would lead to a corresponding decrease in their social and political power appears unwarranted; so does the assertion that universally competitive markets would end the social and political power of business. But there are important connections. Part of the power of the business leaders comes from the size of the enterprises they operate and the number of people they influence directly as employees, suppliers, customers; absolute size, in turn, is highly correlated with relative size and market power. Freedom in spending money is connected with both absolute size, and the security of income which market power provides. The initiative in the complex process of taste formation might shift away from smaller and more competitive businesses toward other institutions to a substantial extent; and the ability of firms to spend large resources on shaping demand would be lessened by reductions in their market power. Thus diminution of the economic power of large firms would have a more-than-trivial effect on their power in other spheres, even if we cannot state firmly the law that relates them.

The reasons for concern about the social and political power of business are also worth consideration, since they are not obviously the same as those which the concentrated economic power of large corporations raise. There are two aspects of this question which appear worth distinguishing. The first is the already-mentioned point of the irresponsibility of business power. Its exercise with respect to choices which are themselves far from the matters of meeting the material needs of society that are the primary tasks of business further emphasizes this point. The process of selection of business leaders may be adaptive with respect to their performance of the economic function of business; there is no reason to expect that it should be with respect to the exercise of power in other realms. In short, why should we entrust to the judgement of business leaders decisions of this kind, when we have neither a mechanism for ratifying or rejecting their judgements and them, nor any reason to believe them particularly suited to make these judgements? Second, we can go further than merely to raise the question of whether the training and selection of business leaders qualifies them to make the kinds of decisions and exercise the kinds of power we have discussed. In some quite important respects, it is clear that business values and business attitudes are dysfunctional in meeting our national needs. This is true both with respect to the many problems which we face in our international relations, and with respect to important domestic problems as well. If we look on our economic relations with the under-developed nations, especially those of Asia and Africa, as primarily tasks of business firms to be met through the market under the stimulus of market incentives, supported to some extent by special subsidies, it appears unlikely that we will succeed in achieving our political and security goals. If our attitudes toward other governments are heavily colored by ideological evaluations of the kind of economic organization they favor, from the standpoint of our own business ideology, our world problems will be made no easier. And in the domestic sphere, there is a range of problems from education to metropolitan organization and urban renewal which cannot be dealt with adequately if viewed in business perspective and under business values.

We can sum up these points by saying that the position of big businesses and their leaders contributes significantly to our being a 'business society'. Do we want to be? Can we afford to be?

These rhetorical questions indicate clearly enough my own view on whether or not we should try to limit or control the power of large corporate enterprise. The crucial question, however, is whether such power can be limited or controlled. Broadly, there are three alternative possibilities. The first is limitation of business power through promoting more competitive markets; the second is broader control of business power by agencies external to business; the third, institutionalization within the firm of responsibility for the exercise of power. Traditionally, we have purported to place major reliance on the first of these alternatives, in the shape of antitrust policy, without in practice pushing very hard any effort to restrict market power to the maximum feasible extent. I have argued elsewhere that it is in fact possible to move much further than we have in this direction, without either significant loss in the over-all effectiveness of business performance or the erection of an elaborate apparatus of control (Kaysen and Turner, 1959). While this, in my judgement, remains the most desirable path of policy, I do not in fact consider it the one which we will tend to follow. To embark on a determined policy of the reduction of business size and growth in order to limit market power requires a commitment of faith in the desirability of the outcome and the feasibility of the process which I think is not widespread. What I consider more likely is some mixture of the second and third types of control. Business itself has argued vehemently that a corporate revolution is now in process, which has resulted in a redirection of business goals and conscious assumption of responsibility in broad social spheres. This theme has been put forward by academic writers as well (Berle, 1954; Kaplan, 1954; Kaplan, Dirlam, Lanzilloti, 1958). To whatever extent such a 'revolution' has taken place, it does not meet the need for the institutionalization of responsibility which the continued exercise of wide power demands. It is not sufficient for the business leaders to announce that they are thinking hard and wrestling earnestly with their wide responsibilities, if, in fact, the power of unreviewed and unchecked decision remains with them, and they remain a small, self-selecting group (Mason, 1958). Some of the more sophisticated accounts of the revolutionary transformation of business identify business as a 'profession' in the honorific sense, and imply that professional standards can be relied on as a sufficient social control over the exercise of business power, as society does rely on them to control the exercise of the considerable powers of doctors and lawyers. This is a ramifying problem which we cannot here explore; it is sufficient to remark that there is, at least as yet, neither visible mechanism of uniform training to inculcate, nor visible organization to maintain and enforce such standards; and, further, that even if business decisions in the business sphere could be 'professionalized' and subject to the control of a guild apparatus, it seems less easy to expect that the same would be true of the exercise of business power in the social and political spheres.

Some likely directions of development of explicit control can be seen in the kinds of actions which now provoke Congressional inquiry, and the suggestions which flow from such inquiries. Concern with the wage-price spiral has led to Congressional investigation of 'administered prices' and to suggestions that proposed price and wage changes in certain industries be reviewed by a public body before becoming effective. A combination of the increase of direct regulation of some of the economic choices of powerful firms with an increase in public discussion of the choices which are not explicitly controlled, appears probable. Such a program will, in effect, do by a formal mechanism and systematically what is currently being done in a somewhat haphazard way by Congressional investigation. On the whole, it is this which has been the active front. The development of mechanisms which will change the internal organization of the corporation, and define more closely and represent more presently the interests to which corporate management should respond and the goals toward which they should strive is yet to begin, if it is to come at all.

References

ADELMAN, M. A. (1951), 'The measurement of industrial concentration', *Rev. Econ. Stats.*, no. 23, pp. 269–96.

BERLE, A. A. (1954), *The Twentieth-Century Capitalist Revolution*, Harcourt, Brace & World.

ECKSTEIN, O. (1958), 'Inflation, the wage-price spiral and economic growth', *The Relationship of Prices to Economic Stability and Growth*, Joint Economic Committee.

FRIEDLAND, S. (1957), 'Turnover and growth of the largest industrial firms, 1906–50', *Rev. Econ. Stats.*

GORDON, R. A. (1946), *Business Leadership in the Large Corporation*, University of California Press.

KAPLAN, A. D. H. (1954), *Big Enterprises in a Competitive System*, Brookings.

KAPLAN, A. D. H., DIRLAM, J., and LANZILLOTI, R. (1958), *The Pricing Policy of Big Business*, Brookings.

KAYSEN, C., and TURNER, D. F. (1959), *Antitrust Policy, an Economic and Legal Analysis*, Harvard University Press.

MASON, E. S. (1958), 'The apologetics of managerialism', *J. Bus.*, vol. 31, no. 1.

US DEPARTMENT OF COMMERCE (1955), *Survey of Current Business*, Office of Business Economics.

US DEPARTMENT OF COMMERCE (1957), *Statistical Abstract of the United States*, Bureau of the Census.

US DEPARTMENT OF COMMERCE (1958), *Company Statistics 1954*, Bureau of the Census.

US DEPARTMENT OF DEFENSE (1957), 'A hundred companies and affiliates listed according to net value of military prime contract awards, July 1950–June 1956', Washington DC.

US NATIONAL SCIENCE FOUNDATION (1956), *Science and Engineering in American Industry*, Washington DC.

US TREASURY (1958), *Statistics of Income Part 2, 1955*, Internal Revenue Service.

WESTON, J. F. (1953), *The Role of Mergers in the Growth of Large Firms*, University of California Press.

12 Edward C. Banfield and James Q. Wilson

The Centralization of Influence

Excerpt from Edward C. Banfield and James Q. Wilson, *City Politics*, Harvard University Press and MIT Press, 1963, pp. 101–7.

In order for anything to be done under public auspices, the elaborate decentralization of authority must somehow be overcome or set aside. The wide diffused *right* to act must be replaced by a unified *ability* to act.[1] The many legally independent bodies – governments or fragments of government – whose collaboration is necessary for the accomplishment of a task must work as one. If, for example, the task is an urban renewal program, the various possessors of authority – say the mayor, the city council, the redevelopment authority, the legislature, the governor and perhaps also the voters – must act concertedly. If any possessor of authority refuses to 'go along' with the others, if they will not exercise their authority in the ways that are necessary, nothing can be done. For example, if the mayor will not collaborate with the redevelopment authority, there can be no renewal program, for he alone has authority to do certain things that must be done.

If all possessors of authority subscribe to a common purpose, this may conceivably be enough to bring about the necessary collaboration, each actor 'voluntarily' exercising his authority as the common purpose requires. Such voluntary concerting of action is a very important element in most governmental action, but it is rarely sufficient to overcome the decentralization of authority in the city. In almost every situation there are some

1. We use 'authority' to mean the *legal right* to act or to require others to act. We use 'influence' to mean the *ability* to act, or to cause others to act in accordance with one's intention. (Authority, then, may or may not give rise to influence: i.e. the legal right to require action may or may not suffice to evoke it.) We use 'power' to mean influence the basis of which is something other than authority (e.g. the promise of favors and the threat of injuries).

possessors of authority who either do not see the common purpose in the same way as the others or have some contrary purpose of their own. The mayor may withhold cooperation from the redevelopment authority because he thinks its plans unwise or because he thinks that they will hurt him politically. But even if he does not, some other possessor of authority – say the city council – probably will. Therefore if the action of the various independent possessors of authority is to be concerted, mechanisms must exist which in one way or another render nugatory the decentralization of authority.

Mechanisms of centralization

In city government, this is accomplished mainly through the operation of these mechanisms: indifference and apathy; deference; party loyalty; inducements, either specific or general; salesmanship.

Here is how the mechanisms work:

Indifference and apathy. Some people in effect give over their authority to others by failing to exercise it because they do not care what happens. A voter who fails to vote, for example, in effect gives his authority (vote) to those who do vote. An actor's indifference may extend to all of the affairs of the city (apathy) or only to those which he thinks do not affect him. Except for politicians and bureaucrats, few people have a very active interest in most city affairs. To the extent that there is indifference or apathy, the decentralization of authority is overcome and action is made easier.

Deference. Some possessors of authority may in effect lend it to others because they feel that they ought to do so. The members of a board of education, although disagreeing with the mayor, may feel that they ought to defer to his wishes; in such a case, the decentralization of authority to them is overcome by their action in deferring. This happens often. People see that the particular circumstances require more centralization than the law provides and they act accordingly. Of course, *pretended* deference may be used to avoid responsibility; 'Let the mayor have his way' may be a way of saying 'Let the mayor take the blame.'

Party loyalty. Possessors of authority may abdicate the use of it because of loyalty to party. This is really a special case of the class just described; the possessor of authority, instead of giving it over to the one who wants to act, gives it over on a continuing basis to the party managers who dispense it as they see fit. Party 'loyalty' thus transfers authority from many hands into few.

Inducements. A promise of reward (or threat of punishment) may induce the possessor of authority to exercise it in the way someone else demands, thus in effect turning the authority over to that someone else. This happens, for example, when a politician agrees to 'take orders' from one who can assist his political career.

A *specific* inducement can be given to (or withheld from) a specific individual. A *general* one can be given only to all members of a given group; if one gets it, all must get it by the nature of the case. Jobs, favors and bribes (but also intangibles like friendship) are specific inducements (Barnard, 1938, chs 7 and 11). Generous welfare payments, able administration and an attractive public personality are general inducements. The importance of the distinction is that specific inducements, where they can be used at all, are more dependable and effective in their operation. A politician who promises someone a particular job can count on his support because if the support is not forthcoming the job will not be either. But a politician who promises a whole class of people jobs cannot count on their support; each member of the class knows that even if he opposes the politician he will share in any benefits of a kind (full employment, for example) that must accrue, if they accrue at all, to the whole group.

It is useful to distinguish inducements that involve compromise of measures from ones that do not. A mayor who can induce councilmen to vote for his measure only by accepting certain crippling amendments that they want to make in it is in a very different position from one who can get their votes by giving inducements (such as patronage) that are unrelated to the measure. A particularly important way of generating inducements that do not involve the compromise of measures is 'log-rolling' – the arrangement by which A supports B's measure as a means of inducing B to support his.

Salesmanship. The possessor of authority may be induced by the arts of rhetoric or by the exercise of charm or charisma to put it at the service of another. A mayor who 'sells' an independent board of education on doing what he wants done in effect overcomes the decentralization of authority. Moses has described how Mayor Fiorello La Guardia used a familiar sales approach – the appeal to ethnic attachments – to help centralize the power that he needed to govern New York City:

It must be admitted that in exploiting racial and religious prejudices La Guardia could run circles around the bosses he despised and derided. When it came to raking ashes of Old World hates, warming ancient grudges, waving the bloody shirt, tuning the ear to ancestral voices, he could easily out-demagogue the demagogues.... He knew that the aim of the rabble-rousers is simply to shoo into office for entirely extraneous, illogical and even silly reasons the municipal officials who clean city streets, teach in schools, protect, house and keep healthy, strong and happy millions of people crowded together here (1957, pp. 7–8).

Patterns of centralization

Most of these ways of overcoming the decentralization of authority are used in most cities most of the time. There are important differences among cities, however, both in the combination of methods that is used and in the amount of centralization that is achieved. In the rest of this chapter, we shall describe and compare the ways in which influence is centralized in the nation's three largest cities. The result, we think, will be a simple typology into which most other cities could reasonably well be fitted.

Extreme centralization of influence (Chicago)

Chicago is a city in which an extreme decentralization of authority has been overcome by an extreme centralization of power, the power being based mainly on specific inducements. The mayor of Chicago is a boss. That is to say, he is a broker in the business (so to speak) of buying and selling political power. He performs an entrepreneurial function by overcoming the decentralization of authority that prevents anything from being done, and in this his role is very like that of the real-estate broker who assembles land for a large development by buying up parcels here and there. Much of what the political broker gathers up is on speculation: he does not know exactly how it will be used, but he is confident that someone will need a large block of power.

As a rule, the boss gets his initial stock of influence by virtue of holding a party or public office. He uses the authority of the office to acquire power, and then he uses the power to acquire more power and ultimately more authority. By 'buying' bits of authority here and there from the many small 'owners' (voters, for example) who received it from the constitution-makers or got it by being elected or appointed to office (strictly speaking, it is control over the use of authority, not authority itself, that he 'buys'), the boss accumulates a 'working capital' of influence. Those who 'sell' it to him receive in return jobs, party preferment, police protection, other bits of influence and other considerations of value. The boss, like any investor, has to invest his influence shrewdly if he is to maintain and increase it.

The Chicago city council, which has the authority to be a powerful check on the mayor, hardly exists as a real influence. All but three of the fifty members of the council in 1961 were Democrats, and Democrats hardly ever vote contrary to the mayor's wishes. He can use specific inducements, especially patronage and party preferment and the threat of 'dumping' a rebel (removing his name from the ballot in the next election) to maintain strict discipline. Here is a newspaper's account – somewhat exaggerated perhaps, but certainly true in the main – of the way that discipline may be exercised:

Ald. Keane (31st) arrived eleven minutes late for a meeting Tuesday morning of the council committee on traffic and public safety, of which he is chairman. The committee had a sizeable agenda, 286 items in all to consider.

Ald. Keane took up the first item. For the record, he dictated to the committee secretary that Ald. A moved and Ald. B seconded its approval, and then, without calling for a vote, he declared the motion passed. Neither mover nor seconder had opened his mouth. He followed the same procedure on six more proposals, again without a word from the aldermen whose names appeared in the record. Then he put 107 items into one bundle for passage, and 172 more into another for rejection, again without a voice other than his own having been heard.

Having disposed of this mountain of details in exactly ten minutes, Ald. Keane walked out. The aldermen he had quoted so freely, without either their concurrence or their protest, sat around looking stupid.

Most likely they are (*Chicago Tribune*, 13 April 1955).

The mayor has a big block of votes in the legislature. Few Cook County Democrats would dare to go against him and many Cook County Republicans get patronage or other favors from him. (He expects these Republicans to vote with him only when they can get away with it, or only on something that is very important to him and not very important to them.) He controls indirectly the votes of many downstate Democratic legislators who are beholden to downstate bosses who must bargain with him. So strong is the mayor in the legislature that even when both houses are Republican a Republican governor must bargain with him. There are always some occasions when a Republican governor needs help from outside his party; when these occasions arise and the mayor sees fit to give the help, he gets something in return. A few years ago, a Republican governor wanted to increase the state police force. His bill was opposed by the county sheriffs' association, and the legislature was about to turn it down. The mayor came to the rescue, and in return the governor gave the mayor a city sales tax. Thus the authority of the legislature over the city is mitigated or overcome by the influence of the 'boss'. There are times when the city (the mayor, that is) comes closer to running the state than the state to running the city.

Even the decentralization of authority to the voters is largely overcome in Chicago. Through his control of the party machinery, the mayor can usually get his proposals approved by the electorate. If an unpopular public expenditure is to be voted upon, he can have it put on the ballot at an election for minor offices when the vote is light and only the party regulars come out.

Having this influence, the mayor can use it to acquire more. Formally independent agencies like the Park District, the Board of Education and the Housing Authority are well aware that without the mayor's help in the council and in the legislature and sometimes with the voters, they are helpless. So far as the law is concerned, there is nothing to stop them from crossing the mayor at every turn. But as a practical matter they are compelled to look to him for help and support and therefore to follow his lead.

In some matters and within certain limits, the mayor is a kind of informal metropolitan-area government. His influence in the legislature is so great that the suburbs, most of which want something from the central city or from the legislature, occasionally take their cues from him.

As all this suggests, the mayor of Chicago is rarely under the necessity of compromising his measures in order to 'buy' support for them. Having an ample supply of other inducements, he can usually insist that they be adopted without crippling amendments.

Nor need he employ the arts of salesmanship. He does not try to make himself a 'personality' (no machine politician would read the funny papers over TV, eat blintzes and pizzas on the sidewalk, or rush to fires in a fireman's uniform). For his purposes, the 'organization' is a more effective way of accomplishing the end in view, i.e. the centralization of influence.

The importance of this high degree of informal centralization to the functioning of Chicago's government can perhaps best be seen from what happened when the centralization temporarily ceased to exist. In 1947, the Democratic party, beset with scandals, found it expedient to elect a 'reform' mayor. Martin Kennelly, a businessman without political experience, took the nomination with the understanding that the party would not interfere in city affairs and he would not interfere in its affairs. In other words, there was to be no 'boss'; the mayor's influence would depend entirely upon the authority of his office and such support as he might attract on other than party grounds and without the help of the party machinery.

The result was a weak and ineffective administration. The mayor did not have enough power to run the city; important matters were decided by default or else by an informal coalition of councilmen – the Big Boys, they were called – whose authority and party-based influence made them independent of the mayor. When a controversial public housing proposal came before the city, Mayor Kennelly stood by while the council, after much delay, compromised and curtailed the program in response to neighborhood pressures. There was no doubt, the housing officials thought, that under Boss Kelly, Kennelly's predecessor as mayor, the city would have got a better housing program and would have got it quicker (Meyerson and Banfield, 1955, pp. 128–9).

References

BARNARD, C. I. (1938), *The Functions of the Executive*, Harvard University Press.

MEYERSON, M., and BANFIELD, E. C. (1955), *Politics, Planning and the Public Interest*, Free Press.

MOSES, R. (1957), *La Guardia: A Salute and a Memoir*, Simon & Schuster.

13 Jerzy J. Wiatr and Adam Przeworski

Control without Opposition

Jerzy J. Wiatr and Adam Przeworski, 'Control without opposition', *Government and Opposition*, vol. 1, 1967, no. 2, pp. 124–39.

In all organizations but especially in the States, the problem of government is twofold. From the point of view of the government, the problem is to secure acquiescence from the governed; from the point of view of the governed, the problem is to make the government take account, not only of its own interests, but also of the interests of those over whom it has power. If either of these problems is completely solved, the other does not arise; if neither is solved, there is revolution. But as a rule a compromise solution is reached (Russell, 1957, pp. 187–8).

The historical development of the western civilization produced several patterns of political opposition deeply rooted and relatively well established in the political systems. This opposition is usually identified with the control of the governed over the government: it is maintained that opposition is at the same time a sufficient and a necessary condition for the existence of such control. Opposition, as the term is commonly used, has the following characteristics:

1. It is political.

2. It is institutionalized in the form of a party or parties.

3. It is often said that it is also 'responsible', i.e. it does not extend to obstruction of the government's actions.

In order to ask more precisely the question concerning the relationship between opposition and control, we must pose two questions of a more specific nature: is opposition a sufficient condition for effective control; and is it a *sine qua non* condition? In spite of some ideological assertions, it seems clear that the answers to both questions are negative. Since the problems of opposition in the two and multi-party systems are treated elsewhere, we shall focus here on those mechanisms of control which present an alternative to opposition as institutionalized in the party system.

The development of institutionalized opposition in the western countries is a historical regional phenomenon. This pattern of opposition is not successfully repeated in other parts of the world. Neither the socialist countries of eastern Europe and Asia nor the majority of the so-termed 'developing' nations have had a successful experience with political opposition similar to that known in western Europe and North America. Is this a proof that the 'new nations' have not learned the lesson offered to them by the 'older nations', for example by the United States (Lipset, 1963)? Or is it a result of a diabolic conspiracy which deprives the western-type democracy of its position outside the economically developed region of the world? Since both explanations seem somewhat naïve, we are inclined to seek understanding of this phenomenon in the economic and social conditions prevailing in the 'non-western' world. Four hypotheses on the emergence of one-party systems in the underdeveloped countries are most often cited:

1. Multi-party systems are associated with high levels of economic development (Lipset, 1960; Almond and Coleman, 1960).

2. Multi-party systems are said to slow down the process of economic development (UNESCO 1963; Galenson, 1959, p. 16; Heilbroner, 1959, p. 35; Duverger, 1960a, p. 104).

3. Multi-party systems cannot function effectively when the country is not integrated ethnically and linguistically (Emerson, 1960, pp. 329–30; Lipset, 1963, p. 11; Wriggins, 1961).

4. Multi-party systems cannot function effectively if they are alien to the cultural traditions of a nation (Gray, 1963; Emerson, 1960, p. 284).

The extent to which these hypotheses have been confirmed varies and is still not sufficient. Przeworski has demonstrated that the correlations between the type of party system and the level of economic development, as well as between the party system and the rates of economic development are non-linear (Przeworski, 1965). Nevertheless, it can be assumed that a minimum level of economic growth must be achieved before a country can successfully develop a pluralistic party system. It can also be expected that the absolute level of economic development does not provide a sufficient explanation of the type of party system existing in a given society; other factors, especially stability of the socio-economic conditions, should also be taken into account.

The degree of ethnic and political integration of a society is an important determinant of control. It should be noted that not every kind of pluralism is functional for this purpose, at least not when pluralism means disintegration. A political system must exist if control is to be exercised within this system. This is often not the case in those countries in which pluralism is still 'pre-modern'. This is true, for example, in such multi-party systems as those of the Congo, Nigeria or Sudan where the parties are organized on tribal bases. When no authoritative decisions are considered binding, it is difficult to speak about control over the government.

Whatever the reason, it is clear that opposition is a phenomenon limited to a minority of political systems. We are concerned with the possibilities for effective control in those systems where the opposition is not institutionalized in the form of parties but absent. Therefore, we shall focus on those channels of control beyond the realm of the party system. These systems can be grouped into three categories based on their respective party system (Duverger, 1951; 1960b; Blanksten, 1960; Wiatr, 1964):

1. Dominant party systems.
2. Hegemonic party systems.
3. Mono-party systems.

The dominant party systems constitute a border case between 'opposition' and 'non-opposition' systems since in some cases the potential of the smaller parties is sufficiently large to constitute a mechanism of control. However, in general such systems conform to the description by Blanksten:

A single political party holds an *effective* monopoly of public power and controls access to government offices. In some one-party systems, this may be provided by law, in which case other political parties are considered illegal or subversive; in another type of one-party system, other parties may exist legally but, for reasons largely unrelated to legal questions or government coercion, find themselves unable to challenge effectively the dominant party's hold on public power (1960, p. 479).

However, the typologies based exclusively on the form of a party system are clearly one-sided. Taking into account the nature and the ideology of the ruling party and the relationship between the party and the society, we may introduce another typology of political systems without opposition. As an illustration we may distinguish here such systems as the 're-volutionary movement-regime' described by Tucker (1961), the conservative 'authoritarian regimes' of which Spain may be a good example (Linz, 1964), and oligarchical regimes existing in many underdeveloped countries, especially in those Latin American countries where the process of development has been very slow.

'Control' may have at least two meanings. In the legal sense of the word, 'control' means the legal power to supervise the controlled domain, to delegate power and withdraw such a delegation, to make final decisions in controversial issues, etc. In this sense of the concept we can speak of judicial control of the constitutionality of political decisions, civilian control over the military, the control of the central government over local authorities. Such forms of control do exist in some countries where the opposition is not present, but they do not constitute the main and politically most important aspect of control. In the political sense, by 'control' we mean the possibility of influencing those who hold power in such a way that they take into account the interests of groups exerting this control. Thus control is a very general notion. It must remain general because the actual forms of control in various systems are greatly differentiated. Nevertheless, one aspect should be made clear. Control means an actual and not only a formal possibility of exercising influence. Those who 'control' may sometimes be unsuccessful. But if they are never successful it means that control has ceased to exist. The test of political control must be sought in the actual functioning of the political system, not in the laws.

Control over the government is not possible if the system is completely monolithic. On the other hand, any elements of pluralism are by their very existence a basis of some kind of control over those who hold power. The problem of control is a quantitative one: since absolutely monolithic systems are a nightmare rather than reality, we should attempt to identify not the mere fact of existence of control but its nature and degree.[1]

Since, as was said above, one-party systems generally occur in the less developed countries, we should make some observations concerning the matters which are under control in these countries. The concept of 'control' should not be considered merely in political categories but should be placed in the concrete socio-economic setting in which it occurs. It seems that in the underdeveloped countries, control is basically limited to the issues of allocation of the scarce resources to the various politically significant sectors of the population and to the issues connected with the projected pace and character of change.

Having defined 'control' in terms of political (but not only party) pluralism and pressures exercised by the 'ruled' on the 'rulers', we should distinguish two basic channels of pressures to be found in the political systems considered here. The first channel includes pressures and influences exerted *within the ruling party*, the second those exercised *outside this party*.

Control within party

The role of the ruling party in the regimes in which it does not face an opposition is twofold. On the one hand, the ruling party acts as the center of power and in this character it bears the responsibility for the functioning of the entire system, and attempts to represent the comprehensive national interests. On the other hand, in some systems simultaneously with the general interests, the ruling party represents some interests of particular

1. Moore (1958) points to the limitations of pluralism – therefore in our terms, political control too – due to mass hysteria widespread in some western democracies.

groups and social strata. Either they exclude some groups from the comprehensive coalition or they feel more responsible for the interests of some groups within the coalition than of other groups. The dominant and the hegemonic parties are the most comprehensive: they perceive themselves to be the representatives of the entire nation and assume in their official ideology a basic harmony of interests of the entire nation. The broad range of such a coalition results in the situation in which the party is both a representation of some sectors of the population and the forum where interests of various groups are balanced against each other. The revolutionary mono-party systems in their early stages are usually less aggregative: official ideology assumes a basic struggle against the 'reactionary' forces, and the criteria for inclusion in the coalition are distinctly narrower than in the former systems. Finally, the oligarchical mono-party systems have the narrowest social support. However, no party is so parochial that it represents only one group of interests. The empirical question is to find to what extent and in what fashion the various interests are expressed and balanced within the party.

In posing these questions we challenge a simplified view of the nature of the ruling parties in the regimes under discussion. Those who accept the extreme version of the division between those 'in power' and those 'out of power' see the ruling party as an apparatus through which the collective interests of the power elite are expressed and realized. If this is true, the problem of control would be limited only to the question of how far those in the positions of authority would submit themselves to the influences of the social group to which they belong. But the problem is much more complex. The group interests of those who hold power certainly influence the decisions they make but the interests of other groups significantly influence those decisions. Moreover, those who actually hold power very often consider themselves as merely representatives of the broader groups of the population or, eventually, of the entire population. There is no convincing argument that such a feeling is solely a false pretention: on the contrary, the inner differences within the ruling groups do not represent their own interests only and the empirical data seem to indicate that they are subject to pressure from various 'outside' groups. In this sense, the interests of the stratum of professional politicians should be considered as being only a part of those different interests which are expressed within and through the party. The party itself attempts to combine in its ideology the traditional liaison for a given part of society with the attempt to serve as a representation of the interests of all, or nearly all, segments of the population. In the case of the communist parties, this is the antimony between their role as workers' parties and their role as representative of the socialist society as a whole. This is the way in which the Yugoslav Communist program perceives this dual function:

The Communist Party of Yugoslavia always faithfully served working-class interests and aspirations which themselves correspond to the objective interests of all other sections of the working people of Yugoslavia. The league of Yugoslav Communists has been, and continues to be under present conditions, the representative of the interests and aspirations of the working class and all other working people in Yugoslavia (Programme of the League of Yugoslav Communists, 1958).

For the majority of the movement-regimes in the developing countries the problem does not exist on the level of ideology: the ruling parties act officially as representative of all the people. However, to the extent to which the societies are differentiated, the same problem of balancing conflicting interests also appears in those parties.

For political scientists the most interesting is the problem of open expression of interests. The extent and the forms in which interests are openly expressed vary. Where factionalism exists and is officially accepted, it functions as a substitute for multi-partism, although the factions are less free in their appeal for outside support. Where factionalism is banned groups, tendencies or 'cliques' may operate at various levels of the political systems. Indirectly, they may also represent the interests of various groups located outside the party. To use an example, we may recall the history of pro-peasant opposition within many communist parties in the period of rapid collectivization.

Thus the controversial problem is not whether such differences and divisions within the party exist, but whether they may be sufficiently strong to exercise effective control. Does the expression presuppose control? In the long term, the answer is affirmative. Those who hold power may not respond immediately to various kinds of criticism but such criticism, supported by electoral pressure inside the party, influences decision-making.[2] In extreme cases, we observe drastic changes in policy under the influence of the rank and file members or more specifically from the middle levels of the party hierarchy, as in Poland in 1956.

The control exercised within the party constitutes at the same time a control of the state administration. The ruling party is nearly identical with the government and comprises within its ranks a great proportion (often a majority) of those who hold public power. However, in a much greater proportion, the party also includes persons who occupy subordinate positions in the administration. Thus the articulation within the party constitutes an instrument for control of the government when, within the party, the political and professional interests and opinions diverge. The influence of the rank and file on the party leadership constitutes indirectly a kind of control over the functioning of the state administration at various levels.

Control outside the party

When political participation becomes widespread, the popular control over the administration may assume two basic directions, depending upon the intensity of articulation through the various channels of the political system. Assuming that a political system which has a high degree of mobilization comprises a set of vertically organized social and political organizations with a mass membership and that these organizations interact horizontally at various territorial and administrative levels of the political system, we can examine the direction of integration of interests, their articulation and aggregation. Traditionally, we are inclined to think of a political system in which

2. Cases of party elections in which former office-holders or officially supported candidates were defeated are not infrequent in Poland and Yugoslavia. The 'rotation' system, recently introduced in the latter country, may intensify this phenomenon but it is still too early to anticipate its consequences.

the government is under pressure of parties and interest groups which transmit vertically the interests articulated at the lower levels of the political system. However, it seems that such a model of a political system, which puts emphasis on vertically rooted pressure groups organized around the government corresponds only to these societies which either have a low degree of political participation or are permeated with class and functional conflicts. In the countries where participation is high and in which there are no basic conflicts of interests among the various groups of the population, the integration of interests is much more likely to occur horizontally at each separate level and independently of the structure of political organizations. In such a situation, opposition and control are decentralized: competition takes place at each level of the political system but it is not integrated nationally along the vertical lines of political organizations, whether these are parties or other political and social institutions. The recent election which took place in Poland in May 1965 provides an illustration of such a competition. According to the speech of the First Secretary of the Polish United Workers' Party, Wladyslaw Gomulka, 7 per cent of the candidates to the village councils were rejected at the preelectoral meetings. These candidates were replaced by persons who were put on the slate during these meetings. However, the structure of party membership of those candidates rejected and those added was nearly identical. Control and competition were independent from the party structure.

Interests are often integrated horizontally at the local level. This is particularly true when a local community decides to enter competition with other communities for allocation of investment in their territory. Narojek describes the mechanism of articulation of such interests:

a common front of a local community is formed. Proper supra-local authorities which are competent to decide a given matter are constantly visited by local delegations or population representatives. All channels of influence are used: through the PZPR [Polish United Workers' Party] and other parties, through poviat and voivodship authorities, through former citizens of the town who are at present persons of influence in higher level authorities, etc. (1965).

The horizontal expression of interests finds its stronger expression in the factories. Although some socio-economic differences between the managerial and the engineering staff, on the one hand, and the workers, on the other hand, do exist, both groups are economically motivated to have an optimal plan. The basic economic incentives depend upon the fulfilment of the plan, and this concerns all employees regardless of their position in the factory. Thus, to an extent, in the countries where the basic industries are socially owned, the interests of all employees of a factory are identical. On the other hand, the massive participation is organized in the form of Workers' Self-Government. The Conferences of Workers' Self-Government exist in 9,426 factories and involve participation of 219,025 persons. The most important decisions taken at the level of an enterprise – those concerning the plan – are discussed in the factories with widespread participation, at least passive, of the workers (Ostrowski and Przeworski, 1967).

Integration of interests within a local political system or within a factory merits special attention. It evidences important channels of control and an important dimension of competition in those countries where control is not institutionalized in the form of nationally organized opposition.

However, in every political system some interests are expressed and transmitted vertically through the political and social organizations. In so far as control is exercised through such vertical national organizations, we can speak of interest groups and their control over the government. However, the role of specialized groups of interests must be re-examined in those countries in which the ruling party is a broad national coalition oriented toward rapid economic development and assumes a harmony of interest of the entire nation. In the multi-party systems, particularly those of the highly developed countries, interest groups are synonymous with 'pressure groups', i.e. groups operating outside the immediate scope of the government and attempting to exert pressure on the government to accommodate the interests they represent. In the one-party systems, interest groups are located within, not outside, the government. Their functions are twofold. On the one hand these groups articulate the interests which they represent, functioning to that extent as 'pressure groups'. The contents of the demands vary, obviously, with the nature of the interests represented, but in general these demands concern specific issues of economic, social and cultural policies and are based on the consensus regarding the ideological and political bases of these policies. On the other hand, the specialized groups perform the mobilizing and educating functions. They mobilize the social initiative in seeking the reserves which could be used for a more rapid economic development. And they are an instrument of political education – translating to the represented groups the general issues of national policies.[3]

The minor parties functioning in the dominant and hegemonic one-party systems provide illustrations of the functioning of such specialized groups of interest. The minor parties in the dominant systems do not constitute alternatives to the major party. They function as interest groups. According to Kothari, the role of the minor parties in India is to:

constantly pressurize, criticize, censure and influence it [the dominant party] by influencing opinion and interests inside the margin [of consensus] and, above all, exert a latent threat that if the ruling group strays too far from the balance of effective public opinion, and if the factional system within it is not mobilized to restore the balance, it will be displaced from power by opposition groups (1964, p. 1162).

On the national level, the position of dominant parties is so stable that the 'opposition' cannot hope for success in the foreseeable future. However, on the local levels the situation may be very different, as evidenced by the Indian experience.

In the hegemonic party systems the parties forming the coalition accept the dominance of one party, for example, communist parties in the socialist countries.[4] But in those countries

3. For example, in Mexico 'virtually all types of firms are required to belong to one or another trade organization which represents that trade to the government and through which the government can make its policy known to the industry' (Edminster, 1961).

4. In Poland, United Peasants' and Democratic Parties; in Bulgaria, Peasant Party, Slovak Rebirth Party and Slovak Freedom Party. In addition some of these countries have political organizations which formally are not parties but which jointly with other parties and organizations participate in the elections, publish newspapers, etc. In Poland, for example, there are three political organizations of Catholics differing in political philosophy, tactics and affiliations.

where the ruling party is hegemonic (as opposed to being the only one) the existence of a coalition helps to exert influence or pressure on the ruling party. The allied parties do not compete for power but present their candidates jointly with the hegemonic party. They do not challenge its leadership in those fields which are vital for the state. But they are officially recognized as representatives of selected sectors of the population such as the peasants, craftsmen, etc. and they are consulted whenever a decision concerns issues of vital interest for the groups they are supposed to represent. Occasionally the minor parties exert pressure on the hegemonic party with regard to policies outside their scope of representation. However, since there is no competition for power, the pressures are exercised through delicate negotiations and bargaining rather than public debate. As a result, the public is not aware of the role of the minor parties and their political potential is low since they do not have a popular appeal. But on the other hand, this type of bargaining provides the minor parties with a powerful triumph in any negotiation: the hegemonic party would treat an open conflict as a collapse of the coalition and would, therefore, try to avoid it even at the cost of far-reaching compromise. In general, little is still known about the role of the minor parties in the hegemonic party systems and any generalization would still be premature.

Among the other groups of interest which can be expected to exert some control over the government, the bureaucracy, the trade unions, the army, mass media and universities usually enter the hegemonic coalition. Since research concerning the pressure and the mobilizing functions of these groups is still very scarce, a detailed analysis of the functioning of these groups is premature at this point.

Special attention should be devoted to the problem of elections as they occur in the one-party system. We have indicated above that elections do involve some competition on the local level. However, it seems that the very function of elections is different in the one-party systems and in multi-party systems. Elections serve as an occasion for expressing demands and for a review of the basic policies of the government. Thus, particularly in so far as the elections to the national bodies are concerned, their basic role is that of a referendum rather than of competition between parties. The meaning of elections for the Soviet society has been described as follows:

It should be borne in mind that the Soviet people traditionally regard polling not only as an act of election of specific persons to a representative organ, but also as an act of appraisal of the Soviet Government's activity for the past period and of launching a programme for the future. Having several candidates in one constituency would mean an artificial scattering of the votes and would run counter to this tradition (Kotok, n.d.).

Both the Yugoslav and the Polish electoral systems allow for several candidates running for the same seat (Godić, 1965; Neal, 1958; Pelezynski, 1959). The electoral research conducted in Poland (Wiatr, 1959; 1962) emphasized the semi-plebiscitary aspect of the elections. While elections serve as an important instrument for popular participation, they also constitute a channel of expression and articulation of attitudes toward the government and its policies. Therefore, the frequency of voting, the proportion of votes cast for the lists of the Front for National Unity, and the extent to which people voted for the list candidates were studied as indicators of the public attitudes toward the government. These studies evidenced the importance of the electoral process as one of the channels of political control.

Other channels may also exist and should be studied. It should be observed in general that the knowledge concerning the process of articulation and control in the one-party systems is still greatly limited. The present paper attempts to provide some guide-lines for the study of political control in the countries which do not have institutionalized opposition. Since a systematic analysis of these phenomena is not yet possible, the tentative character of this paper should be strongly emphasized.

References

ALMOND, G. M., and COLEMAN, J. S. (eds.) (1960), *Politics of the Developing Areas*, Princeton University Press.
BLANKSTEN, G. I. (1960), 'The politics of Latin America', in G. M. ALMOND and J. S. COLEMAN (1960).
DUVERGER, M. (1951), *Les Partis Politiques*, Paris.

DUVERGER, M. (1960a), *La Dictature*, Milan.

DUVERGER, M. (1960b), 'Sociologie des partis politiques', in G. Gurvitch (ed.), *Traité de Sociologie*, vol. 2, Paris.

EDMINSTER, R. (1961), 'Mexico', in A. Pepelasis, L. Mears and I. Adelman (eds.), *Economic Development*, Harper & Row.

EMERSON, R. (1960), *From Empire to Nation*, Harvard University Press.

GALENSON, W. (ed.) (1959), *Labor and Economic Development*, Wiley.

GODIĆ, D. (1965), 'April elections', *Review, Yugoslav Monthly Magazine*.

GRAY, R. F. (1963), 'Political parties in new African nations: the case of Ceylon', *APSR*, no. 55.

HEILBRONER, R. (1959), *Future as History*, Harper & Row.

KOTHARI, R. (1964), 'The congress system in India', *Asian Survey*, no. 4.

KOTOK, V. (n.d.), *The Soviet Representative System*, Progress Publishers, Moscow.

LINZ, J. J. (1964), 'An authoritarian regime: Spain', in E. Allardt and Y. Litturen (eds.), *Cleavages, Ideologies and Party Systems*, Helsinki.

LIPSET, S. M. (1960), *Political Man*, Doubleday.

LIPSET, S. M. (1963), *The First New Nation*, Basic Books.

MOORE, B. (1958), *Political Power and Social Theory*, Harvard University Press.

NAROJEK, W. (1965), 'The structure of local power', in K. Ostrowski and A. Przeworski (eds.), *Local Political System in Poland*, Institute of Philosophy and Sociology, Warsaw.

NEAL, F. W. (1958), *Titoism in Action: The Reforms in Yugoslavia after 1948*, University of California Press.

OSTROWSKI, K., and PRZEWORSKI, A. (1967), 'Trade unions and economic planning in Poland', *Polish Roundtable*, no. 1.

PELEZYNSKI, Z. A. (1959), 'Poland 1957', in D. Butler (ed.), *Elections Abroad*, Macmillan.

PRZEWORSKI, A. (1965), *Party System and Economic Development*, unpublished Ph.D. thesis, Northwestern University.

RUSSELL, B. (1957), *Power: A New Social Analysis*, Allen & Unwin.

TUCKER, R. C. (1961), 'Towards a comparative politics of movement-regiment', *APSR*, no. 55.

UNESCO (1963), 'Rapport de la réunion d'experts sur les conditions sociales de la croissance economique'.

WIATR, J. J. (1959), 'Some problems of public opinion in the light of elections of 1957 and 1958', *Studia Socjologiczno Polityozne*, no. 4.

WIATR, J. J. (1962), 'Election voting behaviour in Poland', in A. Ranney (ed.), *Essays on the Behavioural Study of Politics*, University of Illinois Press.

WIATR, J. J. (1964), 'One-party systems: the concept and issue for comparative studies', in E. Allardt and Y. Litturen (eds.), *Cleavages, Ideologies and Party Systems*, Helsinki.

WRIGGINS, W. H. (1961), 'Impediments to unity in new nations: the case of Ceylon', *APSR*, no. 55.

14 Franz Schurmann

The Communist Party and the State

Excerpt from Franz Schurmann, *Ideology and Organization in Communist China*, Cambridge University Press, 1966, pp. 105–14.

Soviet and Chinese conceptions
The party as organization

In our study of ideology and organization in Communist China the Chinese Communist party occupies a central place. All Communist parties arise in situations of actual or potential revolution. The ultimate aim of all Communist parties, regardless of internal disputes over the means, is the seizure of state power. But what role does it play in society after that aim has been achieved? Where Communist parties seize power, they set up complex structures of organization. Could these structures continue to function without the Communist party – is the Communist party the keystone to the whole structure, so that its disappearance would mean the collapse of the structure? The weight of evidence, in my opinion, is that this is so: given Communist-type organization of state power, a Communist party would have to be created if it did not exist.

This may sound paradoxical, but Cuba provides a case in point. Cuba had an old-line Communist party which was not directly involved in the revolution. On the contrary, Communist-dominated sections of the organized working class appear to have collaborated with Batista to some extent. When Castro came to power, two revolutionary organizations existed: the Castroites who emerged from the Sierra Maestra as an organized revolutionary force led by urban intellectuals and supported by sections of the peasantry; and the old-line Communist party deriving its strength mostly from the urban working class. The existence of two revolutionary organizations prevented the formation of a unified organizational instrument. Nevertheless, Castro created a political system increasingly similar to that of the Communist countries. Since such a political system demanded a true Communist-type party, Castro proceeded gradually toward the formation of a single unified party, the United Party of the Cuban Socialist Revolution. The UPCSR has now begun to play a role in Cuban society comparable to the role of the Chinese Communist party (*New York Times*, 7 July 1964). In Cuba, organizationally speaking, it was the revolution which created the party, and not the party that created the revolution.

This was obviously not so in China, yet there are some similarities between China and Cuba. The Chinese Communist party directed the revolution and war that led to the seizure of state power in 1949. After that, the new regime created military and bureaucratic structures. These developed so rapidly that for a time they began to obscure the role of the Party. Victory had brought the Party into an environment, the cities, in which it lacked strength. But the Party quickly started to build up organization in breadth and depth until it was able to take over active leadership and coordination at all levels of the system. This was called the process of Party construction (*chientang*), and was similar to the building of the UPCSR in Cuba.

People from Communist countries speak of 'the Party' as if it had a life of its own, transcending the individuals in it. In many interviews with refugees from Mainland China, I asked them to specify whom they meant when they talked abstractly of the 'Party'. Most of them vigorously defended the abstract reality of the Party by pointing out that when problems arise in an organizational context, you 'call the Party' and not a specific individual. Different individuals may appear on call, not as persons but as representatives of the Party. The Party has such clearly perceived functions that the differences of individual personality are submerged, just as with priests administering sacraments.

In some highly routinized organizations the human relationships provide the dynamics the organization needs to function; such organizations often continue to function precisely because of the particular individuals in it who play the leading roles – if they are transferred, it usually has significant consequences for the functioning of the organization; men are more important than the roles they are required to perform.

Yet there are other organizations where the dynamism flows from the organization itself, where the prescribed roles can be effectively assumed by men of different personality and temperament. In these organizations, values and norms are powerful enough to make men act in strict compliance.

Every Communist party relies heavily on ideology. In parties, such as the Chinese, where the revolutionary tradition has remained alive, ideological indoctrination has a distinct function. Party members are subjected to intensive indoctrination to keep their beliefs effective. In the more bureaucratized Communist parties, ideological indoctrination is less important. Nevertheless, even in such parties, ideology remains a latent instrument which can be reactivated if the leaders, and the external situation, call for it. Khrushchev's attempt to make the Soviet Communist party into a more active organizational instrument was accompanied by a renewed stress on ideology. All organizations tend toward routinization; Communist parties are no exception. Ideology gives the Party's leaders an instrument for combating such tendencies.

The Party has no specific concrete task, such as, let us say, a ministry has. It is an organization in which the leaders are gathered in a context which strengthens their capacity to lead; it is a unique training ground for moral-political leadership, actualized in some other organizational role, not in the Party itself. Party members go forth from Party meetings armed with new policy instructions from the leadership and activated by new ideological and political indoctrination. Routinization of such an organization would simply make the Party into an elite club in which the political leaders meet to renew their solidarity. Routinization would make men more important than their roles; it would make the Party a pluralistic entity held together by interpersonal relationships, somewhat like the Partido Revolucionario Institucionalista in Mexico; it would do away with the unity which gives the Party its unique leadership role in a Communist society, namely that at any time all its members act in a unified fashion throughout the society to carry out policy determined by the top leadership.

In an organization characterized by powerful values and norms, the factor of consciousness becomes important. Values can only be held consciously, and norms can only be acted on if people understand them. All Communist parties have a revolutionary history, even though power itself may have been seized in 'old-fashioned' political and military ways. The Party member must be conscious of the values and norms of the system.

Another object of consciousness is the nature and role of the Party. Chinese Communist teachings on 'thought' compel the individual to be conscious of the external world, but also to be conscious of himself. In a broader sense, this is true of the Party as well. Periodically its ideologists try to see the Party within the larger context. Such self-reflection can be dangerous, for it has often led to crystallization of different views and factionalism. Self-reflection was extremely dangerous during the Stalin period, in view of the chasm between theory and practice. Yet there always has been this will to explain the nature of the Party, state its position, formulate rationally its role in society. Such self-definitions have usually been tortured and evasive, but they have been necessary. Party self-definition can be seen as an inevitable consequence of commitment to the importance of ideology.

In a traditional, routinized organization, periodic self-definition means little, because what counts are not so much the values and norms governing the organization but the men in key positions. But, as we have said, Communist parties have always resisted routinization, sometimes by purges, more often by renewed outbursts of ideological activity. If the Communist party plays the role of unified leadership and coordination in society, then it is only the ideology, ultimately, which provides the cement for such unity. The Party is an organization that fulfils executive roles in society. It must provide leadership in a context that not only does change but is supposed to change. Any executive decision-maker in a rapidly changing organization must be able to justify his impulses leading to certain decisions on the basis of general values and norms. In routinized organizations, it is the advisory and supervisory personnel – 'the staff and line of bureaucracy' – that ensures continued operation. In a dynamic organization the leader may have a sudden insight of what to do; but the legitimacy for transforming that insight into decision depends on his ability to link it to the broad values and norms that everyone more or less accepts. The more unified such decision-making is supposed to be, the greater number of discrete organizational units it involves, the more important are values and norms. The maintenance of ideology is therefore crucial to executive function and to the continued role of a Communist party. But men do not just manipulate ideology to justify their impulses toward decision. The ideology gradually takes on more concrete form as a body of teaching and policy, and begins to have a reverse forcing effect on the decision makers. Cynical playing with ideology has often had disastrous results for those who saw it simply as a useful tool. Despite the manipulation of ideology during the Stalinist period, the Communist party in the Soviet Union has continued to feel the need for meaningful ideology, not just as a façade but as an indispensable part of the whole process of organizational operation. In this sense, it is important to see what sort of self-definition the Party has evolved. If the Party remains the keystone of organization in a Communist society, the way it defines itself throws sharp light on its function.

Party and state

A brief look at the self-definition of the Soviet Communist party should add perspective to that of the Chinese Communist party. In the ideological literature of the Soviet Union, the Party is not construed as an element of the apparatus of state, but as the organized expression of the will of the dominant class of society, namely the proletariat. But it is the Party which leads and controls the state. The 1958 edition of the official primer of Soviet philosophy published at the height of the anti-Stalin campaign, states the function of the Communist party in the following words:

All these state and public organizations can only function successfully under the leadership of the Communist party, which works out the correct political line, and determines the direction of their practical activity. . . . Only the Party, expressing the interests of the entire nation, embodying its collective understanding, uniting in its ranks the finest individuals of the nation, is qualified and called to control the work of all organizations and organs of power. ... The Party realizes the leadership of all state and public organizations through its members who work in these organizations and who enter into their governing organs (*Osnovy marksistskoi Filosofii*, pp. 549–50).

State and Party are therefore linked but not identical. The distinctions between state and Party seem to be scholastic, but an examination of the organizational history of the Soviet Union and Communist China shows that this is not so. All Communist countries accept the fact that under 'socialism' a distinction remains between state and Party. To define the state has been a thorny problem in Marxist polemics since the days of Marx. Nevertheless, Soviet and Chinese Communist literature makes it clear that 'state' (*gosudarstvo* or *kuochia*) means the formal organization which dominates society. The state is a conscious contrivance. It is the most important element of the superstructure of society, the instrument of its ruling class; in the dictatorship of the proletariat, it is the instrument of the proletariat. As an instrument it has 'structure' – a word commonly used in Communist lexicons in association with the concept of state. The state is bureaucracy, army, law; the body of organized formal instruments from which command flows.

The Party, on the other hand, is the organized expression of the will of society. For the Soviets, it is the expression 'of the interests of the entire nation'; for the Chinese it represents 'the interests of the people'.[1] The Party actualizes the control of

1. It is significant that the ambiguity of the Russian word *narod* is absent in the Chinese. The official ideological literature of the Chinese Communists states explicitly that the Party is the organized expression of 'the interests of the people' (*jenmin*). In other words, the Party is clearly the expression of the will of society, and not of a political entity, the nation. In the Soviet Union, the will of the people and the will of the nation are theoretically identical because all exploiting classes have been eliminated. The Chinese do have a concept of nation, expressed in the word *kuomin*, but the Chinese Communists do not make use of it, because *kuomin* includes exploiting classes which have not yet been fully eliminated from Chinese society. Therefore, the Communist party cannot yet be the expression of the will of the nation, but only of the people *jenmin*. These remarks, too, may appear to be scholastic, but they illustrate something which I feel to be an important aspect of the Chinese Communist self-conception, namely, that

society over the state. But the Party, theoretically, does not command, for formal command must flow from some instrument of the state. The Communist party may propound policy, but technically it cannot issue orders. These must come from an organ of the state. As long as this fine distinction is maintained, the Party cannot be regarded as an instrument of the structure of state power.

This distinction is not so scholastic as to be meaningless. Any organization must try to maintain a separation between executive functions on the one hand and staff-and-line functions on the other. The task of staff and line is to translate the policy directives of the executive into concrete commands. In the Soviet Union and China, the actual commands come from an organ of state, although they may follow long after the policy has already been announced and wheels have begun to turn at lower levels without waiting for formal communication from the government. Even during the Great Leap Forward, when the Chinese Communists believed that policy could be directly translated into action and deprecated the technical command functions of the state administration, formal commands, such as they were, still came from the state organs, though often jointly with the Central Committee.

There are powerful ideological reasons for maintaining the principle that the Party is not a state organ, but there are also practical reasons. The more an organization turns into a command-issuing body, the more it has to grapple with the concrete technicalities of command. This inevitably begins to limit the freedom needed for a wide range of innovative and creative decisions. The Chinese Communists in particular have sharply fought any tendencies toward bureaucratization of the Party, and so have had a strong material interest in maintaining the ideological principle that the Party is not part of the apparatus of state. In the Soviet Union under Stalin where extreme centralization of policy-making functions prevailed, the major concern was that the ministries adequately performed their

they are still involved in a process of nation-building. This means, concretely, that the Chinese Communist leadership regards the revolution as still in progress. In the Soviet Union, the revolution was concluded with the consummation of the October Revolution.

staff-and-line functions of issuing effective commands. Stalin encouraged far-reaching bureaucratization of the Party (apparatization, so to speak), but theory held that it was still qualitatively different from an organ of state.

State and society

Soviet and Chinese Communist theorists agree that the Party is the expression of the will of the proletariat, and in a broader sense expresses the will of the nation or the people. The Party may lead the state, but it has its roots in society. The intimate involvement with society, so characteristic of the Chinese Communist party, may be seen as a consequence of this belief. The core of society, for the Chinese Communists, are the masses. In China, the mass line has been a continuing feature of Communist organizational philosophy since Yenan times. The mass line demands that the Party be physically close to the masses. In the Soviet Union, something in the nature of a mass line has been emerging in recent years in the policy of 'social will' (*obshchéstvennost'*), which has already had concrete expression in the popular militia, the comrades courts, Party control commissions, and the like. As the Chinese see it, the Party must be close to the masses, for the state has an inherent tendency to become alienated from the masses. One might cite a passage from Friedrich Engels's *Origin of the Family, Private Property and the State* which the Chinese have often quoted during their antibureaucratic periods:

The state is therefore by no means a power imposed on society from without; just as little is it 'the reality of the moral idea', 'the image and the reality of reason', as Hegel maintains. Rather, it is a product of society at a particular stage of development; it is the admission that this society has involved itself in insoluble self-contradiction and is cleft into irreconcilable antagonisms which it is powerless to exorcise. But in order that these antagonisms, classes with conflicting economic interests, shall not consume themselves and society in fruitless struggle, a power, apparently standing above society, has become necessary to moderate the conflict and keep it within the bounds of 'order'; and this power, arisen out of society, but placing itself above it and increasingly alienating itself from it, is the state.[2]

2. Quoted in *Hsienfa went'i ts'ank'ao wenchien* (Peking, 1954), pp. 14–15.

The last sentence conveys a feeling that runs through Mao's 1957 speech on internal contradictions within the people. Bureaucracy (an arm of the state) inevitably leads to alienation from the masses, unless a corrective is applied. Mao proclaimed, to the chagrin of the Soviets, that contradictions continue to exist within socialism. One of these is the contradiction between bureaucracy and masses or, more broadly speaking, between state and society. Mao's solution was simple: *the Party is the instrument that forges the resolution of the contradiction between state and society in socialism.*

Since the Marxists regard the state as an instrument of oppression, Soviet theorists have found it difficult to establish the positive role of the state under socialism, especially with the immense growth of formal state power in the Soviet Union. The Chinese Communists have accepted standard Soviet formulations of the role of the state under socialism, but appear to be much less bothered about this question than the Soviets. Both the Soviet and Chinese Communists periodically attack bureaucratism, but the type of attack differs. For the Soviets bureaucratism means the immoral use of state power. For the Chinese Communists, bureaucracy seems inherently evil. This is an expression of the populist strain in the Chinese Communists and also has roots in Chinese revolutionary history. The most terrifying slogan of the Tai-ping rebels was the cry *to-kuan*, 'Smash the Officials'. Hostility to bureaucracy crops up again and again in Chinese Communist history and reached its high point during the Great Leap Forward when the leadership appeared convinced that the economic revolution could more or less dispense with the instruments of formal administration.

The state under capitalism 'disposes over the instruments of power: army, police, gendarmerie, court organs, prisons, etc., for the preservation of the economic dominance of the governing class and for the subjugation of contradictions between different classes', but under socialism its role changes (*Osnovy*, p. 477). Under socialism, 'the army, punitive organs, intelligence are turned against external enemies. It is economic-organizational and culture-educational work which occupies the main place in the activity of the socialist state' (*Osnovy*, p. 543). But once communism has definitively triumphed, 'in place of administration by people there will come, as Engels has said, administration by things and leadership by productive processes. Then the leadership of the economic and cultural life of society will not have political character, but will be realized without the state' (*Osnovy*, p. 544). Yet, 'under socialism, this leadership still has political character'. One might illustrate this Soviet conception of the difference between socialism and communism by the nature of economic planning. When economic planning has become perfect, the command component of planning will vanish and perfect information alone will govern men's decisions. This is the 'administration by things and leadership by productive processes' of communism. But under socialism, the command (or political) component in planning is still necessary. Hence there is objective need for state power. State power under socialism, however, means 'administration by persons', and, by implication, rule through arbitrary will.

If the Soviet theorists accept 'administration by persons' as a necessary evil under socialism, the Chinese Communists in practice have shown far greater reluctance to accept it for socialism in China. One of the cardinal sins of leadership behavior in Communist China is 'commandism', a theme which usually arises when the bureaucracy is under attack or when bureaucratic tendencies within the Party are being criticized. But Party leadership, as the Chinese Communists see it, does not mean what the Soviets see as the only alternative to administration by persons, namely leadership through impersonal objective processes. The Marxist distinction between leadership by persons and by things is somewhat similar to the distinction made by some sociologists between personal and institutional leadership. If the state can only rule through personal or institutional leadership, society has other choices for governing itself. The Party, by reaching down into society can tap these instrumentalities of rule, and in so doing needs not make maximal use of formal state power for achieving the development of society. If Soviet theorists are concerned with explaining the role of the state under socialism, the Chinese Communists stress the role of the masses under socialism.

Many contemporary sociologists see society as an integral entity in which the political 'subsystem' is a functionally necessary sector. There is no way in which a theory on 'the withering away of the state' can be derived from such a conception. But both Soviet and Chinese theorists distinguish between state and society, accepting the Marxist distinction between substructure and superstructure. In effect, they accept Engels's statement that the state is 'that force which arises from society but stands above it and daily becomes more distant from society'. In class societies, the alienation of the state from society leads to tyranny. Under socialism, the alienation of the state from society leads to its redundancy, climaxed by its withering away. The withering away of the state is not brought about by its becoming closer to society and thus turning into a functionally integral element of society, but – to the contrary – by the constant diminishing of its functional importance in the operations of society.[3] Soviet theorists do not say much about the distinctions between state and society, at least not for socialist societies. They usually revert to the substructure and superstructure conceptions of classical Marxism: 'The substructure of society includes the totality of economic relationships between people that are formed in the process of material production and reproduction of their life.' (*Osnovy*, p. 441.) But society is more than a network of economic relationships. The Soviet theorists state:

Economic relationships in real life are tightly interwoven with political, legal, customary, familistic, national, religious, moral and other relationships. Let us take as an example the nation or the family. Characteristic of the nation is the commonness of language, of economic life, of territory, of psychic mentality, of culture. Nations in bourgeois society consist of antagonistic classes – the bourgeoisie and the proletariat. In the family we find elements of economic, customary, work, legal, moral and other relationships between their members. It would be imperative to have a vast force of scientific abstraction so that in all the complex networks of social relationships one could sort out productive, economic relationships as the primary and basic ones, and establish that ideological relationships are dependent on them (*Osnovy*, p. 441).

One may not have 'a vast force of scientific abstraction'

3. Soviet theory, following some of Stalin's latter-day contributions on the subject, nevertheless maintains that 'the state is vitally necessary in the first phase of communism'.

available, but one can deduce from the statement that the 'nation', whether in bourgeois or socialist society, does include the state. The 'nation' is an organic conception that implies some essential unity between all elements that make it up. Indeed, in this sense it is like the family.

Part Three Groups and Parties

While characteristics of governments, parliaments and even
bureaucracies are relatively constant, those of pressure groups
and political parties frequently vary. The nature of the political
system, then, is very much affected by the type of pressure
groups and political parties operating within it. Beer's article
begins to describe a type of political system which can be
fruitfully compared to the contemporary economic system.
Thus parties and pressure groups, mechanisms of the political
system, parallel the function of oligopolies, the equivalent
mechanism in an economic system of imperfect competition.

But political parties do not belong entirely, and to the same
extent, to a system; they are always partly within it, partly
without it. Duverger suggests that parties born outside the
boundaries of the parliamentary system can be absorbed into it
while retaining the mark of their external origin. And Michels
illustrates how a party struggling against the system can be led,
by the very use of bureaucratic machinery, far from its original
non-negotiable ends.

What social factors influence the decision to join or vote for a
particular party? Lipset tries to provide an answer by testing the
hypothesis that social class is the main influence; Campbell
and Rokkan describe a situation in which a working-class
party has created a subculture which modifies the pattern of
political participation.

15 Samuel H. Beer

Group Representation in Britain and the United States

Samuel H. Beer, 'Group representation in Britain and the United States', *Annals of the American Academy of Political and Social Science*, vol. 319, 1958, pp. 130–40.

We usually think of Great Britain as a country of strong parties and weak pressure groups; the United States as a country of weak parties and strong pressure groups. I wish to suggest some contrary views: that not only are British parties strong, but so also are British pressure groups; that in comparison both American parties and pressure groups are weak. The terms 'strong' and 'weak' cry out to be defined. The meanings I give them derive from a historical development – the rise of 'collectivism' – that has similarly affected both parties and pressure groups.

What are the consequences for policy? Strong parties can more readily resist pressure groups. They can also more readily yield them what they want. On the other hand, the dispersion of power may simply produce a self-defeating war of all against all in which even the special interests suffer. Centralized power at least creates the possibility of deliberate and orderly solutions.

The collectivist economy

The virtue of centralized power is worth examining if for no other reason than that the opposite doctrine holds so high a place in liberal democratic thought. Liberals and Radicals in both Britain and America have applied the doctrine of dispersed power to both the economy and the polity. In the Smithian model of the economy, for instance, the wealth of the nation and the satisfaction of consumers' wants will be maximized if the market is free. No unit, not even government, is to exercise 'market power'. Once power is removed, rational and voluntary exchange will result and along with it other desirable consequences in the allocation of resources and the satisfaction of the consumer.

Very similar is the Liberal-Radical model of the polity. Remove Burke's 'established' aristocracy and all other agents of power that had historically guided the political process; reduce society to its individual, rational atoms; then, power removed, reason will reign. A free, competitive marketplace of ideas, automatic and self-regulating like the marketplace of the *laissez-faire* economy, will test the truth of opinions. Upon opinions so tested, popular government will base public policy.

In both the British and American economies in the nineteenth century, the market conditions required by the self-regulating model did actually exist in very great degree. And in both, to no inconsiderable extent, these conditions still exist. But in the past two generations or so, certain structural changes have taken place – reaching a further point of development in Britain than in the United States – that depart radically from this model. These developments, which we may call 'collectivism', can be summarized under four headings. One is the tendency to a concentration of economic power among a few large buyers or sellers in a particular industry or complex of industries. Along with the increase in size of units has gone a change in internal structure that is referred to by terms such as bureaucracy and managerialism. Moreover, where such large units have grown up, they tend to deal with one another by a process of 'bargaining' – or perhaps it is better to say, 'collective bargaining'. Finally, while bargaining tends to be confined to the relations of producers – whether business firms or trade unions – in their dealings with the mass of ultimate consumers, large units have learned to shape, even to create, the very 'wants' that presumably they have come into existence to satisfy.

Collectivist parties

In the polity as in the economy, there have been similar tendencies toward collectivism. By this I do not mean the increase in government intervention – the rise of the welfare state and the controlled economy. I mean rather that in the political structure have occurred certain changes analogous to those changes in economic structure summarized above. Starting from these contrasting models of the polity, the self-regulating and the collectivist, we may compare the distribution of power in Britain and the United States. It would appear that, as economic collectivism has proceeded farther in Britain than in the United States, so also has political collectivism.

We may look first at the relative number of units and their internal structure. Examined in the light of these criteria, both British parties and pressure groups present striking contrasts with the American models. While in both polities there are two major parties, the loose and sprawling parties of American politics make the British appear highly concentrated. In the American party, power is dispersed among many units – for example, personal followings or state and local machines – with the result that only occasionally and for limited purposes, such as nominating a Presidential candidate, does the national party act as a unit. In terms of density – that is, the percentage of eligibles organized as party members – American parties exceed British. But if we apply a measure of intensity, such as payment of dues, it is clear that British parties have mobilized the electorate far more highly than have American. In the British party, moreover, this membership is brought together for unified action by an elaborate and effective system of articulation, in particular active representative bodies extending from bottom to top and a bureaucratic staff running from top to bottom. There are still semiautonomous centers within the party that a perfected merger would obliterate. But to an American, a British party is a highly unified social body, remarkably well equipped for coordinated action: we think, for instance, of the fact that all candidates must be approved by a central-party agency and that they will all run on the same platform. No doubt, the most striking expression of this power of united action is the extent of party voting in the House of Commons. Judged even by Lowell's strict criteria, party voting has been on the increase for a hundred years and today reaches nearly one hundred per cent.[1]

Along with such concentration, and perhaps making it possible, goes a high measure of political homogeneity. (I do not

1. Lowell (1902) counted as a party vote a division in which at least 90 per cent of one party voted in favor and at least 90 per cent of the other party voted against.

mean social homogeneity, for, measured by nonpolitical criteria, the British are a very heterogeneous people.) This political homogeneity in the electorate as a whole is reflected in what students of voting behavior call the 'nationalizing' of British politics. When political opinion moves, it moves in unison throughout the country: in a general election the 'swing' from one party to the other is much the same in every constituency. In the United States, as Schattschneider and David have shown, voting has also tended in this direction (1956, pp. 194–215; 1957). Sectionalism and the number of one-party states are on the decline. But – as 1956 illustrates – nothing like the uniformity of swing in British voting has been reached.

In spite of mass membership and representative bodies, however, the internal structure of the British party gives great power to central party leaders – far more, of course, than that possessed by American leaders. It is rather as if the Congressional caucus of post-Federalist days had been imposed upon the Jacksonian party system. In both British parties, as McKenzie has shown, the leaders of the parliamentary party, and especially the Leader, are dominant (1955). That is a loose description and needs must be, since the Leader's power is complex and certainly far from dictatorial. He must continually practice 'the art of management', appeasing a dissident faction, finding a formula, keeping up party morale. Indeed, he is a 'manager' – a modern-day manager committed to party principle, of course, but by his function compelled above all to think of the continuation of the organization.

Collectivist pressure groups

Turning from parties to pressure groups, we find that in Britain as in the United States, the center of the stage is occupied by organizations based on the great economic interest groups of modern society, especially the big three of business, labor and agriculture. Given the nature of public policy, which affects these interests so often and so intimately, pressure groups claiming to speak for them are bound in turn to influence policy making more frequently and on the whole more effectively than pressure groups of other types.

In Britain as well as in the United States, in addition to such 'self-oriented' pressure groups, we must also deal with what Finer calls 'promotional' groups (1958). Among the former we may classify such organizations as the Federation of British Industries, the Trades Union Congress, the National Farmers Union, the British Medical Association, the National Union of Teachers, the British Legion, the National and Local Government Officers' Association. The 'promotional' groups include the Howard League for Penal Reform, the National Council for Civil Liberties, the Peace Pledge Union, the Campaign for the Limitation of Secret Police Powers. As compared with the self-oriented groups, writes Finer, the latter 'do not represent "interests" in the same sense at all. They represent a cause, not a social or economic "stake" in society' (1958).

Such a broad distinction in the character of goals tends to have important consequences for structure and behavior. The promotional group, for instance, tends to be open to all like-minded persons, while the self-oriented group has, so to speak, a fixed clientele. By and large the self-oriented group can more readily extract money and work from its members on a continuing and regularized basis. It may also be less subject to splintering and more capable of continuous, unified action. At least in part for such reasons, the more powerful pressure groups of the British polity are self-oriented groups, based on a vocational interest, bureaucratic in structure, and continuing over a long period of time. While some form of group politics has long flourished in the British as in other polities, this modern, collectivist type has emerged only in recent generations (Beer, 1956; 1957). There is some sense in saying that one line of development in the history of British pressure groups has been from the promotional to the self-oriented, vocational type. Possibly a similar development has taken place in the United States, although here the third party has often played the role of the promotional group in Britain. We might also find that the promotional group remains a more important feature of the American polity than of the British.

Farm, labor and business organizations

Concentration and bureaucracy characterize British pressure groups as well as parties. Hardly without exception the big vocational pressure groups in Britain have a higher index of density and concentration. There, for instance, the National Farmers Union is the only significant organization of farmers and includes 90 per cent of its potential membership. In the United States, of course, only a fraction – no more than 30 per cent – of all farmers are organized and these are divided among three main groups and various minor ones. While absolute numbers are much smaller in Britain, we must remember that British agriculture is highly diversified as to crops, size of farms and location. Yet through the NFU British farmers speak with one voice to a degree rarely achieved by farmers in the United States. No doubt this is true because to no small extent the organization is run from the top. In Bedford Square is a large and able bureaucracy and at its head stands one of the ablest managers in modern Britain, Sir James Turner – sometimes known as the 'Sacred Bull of British Agriculture'.

In the field of trade unions, just a little less than half the total working force has been organized, while in the United States the figure is around a quarter. To one peak organization, the TUC, nearly all unions are affiliated and it has been the undisputed spokesman for organized labor for generations. Its permanent secretary, even when Walter Citrine held the post, has never occupied the position of, say, a Gompers. The heads of the Big Three,[2] however, have as prominent a political role as our Reuther, Meany and Lewis. The British labor leaders of this generation are more likely to have worked their way up the bureaucratic ladder by long and able management than to have emerged from heroic struggles for the right to organize or for better contracts. Contrary to popular impression and in strong contrast with American experience, the strike has almost ceased to be an instrument of labor-management relations in Britain since as far back as 1932 (Clegg, 1956). If by bureaucracy, however, we mean full-time paid staff, then British unions generally are far less well endowed than American. The reluctance of the rank and file to pay dues sufficient to employ such staff –

2. The Transport and General Workers' Union; the National Union of General and Municipal Workers; the Amalgamated Engineering Union – which among them include 30 per cent of all unionists affiliated to the TUC.

and to pay substantial salaries to any permanent official – seriously handicaps British unions (Mack, 1956).

In the field of business, in Britain as in the United States the basic unit of political action is the trade association. Comparison is made a little easier if we consider only national manufacturing trade associations (PEP, 1957). Of these there are 1,300 in Britain and some 950 in the United States. Density is high: a sample survey showed that 90 per cent of larger firms and 76 per cent of smaller firms in Britain belong to such associations. Concentration among manufacturing trade associations is considerably greater in Britain. The peak association is the Federation of British Industries (FBI) which represents, through its affiliated trade associations and directly through member firms, some 85 per cent of all manufacturing concerns employing ten or more workers (Finer, 1956). In the United States, on the other hand, the National Association of Manufacturers has never represented more than 6 per cent of all manufacturing concerns (Gable, 1953). If the same base as that used for the FBI were taken, however, there is reason to think that the NAM figure would be more like 20 per cent to 25 per cent. The contrast would still be striking.

Bargaining in the polity

So much for the briefest sort of sketch of collectivism in the structure of the British polity. Let us turn to the modes of interaction of these massive unit actors, in particular the political party and the pressure group.

What we have called bargaining is a principal trait of the relationships of large producers in the collectivist economy. Its essence is that each of the negotiating units is highly dependent on the other as a seller or as a buyer. In a free market, on the other hand, each seller can turn to other buyers and each buyer to other sellers and none have significant market power. In bargaining, however, each unit has substantial market power; hence, the ultimate decision is made as a result of negotiations in which each gauges his offers in the light of expectations about the possible offers of the other (Schelling, 1956).

A similar kind of decision making occurs where a party

enjoys large power over the authority of government, while a pressure group with which it deals enjoys similar power over something – such as votes – that the party wants. Such a situation is very different from one in which government authority is dispersed among many elected office-holders and voting power among an unorganized electorate. In the latter situation, there is a kind of bidding for votes on one side and for promises or policies on the other that has a limited, but real, analogy with the economic free market. Where the centralized party in office confronts the massively organized pressure group, decisions are made quite differently. Indeed, some who have sat in on the annual price review between the National Farmers Union in Britain and the Ministry of Agriculture have reported that the proceedings and the way in which a settlement is reached resemble nothing so much as collective bargaining. For both the farmers and the ministry there is a range of outcomes that would be better than no agreement at all. Each opponent pretty well knows what this range is. No wonder it has sometimes taken four months for a decision to be reached!

Consultation with interests is a feature of all modern Western democratic governments. Some years ago Leiserson, writing of representative advisory committees, traced their origin to 'the delegation of discretionary rule-making powers under legislative standards to administrative agencies executing various types of social legislation' (1942). Leiserson's statement, broadened somewhat, is a generalization valid for not only American, but also for Western European government: increasing government intervention for such purposes as social reform, economic stability and national defense has led to the grant of rule-making power to administrative agencies and to increasing participation of interested groups in decision making at that level.

Different stages in this development, however, can be distinguished, depending upon how far the scope of policy has been expanded and the polity has become collectivist. The extent to which power has been mobilized and unified on each side – on the side of the party in power and on the side of the pressure group with which it deals – will determine whether bargaining predominates in the relationship. In the United

States, we find administrative consultation on a vast scale both in Washington and in the state capitals. In Britain, a more collectivist polity, the situation is better described as 'quasi-corporatism'.

It is against the background of this power pattern that we must examine the emphasis that British pressure groups give to the various points in the process of decision making. The formal structure of authority – British parliamentary government as compared with the American separation of powers – will play its role. But we must recall that a hundred years ago Britain also had parliamentary government, yet pressure groups then gave far more attention to the legislature than they do now.

Administrative consultation

In each polity we may distinguish four main phases of policy making: at elections, in the legislature, within the party and at the administrative level. British pressure groups exert their major influence at the administrative level, taking this to include both ministerial and official contacts. Perhaps their second most important point of influence is within the party. In contrast American pressure groups, by and large, concentrate on the first two points: the electorate and the legislature.

There are, of course, many variations within these two broad patterns. A very important difference may result from the character of the power base of a group. There is a kind of power – and this is particularly important in Britain – that is created by the expansion of policy itself. 'The greater the degree of detailed and technical control the government seeks to exert over industrial and commercial interests,' Herring wrote, 'the greater must be their degree of consent and active participation in the very process of regulation, if regulation is to be effective or successful' (1936). This generalization, I should think, holds for most Western democracies and surely for Britain. There, certain types of control exercised in recent years – price control, materials allocation, tariffs, import control and the encouragement of exports and productivity are only some of the more striking examples – simply could not be enforced effectively without the substantial cooperation of the groups concerned. The group's technical advice is often well-nigh indispensable. But cooperation – something more than grudging consent to 'the law' – is a further necessity. Our farm programs with their referenda and farmer-elected committees recognize this necessity. But in Britain the far wider scope of regulation and planning – even after the various 'bonfires of controls' – gives this power factor far greater weight.

A few examples: The farmers – meaning in effect the NFU – are represented on a set of local committees that have had important administrative duties under various agricultural programs, and the chance that the NFU might encourage these farmer representatives to withdraw from the committees has been a force in the annual price reviews. When the Conservatives in denationalizing part of the transport industry in 1952 dismantled the government haulage (that is, trucking) system, a standby scheme was organized by the industry itself. The Labour government's limitation of advertising expenditure was policed by the organized advertisers, and its important anti-inflationary effort to restrain both dividends and wage increases was carried out – and with remarkable success – on a voluntary basis by organized business and labor.

Neither the British nor the American system of consultation between government and pressure groups has been fully described. Some rough impressions, modestly intended, may be in order. In both countries the central device is the representative advisory committee. British examples range from high-level bodies such as the Economic Planning Board, the National Joint Advisory Council of the Ministry of Labour, the National Production Advisory Council on Industry, on which the relevant peak organizations, the FBI, BEC and TUC, are represented, to the multitude of advisory committees of the main economic departments to which trade associations send representatives. The latter are connected with the system of 'sponsoring' departments which grew up during and after the Second World War and which means today that every industry and every branch of it, no matter how small, has a sponsoring department or section of one, somewhere in the government machine. Apart from such committees, although often around them, a regular system of informal consultation has grown up

Private and public bureaucrats continually call one another on the telephone or meet for luncheon and discuss a problem on a first-name basis. Often several departments and several groups are concerned.

On the American side, the immense documentation on advisory committees in the federal government that was assembled by a subcommittee of the Government Operations Committee in 1957 has not yet been analysed by political scientists (House Committee on Government Operation, 1956 and 1957). But it is clear that from the time of the National Recovery Administration, the use of this device, from being relatively rare, has immensely increased. The number of advisory committees associated with government departments at the center – and in addition to many more at the local or regional level – runs into the hundreds. One major set established by statute are in the Department of Agriculture – for instance, the Commodity Stabilization Committees. Of the remainder, the vast majority it seems are associated principally with the defense effort – procurement, development, standards, stockpiling and so on – and consist of industry advisory committees. In comparison with similar British industry advisory committees, the American appear to depend less on trade associations, the result at least in part of the Defense Production Act of 1950 that requires that non-members as well as members of trade associations be included. The peak associations – the NAM and United States Chamber of Commerce – also play a much less prominent role than their British counterparts, not being represented, as such, on even the Business Advisory Council. Certainly trade unions are not called in for advice so frequently or on so broad a front in the United States as in Britain. The TUC alone, for instance, is represented on some sixty committees touching all aspects of social and economic problems.

Of the broad character of the power relationship we can speak with confidence: the American executive possesses far less actual power than the British. Quite apart from the degree of delegated powers in this country, the political independence of Congress and the exercise of administrative oversight by Congressional Committees mean that the group interested in influencing policy must give great attention to the legislature.

Some years ago Blaisdell found that pressure groups, while concerned with the administration, focused their attention principally upon Congress (Blaisdell, 1941). Broadly this must still be the case, although it would be interesting to know how far the defense effort may have shifted the balance.

Pressure on parties

At the Democratic National Convention in 1956 the number of trade-union officials sitting as delegates ran into the hundreds, while at the Republican Convention there was no more than a scattering. Generally, however, in both national and state parties in the United States, the connection of pressure groups and parties is less close than in Britain. We do not have the formal affiliation of the trade-union movement with one party. But the more important difference arises from the fact that American parties are so poorly unified that they do not provide an effective channel for influencing the use of government authority. In Britain, on the other hand, the party ranks second – although perhaps a poor second – to the administration as an object of pressure.

Where the power is, there the pressure will be applied. Where we see the pressure being applied, therefore, we shall probably find the seat of power. Judged by this rule, the central organs of the British party, especially the parliamentary party, are far more powerful than the party's representative assemblies. Pressure groups do not openly descend on a British party conference as they do on the platform hearings of an American party convention. Their representatives, however, may be present and spokesmen for various special interests – farmers, trade unionists, veterans, teachers, old-age pensioners, advertising men with a concern for commercial broadcasting – will take up a good deal of time at a party conference.

The important point of influence, however, is the parliamentary party – its regular, full meetings and its specialized committees – and to a lesser extent the party's central office. We are familiar with the way leaders of the Labour party while in power or in opposition will frequently consult with the trade unions on pending decisions. There is also an active alignment, if not formal affiliation, of organized business with the Conservatives. During the passage of the bill nationalizing transport in 1946–7, for instance, the Conservative opposition tabled several hundred amendments. Where had they come from? In practice the party's Parliamentary Secretariat – a body of party employees, not MPs – acted as intermediary between the transport committee of the parliamentary party and the various pressure groups, especially the General Council of British Shipping, the Dock and Harbours Association and a joint committee of the Federation of British Industries, National Union of Manufacturers and the Association of British Chambers of Commerce (Finer, 1956).[3]

Inseparable from these channels of influence is one of the, to an American, most curious phenomena of British politics. He is the 'interested MP' – that is, the member who is connected with an outside interest group by direct personal involvement, such as occupation or ownership of property, or by membership or office holding in an outside organization speaking for an interest group. Today and for generations the House of Commons through the personal involvement of its members has represented a far wider range of interests than has the American Congress, notoriously inhabited by lawyers.

In Britain such personal involvement was a principal way in which interest groups of the nineteenth century made themselves heard in government. Of more importance in today's collectivist polity is the member connected with an outside organization. The MPs sponsored and subsidized by the trade unions are the best-known examples. But there is also a host of others: a joint Honorary Secretary of the Association of British Chambers of Commerce, the Chairman of the Howard League for Penal Reform, a Director of the Society of Motor Manufacturers and Traders, the President of the British Legion, the Secretary of the National Tyre Distributors Association – there seems to be hardly a member who fails to note some such connection in his biography in the *Times' House of Commons*. Perhaps some Congressmen also have similar connections.

3. For other examples of pressure group activity in the House of Commons see Stewart (1958).

Amid their wide membership in churches, fraternal organizations and 'patriotic' groups as recorded in the *Congressional Directory*, however, they fail to mention them.

Perhaps, as Finer has suggested, the absence of such interested members from the Congress is one reason why American pressure groups must make up the deficiency by hiring lobbyists in such large numbers. For the interested MP is an active lobbyist within the legislature. His principal role is played within the parliamentary party, but his activity in the House itself is more observable. He may speak openly as the representative of a group, as the President of the British Legion often does in forwarding the Legion's campaign to increase disability pensions (Millett, 1957). He is more likely to be effective at the amendment stage of a finance or other bill when, briefed by his association, he suggests changes, which perhaps at the same time are being urged on the Minister and civil servants by officers or staff of the pressure group.

Influencing public opinion

Herring long ago observed how American pressure groups direct great attention to influencing public opinion: not only to win support for some immediate objective, but also to build up generally favorable attitudes. This he found to be a trait of the 'new' lobby, and it is not irrelevant that this technique arose along with the development of modern mass-advertising methods and media. A major difference in Britain is that the big vocational pressure groups rarely mount such public campaigns. In the nineteenth century, this was not so. Beginning late in the century, however, this propagandist function seems more and more to have passed to political parties. Today and for many years now, the parties, in contrast with the pressure groups, have virtually monopolized communication with the voters as such – that is with the general public as distinguished from communication by a pressure group with its clientele.

This differentiation of function in political communication has gone very much farther in Britain than in the United States. A striking feature of nearly all the vocational pressure groups there is the extent to which they urge their demands simply and frankly as special interests. There is a significant contrast, I think, with American pressure groups which tend to base their claims on some large principle of social philosophy or national policy – as, for example, in the vast public-relations program of the NAM.

Yet the public campaign has sometimes been used by the big pressure groups of British politics and its use may be on the increase. Examples are the anti-nationalization campaign launched by the Road Haulage Association in 1946–7; Tate and Lyle's famous 'Mr Cube' campaign against the nationalization of sugar refining in 1949–50; and in general the growing use of Aims of Industry, a public-relations agency founded to defend and advocate free enterprise. Lesser efforts have been pressed by the National Union of Teachers and the British Legion. If this practice grows greatly, one might well expect it to weaken the position of the parties.

Such a development – which I do not expect – could have great consequences for the British polity. For without in any degree being cynical, one must acknowledge the large part played by British parties in creating the present political homogeneity of the British electorate – the national market for their brand-name goods. The British party battle is continuous and highly organized and so also is the stream of propaganda directed at the voter. Through it the party voter is strengthened, if not created, and the tight party majority in the legislature prepared. Even more important, the framework of public thinking about policy, the voter's sense of the alternatives, is fixed from above. Popular sovereignty in the polity has been qualified by the same means that have qualified consumers' sovereignty in the economy.

In this Americans are not likely to find much cause for self-congratulation. We will hardly say that we are more free of political propaganda. As in other aspects of the American power pattern, the difference is that the centers from which this weighty influence emanates are far more dispersed and uncoordinated. Is this necessarily to our advantage? Some words of Herring's suggest an answer:

A democracy inclines toward chaos rather than toward order. The representative principle, if logically followed, leads to infinite diversity rather than ultimate unity. . . . Since the 'voice of the people' is a pleasant fancy and not a present fact, the impulse for positive political action must be deliberately imposed at some strategic point, if democracy is to succeed as a form of government (Herring, 1936, p. 377).

References

BEER, S. H. (1956), 'Pressure groups and parties in Britain', *Amer. polit. Sci. Rev.*, vol. 50, no. 1, p. 4.

BEER, S. H. (1957), 'The representation of interest in British government: historical background', *Amer. polit. Sci. Rev.*, vol. 51, no. 3, pp. 635–45.

BLAISDELL, D. C. (1941), *Economic Power and Political Pressures*, monograph 26 TNEC.

CLEGG, H. A. (1956), 'Strikes', *Polit. Q.*, vol. 27, no. 1, pp. 31–5.

DAVID, P. (1957), 'Intensity of inter-party competition and the problem of party realignment', *American Political Science Association*.

FINER, S. E. (1956), 'The Federation of British Industries', *Polit. Stud.*, vol. 4, no. 1, p. 62.

FINER, S. E. (1958), *Anonymous Empire: A Study of the Lobby in Great Britain*, Pall Mall Press.

GABLE, R. W. (1953), 'NAM: influential lobby or kiss of life?', *J. Polit.*, vol. 15, p. 257.

HERRING, E. P. (1936), *Public Administration and the Public Interest*, McGraw-Hill.

HOUSE COMMITTEE ON GOVERNMENT OPERATIONS (1956 and 1957), *Advisory Committees* (Pts 1–4), 84th Congress, 2nd Session; 85th Congress, 1st Session.

LEISERSON, A. (1942), *Administrative Regulation: A Study in Representation of Interests*, University of Chicago Press.

LOWELL, A. L. (1902), 'The influence of party upon legislation in England and America', *Annual Report of the American Historical Association for 1901*, vol. 1, pp. 319–542.

MACK, J. A. (1956), 'Trade-union leadership', *Polit. Q.*, vol. 27, no. 1, p. 77.

MCKENZIE, R. T. (1955), *British Political Parties*, St Martin's Press.

MILLETT, J. H. (1957), 'British interest group tactics: a case study', *Polit. Sci. Q.*

PEP (1957), *Industrial Trade Associations: Activities and Organization*, Political and Economic Planning.

SCHATTSCHNEIDER, E. E. (1956), 'The United States: the functional approach to party government', in S. Neumann (ed.), *Modern Political Parties*, University of Chicago Press.

SCHELLING, T. L. (1956), 'An essay on bargaining', *Amer. Econ. Rev.*, vol. 45, no. 3, pp. 281–3.

STEWART, J. D. (1958), *British Pressure Groups: Their Role in Relation to the House of Commons*, Oxford University Press.

16 Robert Michels

Principles and Bureaucracy in Political Parties

Excerpt from Robert Michels, *Political Parties*, translated by
Eden and Cedar Paul, Free Press, 1915, pp. 185–8. First published in
French in 1911.

The organization of the state needs a numerous and complicated bureaucracy. This is an important factor in the complex of forces of which the politically dominant classes avail themselves to secure their dominion and to enable themselves to keep their hands upon the rudder.

The instinct of self-preservation leads the modern state to assemble and to attach to itself the greatest possible number of interests. This need of the organism of the state increases *pari passu* with an increase among the multitude, of the conviction that the contemporary social order is defective and even irrational – in a word, with the increase of what the authorities are accustomed to term discontent. The state best fulfils the need for securing a large number of defenders by constituting a numerous caste of officials, of persons directly dependent upon the state. This tendency is powerfully reinforced by the tendencies of modern political economy. On the one hand, from the side of the state, there is an enormous supply of official positions. On the other hand, among the citizens, there is an even more extensive demand. This demand is stimulated by the ever-increasing precariousness in the position of the middle classes (the smaller manufacturers and traders, independent artisans, farmers, etc.) since there have come into existence expropriative capitalism on the grand scale, on the one hand, and the organized working classes on the other – for both these movements, whether they wish it or not, combine to injure the middle classes. All those whose material existence is thus threatened by modern economic developments endeavour to find safe situations for their sons, to secure for these a social position which shall shelter them from the play of economic forces.

Employment under the state, with the important right to a pension which attaches to such employment, seems created expressly for their needs. The immeasurable demand for situations which results from these conditions, a demand which is always greater than the supply, created the so-called 'intellectual proletariat'. The numbers of this body are subject to great fluctuations. From time to time the state, embarrassed by the increasing demand for positions in its service, is forced to open the sluices of its bureaucratic canals in order to admit thousands of new postulants and thus to transform these from dangerous adversaries into zealous defenders and partisans. There are two classes of intellectuals. One consists of those who have succeeded in securing a post at the manger of the state, whilst the other consists of those who, as Scipio Sighele puts it, have assaulted the fortress, without being able to force their way in (1903, p.160). The former may be compared to an army of slaves who are always ready, in part from class egoism, in part for personal motives (the fear of losing their own situations), to undertake the defence of the state which provides them with bread. They do this whatever may be the question concerning which the state has been attacked and must therefore be regarded as the most faithful of its supporters. The latter, on the other hand, are sworn enemies of the state. They are those eternally restless spirits who lead the bourgeois opposition and in part also assume the leadership of the revolutionary parties of the proletariat. It is true that the state bureaucracy does not in general expand as rapidly as do the discontented elements of the middle class. None the less, the bureaucracy continually increases. It comes to assume the form of an endless screw. It grows ever less and less compatible with the general welfare. And yet this bureaucratic machinery remains essential. Through it alone can be satisfied the claim of the educated members of the population for secure positions. It is further a means of self-defence for the state. As the late Amilcare Puviàni of the University of Perugia, the political economist to whom we are indebted for an important work upon the legend of the state, expresses it, the mechanism of bureaucracy is the outcome of a protective reaction of a right of property whose legal basis is weak, and is an antidote to the awakening of the public conscience (1903, p. 258).

The political party possesses many of these traits in common with the state. Thus the party in which the circle of the elite is unduly restricted, or in which, in other words, the oligarchy is composed of too small a number of individuals, runs the risk of being swept away by the masses in a moment of democratic effervescence. Hence the modern party, like the modern state, endeavours to give to its own organization the widest possible base, and to attach to itself in financial bonds the largest possible number of individuals.[1] Thus arises the need for a strong bureaucracy and these tendencies are reinforced by the increase in the tasks imposed by modern organization.[2]

As the party bureaucracy increases, two elements which constitute the essential pillars of every socialist conception undergo an inevitable weakening: an understanding of the wider and more ideal cultural aims of socialism, and an understanding of the international multiplicity of its manifestations. Mechanism becomes an end in itself. The capacity for an accurate grasp of the peculiarities and the conditions of existence of the labour movement in other countries diminishes in proportion as the individual national organizations are fully developed. This is plain from a study of the mutual international criticisms of the socialist press. In the days of the so-called 'socialism of the émigrés', the socialists devoted themselves to an elevated policy of principles, inspired by the classical criteria of internationalism. Almost every one of them was, if the term may be

1. The governing body of Tammany in New York consists of four hundred persons. The influence of this political association is concentrated in a sub-committee of thirty persons, the so-called Organization Committee (Ostrogorsky, *La Democracie*, vol. 2, p. 199).

2. Inquiries made by Lask have shown how deeply rooted in the psychology of the workers is the desire to enter the class of those who receive pensions. A very large number of proletarians, when asked what they wished to do with their sons, replied: 'To find them employment which would give them right to a pension.' Doubtless this longing is the outcome of the serious lack of stability characteristic of the social and economic conditions of the workers (Schulze-Gaevernitz, 'Nochmals: Marx oder Kant?', *Archiv für Sozialwissernschaft*, fasc. 2, p. 520, 1900).

used, a specialist in this more general and comprehensive domain. The whole course of their lives, the brisk exchange of ideas on unoccupied evenings, the continued rubbing of shoulders between men of the most different tongues, the enforced isolation from the bourgeois world of their respective countries, and the utter impossibility of any 'practical' action, all contributed to this result. But in proportion as, in their own country, paths of activity were opened for the socialists, at first for agitation and soon afterwards for positive and constructive work, the more did a recognition of the demands of the everyday life of the party divert their attention from immortal principles. Their vision gained in precision but lost in extent. The more cotton-spinners, boot and shoe operatives or brushmakers the labour leader could gain each month for his union, the better versed he was in the tedious subtleties of insurance against accident and illness, the greater the industry he could display in the specialized questions of factory inspection and of arbitration in trade disputes, the better acquainted he might be with the system of checking the amount of individual purchases in cooperative stores and with the methods for the control of the consumption of municipal gas, the more difficult was it for him to retain a general interest in the labour movement, even in the narrowest sense of this term. As the outcome of inevitable psychophysiological laws, he could find little time and was likely to have little inclination for the study of the great problems of the philosophy of history, and all the more falsified consequently would become his judgement of international questions. At the same time he would incline more and more to regard every one as an 'incompetent', an 'outsider', an 'unprofessional', who might wish to judge questions from some higher outlook than the purely technical; he would incline to deny the good sense and even the socialism of all who might desire to fight upon another ground and by other means than those familiar to him within his narrow sphere as a specialist. This tendency towards an exclusive and all-absorbing specialization, towards the renunciation of all far-reaching outlooks, is a general characteristic of modern evolution. With the continuous increase in the acquirements of scientific research, the polyhistor is becoming extinct. His place is taken by the writer of monographs. The universal zoologist no longer exists, and we have instead ornithologists and entomologists; and indeed the last become further subdivided into lepidopterists, coleopterists, myrmecologists.

References

PUVIANI, A. (1903), *Teoria della Illusione Finanziaria*, Sandron.
SIGHELE, S. (1903), *L'Intelligenza della Folla*, Turin.

17 Maurice Duverger

The Origin of Parties

Maurice Duverger, Introduction to *Political Parties*, translated by
Barbara and Robert North, Methuen, 2nd edn, 1959, pp. xxiii-xxxvii.
First published in French in 1951.

We must not be misled by the analogy of words. We use the
word 'parties' to describe the factions which divided the Republics of antiquity, the troops which formed round a condottiere
in Renaissance Italy, the clubs where the members of the Revolutionary assemblies met, and the committees which prepared
the elections under the property franchise of the constitutional
monarchies as well as the vast popular organizations which give
shape to public opinion in modern democracies. There is some
justification for this identity of name, for there is a certain
underlying relationship – the role of all these institutions is to
win political power and exercise it. Obviously, however, they
are not the same thing. In fact it is hardly a century since
parties, in the true sense of the word, came into being. In 1850
no country in the world (except the United States) knew political parties in the modern sense of the word. There were trends
of opinion, popular clubs, philosophical societies and parliamentary groups, but no real parties. In 1950 parties function
in most civilized nations, and in others there is an attempt to
imitate them.

How did we pass from the system of 1850 to that of 1950?
The question is not prompted solely by pure historical curiosity.
Just as men bear all their lives the mark of their childhood, so
parties are profoundly influenced by their origins. It is impossible, for example, to understand the structural difference between the British Labour party and the French Socialist party
without knowing the different circumstances of their origin. It is
impossible to make a serious analysis of the multi-party system
in France or Holland, or the two-party system in America,
without referring to the origins of parties in each of these coun-

tries, which explain their proliferation in the first two and their restriction in the last-named. On the whole the development of parties seems bound up with that of democracy, that is to say with the extension of popular suffrage and parliamentary prerogatives. The more political assemblies see their functions and independence grow, the more their members feel the need to group themselves according to what they have in common, so as to act in concert. The more the right to vote is extended and multiplied, the more necessary it becomes to organize the electors by means of committees capable of making the candidates known and of canalizing the votes in their direction. The rise of parties is thus bound up with the rise of parliamentary groups and electoral committees. Nevertheless some deviate more or less from this general scheme. They originate outside the electoral and parliamentary cycle, and this fact is their most outstanding common characteristic.

The electoral and parliamentary origin of parties

The general mechanism of this genesis is simple. First there is the creation of parliamentary groups, then the appearance of electoral committees and finally the establishment of a permanent connection between these two elements. In practice there are various departures from this strict theoretical scheme. There have usually been parliamentary groups before electoral committees. Indeed there were political assemblies before there were elections. Parliamentary groups can be formed in an autocratic chamber just as well as in an elected chamber. In fact the struggle of 'factions' is generally to be seen in all hereditary or coopted assemblies, whether it be the Senate of classical Rome or the Diet of Poland. Certainly 'faction' is not the same thing as 'parliamentary group'. Between the two there is all the difference which exists between the inorganic and the organized. But the second evolved from the first more or less gradually.

A priori it would seem that community of political doctrine has constituted the essential impulse in the formation of parliamentary groups. Yet facts do not always confirm this hypothesis. Often geographical proximity or the desire to defend one's profession seems to have given the first impulse. Doctrine only came afterwards. Thus in certain countries the first parliamentary groups were local groups which eventually became ideological groups. The rise of parties in the French Constituent Assembly of 1789 is a good example of this kind of development. In April 1789 the provincial representatives to the Estates General began to arrive at Versailles, where they felt rather bewildered. Quite naturally the representatives of the same region tended to meet together so as to escape from the feeling of isolation which assailed them, and at the same time to make preparations for the defence of their local interests. The initiative was taken by the Breton deputies, who hired a room in a café and organized regular meetings among themselves. They then perceived that they shared certain ideas not only on regional matters, but also on the fundamental problems of national policy. So they tried to enrol the deputies from other provinces who shared their views, and in this way the 'Breton club' became an ideological group. When the Assembly was transferred from Versailles to Paris the meetings of the club were at first interrupted and a new meeting-place had to be found. This time, no room in a café being available, the leading spirits hired the refectory of a convent, and it was under the name of this convent that they were to become famous in history. Almost everybody has forgotten the 'Breton club', but who does not know of the Jacobins? An analogous process, transforming a local group into the nucleus of an ideological faction, was later to give rise to the Girondin club.

There should be no confusion between such local groups and those whose name is derived from their meeting-place. The example of the Jacobins is worth quoting here too, since it seems to be typical of a whole phase of the very beginnings of party development. Similarly, in the French Constituent Assembly of 1848, there were the groups of the Palais National, the Institut (Moderate Republicans), the Rue de Poitiers (Catholic Monarchists), the Rue de Castiglione and the Rue des Pyramides (Left). In the Frankfurt Parliament there were the parties of the Café Milani (Extreme Right), the Cassino (Right Centre), the Hotel de Wurtemberg (Left Centre, from which the party of Westendhal and that of the Hotel d'Augsburg broke away), the Hotel d'Allemagne (Left), and the Hotel du Mont-Tonnère (Extreme Left). We have here a very different phenomenon from that of the Breton club or the Girondin club. The deputies meet in the same place because they have ideas in common, instead of becoming aware of their community of ideas after meeting as a result of their common origins. This is an ideological group and not a local group, but the fact that the name is derived from the meeting-place shows that the doctrines are still too vague to be used to define the party.

Next to local and ideological factors personal interest finds a place. For example certain groups are more or less obviously parliamentary unions for common defence. The desire for re-election has naturally played a great part: it never completely disappears from parliamentary groups, even when they have reached maturity. Obviously, voting techniques which require a collective effort, for example voting by list (*scrutin de liste*) and proportional representation, strengthen this general tendency: in some countries (e.g. Switzerland and Sweden) the formation of the first really organized parliamentary groups coincided with the adoption of the proportional system. Hope of a ministerial post is also an important factor leading to the coagulation of parliamentary energies: several Centre groups in the French Assemblies are nothing but coalitions of candidates for office (*ministrables*). Nor do they succeed in passing beyond this stage to become real parties. If we are to believe Ostrogorsky,[1] corruption has played quite a large part in the development of British parliamentary groups. Over a long period, English ministers made sure of substantial majorities by buying the votes, if not the consciences, of Members of Parliament. The procedure was semi-official: in the House itself there was a desk where members came to receive the price of their vote on a division. In 1714 the post of Political Secretary of the Treasury was set up to take charge of these financial operations; the secretary in question soon became known as the 'Patronage Secretary' because for purposes of corruption he had at his disposition the nominations to government posts. Responsible for distributing the government's largesse to the members of the majority party, the Patronage Secretary kept a close watch on their votes and their speeches. He thus became in their eyes the man with a

1. But this interpretation is far from commanding general assent amongst English scholars.

whip, 'the Whip', just as in hunting the 'whips' gather hounds into a pack. Strict discipline was in this way gradually instituted in the majority party. It was in the nature of things that the minority should adopt in self-defence a similar discipline – although it was based on different methods. Later, when parliamentary morality had been gradually improved, the structure of the groups in Parliament, including their strong organization and the authority of the whip, outlived the causes which had given it birth.

It would be interesting to discover whether the British system has been used in other countries and whether parliamentary corruption produced, either by action or in reaction, a strengthening of the internal organization of the groups of members. It has been recognized that phenomena like corruption have been important, in a certain phase of the development of democracies, as a means whereby the government could resist growing pressure within the assembly: the examples furnished by Guizot in France and Giolitti in Italy are well known. But have they had everywhere else the same effect on the development of parties as in England? Any hasty generalization on the question would be best avoided. In Italy, the Giolitti system seems on the contrary to have broken up parliamentary groups that were coalescing and increased the personal nature of political struggles.

The emergence of local electoral committees is directly linked with the extension of popular suffrage; this makes it necessary to bring the new electors into the party. For example, the adoption of universal suffrage brought about the expansion of the Socialist parties that occurred in most European countries as the twentieth century opened. However, such mechanical extension of the suffrage is not the only factor in the birth of local committees: the development of egalitarian feelings and the desire to oust traditional social elites is another without which the first would have had no effect. Consider a political system of very limited suffrage as in France from 1815 to 1830 or in England before 1832. Here no committees were needed to bring together the electors; they were both sufficiently evolved socially and sufficiently few in numbers to be able to make a direct choice between candidates without these being presented by a party: the election took place, so to speak, amongst gentlemen, amongst people of the same world, who were acquainted with one another, or almost. Electoral committees do indeed exist sometimes under such a system of limited suffrage, but they play a very minor part. Imagine however the sudden extension of the suffrage: if, at the same time no one creates or develops active committees capable of securing the confidence of the new electors, these will inevitably tend to vote for the only candidates of whom they have any knowledge, namely the traditional social elites. Thus, at the elections to the French National Assembly in 1871 the suffrage suddenly became free after twenty years of official candidatures, but there were no parties, and so the great mass of voters in country areas turned to the local landlord. The result was the *Republic of Dukes*. The creation of electoral committees tends therefore to be a left-wing effort because fundamentally it is advantageous to the Left: the task is, by means of these committees, to make known new elites which will be able to compete in the minds of the electorate with the prestige of the old elites. But the Right is obliged to follow the example in order to retain its influence; this phenomenon of contagion from the Left will be seen again and again as we analyse the structure of the parties.

The precise way in which an electoral committee is created is difficult to describe in terms of general principles alone, for local conditions here assume a major role. Sometimes it is the candidate himself who gathers around him a few faithful friends in order to ensure his election or his re-election: such a committee is somewhat artificial in character. In some countries, as for example in England, it was not considered right for a candidate to stand for election without backing; he was therefore obliged to persuade a few friends to stand surety for him. Many committees formed in the nineteenth century owed their origin solely to this fact. Sometimes, on the other hand, a few men form a group to launch a candidate and help him in his campaign: take for example the committee formed in 1876 in the sixth *arrondissement* of Paris by a group of students and a few workmen to support the candidature of Emile Acollas, Professor of Law at the Sorbonne, who was the first Socialist candidate under the Third Republic. Very often some previously existing society gives rise to the creation of a committee: during the French Revolution 'philosophical societies' played an active part in elections; in the United States local clubs exercised considerable electoral influence in the early days of the Union. Frequently too newspapers bring about the creation of electoral committees, as witness the well-known cases of the influence exerted by *Le National* and *La Réforme* in France in 1848.

Sometimes particular circumstances have favoured the birth of committees. An example is to be found in the electoral registration system set up by the English Act of 1832 which entrusted the establishment of electoral lists to parish overseers of the poor who were fiscal officers ill-equipped for such tasks; but appeals by individuals were allowed on many counts, with the result that private initiative played a considerable part. It was however slow to act, all the more so because the law had fixed a registration fee of one shilling that many people were reluctant to pay. In consequence Registration Societies rapidly sprang up in association with the candidates to facilitate the procedure of registration and to urge electors to submit to it. The movement was begun by the Liberals, but the Conservatives soon followed suit. At first the Registration Societies did not concern themselves with the nomination of candidates, who retained their freedom entire, but as the Societies grew they entered this field as well.

In the United States electoral committees have similarly benefited from special conditions. Since a large number of public posts are elective, the mass of voters would find themselves at a loss were they not guided by some selecting organization. Moreover, since the Presidential election was based on a single ballot, the intervention of well-organized committees was essential to avoid any splitting of votes. Furthermore the constant stream of immigrants was perpetually introducing into the voting body a mass of newcomers completely ignorant of American politics: their votes had to be directed towards candidates of whom they knew nothing apart from the fact that they were recommended by the committee. Finally the establishment from the time of Jackson onwards of the Spoils system, which allotted to the victorious party all the Civil Service posts, placed at the disposal of the committees powerful material means: just as corruption strengthened the structure of parliamentary groups in England, so in America it consolidated that of the electoral committees.

Once these mother-cells, parliamentary groups and electoral committees, have come into being, it is enough that some permanent coordination be established between them and that regular connections unite them, for us to find ourselves faced with a true political party. In general the parliamentary group has played the essential role in this particular phase. From above, the group coordinated the activity of parliamentary representatives, but each of these, on the other hand, was eager to develop his connections with his own electoral committee, on which would depend at some time in the future the renewal of his mandate. The result was that the different committees found themselves federated indirectly because their nominees collaborated within the parliamentary group. It only needed these relationships to become institutional instead of personal for the birth certificate of a party to be officially delivered. However, the legal registration of the facts is less important than their sequence in practice. To complete the description we must add that the first effort of a party after its creation normally consists in sponsoring the creation of electoral committees in constituencies where it still has none. In contrast with the earlier ones, these are created as a result of an impulse from the centre. The mechanism of party evolution is thus reversed. The full importance of this observation will become apparent when we attempt to determine how far any party is centralized or decentralized, or the respective influence of parliamentarians and 'inner leaders' in its direction. In the second stage the creation of committees in constituencies not represented in parliament usually leads to the setting up of a party administration distinct from the parliamentary group: the party grows away from its origins (although it remains strongly marked by them). It then tends to resemble parties of the second type which are by their structure at several removes from this electoral and parliamentary mechanism, having been created outside it: these are the externally created parties.

Extra-parliamentary origins of parties

In the course of our examination of the genesis of parties within the electoral and parliamentary framework we have noted the intervention of outside organizations: philosophical societies, working-men's clubs, newspapers and so on. The distinction between externally created parties and parties created within the electoral and parliamentary framework is not rigorous: it denotes general tendencies rather than clearly differentiated types, with the result that it is often difficult to apply in practice. In a fairly large number of cases, however, the shape of a party is essentially established by a pre-existing institution of which the true activities lie outside elections and parliament: it is then accurate to speak of creation from without.

The groups and associations which may thus bring about the birth of a political party are very numerous and most varied. It is out of the question to draw up an all-embracing list: we shall limit ourselves to a few examples. The activity of the trade unions is best known: many Socialist parties have been directly created by them and have moreover retained for varying periods the character of 'secular arm' of the trade unions in electoral and parliamentary matters. The British Labour party is the most typical example: its birth was the result of a decision taken by the Trades Union Congress in 1899 to create a parliamentary and electoral organization (Holmes's motion, passed on a card vote by 548,000 to 434,000). Undoubtedly there already existed the Independent Labour party (ILP), led by Keir Hardie, and especially the Fabian Society: both played a very important part in securing the adoption of Holmes's motion (he was in fact a member of the ILP). But the decisive factor was the action of the trade unions: the consequence is that the party remains closely dependent upon them. Here is a measure of the influence exerted on structure by origins. James Bryce rightly proposed a distinction between two categories of Socialist parties: Workers' parties, created by trade unions, and Socialist parties proper, created by parliamentarians and intellectuals, the second being much more doctrinaire and much less realist than the first.

With the influence of trade unions in the creation of parties must be compared that exercised by Agricultural Cooperatives and by Peasants' Associations. Although fewer agrarian than Labour parties have developed, they have none the less displayed great activity in certain countries, particularly in the Scandinavian democracies, Central Europe, Switzerland, Australia, Canada and even in the United States. Sometimes they are but simple electoral and parliamentary organizations conforming to the first type described (e.g. France). Elsewhere, on the contrary, they resemble in the circumstances of their creation the British Labour party: agrarian trade unions and groups decide on the creation of an electoral organization or else transform themselves directly into a party.

The activity of the Fabian Society in the creation of the Labour party illustrates the influence of philosophical societies, as they were called in the eighteenth century, and of groups of intellectuals on the genesis of political parties. The part played by students' associations and university groups in nineteenth-century European popular movements and in the emergence of the first left-wing political parties is well known. A similar phenomenon is at work today in some Latin-American states. In the same way Freemasonry seems to have played a part in the genesis of the Radical party in France and of various Liberal parties in Europe. In Belgium, there is clear evidence of the nature of its action: the Grand Master of Belgian Freemasonry, Defacqz, had in 1841 founded a political association, the *Alliance*, which set up local societies throughout the country. In 1846 the Alliance called a congress of all these provincial societies in the Hôtel de Ville at Brussels; there were 320 delegates. Under the presidency of Defacqz the Congress decided to set up permanent Liberal associations in the cantons. Similarly there must be a fairly large number of cases of political parties created by groups of intellectuals: it is, however, very rare for such a party to enlist sufficient popular support for it to be successful in countries with universal suffrage. The recent failure in France of the attempt by Jean-Paul Sartre and a few left-wing writers to found the *Rassemblement démocratique révolutionnaire* (RDR, Revolutionary Democratic party), is a good example. This method of creating parties would appear more suited to a system of limited suffrage.

On the other hand the influence of the Churches and of religious sects is always considerable. For example in the Nether-lands the Anti-Revolutionary party was set up by the Calvinists in opposition to the Catholic Conservative party; in 1897, even more intransigent Protestants created the Christian Historical party to protest against the collaboration of the Catholics and the Anti-Revolutionaries. Catholic organizations, if not the clergy itself, played a direct part in the creation of the right-wing Christian parties that emerged before 1914, and in the contemporary rise of Christian-Democratic parties. In Belgium, the action of the religious authorities was a decisive factor in the development of the Catholic Conservative party. In order to campaign against the 'calamitous' laws of 1879 concerning secular teaching and to protect religious education, the clergy brought about the creation of 'Catholic school committees' throughout the country. They led to the withdrawal of children from the State schools and an increase in the number of con-fessional schools. In 1884, these committees transformed them-selves into local sections of the Catholic party, which thus became one of the most highly organized in Europe. The influence of the Church in the creation of Christian-Democratic parties in 1945 seems to have been less direct. In France, for instance, the ecclesiastical authorities took no initiative in the matter (emphasis must however be laid upon the catalysing action of the *Association catholique de la jeunesse française* (ACJF, Catholic Association of French Youth) and of its various specialized branches: Young Christian Workers, JOC; Young Christian Students, JEC; Young Christian Farmers, JAC). Although the ACJF did not intervene as an organiza-tion, it supplied the party leaders and workers, both at the national and at the local level. In Italy, Catholic Action seems to have played a similar role, the intervention of the clergy being often more direct; so, too, in Germany.

To the list of organizations such as trade unions, philosophi-cal societies and Churches, which are capable of giving birth to parties, must be added Ex-Servicemen's Associations. On the morrow of the 1914 war they played a great part in the creation of Fascist or pseudo-Fascist parties. Well-known examples are the influence exerted by the former Baltic *freikorps* on the origins of National Socialism and the role of Italian Ex-Servicemen's Associations in Fascism. A yet more definite example occurred in France in 1936 when an association of ex-servicemen – the *Croix de Feu* – transformed itself openly and directly into a political party, the *Parti social français* (PSF, French Social party). It is true that some two years previously the Croix de Feu had in part lost its character of Old Comrades' Association to take on that of a 'league' in the special sense of the word in French politics. Like parties, 'leagues' are associations set up with political aims, in contradistinction to the other 'external organizations' studied so far, but they do not employ the same means to attain their ends. Party action is always exerted on the electoral and parliamentary plane, if not exclusively, at least to a very great extent; on the contrary, 'leagues' do not put forward candidates at elections and make no attempt to group parliamentary representatives; they are solely organizations for propaganda and agitation. Consequently, by their very nature, leagues are violently anti-parliamentary: they refuse to play the parliamentary game, differing in this from Fascist and Communist parties which are equally hostile to parliament in doctrine but make use of parliament to conquer power. The league phenomenon corresponds to a politically primitive method, for in a democracy it is obviously more efficacious to use electoral and parliamentary methods to destroy the system than to act from without. The line of development natural to the league is thus a transformation into an extremist party and it is a fact that some such parties, notably the Italian Fascist party, were leaguist in character before becoming true parties.

With the influence of leagues on the formation of parties may be compared that of secret societies and clandestine groups. In both cases in fact we are concerned with organizations having a political aim but which do not function on the electoral and parliamentary plane, the former because they do not wish to, the latter because they cannot, since they are banned by law. (This definition of secret societies, it will be noted, excludes Freemasonry which properly speaking is not secret but discreet.) When the legal ban disappears the clandestine groups tend to be transformed into parties. Thus in 1945 Resistance movements in many formerly occupied countries were to be seen attempting to change themselves into parties, generally without succeeding. However the French *Mouvement républicain populaire* (MRP, People's Republican party), and even more the Italian Christian Democratic party can be considered very largely to have issued from former clandestine organizations. Such too were the origins of the Russian Communist party which in 1917 passed direct from illegality to power, retaining moreover certain notable features of its former organization (subsequently introduced into all the Communist parties throughout the world which were reorganized after the pattern of the first one). Here again we note the influence exerted by genesis upon permanent structure. In the case of Communism it is true that the retention of the organization due to clandestinity was also justified by the possible need to reassume speedily the structure of a secret group should governmental persecution make it necessary.

Finally, this enumeration of the different 'external organizations' which may bring about the creation of a political party would not be complete without mention of the action of industrial and commercial groups: banks, big companies, industrial combines, employers' federations and so on. Unfortunately here it is extremely difficult to pass beyond the bounds of generalizations and hypotheses, for such action is always cloaked in great discretion. In the *Encyclopedia of Social Sciences*, E. H. Underhill demonstrates the part played in the birth of the Canadian Conservative party in 1854 by the Bank of Montreal, the Grand Trunk Railway and by Montreal 'big business' generally. Similar influences could no doubt be discovered at work in the formation of almost all right-wing parties; but on this point we have for the most part at our disposal only presumptions (well-founded, it is true) but not evidence: very tactful investigations would be required to make clear the forms and degrees of influence exerted by capitalist groups on the genesis of political parties.

Whatever their origin parties which have come into being outside parliament offer a marked contrast with parties arising within the electoral and parliamentary cycle. To begin with they are generally more centralized than the latter. In fact, their development begins at the top whereas that of the others starts at the base. Their committees and local groups are set up through the drive from a pre-existent centre, which can therefore restrict their liberty of action as it pleases; but in the case of parties of parliamentary or electoral origin it is the local committees which are in existence first and which create a central organism to coordinate their activity and consequently limit its powers so as to preserve the greatest possible amount of autonomy. The extent to which the extra-parliamentary institution creating the party is decentralized obviously has an influence on the degree of decentralization of the latter: for example Labour parties are less centralized than Communist parties; parties created by capitalist groups are less centralized than Labour parties, and so on. None the less there is a certain correlation between extra-parliamentary origin and centralization. For analogous reasons, parties arising outside the cycle are generally more coherent and more disciplined than parties of electoral and parliamentary origin. The former have at their disposal an organization already in existence which binds together naturally all the cells at their base; the latter have all these bonds to create with no other starting-point than the coexistence of a few representatives within the one parliament.

Similarly the influence of the parliamentary group is very different in the two types of parties. It is immense in the case of parties of parliamentary or electoral origin. The parliamentary representatives play an essential part whether they as a body constitute the directing organization of the party or whether as individuals many of them are members of a controlling committee theoretically distinct from the parliamentary group. This preponderance of the elected representatives is easily explained by the mechanism of the party's development in which the greatest part was played by the members of parliament. On the other hand parties of extra-parliamentary origin were set up without their intervention, so it is easy to understand that their influence is always less there. In fact in such parties there is a certain more or less open mistrust of the parliamentary group, and a more or less definite desire to subject it to the authority of an independent controlling committee. Certainly many other factors enter into the explanation of this phenomenon. For example it happens in all Socialist parties, whether of parliamentary origin, as in France, or of extra-parliamentary origin, as in England. This example, however, does not invalidate the preceding statement. On the contrary, is it not striking to note that the practical influence of the parliamentary group is much more developed in the French Socialist party than in the Labour party? And have not all Socialist parties, even those closest to the electoral and parliamentary cycle, been more or less subjected to the influence of extra-parliamentary elements? Among the factors determining the influence of parliamentary representatives on a party the origin of that party remains a fundamental one.

The scope of the discussion needs to be enlarged. It is the whole life of the party which bears the mark of its origin, and its attitude with regard to the elected representatives is only one particular manifestation of the general importance accorded to electoral and parliamentary activities in relation to the others. Parties of extra-parliamentary origin show a much greater independence of them than those born and bred in the shade of the Chamber. For the latter the winning of seats in political assemblies is the essence of the life of the party, the very reason for its existence and the supreme purpose of its life. On the other hand, for the former, the electoral and parliamentary struggle remains very important, but it is only one of the elements in the general activity of the party, one of the means, among others, that it uses to realize its political ends. For example, for the Radical party in France the main question is the winning of the greatest possible number of seats in parliament; for the MRP the essential is, on the other hand, the promotion of certain spiritual and moral values in political life, and this lays as much stress on educational work as on electoral campaigns: finally, for the Communist party, the electoral campaigns are only one element, and that often a very secondary one, of an all-embracing strategy aiming at the complete seizure of power and the exercising of it in totalitarian form. Certainly these differences cannot be explained entirely by dissimilar origins, but their influence is incontestable. The result is that parties of extra-parliamentary origin, even when attached by their doctrine to the parliamentary system, never allot to it the same value as do parties of the first type. Their development therefore entails a certain independence in fact (often unconscious and repressed) with regard to parliaments and elections.

This point gains in seriousness from the fact that electoral and parliamentary creation seems to correspond to an old type and extra-parliamentary creation to a modern type. Up to 1900 the greater number of political parties arose in the first way: apart from the influence of the Church on certain Catholic parties (notably the Belgian Conservative party), that of industrial and financial groups on the parties of the Right, and that of intellectual circles (and Freemasonry) on some Liberal parties, we find very few extra-parliamentary interventions before the birth of Socialist parties at the beginning of the century. From that time on, however, creation outside parliament becomes the rule and creation within parliament becomes the exception: the recent example of the *Parti Républicain de la Liberté* (PRL, Republican party of Liberty) in France, and its failure, is a good illustration of the unwonted nature of such a procedure at the present time. Nevertheless exception must be made of countries new to democracy, that is to say, countries where political assemblies and universal suffrage have scarcely begun to function properly: here the development of parties conforms to the first type described. This does not contradict the preceding affirmation – on the contrary it emphasizes its truth by showing that the electoral and parliamentary creation of parties corresponds to a certain phase of democratic evolution, that of the progressive establishment of universal suffrage (in practice, and not only in legal texts, the latter usually preceding the former). The question is then to organize progressively a mass of new electors, by passing from a personal vote to a collective vote: the development of local committees is the natural answer to this. But once this first phase is passed, once parties are firmly constituted, fresh parties as they appear beat against the barrier of the old ones: separate local movements no longer suffice to break down this barrier; these movements cannot pass beyond their birthplace, and remain incapable of giving rise to a truly national party. In other words, the first type described corresponds to the creation of political parties in a country where no system of organized parties yet exists. As soon as such a system is at work, the second type of creation becomes the more usual.

18 Stein Rokkan and Angus Campbell

Citizen Participation in Political Life

Excerpts from Stein Rokkan and Angus Campbell, 'Citizen participation in political life: Norway and the United States of America', *International Social Science Journal*, vol. 12, 1960, pp. 69–99.

We shall present in this article a set of findings from parallel analyses of data from election surveys in two Western democracies: Norway and the United States. Our analysis will be concerned with similarities and differences in the recruitment of active participants in electoral contests in these two political systems: What kinds of citizens are most likely to become active in politics and to take a personal interest in public affairs? What are the primary channels of recruitment of such 'activists'? How do the different parties compare in their patterns of recruitment?

In any such confrontation of data on citizen behaviour in different political systems the fundamental problem is to find meaningful ways of relating variations at this 'micro' level of individual reactions and choices to differences in the 'macro' properties of the structures within which they occur and to the differences in the range and character of the alternatives set for the citizen by the institutional arrangements and by the constellation of competing forces in his society. In a rigorous analysis design, such macro-properties would have to be varied systematically and related to differences in patterns of citizen reactions and preferences. Such rigour is hardly practicable in the comparison of such units differing in such complex ways along a variety of dimensions, but step-by-step approximations should be within the range of the possible. [...]

Differences in the conditions for citizen participation

We felt tempted to set beside each other data from Norway and the United States both because of the basic similarities in political values, and because of the salient differences in the con ditions for citizen participation in the two systems: we felt that the two systems were similar enough to make it meaningful to attempt such comparisons at the 'micro' level, yet differing so markedly in the setting of their politics as to open up interesting opportunities for an analysis of factors affecting the levels of citizen participation.

Our two systems have very much in common: they are both within the Western family of economically-advanced pluralist democracies, they have both developed complex networks of organizations and associations actively influencing the processes of decision-making, and they are both dominated by political cultures giving strong encouragement to citizen participation in public affairs.

Geography and history have combined, however, to produce markedly different conditions for individual participation in the processes of politics in the two systems. [. . .]

Differences in the overall levels of participation in the two systems

Estimates from official statistics and from documentation from the parties indicate some differences between the two countries in the proportion of active citizens: the proportion of regular voters and the proportion of registered party members both appear to be markedly higher in the Norwegian electorate than in the United States.

There are a number of intricate questions to be asked about these differences: (a) How far can they be accounted for by differences in the definition of the total electorates and in the procedures of enumeration? (b) How far does it make sense to compare such proportions of individual acts when they occur in systems differing so clearly in the ranges of alternatives set for the citizen? (c) Granting that there are genuine differences between the systems in such overall proportions, how far can these be explained by the contrasts at the 'macro' levels of the total systems and how far can they only be accounted for by breakdowns within each system?

We cannot deal exhaustively with these problems in this context, but will discuss the questions briefly for each of the two categories of participation: voting and party membership.

Voting

In Norway the average turnout at the four Storting elections since the Second World War has been 79 per cent (82 per cent for men and 76 for women); the corresponding figure for the four last communal elections is 70 per cent (74 per cent for men and 69 for women).

In the United States the 'raw' participation figures for the three presidential elections after the war have averaged 58 per cent and the corresponding figure for the last four 'off-year' elections has been 41 per cent.

These figures would indicate a substantially higher level of electoral participation in Norway than in the United States. The data, however, cannot be compared without adjustments and qualifications: the two countries differ a great deal in the procedures used for registering and enumerating the electorate and in the availability of accurate statistics for turnout variations. [. . .]

Party membership

The difficulties of direct cross-system comparison increase dramatically as we move higher on the political activity scale: they are largely of a technical nature at the level of electoral participation, but raise serious conceptual problems as soon as we try to compare data on the proportions of citizens who in some way or other have joined one of the conflicting parties in each system.

In Norway, all the six parties have provisions for formal affiliation and regular dues-paying: they are, in Duverger's terminology, 'mass parties' (1954, pp. 63–71). This does not mean that party member is a clear and unambiguous term: there are variations in the procedures for affiliation and in the strictness of the dues requirements; there are also differences between the main party organizations and the auxiliary associations for young people and for women. Barely 10 per cent of the party members are 'militants' in the sense that they are active party workers, but even the less active members differ markedly from the 'rank-and-file voters' in their commitment to the party, in the interest they manifest in political affairs, and in their level of informedness (Rokkan, 1959).

The membership figures published or otherwise made available by the central party secretariats are not always based on accurately kept local records, but can be taken to be fair estimates of the situation in the electorate. The total individual memberships reported for the six parties in 1957 were about 390,000:[1] the electorate amounted to 2,298,000. A small, but unknown, proportion of the reported members were not yet of voting age and there are also possibilities of over-reporting because of double affiliations between the main organizations and the auxiliary associations. The percentage of party members in the electorate may therefore be evaluated at a maximum of 15 per cent: this corresponds almost exactly to the proportion reporting individual party membership in the 1957 election survey.

In the United States the term 'party member' does not have a settled political connotation: it may indicate any degree of commitment to a party, from simple registration at primaries or elections to active campaign work (Berdahl, 1942; Epstein, 1956). The American parties have not built up the mass memberships characteristic of the dominant parties in western Europe: they are, in the Duverger terminology, 'cadre parties' based on localized caucus organizations. It is technically difficult to assess the proportions of citizens who thus qualify as 'party members' in the strict sense. The Survey Research Center at the University of Michigan asked questions about membership in 'political clubs or organizations' in the national sample surveys before the presidential elections in 1952 and 1956: the proportions claiming such membership were 2 per cent and 3 per cent. Membership of this kind is clearly much less common in the United States than in Norway, but it would be misleading to take this as the ultimate measure of the overall difference in political participation in the two countries. Political activity is definitely more widespread in the United States than is indicated by the low proportion of party 'members' in the electorate.

1. The Communist Party membership has been estimated at around 6000; the Labour Party recorded 163,000 individually affiliated members plus 3,000 affiliated via collective trade union membership; the Liberals indicated 28,000 members, the Christians 30,000 (approximate figure), the Agrarians 64,000 and the Conservatives 96,000.

The design of the comparative survey analysis

Direct comparisons of overall levels of participation may prove inconclusive because of the difficulties of establishing equivalences, but indirect, 'second-order' comparisons of regularities in the differences within the system may still prove of great theoretical interest.

The present analysis focuses on such 'second-order' comparisons and for two major reasons:

1. It is clearly easier to establish differences between groups within the same political systems than to compare across entirely different systems: in the one case we have very good reasons for interpreting participation as a response to similar ranges of political alternatives while in the other any such assumptions are problematic.

2. Any between-system differences in overall levels of participation must be the resultants of the interaction of a variety of factors and these cannot be disentangled without detailed breakdowns by groups within each system.

In this analysis we are no longer concerned with the proportions of active citizens in the total electorates but with the recruitment of such participants from the different groups within each system. We do not compare 'party membership' in Norway with 'party membership' in the United States because it proves so difficult to establish equivalent categories. Instead we choose our 'dependent' variables, our participation indicators, within each system and compare the differences in the levels of participation between comparable groups within each of them: differences in participation between men and women, country folk and city dwellers, farmers, manual workers and salaried employees, and so on. . . . Our 'dependent' variable, the indicators of individual participation, are system-specific while our 'independent' and 'intervening' variables, the causal factors we seek to identify, are roughly comparable characteristics of groups within each system: sex, rural-urban residence, education, occupation, party preference. . . .

We shall base our analysis on two sets of interview data from cross-sectional surveys: for Norway, a sample of 1406 citizens drawn by random probability methods from the registers in 99 *kommuner* and interviewed before and after the election for the Storting on 7 October 1957;[2] for the United States, a sample of 1772 persons interviewed before and after the presidential election on 6 November 1956.[3]

The analysis will proceed as follows: (a) we shall present, for each country, two indexes of political activity derived from a combination of several indicators in the survey responses; (b) we shall present and discuss comparative tables indicating similarities and differences shown by these indexes between the sexes, between communities at different levels of urbanization, between educational and occupational strata in each electorate; and (c) we shall present and discuss differences in the recruitment patterns for the major party groupings in the two countries.

Two indexes of political activity

Both nation-wide surveys included a number of questions about the politically relevant activities engaged in by the citizens to be interviewed. In comparing the data from the two surveys we tried to summarize this information in two simple indexes: one for organizational participation and another for the attention paid to politics in the mass media. The indexes cannot be compared directly between the systems but they allow analysis of the differences between the two electorates in the recruitment of the 'actives' in each system, in their demographic and socio-economic background and in their party attachments.

Organizational participation

The index of organizational participation summarizes information about energy inputs into some organized political framework: from the act of voting to direct campaign work.

The index has a very simple structure, it divides the samples into three groups: the 'non-voters', the 'only-voters' who

2. For a general account of this inquiry, see Rokkan (1959); details of the sampling procedures are given in a mimeographed report, *The Nationwide Survey: Basic Tables I*, Bergen, August 1958.

3. The findings of this survey are presented in Campbell, Miller, Converse and Stokes (1960).

indicate no other political activity, and the 'organizationally active' who indicate one or more activities beyond voting.

Sample surveys generally fail to produce reliable estimates of the proportion of non-voters in a given electorate. We cannot cite any exception to the rule that the proportions reporting abstention in cross-sectional samples of interviewed citizens will be lower than the officially reported or estimated proportions of non-voters in the total electorate.

It is not difficult to account for these regular discrepancies between sample proportions and proportions for the total electorates.

First, it must be remembered that the proportions of non-voters in a survey are always given as percentages of the number of obtained interviews: these figures cannot be compared with the official turnout estimates without controls for the coverage of the sample (does it deliberately exclude or for other reasons fail to cover any identifiable sections of the given electorate?), and the non-response (do those interviewed differ significantly from those not interviewed within the given example?). . . . The citizens not reached by sample surveys are exactly the citizens least likely to vote: this clearly biases the samples in the direction of higher turnout levels.

Secondly, there is also some evidence of a culturally determined reluctance to admit a failure to vote: the majority of the citizens contacted in a survey will consider it a definite duty to vote and may not be willing to tell an interviewer that they have been negligent in this duty.

These difficulties do not necessarily jeopardize our analysis. Our index only assumes the validity of the reports on non-voting: these are taken to indicate the lowest level of political participation. The reported voters are subjected to a number of further tests to sort out the 'actives': the remaining group of 'only-voters' may include some actual non-voters but this is not a serious drawback since all the analysis focuses on the differences at the extremes of the distribution.

In the Norwegian survey, the number of respondents who admitted that they had not voted was too small to allow extensive analysis. It was therefore decided to establish a broader category of 'probable non-voters' by taking into account not

only the report after the election, but also the expressed intention before the election and the report given on the regularity of
official turnout figures, but some of these respondents must
clearly have voted in 1957, however poor their previous
turnout at previous elections: this gives a group of 'low-prob-
ability voters' with a record of erratic turn-out and chronically
low interest in participation. This group was found to make up
21 per cent of the sample: this corresponds very closely to the
record.

The next step in the construction of the index was to identify
the 'organizationally active' within the groups of reported
voters. In the Norwegian survey, the 'actives' were sorted out
on the basis of responses to three questions, in the United States
on the basis of four questions (see Table 1).

The percentages given for each question are for those
classified as voters, not for the entire samples. Naturally, only

Table 1

Norway		United States	
Question	Per cent positive among voters	Question	Per cent positive among voters
Are you a member of any political party?	23	Do you belong to any political club or organization?	4
Were you yourself present at one or more election meetings or political rallies this autumn?	8	Did you go to any political meetings, rallies, dinners, or things like that?	9
(Not asked)		Did you give any money or buy tickets or any-thing to help the cam-paign for one of the parties or candidates?	12
Did you yourself take an active part in the election work for any of the parties this autumn?	3	Did you do any other work for one of the parties or candidates?	4

very few of the non-voters report any such activities. The Norwegian percentage for party membership is particularly high: it includes not only those reporting individual membership, but also those who said they were collectively affiliated through their union. Cross-tabulations against other activity indicators showed little difference between these two membership categories: they were therefore grouped together.

To simplify the analysis our index of organizational participation assembles in one 'active' category all those who indicated at least one of the activities listed. Table 2 gives the resulting distribution, for the two countries. It will be seen that sizable proportions of the 'actives' thus defined have reported two or more activities: in Norway, this was the case with 18 per cent of all 'activities', in the United States with as many as 32 per cent. Political activities of these kinds are clearly cumulative:[4] a citizen engaging in one given type of activity is much more likely than other citizens to engage in another type of activity in the sphere of politics.

Table 2 Levels of Organizational Participation in Politics: Men and Woman Compared in Norway and the United States

Percentage of Respondents classified as:	Norway			United States		
	Total Sample (1406)	Men (688)	Women (718)	Total Sample (1772)	Men (791)	Women (981)
'Non-voters'	21	15	26	27	20	33
'Only-voters'	57	55	60	59	64	55
'Organizationally active'	22	30	14	14	16	12
	100	100	100	100	100	100

The table shows that 22 per cent of the Norwegian sample and 14 per cent of the United States sample indicated one such

4. This characteristic of community activities is discussed in some detail by Allardt (1958).

activity beyond voting. The reader is again warned against direct comparisons between such percentages: the categories are clearly relative to each system and to the content of the questions asked in order to identify the 'actives'.

The originally constructed index for the United States data took into account two further categories of political activity: efforts of informal persuasion and visible manifestations of political preference (wearing a campaign button or putting a 'sticker' on one's car). This allowed further differentiation within the group of organizationally passive voters: altogether 20 per cent out of the 59 per cent in the present 'only-voter' category were found to be 'informally active'. This distinction is clearly of great relevance in any analysis of participation, but unfortunately there were no directly comparable questions in the Norwegian survey: our present efforts will therefore have to be concentrated on the comparison of 'organizationally active' and 'non-voters'.

Attention to politics in the mass communication media

Our second index of activity is different in structure and serves to measure another dimension of participation: the citizen's private efforts to keep abreast of what is happening in local and national politics and to seek information about matters of public concern.

A score for the attention paid to the campaign was made up by the simple procedure of counting the number of media in which the campaign was followed: the resulting distribution will be found in Table 3.

In the Norwegian survey there was unfortunately no equivalent sequence of questions about the attention given to the campaign in the media, but it was possible to construct an index of similar dimensions by combining the responses to questions about radio listening, newspaper reading and acquaintance with party pamphlets. There were no regular television programmes in Norway in 1957 and there was no point in asking about politics in magazines since these were too unimportant to matter in a cross-sectional survey. The questions were not phrased in the same way as in the United States study and it was difficult to decide on distinctions between those who 'followed the campaign' in the medium and those who simply paid some attention to it. In the case of newspaper reading, we classified as 'following the campaign' all those who reported that they read the editorials or the campaign news in the newspaper most days of the week: they amounted to 27 per cent of the sample. The party pamphlet item caused the greatest difficulty: 78 per cent

Table 3 Levels of Attention to Politics in the Mass Communication Media: Men and Women Compared in Norway and the United States

	Norway			*United States*		
Percentage of respondents who report that they follow campaign in:	*Total sample (1406)*	*Men (688)*	*Women (718)*	*Total Sample (1772)*	*Men (791)*	*Women (981)*
No media	19	12	26·5	8	6	11
One (N) or two (US)	35	28·5	41	51	48	53
Most (N: two, US: three)	32	38·5	25·5	28	31	25
All the media inquired into:	14	21	7	13	15	11
	100	100	100	100	100	100

of the sample reported that they had received or seen one or more mass distributed items of party literature during the campaign, but the questions asked in this area did not readily allow an analysis of the relative attention paid to this medium of communication. It was decided to classify as 'following the campaign' all those who reported seeing or receiving two or more items, but this procedure can clearly be questioned. In the circumstances, we nevertheless found it worth while to use this index for exploratory purposes. We shall therefore confine ourselves to the analysis of group differences on the indexes set beside each other in Table 3: the steps in these indexes cannot at all be compared across the countries, but there is a good deal of evidence to show that the indexes produce reliable system-specific measures of the relative attention paid to politics within each electorate.

The relationship between the two indexes

The two indexes constructed for the two samples could clearly be expected to be correlated with each other: we should expect the 'organizationally active' citizen to pay more attention to politics in the media than the 'only-voter' and, even more, the non-voter. The correlations between the indexes are significant in both countries ($r=0.18$ for the Norwegian sample, $r=0.37$ for the United States), but they are far from perfect: we find quite a few 'organizationally active' who pay little attention to the media, and we find substantial proportions of 'only-voters' and 'non-voters' who nevertheless manifest considerable interest in the media. The indexes clearly measure *different dimensions of participation*: the circumstances and the motives behind a decision to take on an organizational role in politics will differ from those behind decisions about the consumption of mass-directed information. We shall therefore take both the indexes into account in our analysis and pay particular attention to the patterns of differences between groups in the electorates in their scores on the two indexes.

The correlation between the two indexes is lower in Norway than in the United States. This clearly reflects the lower level of urbanization in Norway: the smaller local units and the strong working-class organizations make it possible to take on active organizational roles without depending to the same extent as in the United States on the urban system of mass communications. We shall see in our further analysis how this difference comes out again and again in the parallel tabulations for the two indexes. [...]

Differences between lower and higher educational and occupational strata

With the contrast in the degree of urbanization goes a marked difference in the socio-economic structure of the two electorates: Norway lags far behind the United States in economic growth, has a larger proportion of its labour force in the primary economy as farmers, forest workers and fishermen, and has a smaller proportion in the tertiary sector of its economy as salaried employees in 'white-collar' occupations.

With this difference in socio-economic structure goes a clear contrast in the character of the cleavages between the political parties: the Norwegian parties correspond much more closely than the United States ones to the major economic divisions in the population and fit much more definitely in with the dominant interest organizations. The Norwegian parties all have their distinctive electoral clientele: each body of party supporters differs pronouncedly from the total electorate in socio-economic structure, in organizational affiliations.[5] In the United States the two contending political parties are both near the 50 per cent mark: they are highly heterogeneous in the composition of their clientele and they appeal for support from all major sectors of the electorate.[6]

How would we expect these differences in socio-economic structure and party divisions to be reflected in the levels of political activity within the two systems?

This question gets us into the heart of the problem of identifying the major channels of recruitment to the ranks of the politically active in a system.

It is analytically convenient to distinguish four such channels: (a) the learning of politics in the family; (b) the development of skills for public life through formal education; (c) the strengthening of political commitments through roles in occupational life and through the growth of loyalties in one's econ-

5. In the Norwegian 1957 survey, 48 per cent of the heads of all the households interviewed were classified as manual workers; the corresponding proportion for Social (Communist and Labour) voters was 70 per cent, for Liberal voters, 30, Christians, 30, Agrarians, 14 and for Conservatives, 21.

6. In the United States presidential election survey in 1956, 44 per cent of the nation-wide sample were classified as belonging to 'blue-collar' households: of those who identified with the Democrats there were 47 per cent in this blue-collar category and of those identifying with the Republicans, 38 per cent. The deviations from the national average were thus markedly smaller in the United States than in Norway. There is evidence of significant changes in the degree of 'status polarization' of United States politics Converse (1958). A detailed analysis of the contrast between Norway and the United States has been undertaken by Angus Campbell and Henry Valen: 'Party Identification in the United States and in Norway: A Comparative Analysis.'

omic career; (d) the encouragement of political activity through membership in economic, social and cultural organizations and associations. . . .

In the Norwegian survey we asked questions about the political activities of the parents and found a distinct relationship between the level of activity in the family of origin and the current participation of the offspring: the 12 per cent who said their fathers had been 'very active' were found to be about twice as likely as the others to be 'organizationally active' themselves. A tabulation from the Survey Research Center study of the 1958 congressional election indicates a similar relationship.

Our hypothesis is that *formal education and occupational position will make less of a difference in the level of political activity in a class-distinct party system such as the Norwegian and more of a difference in a system of two socially and economically highly heterogeneous parties such as the American.*

In general terms, we might say that we shall seek to use the contrast between the two countries to test a set of hypotheses about the effects of the status distinctiveness of the parties in a system on the recruitment of active participants from the strata of the less educated and of the holders of lower occupational statuses: (a) the greater the distinctiveness of the electorates of each party in the system, the better the opportunities and the stronger the net incentives for active participation within the lower strata; (b) the greater the status heterogeneity of the electorates of the major parties in the system, the greater the importance of formal education and occupational status in the recruitment of active participants in politics.

In the Norwegian setting, workers and farmers get activated for politics through strong economic organizations dominating distinctive parties of their own: the trade unions in the Labour Party and the farmers' associations in the Agrarian Party. Family traditions certainly count in the recruitment of 'actives' among workers and farmers, but the decisive influences are organizational: the unions and the economic associations create incentives for active participation in party politics and open up opportunities for promotion to positions of trust in the party organizations. What counts in the recruitment of militants and leaders in these parties is the learning process in the economic organizations: formal education may of course be a prerequisite for positions in the central party bureaucracies and probably increasingly so as the organization grows in complexity, but education counts very little in the recruitment of local party workers.

In the United States, the workers and the farmers have large and efficient organizations but none of them has achieved any position of dominance in any of the national parties. The trade-union leadership has strong influence on the Democratic Party organizations in several states, but there are few open channels of recruitment from the unions to the party. . . . The American parties are complex alliances of interest alignments and this very complexity tends to discourage the recruitment of active participants from the strata of the less educated and the lower status-holders.

Table 4 presents evidence for the differences in the conditions for the recruitment of active participants in the two systems: it divides the cross-sectional samples according to the level of formal education.

Electoral turnout

Table 4 shows very similar trends in the variations in the proportions of non-voters in the two countries. Electoral turnout is regularly lowest among citizens with little education beyond the primary level, among manual workers, fishermen and smallholders; it is regularly higher among citizens with higher education, among salaried employees, managers and businessmen.

These survey findings accord very well with regularities found in analyses of official voting registers in a number of countries (Tingsten, 1957; Lane, 1959).

Organizational activity

Table 4 shows a definite contrast between Norway and the United States in the educational bases for the recruitment of the 'organizationally active'. In the Norwegian sample there is no regular increase in the proportions of 'actives' from one educational level to another. What is perhaps most interesting in the table for the Norwegian data, however, is the lower proportion of participants among the citizens with higher formal education: this seems to reflect the current trends toward increasing political 'disengagement' within the professional elite.[7]

We may compare with this complex recruitment pattern in Norway, the very straightforward progression in the United States data: for these, the table shows substantial and consistent increases in the proportions of 'actives' from one educational level to the next.

In Norway we find the highest proportions of actives among the male farmers and workers and lower proportions within the middle-class groups: in the United States the trend is the other way, 'white-collar' citizens highest in participation, manual workers and farmers lowest.

There are important differences, however, between men and women and between economically active and economically dependent women: these are of sufficient theoretical interest to warrant detailed analysis in a separate section.

Media attention

There is no similar contrast in the findings for the other index: for the attention to politics in the mass media.

The findings for the Norwegian sample run very much along the same lines as for the United States data: the higher the level of education and the higher the occupational status the greater the average number of media attended to.

There is a clear contrast between the findings for the two indexes of activity in the Norwegian data: the lower strata have a higher proportion of organizationally active but a lower proportion of alert media consumers while the higher strata have a lower proportion of active party supporters and a higher proportion of passive information gatherers.

Data from a variety of sources offer evidence of the limited influence of the mass media on the political motivations of working-class citizens: they may be exposed to a continuous

7. Aubert (1959) has analysed data on publicly-recorded political participation among lawyers in Norway and has found a decrease in the proportions of politically active from 17 per cent in 1932 to 7·5 per cent in 1950.

Table 4 Organizational Participation and Media Attention: Differences between Men and Women by Level of Education.

Norway

Sex	Number of persons	Non-voters %	Actives[1] %	Mass media None %	Mass media Most or all[1] %
Primary education only					
Men	300	27	28	17	49
Women	399	30	10	31	28
Primary plus vocational					
Men	245	18	33	9	68
Women	165	24	18	22	38
Christian Youth or Folk High School					
Men	43	9	44	14	68
Women	59	27	19	15	32
Secondary					
Men	50	2	22	2	66
Women	72	17	25	21	34
Gymnasium, university					
Men	50	8	26	8	76
Women	23	13	9	17	39

United States

Sex	Number of persons	Non-voters %	Actives[1] %	Mass media None %	Mass media Most or all[1] %
Grade school					
Men	253	30	10	11	31
Women	290	48	7	20	20
High School					
Men	357	19	16	4	45
Women	533	30	11	8	36
College					
Men	178	9	25	2	69
Women	153	12	27	1	68

1 Percentages for each index do not add up to 100 because middle categories have been left out.

flow of stimuli from mass media such as newspapers, magazines, radio and television but the messages they expose themselves to are of little political relevance to them. We know from
a study of the readership of the political press in Norway
(Rokkan and Torsvik, 1959) that about two-thirds of the
Labour Party voters read newspapers opposed to or indifferent
to their party. Their political loyalty is developed and maintained in the face-to-face environments of the kin group, the
workplace and the secondary organizations and is seldom decisively influenced by the mass-directed messages in the
press. . . .

Differences between men and women in the lower and in the higher strata

Our analysis of the differences in the levels of political activity
in communities of different size and complexity indicated a
striking similarity between the two countries in the distributions
for the two sexes: the differences between men and women in
the proportions of actives tended to even out with increasing
urbanization. In Norway, this was found to be the case both for
differences in turnout and for differences in organizational activity. In the United States the trend was found to be the same
for turnout but not for organizational activity.

If we look at Table 4 we find evidence of similar trends of
narrowing differences in comparisons for educational level. The
difference between the sexes tends to be largest in the lower
strata and tends to disappear in the higher strata. The trends are
on the whole similar in the two countries but the data do not
coincide completely. . . .

Organizational activity

In the Norwegian data, the differences between men and
women in the proportions of organizationally active follow
much the same trends as for turnout: the difference is largest in
the rural occupations and among the workers, smallest within
the higher urban occupations. We find this reflected in the composition of the active cores of the voters for the different
parties: The active cores of supporters are predominantly male
in the parties with strongholds in the rural districts and in the

parties of the working class. In the Conservative Party, on the other hand, we find a completely even distribution between the sexes: this is predominantly a party of the urban middle class of business and professional families and salaried employees and in these strata there is a pronounced trend toward equal participation from men and women.

In the United States data, the trends for organizational activity are not very easy to interpret in the direct tabulations. Our further analysis will show that a clear trend emerges in the sex differences as soon as we classify by education or by occupation within party identification groups: the difference between men and women in the proportion of actives tends to disappear within the higher strata of the Republican identifiers. This finding is of considerable theoretical importance: it will be dealt with in a wider context in a subsequent section.

The recruitment of active participants within the major party groupings

We have found evidence of marked differences between our two countries in the recruitment of active participants in politics from the lower and from the higher socio-economic strata and we have formulated a set of general hypotheses about the conditions making for such differences: these hypotheses focused on the degree of class distinctiveness of the party systems and the consequent differences in the character of the alternatives facing citizens at similar socio-economic levels in systems differing in the average class distinctiveness of their parties.

We have so far formulated these hypotheses for comparisons between the entire samples of the electorates and in fact stayed at this level in our discussion of the evidence: Table 4 gives the variations on our indexes within the entire samples by sex and education.

Our analysis so far has offered some evidence that the hypotheses hold at this overall system level but also underscored the need for detailed breakdowns by the major party preference alignments within each system.

At this level it is possible to specify our initial hypotheses in terms of comparisons, not between systems, but between parties: (a) the more a party is dominated by lower-stratum economic organizations the less the importance of formal education and occupational position in the recruitment of active participants among its voters; (b) the less a party is dominated by lower-stratum economic organizations the greater the importance of formal education and occupational position in the recruitment of actives among its voters.

It was technically impossible, as a means of testing these hypotheses on the data for Norway and the United States, to compare each of the six parties in the one country with the two in the other: the size of the Norwegian sample would have had to be several times larger for that to be possible. Instead we found it justifiable to divide the Norwegian parties into Socialist and non-socialist and to compare the intended voters for these two party groups with the potential voters for the Democratic and the Republican parties.

The non-socialist voter group established in the Norwegian sample is highly heterogeneous. The four parties grouped together in this way differ considerably in the proportions of active participants and, what is very important in the analysis, quite particularly in the sex composition of these nuclei of supporters: the two older parties, the Liberals and the Conservatives, have a relatively low ratio of activists to voters while the newer 'interest group parties', the Christians and the Agrarians, have higher proportions of actives: these parties are the political expression of important networks of associations and recruit their actives directly through such organizational channels. In this they resemble the 'lower stratum' Socialist parties: formal education is not a very important factor in the recruitment of actives in these parties. The Agrarian Party also comes close to the Socialist parties in the sex composition of its active core: half of the men intending to vote for the party reported organizational activities as against only 15 per cent of the women. We nevertheless decided to contrast Socialist and non-socialist voters in a first approximation to a test of our hypotheses: we have since endeavoured to guard ourselves against over-interpretation by checking our findings against alternative procedures of tabulations. Table 5 excludes all citizens in the primary economy: this should make for a purer test of our hypotheses since the status contrast comes out so much more clearly outside agriculture, forestry and fisheries.

Theoretically, the party dichotomies in the two national samples give us six possibilities of paired comparisons, but only three of these are of direct relevance in the testing of the hypotheses: (a) Socialist voters versus non-socialist voters in Norway; (b) Democrats versus Republican identifiers in the United States; (c) Socialists in Norway versus Democrats in the United States.

This is borne out quite clearly by Table 5.

For education we find in Norway a 25–33 per cent differential among the Socialist voters, but 14–34 per cent among the non-socialist: this compares to a 11–19 per cent differential for the Democrats against a 9–36 per cent differential for the Republicans.

For occupation we find for the Socialists in Norway a higher proportion difference in the opposite direction for the non-socialist voters: this compares to a 14–19 per cent differential for the Democrats as against a marked 10–30 per cent differential for the Republicans.

Comparison (c) cuts across the systems and serves to test the hypotheses for different degrees of lower-stratum dominance within the parties: very strong in the case of the Socialist parties in Norway, only moderate in the case of the Democratic Party in the United States. Our expectation would be that the status differentials would be even less marked among the Socialists than among the Democrats.

This is again borne out by the tables, not very clearly for education but remarkably clearly for occupation: among the Socialists there is actually a higher proportion of actives among the workers than among the middle-class voters, while among the Democrats there is a tendency in the opposite direction.

Perhaps the most interesting feature of these tables is the contrast they show in the status differentials for the women: in the lower-stratum parties status makes very little difference in the proportions of organizationally active among the women while in the middle-class parties the status differentials for women tend to be more marked than for men.

We have already seen from Table 4 that the differences between men and women in the proportions of actives tend to

Table 5 Organizational Participation and Media Attention: Differences between Men and Women by Occupational Level within Major Party Groupings

Norway

Occupation of head	Number of persons	Actives[1]	Mass media None	Mass media Most or all[1]
		%	%	%
Intended to vote Socialist				
Manual worker[2]	363	30	17	49
Men	194	43	13	61
Women	169	16	22	36
Salaried, self-employed[2]	105	20	16	49
Men	56	25	7	63
Women	49	14	27	32
Non-socialist				
Manual[2]	98	21	23	43
Men	44	27	20	53
Women	54	17	20	36
Salaried, self-employed[2]	214	30	14	53
Men	110	32	9	63
Women	104	28	18	43

United States

Occupation of head	Number of persons	Non-voters	Actives[1]	Mass media None	Mass media Most or all[1]
		%	%	%	%
Indentification: Democrat					
Manual workers	358	29	14	11	32
Men	170	28	18	6	32
Women	188	31	11	16	25
'White collar'	232	19	19	3	54
Men	106	11	25	2	50
Woman	126	25	14	3	52
Republican					
Manual	197	29	10	10	39
Men	84	19	9	6	42
Women	113	37	10	13	37
'White-collar'	186	10	30	3	61
Men	74	12	31	3	66
Women	112	14	29	3	57

1 Percentages for each index do not add up to 100 because some categories are left out.
2 Outside agriculture and fisheries.

disappear in the higher status groups and we find this reflected again in the figures for the proportions within party groups . . . in the typical middle-class parties, the Conservatives in Norway and the Republicans in the United States, the differences between men and women in the proportions of actives are clearly smaller than in the 'lower-stratum' parties. Table 5 makes it possible for us to clarify these findings further.

The tables show very clearly that it is only in the non-socialist and Republican parties that the higher-status women reach near-equality with the men in the proportions of actives: in the Socialist and the Democratic parties women at a higher educational or occupational level still differ markedly from men at the same level in the proportions of actives.

Women are definitely more 'status sensitive' than men in their political orientations: higher education and higher economic status is only likely to make a significant difference in their motivation for participation in parties dominated by middle-class voters, in the 'parties of respectablity'. A variety of experiences and environmental forces may make them feel at home in and vote for 'lower-stratum' parties but their organizational participation in such parties will stay relatively low whatever their level of education or their economic status. Within the middle-class parties, on the other hand, women at the higher levels of education and economic position are markedly more likely to approach positions of leadership; the lower status women voting for such parties definitely do not feel stimulated to participate actively themselves.

References

ALLARDT, E. (1958), 'On the cumulative nature of leisure-time activities', *Acta Soc.*, vol. 3, no. 1, pp. 165–72.

AUBERT, V. (1959), *Norsk Sakforerblad*, vol. 26, pp. 73–82.

BERDAHL, C. (1942), 'Party membership in the United States', *Amer. polit. Sci. Rev.*, vol. 36, pp. 16–50, 241–62.

CAMPBELL, A., MILLER, W., CONVERSE, P., and STOKES, D. (1960), *The American Voter*, Wiley.

CONVERSE, P. E. (1958), 'The shifting role of class in political attitudes and behavior', in E. Maccoby (ed.), *Readings in Social Psychology*, Holt, Rinehart & Winston.

DUVERGER, M. (1954), *Political Parties*, Methuen.

EPSTEIN, L. D. (1956), 'British mass parties in comparison with American parties', *Polit. Sci. Q.*, vol. 71, no. 1, pp. 97–125.

LANE, R. (1959), *Political Life*, Free Press.

ROKKAN, S. (1959), 'Electoral activity, party membership and organizational influence', *Acta Soc.*, vol. 4, no. 1, pp. 25–37.

ROKKAN, S., and TORSVIK, P. (1959), 'The voter, the reader and the party press', Fourth World Conference of Sociology.

TINGSTEN, H. (1957), *Political Behaviour*, King.

91 Seymour M. Lipset

Voting Behaviour

Excerpts from Seymour M. Lipset, *Political Man*, Heinemann, 1960, pp. 220–32, 248–52.

In every modern democracy conflict among different groups is expressed through political parties which basically represent a 'democratic translation of the class struggle'. Even though many parties renounce the principle of class conflict or loyalty, an analysis of their appeals and their support suggests that they do represent the interests of different classes. On a world scale, the principal generalization which can be made is that parties are primarily based on either the lower classes or the middle and upper classes. This generalization even holds true for the American parties, which have traditionally been considered an exception to the class-cleavage pattern of Europe. The Democrats from the beginning of their history have drawn more support from the lower strata of the society, while the Federalist, Whig and Republican parties have held the loyalties of the more privileged groups.

There have been important exceptions to these generalizations, of course, and class is only one of the structural divisions in society which is related to party support. In every country which has more than one important religion, or where there is a distinct difference between religious adherents and secularists, religious differences have contributed to the support of one party or another. In some countries religious belief has formed the basis for the formation of religious political parties, dedicated to meeting the needs of specific churches. Similarly, ethnic or nationality divisions within countries have been reflected in group identification with specific parties, or by the formation of ethnic or nationality parties. Religious and ethnic differences, however, have correlated with socio-economic divisions, so that there has been an admixture of class and ethnic support. In the United States, Canada, Great Britain and Australia, the conservative parties have been supported by the more well to do, by the members of the historic privileged religions like the Anglican-Episcopal church and the Congregationalists, and by the ethnic group which has highest status (also disproportionately composed of wealthier individuals).

Regional loyalties are another major factor which has affected party support. In many countries certain regions have developed historic loyalties to one or another political party, which have been maintained long after the specific event which gave rise to the allegiance has lost its relevance.

In practically every country for which we have data (except perhaps the United States), women tend to support the conservative parties more than men do. But this relationship is somewhat different from the preceding four, since the parties which are backed by women cannot be considered as representing women's interests against those of men. The differences are probably due to the different social role of women, and the way in which this leads them to accept values identified with conservative parties.

A sixth distinct factor affecting political opinions and loyalties is age. Unlike the others, however, there is no regular and distinct correlation between age and party support. In some countries and historical periods, the young voters (or the aged) are likely to be found on the left, in others they are more conservative. Different age groups react to their political environment according to the significant experiences of their generation. Any analysis of party support must take age into account as a relevant source of political differentiation, but party conflict cannot be interpreted as an age conflict.

The differences between rural and urban populations have constituted an additional basis of cleavage in many countries. In some the rural population has formed the backbone of an independent agrarian party, while in others farmers have identified with other major parties. The concept of a rural group and its needs opposing the rest of the country often conceals the fact that most rural societies are as internally differentiated as urban areas between rich and poor, and into ethnic, religious and regional groups. Differences between crop areas have also constituted an important source of cleavage. For example, in many countries wheat farmers have often been much more radical than farmers raising mixed crops.

The fact that many interests and groups which are not social classes take part in the party struggle does not vitiate the thesis that 'the rationale of the party-system depends on the alignment of opinion from right to left', as the sociologist and political philosopher MacIver has pointed out.

The right is always the party sector associated with the interests of the upper or dominant classes, the left the sector expressive of the lower economic or social classes, and the center that of the middle classes. Historically this criterion seems acceptable. The conservative right has defended entrenched prerogatives, privileges and powers; the left has attacked them. The right has been more favorable to the aristocratic position, to the hierarchy of birth or of wealth; the left has fought for the equalization of advantage or of opportunity, for the claims of the less advantaged. Defense and attack have met, under democratic conditions, not in the name of class but in the name of principle; but the opposing principles have broadly corresponded to the interests of the different classes[1] (1947, pp. 216, 315).

Such terms as 'left', 'liberal' and 'progressive', and their opposites, 'right', 'conservative' and 'reactionary' have been defined on the basis of many different issues – political democracy versus monarchy, the free-market system versus traditional economic restrictions, secularism versus clericalism, agrarian reform versus landlordism and urban exploitation of the countryside, social reform versus *laissez-faire*, socialism versus capitalism. The parties and social groups which have been 'left' on one of these issues have by no means always been 'left' on another, and the 'center' has emerged to oppose both left and right parties. Nevertheless, at any given period and

---

1. It is interesting to note that Talcott Parsons, whose sociology has often been criticized for deprecating problems of conflict and overemphasizing the degree of cohesion in society, has stressed the need to analyse American political history and voting contests in terms of an enduring conflict between the left and the right: those oriented to the lower strata and change, and those more concerned with stability and the needs of the more well to do (Parsons, 1959, p. 88).

place it is usually possible to locate parties on a left to right continuum (Duverger, 1954, pp. 215–16, 228–39; 1952).[2]

The issue of equality and social change has been a dominant one in most countries over the last two or three generations, and overlaps the older left-right issues like democracy versus monarchy and clericalism versus secularism. The most significant issue cutting across the left-right dimension today is political democracy versus totalitarianism, which was discussed earlier (Shils, 1954, pp. 24–49). In some countries, as I have already documented, the great majority of the traditional leftist vote goes to totalitarian Communist parties, while in others the traditional centrist and rightist vote has gone to various forms of 'fascism'. But even in such cases the economic and stratification left-right issues are probably much in the minds of the rank-and-file voters. More than anything else the party struggle is a conflict among classes, and the most impressive single fact about political party support is that in virtually every economically developed country the lower-income groups vote mainly for parties of the left, while the higher-income groups vote mainly for parties of the right.

The differences in political preference between lower- and upper-income groups which are typical of many countries are illustrated in Tables 1 and 2 which report on the support of French and Italian parties. In both countries the industrial and agricultural workers give strong support to the Communists, and in Italy to the left (Nenni) Socialists as well, and the middle and upper classes back the parties of the center and the right.

Though this broad pattern holds, there is a great amount of variation within income groups. In the middle-income groups white-collar workers and teachers give strong support to the moderate Socialists in France and the Saragat (right-wing) Socialists in Italy. The considerable variation within lower-income groups in the two countries is also shown in these tables.

2. Of course, this groups together parties which have quite different approaches to social change and which may in practice be bitterly hostile toward one another. It ignores the question of the finer degrees of 'left' and 'right' and neglects other issues which at times cut completely across the left-right dimension as defined here, such as regional autonomy v. centralism, national self-determination v. imperialism and, most recently, political democracy v. totalitarianism.

Table 1 Support of Political Parties in France among Different Occupational Groups 1956*

	Industrial workers	Agricultural workers	White collar	Civil servants and teachers	Merchant	Farm owner	Professional
Communist	39%	37%	16%	14%	7%	5%	11%
Socialist	31	19	33	48	21	17	23
Radical	11	13	7	21	12	13	20
MRP (Catholic)	8	9	21	9	17	14	13
Independent	3	17	11	3	21	45	20
URAS (De Gaulle)	4		10	5	3	4	8
Poujade	4	4	2		19	2	5
Total per cent	100	99	100	100	100	100	100
(N)	(169)	(67)	(61)	(58)	(81)	(180)	(64)

* Computed by author from cards of a national opinion survey conducted in May 1956 by the Institut national d'études démographiques. I am indebted to Alain Girard for use of the data.

Table 1 continued
1954†

Occupation	Industrial workers			Farmers		
Economic level	B Above average	C Average	D Poor	A Wealthy	B Above average	C Average	D Poor

Economic level	B Above average	C Average	D Poor	A Wealthy	B Above average	C Average	D Poor
Party choice							
Communist	18%	40%	45%	4%	9%	27%	43%
Socialist	41	27	22	12	28	14	10
Radical	4	7	5	9	12	24	10
MRP	17	7	10	12	12	10	10
Independent	18	15	18	60	30	23	26
RPF (De Gaulle)	2	5		3	8	1	
Total per cent	100	101	100	100	99	99	99

† Recomputed from Stoetzel (1955).

The lower the economic level of the worker, the more likely he is to vote Communist. The higher-income workers prefer the moderate Socialist parties or the center parties.

The same pattern holds in countries with stable two-party systems. As Table 3 shows, in Great Britain the higher one goes in the social structure, the smaller the support for the Labour party, until among top businessmen and higher-level professionals the party is supported by less than 10 per cent of the class. Almost identical patterns differentiate the backing of the Democrats and Republicans in the United States.

Further striking evidence of the pervasiveness of the effect of class position on political attitudes comes from a country in which real party competition does not exist: Communist Poland. In 1967 the young Polish sociologist Andrzej Malewski conducted a public opinion survey on attitudes concerning the proper level of differences in income for different occupations – an issue which in capitalist countries is strongly linked to leftist or conservative views. As in the capitalist countries he found

that there is a strong correlation between the incomes of people and their views concerning a maximum scale of income differences. ... The poll shows that factory workers, technicians and certain groups of the intelligentsia with low salaries (teachers, post office workers, social service officials, etc.) are in favour of egalitarianism. On the other hand, an unfavourable attitude prevails among people of whom many have possibilities of high incomes.

At the extremes, 54 per cent of the Polish workers interviewed favored 'relatively equal incomes' as contrasted with 20 per cent of the executives. Fifty-five per cent of the latter were strongly against sharply narrowing the income gap, as compared with only 8 per cent of the manual workers. So in a Communist country, too, the struggle between the more and the less privileged is reflected in attitudes comparable to those voiced by similarly placed strata in the West. The one major difference is that in a Communist country 'both those in favor of the limitation of income scale span and those opposing it often use the traditional slogans of the left'.[3]

3. The quotations and the statistics are from an apparently as yet unpub lished report by Andrzej Malewski which is translated in part in Lebed (1959, p. 10). A more extensive report of this study may be found in Soch

Table 2 Occupation and Party Choice in Italy* (1953 – males only)

	Occupation			Farm				Workers (socio-economic level)		
	Employers professionals	Large owner	Small owner	Share tenant	Farm labor	Artisan	White collar	Middle	Upper-lower	Lower
Communist	6%	5%	4%	33%	58%	7%	5%	24%	31%	53%
Nenni Left Socialist	11	5	4	10	11	17	3	16	32	25
Saragat Right Socialist	2	5	15	3	2	15	26	12	13	3
Republican		5				4		4	1	
Christian Democrat	41	29	41	33	17	23	42	36	10	9
Liberal	22	29	10	2		4	13	4		3
Monarchist	6	14	10	8		15			5	3
Neo-Fascist (MSI)	11	9	15	11	12	15	11	4	8	3
Total per cent	99	101	99	100	100	100	100	100	100	100
(N)	(46)	(21)	(71)	(61)	(64)	(53)	(38)	(25)	(78)	(32)

* Computed by author from cards of a national opinion survey conducted by International Public Opinion Research for the MIT Center for International Studies.

The simplest explanation for this widespread pattern is simple economic self-interest. The leftist parties represent themselves as instruments of social change in the direction of equality; the lower-income groups support them in order to become economically better off, while the higher-income groups oppose them in order to maintain their economic advantages. The statistical facts can then be taken as evidence of the importance of class factors in political behavior.

This relationship between class position (as measured by education, income, status, power, occupation or property status) and political opinions or party choice is far from consistent, however. Many poor people vote conservative and some wealthy ones are Socialists or Communists. Part of the ex-

Table 3 Estimated Percentages of Persons in Different
Occupations Voting Labour or Conservative, Great Britain, 1951*

Business group	Conservative (%)	Labour (%)
Top business	80	8
Middle business	73	10
Small business	64	15
Managerial	65	19
Professional group		
Higher professional	78	6
Lower professional	52	24
White-collar group		
Higher office	63	13
Lower office	48	29
Intermediate group	41	39
Manual workers	28	51
Whole adult population	40	41

* Bonham (1954, pp. 129 and 173). The figures for the manual workers were compiled from a graph on p. 173. All figures were estimated from survey data from the British Institute of Public Opinion. The difference between the per cent secured by the two main parties and 100 per cent is accounted for by non-voters and third-party voters.

(1959). In Denmark, 'the Social Democratic Party increases monotonically in relative popularity with decreasing social status, while exactly the opposite regularity applies to the Conservatives', Svalastoga (1959, pp. 264–5).

planation of these deviations has already been pointed out: other characteristics and group affiliations such as religious belief are more salient in particular situations than high or low social and economic position. But the deviations are also a consequence of the complexity of the stratification system itself. In modern society, men are subjected to a variety of experiences and pressures which have conflicting political consequences because men have disparate positions in the class structure. Men may hold power, like some civil servants, but have a low income or status; they may enjoy high occupational prestige, like many intellectuals, but receive low incomes; they may enjoy a relatively high income, but have low social status like members of some ethnic minorities or *nouveaux riches* businessmen, and so forth. Some of their social positions may predispose them to be conservative, while others favor a more leftist political outlook. When faced with such conflicting social pressures, some men will respond more to one than to another, and therefore appear to deviate from the pattern of class voting.

These conflicting overlapping social positions probably injure the leftist lower-class-based parties more than they do the conservative right. Men are constantly struggling to see themselves favorably, and some of their status-attributes will produce a favorable self-evaluation, others a negative one. It seems logical to assume that men will arrange their impressions of their environment and themselves so as to maximize their sense of being superior to others. Thus the white-collar worker will stress the identification of white-collar work with middle-class status (a point to be discussed further later); the low-income white worker will regard himself as superior to the Negro, and so forth. A variety of evidence gathered in the course of research on social mobility indicates that those who are occupationally upwardly mobile seek to get rid of the characteristics which still link them to their past status. The man who succeeds will in fact often change his neighborhood, seek to find new, higher-status friends, perhaps leave his church for one whose members are higher in status, and also vote more conservatively. The more conservative parties have the advantage of being identified with the more prestigeful classes in the population, an asset which helps to overcome the left's appeal to the economic interests of the lower strata.

Although it is not always possible to predict whether a right or a left political direction will result from specific status-discrepancies, the concept itself points up sources of change in political values, flowing from the tensions of contradictory social positions. A discrepancy in status may even lead an old but declining upper class to be more liberal in its political orientation. For example, most observers of British politics have suggested that the emergence of Tory socialism, the willingness of British nineteenth-century conservatism to enact reforms which benefited the working class, was a consequence of the felt hostility of the old English landed aristocracy to the rising business class, which was threatening its status and power.

But although variations in the political behavior of the more privileged strata constitute one of the more fascinating problems of political analysis, the available reliable evidence which permits us to specify why people differ in their political allegiances is largely limited to the largest segments of the population, particularly workers and farmers. Public opinion surveys and studies of the voting patterns of different rural districts can deal statistically with different types of workers and farmers in ways that cannot as yet be done on a comparative international level for most sections of the urban middle and upper classes. Discussion, therefore, of variations in the political affiliations of the latter groups has been limited to American materials. This section focuses primarily on the politics of the lower and more numerous strata.

Table 4 presents a summary of the social characteristics that are related to these variations within the lower-income group, i.e. those whose standard of living ranges from poor to just adequate by local middle-class standards – most workers, working farmers, lower white-collar workers, etc. In comparing international political behavior, it is difficult to make a more precise classification.

These generalizations are made on the basis of having examined public opinion or survey data from a large number of countries including the United States, Argentina, Chile, Brazil, Canada, Australia, Japan, India, Finland, Norway, Sweden,

Higher leftist vote	Lower leftist vote
Larger cities	Smaller towns, country
Larger plants	Smaller plants
Groups with high unemployment rates	Groups with low unemployment rates
Minority ethnic or religious groups	Majority ethnic or religious groups
Men	Women
Economically advanced regions	Economically backward regions
Manual workers	White-collar workers
Specific occupations:	Specific occupations:
Miners	Servants, service workers
Fishermen	Peasant, subsistence farmers
Commercial farmers	
Sailors, longshoremen	
Forestry workers	
Less skilled workers	More skilled workers

Denmark, Germany, the Netherlands, Belgium, France, Austria, Italy, Great Britain and Hungary . . . .

Social conditions affecting left voting

Granted that a group of people is suffering from some deprivation under the existing socio-economic system, it does not automatically follow that they will support political parties aiming at social change. Three conditions facilitate such a response: effective channels of communication, low belief in the possibility of individual social mobility, and the absence of traditionalist ties to a conservative party.

Channels of communication

Perhaps the most important condition is the presence of good communications among people who have a common problem. Close personal contacts between such people further awareness of a community of interests and of the possibilities of collective

Table 4 Social Characteristics Correlated with Variations in Leftist Voting in the Lower-Income Groups within Different Countries*

* The major exceptions to some of these patterns are discussed below.

action, including political action, to solve the common problems. When informal contacts are supplemented by formal organization in trade unions, farm groups, or class political movements, with all their machinery of organizers, speakers, newspapers and so forth, political awareness will be intensified still more.

For example, Lazarsfeld has shown that membership in social or other organizations reinforces the tendency to vote Republican among upper- and middle-class people. Similarly, among the lower socio-economic groups 'only 31 per cent of those who were union members, but 53 per cent of those who were not union members voted Republican' (Lazarsfeld, Berelson and Gaudet, 1944, pp. 146–7). The greater political interest and more leftist vote of trade-union members has been documented by studies in a number of countries.[4]

We have already discussed several occupational groups which suffer from severe insecurity of income and which vote strongly leftist in different countries – one-crop farmers, fishermen, miners, sheepshearers and lumbermen. In each of these groups there was not only a strong reason for social discontent but also, as has been pointed out in detail earlier, a social structure favorable to intra-group communications and unfavorable to cross-class communications, an 'occupational community'.

4. Other studies in the United States are Campbell, Gurin and Miller (1954, p. 73). Berelson, Lazarsfeld and McPhee show that the more involved in union activities the members are the more likely they are to vote Democratic (1954, pp. 49–52). This study also shows the reinforcing effect of organization membership upon Republican votes among the middle and upper classes. Kornhauser has demonstrated that the relationship between Democratic vote and union membership holds in all sizes of community, though more strongly in the larger cities (1959).

In Britain, 66 per cent of trade-union members in Droylsden, England, in 1951 voted Labour as against 53 per cent of other employees, Campbell, Donnison and Potter (1952). Milne and Mackenzie found an even stronger relationship between union membership and Labour vote (1954, pp. 62–4); see also Benney, Gray and Pear (1956, p. 112). Data supplied by the Canadian Institute of Public Opinion Research indicate that union members give greater support to the CCF (Socialists) and the Communists than do non-unionized workers. In Germany union members are twice as likely to support the Socialist party as those workers who do not belong to any voluntary associations, Linz (1958, pp. 215, 828–30).

In contrast to such groups the service industries generally are composed of small units scattered among the well-to-do populations they serve, and their workers tend to be not only less politically active but also more conservative. The white-collar workers' well-known lack of organization and class consciousness may also be partly due to the small units in which they work and to their scattering among higher-level managerial personnel (Dreyfuss, 1952, pp. 258–64).

Two general social factors that correlate with leftist voting are size of industrial plants and size of city. We have already noted that there was a correlation between size of plant and leftist vote in German elections before 1933, a finding which was reiterated in a 1953 German survey (see Table 5). Among workers the combined Socialist and Communist vote increased with size of the plants. Twenty-eight per cent of the workers in plants with under ten workers voted left; as contrasted with 57 per cent of those in establishments of over a thousand. Similarly, the vote for the Christian Democrats and the conservative parties was smaller for each larger category of plant size. Interestingly enough, the percentage of workers preferring no party also decreased with increasing plant size, indicating both social pressure to vote left, and simply pressure to vote. The earlier study also found a relation between overall city size and leftist vote (Pratt, 1948, ch. 3).

A later German study (1955) showed that among men the leftist vote increased with size of city in every occupational group except that of people with independent means. But the increase was greatest among manual workers (see Table 5).[5] Similar results are indicated by an analysis of the election returns for Works Councils in Italy in 1954 and 1955. The larger the city and the larger the factory, the more votes received by the Communist-controlled CGIL (General Confederation of Italian Labor) in elections to Works Councils. The Communist union federation secured 60 per cent of the vote in cities with less than 40,000 population and 75 per cent in cities with over a million people. The same pattern held up when comparing union strength by size of factory for the entire

5. See also Linz (1958, p. 347). Both men and women and male workers at each skill level were more leftist in larger cities.

country, and even within most specific industries. For example, in the textile industry, the Communist-controlled union secured 29 per cent of the vote in plants employing fifty to a hundred people (the smallest size reported for this industry) and 79 per cent in plants employing over 2000.[6]

The same relationship between size of community and party choice is to be found in France, Australia and the United States (Centers, 1949, pp. 58, 185–90; Ennis, 1952).[7] The Australian Gallup Poll isolates the responses of those living in mining communities from those living in other smaller communities and finds, as should be anticipated, that the 'isolated' miners are less likely to back middle-class-based parties than are manual workers in large cities (see Table 6). These Australian data further show that, although the skilled workers were less likely to vote Labour than the semi- and unskilled workers, both groups voted Labour more heavily in the large cities than in the small ones.

In all these cases the communications factor may be involved. A large plant makes for a higher degree of intra-class communication and less personal contact with people on higher economic levels. In large cities social interaction is also more likely to be within economic classes. In certain cases the working-class districts of large cities have been so thoroughly organ-

6. For detailed statistical breakdowns of specific cities and plants see *L'Avanzata della C I S L, nelle commissioni interne* (Confederazione Italiana Sindacati Lavoratori, 1955, pp. 46–95). This report was prepared by an anti-Communist labor federation. The categories in which data are given for size of factories for each industry vary from industry to industry so that it was impossible to add the data to get an overall statistic. However, the differences are consistent, and the report in any case does not give all the returns for the entire country. A number of British factory studies by the Acton Society Trust have reported a 'clear relationship . . . between size and sick-leave; between size and the number of accidents . . .' and various other indices of worker morale (Acton Society Trust, 1953); *Size and Morale, II* (1957). Somewhat comparable American findings are reported in Cleland (1955).

7. Epstein demonstrates that in Wisconsin gubernatorial elections, the Democratic vote increased consistently with size of city (1956). Masters and Wright show that though workers are distinctly less inclined to vote Democratic in small cities than in large ones, people in the managerial group tend to vote Republican in the same degree regardless of the size of the city they live in (1958).

ized by working-class political movements that the workers live in a virtual world of their own, and it is in these centers that the workers are the most solidly behind leftist candidates, and, as we have already seen, vote most heavily.

Table 5 Percentage of Male Workers Voting for Different Parties, by Size of City and Size of Plant (Germany – 1955*)

Size of city	Percentage of Socialist and Communist votes	(N)
Less than 2000	43	(453)
2000–10,000	46	(587)
10,000–100,000	51	(526)
More than 100,000	54	(862)

(Germany – 1953)†

Party choice	Size of plant				
	Under 10 workers	10–49 workers	50–299 workers	300–999 workers	Over 1000 workers
Socialist and Communist‡	28	40	45	45	57
Christian Democrat	22	20	18	22	15
Bourgeois Parties	21	16	13	7	5
No Party	26	22	23	22	15
Total	97	98	99	96	92
(N)	(134)	(116)	(163)	(124)	(130)

* EMNID. *Zur Resonanz der Parteien bei Männer und Frauen in den Soziologischen Gruppen* (Bielefeld: mimeographed, no date), p. 4.

† Computed by author from cards supplied by the UNESCO Institute at Cologne, Germany.

‡ Less than 2 per cent Communist.

Table 6 Size of Community and Workers' Party Preference in Australia – 1955*

Party choice	Community size					
	Large cities		Small cities		Mining communities†	
	Skilled workers	Semi- and unskilled workers	Skilled workers	Semi- and unskilled workers	Skilled workers	Semi- and unskilled workers
Liberal	35	19	44	29	15	17
Labour	64	81	56	71	77	83
Total	99	100	100	100	92	100
(N)	(333)	(241)	(96)	(107)	(13)	(6)

* Computed from I B M cards of a 1955 election survey conducted by the Australian Gallup Poll and kindly supplied to the author for further analysis.

† The number of cases is, of course, too small to justify any inferences from one sample, but previous surveys show comparable results. For example, a survey of the 1951 electorate indicates that twelve out of thirteen manual workers living in mining towns were Labour voters.

‡ One respondent preferred one of the minor parties.

References

ACTON SOCIETY TRUST (1953a), *Size and Morale*, Acton.
ACTON SOCIETY TRUST (1953b) *The Worker's Point of View*, Acton.
ACTON SOCIETY TRUST (1957), *Size and Morale II*, Acton.
BENNEY, M., GRAY, A. P., and PEAR, R. H. (1956), *How People Vote: A Study of Electoral Behaviour in Greenwich*, Routledge & Kegan Paul.
BERELSON, B., LAZARSFELD. P. F., and MCPHEE, W. M. (1954), *Voting*, University of Chicago Press.
BONHAM, J. (1954), *The Middle-Class Vote*, Faber.
CAMPBELL, A., GURIN, G., and MILLER, W. E. (1954), *The Voter Decides*, Row, Peterson.
CAMPBELL, P., DONNISON, D., and POTTER, A. (1952), 'Voting behaviour in Droylesden in October 1951', *J. Manchester School Econ. Soc. Stud.*, no. 20, p. 63.
CENTERS, R. (1949), *The Psychology of Social Classes*, Princeton University Press.
CLELAND, S. (1955), *The Influence of Plant Size on Industrial Relations*, Princeton University Press.
DREYFUSS, C. (1952), 'Prestige grading: a mechanism of control', in R. K. Merton (ed.), *Reader in Bureaucracy*, Free Press.

DUVERGER, M. (1952), 'Public opinion and political parties in France', *Amer. polit. Sci. Rev.*, vol. 46, pp. 1069–78.

DUVERGER, M. (1954), *Political Parties*, Methuen.

ENNIS, P. (1952), 'Contextual factors in voting decisions', in W. M. McPhee (ed.), *Progress Report of the 1950 Congressional Voting Study*, Columbia University.

EPSTEIN, L. (1956), 'Size of place and the division of the two-party vote in Wisconsin', *Western Polit. Q.*, vol. 9, p. 141.

KORNHAUSER, R. (1959), 'Some determinants of union membership', Institute of Industrial Relations, Berkeley.

LAZARSFELD, P. F., BERELSON, B., and GAUDET, H. (1944), *The People's Choice*, Duell & Pearce.

LEBEDZ, L. (1959), *Sociology and Communism 1957–1958*, Soviet Survey.

LINZ, J. (1958), *The Social Bases of German Politics*, unpublished Ph.D. thesis, Columbia University.

MACIVER, R. M. (1947), *The Web of Government*, Macmillan Co.

MASTERS, N. A., and WRIGHT, D. S. (1958), 'Trends and variations in the two-party vote: the case of Michigan', *Amer. polit. Sci. Rev.*, vol. 52, pp. 1088.

MILNE, R. S., MACKENZIE, H. C. (1954), *Straight Fight: A Study of voting in the constituency of Bristol North-East at the General Election of 1951*, The Hansard Society.

PARSONS, T. (1959), 'Voting and the equilibrium of the American political system', in E. Burdick and A. Brodbeck (eds.), *American Voting Behaviour*, Free Press.

PRATT, S. (1948), *The Social Basis of Nazism and Communism in Urban Germany*, unpublished M.A. thesis, Michigan State University.

SHILS, E. (1954), 'Authoritarianism: right and left', in R. Christie and M. Jahoda (eds.), *Studies in the Scope and Method of The Authoritarian Personality*, Free Press.

SOCHA, Z. (1959), 'Attitudes towards egalitarianism', *Przeglaad Kulturalny*, no. 3, p. 333.

STOETZEL, J. (1955), 'Voting behaviour in France', *Brit. J. Soc.*, vol. 4, pp. 118–19.

SVALASTOGA, K. (1959), *Prestige, Class and Mobility*, Scandinavian Universities Press.

Part Four Conflict and Change

The problem of conflict and change is the least amenable to rigorous replicable research methods which will yield reliable generalizations. As a result there are many studies of very different character which show the multiplicity of possible approaches to the study of change as a conception of conflict or in which conflict in a specific society becomes virtually stable or a chronic condition. The work of Allardt concerns precisely a case of this last kind, which is included, along with some fairly precise and conclusive results, in a series of investigations on the emergence of the 'culture of opposition'.

Gramsci is perhaps the Marxist theorist who has made the greatest effort to renovate Marx's contributions outside the field of economics and to reduce them to logical propositions. He has done this, on the one hand, by giving more importance to cultural factors in the organization of revolutionary movements and to the transmission of their values, and on the other hand by singling out potentially revolutionary situations which are not strictly determined by economic conditions. Such situations may be called 'organic crises'.

Fanon's writings bear on conditions in developing countries. But his doctrines have been widely diffused, affecting recent movements of the radical Left in Europe and America. What is of interest to this discussion is his analysis of the institutional erosion of traditional revolutionary movements and his evaluation of the force exercised by peasant violence in effecting social and political change.

Amongst all the recent events that have taken place in advanced industrial countries it is May 1968 in France which has brought us closest to the notion we have of revolution. The subsequent debate in France has analysed a great many aspects of the situation but perhaps the most interesting line that has emerged is that put forward by Alain Touraine. This conception puts it in the context of changes in the structure of advanced industrial economies. In a system in which knowledge has become a factor of production, the students, as 'production workers', can be regarded as analogous to the working class of the last century.

This idea of political revolution is comparatively recent, and so is that of revolutionary movements and parties. In 'Revolution of the saints' Walzer shows how the Puritans can be regarded as the first organized revolutionaries of the modern world. But the most stimulating part of his work is the demonstration that religion plays a part in the formulation of a new conception of politics. The politics of the 'instruments of God' are defined as concerned with non-negotiable ends. Walzer gives a completely new point of view, taking up the problem of Tocqueville in the first Reading in this anthology, and presents a fitting commentary on the conclusions set out in the general introduction.

20 Erik Allardt

Types of Protests

Excerpt from Erik Allardt, 'Types of protests and alienation', in
Erik Allardt and Stein Rokkan (eds.), *Mass Politics*, Free Press, 1970,
pp. 45–57.

A basic paradigm

Two basic characteristics of any collectivity, society or group,
are (1) that there is some degree of pressure toward uniformity,
and (2) that there is some division of labor in the collectivity.
Throughout the history of sociology a core theoretical problem
has been to analyse how these two variables explain solidarity
and conflict. It has, however, been pointed out that there are
considerable difficulties in combining theories about pressure
toward uniformity with theories about division of labor (Davis,
1963). The same has been said about solidarity and conflict. It
has been contended that there are difficulties in developing theories that would render good explanations of both solidarity
and conflict (Lipset, 1959). A major point of departure here is
that this position is too pessimistic.

There is, to be sure, also conflicting empirical evidence regarding in particular the relationship between pressure toward
uniformity and solidarity and conflict. Notably within the field
of small group research it has often been shown how group
solidarity and pressure toward uniformity are positively related.
On the other hand, political sociologists dealing with large-scale
and highly industrialized societies have been apt to stress an
almost contrary result: they have emphasized crisscrossing
cleavages and the variety of interests as conditions for solidarity
(Lipset, 1960).

The results stressing the positive relationship between pressure toward uniformity and solidarity have been summarized
and formalized in Festinger's theory on social comparison processes. In small group research the term solidarity is usually
replaced by the term cohesion, and cohesion is usually defined

in terms of the attraction of members to the group. The wish to stay or leave the group is often used as a good indicator of this attraction. In any case, Festinger's central notion is that the individual strives to compare himself with others as regards his abilities and opinions; therefore, situations in which comparisons are possible are attractive. The more uniform the individuals are in their opinions and abilities, the greater the possibility of comparisons. Consequently, the more uniformity in the group, the more attractive it is, and, accordingly, when cohesion is defined through attraction, the more uniformity, the more cohesion in a social group (1954).

An examination of the empirical evidence Festinger cites for his theory indicates that he almost always refers to groups which are very undifferentiated. His theory is not verified in groups requiring a high degree of differentiation such as work groups with a clearcut division of labor. On the contrary, dissimilarity seems to increase cohesion (Turk, 1965). This is even more evident when studying total and differentiated societies; in them strong pressures toward uniformity seem to make for a decrease in solidarity.

Of course, cohesion in small groups and solidarity in large-scale societies have to be defined somewhat differently. The wish to stay or leave the group, used as an indicator for attraction is hardly useful in the study of solidarity in total society. A citizen cannot withdraw from his society in the same way as he can withdraw from a small group or from an association. Solidarity with a society may be defined through the concept of legitimacy. Solidarity prevails as long as people believe that the sociopolitical system of their society is legitimate, or do not act in order to change the system through non-institutionalized means. If solidarity is defined in this fashion then, of course, legitimacy conflicts are simply the obverse of solidarity. The relation between solidarity and conflicts other than those related to legitimacy has to be studied empirically, and such conflicts may very well increase solidarity.

In any case, it seems that Festinger has derived his propositions by excluding one important form of social processes, namely the phenomenon Homans labels *human exchange*. The activities or goods exchanged can, of course, be of many kinds.

One can exchange love, respect, protection, as well as material goods. Of crucial importance here are such exchange relations in which the goods or items exchanged are of many different kinds. There are certainly many situations in which individuals explicitly or implicitly compare themselves with dissimilar persons. In such a situation the question phrased by Homans is apt to arise: does a person's reward for the exchange correspond to his costs and investments? Two persons may help each other precisely because they have strongly dissimilar skills. In such a situation the comparison may focus on the question of whether the Other is able to give as much in exchange as Person gives, but the point is that their behavior may be far from similar or uniform (1961). It is only as regards the result, the ability to match the other in rewards given, that they have to be similar. The exchange of dissimilar items is what we usually call a situation of division of labor. In fact, it seems as if Festinger's main proposition can be applied only to situations where there is no or very little exchange or differentiation within the group. We may, therefore, reformulate Festinger's proposition: when there is a small amount of exchange or division of labor, then the more the uniformity, the stronger the cohesion (or solidarity).

When exchange relations dominate and rewards are principally obtained through exchange of dissimilar activities and goods, the situation is entirely different. Apparently what really counts in an exchange relation is the outcome, the fact that the rewards exchanged between two persons roughly correspond to each other. The question is, what other kinds of behavior are likely to be educed from groups in which there is a great amount of exchange. Since the outcome is what counts, and this can be obtained through an exchange of dissimilar things and goods, some tolerance towards dissimilarity has to be developed. Exchange relations can hardly persist unless people are willing to grant each other great personal freedom. Tolerance toward deviance has to be developed. Therefore, pressures toward uniformity are likely to result in a decrease in the attraction to a situation or a group. We may conclude: the greater the amount of exchange in a group and the less the uniformity, the stronger the cohesion (or solidarity).

The distinction between solidarity through uniformity and

solidarity through variety leads to Durkheim's theory on the division of labor (1960). Durkheim's basic idea is that mechanical solidarity rests on what he calls likeness, whereas organic solidarity is due to the division of labor. A society with mechanical solidarity is held together mainly through normative coercion; deviants are severely punished, and penal, repressive law is important. With increasing division of labor, restitutive law regulating relations of exchange comes into the foreground. The necessity to punish deviants diminishes, and as a consequence, men are willing to grant each other more freedom and equality.

Durkheim's analysis can be seen as resting on the association between three major variables: the degree of solidarity, the degree of pressure toward uniformity and the degree of division of labor. A slight reformulation of Durkheim is, of course, needed. Instead of saying, as Durkheim does, that mechanical solidarity is based on similarity and organic solidarity is based on the division of labor, we can assume that they are two separate variables that can be used together to explain both types of solidarity. Durkheim speaks of uniformity or similarity, but the crucial variable seems to be pressure toward uniformity, as is also indicated by his stress on penal law and punishments. The two independent variables, pressure toward uniformity and division of labor, are theoretical terms and need, of course, a specification when used in empirical studies. As a preliminary and theoretical definition, we may state that division of labor is defined in terms of the number of dissimilar items for exchange: the higher the number of items for exchange, the greater the division of labor. Strong pressure toward uniformity may be defined as having two necessary conditions: (a) existing social norms are specific and related to strong sanctions that are applied with great consistency, and (b) there are no or very few conflicts between norms.

Durkheim not only speaks of the conditions that increase solidarity, but he also mentions situations in which solidarity is weak or lacking. It is perhaps significant for Durkheim that he deals with exceptions as if they were mainly exceptions to organic solidarity. As long as one treats pressure toward uniformity and division of labor as separate variables, it is logical to think of two types of low or weak solidarity, as indicated in the typology of Figure 1.

	division of labor	
	low	high
strong	1. strong solidarity: situation of mechanical solidarity	2. weak solidarity
weak	3. weak solidarity	4. strong solidarity: situation of organic solidarity

pressure toward uniformity

Figure 1

Since solidarity is defined as the obverse of legitimacy conflicts, we may reformulate the contents of the table in the following propositions:

1. The less developed the division of labor and the stronger the pressure toward uniformity, the less the likelihood of legitimacy conflicts.

2. The less developed the division of labor and the weaker the pressure toward uniformity, the greater the likelihood of legitimacy conflicts.

3. The more developed the division of labor and the stronger the pressure toward uniformity, the greater the likelihood of legitimacy conflicts.

4. The more developed the division of labor and the weaker the pressure toward uniformity, the less the likelihood of legitimacy conflicts.

By presenting this crude typology it is by no means maintained that the degree of solidarity is influenced only by our independent variables. The expansion of the typology can be pursued in two major ways. One alternative is to introduce new variables into the typology, whereby the number of major types would greatly increase. Another way is to show that a number of specific situations are really special cases of the major types.

Partly due to the empirical data available, the latter alternative is here judged to be more fruitful.

The two independent variables are of course not very easy to operationalize. In studies of total societies the degree of division of labor can be measured in a number of ways. For gross comparisons between societies and communities, the degree of industrialization or indices of economic development may be taken as sufficiently precise indicators.

Pressure toward uniformity is a more difficult concept to operationalize, and it seems also difficult to find an overall indicator useful in different social systems.[1] It is however, possible to indicate types of societies and communities in which the pressure toward uniformity may be regarded as particularly strong:

1. Tribal societies. Many, if not all, tribal societies can be characterized as having strictly enforced and severe social norms. There are non-specialized and diffuse pressures directed toward large, rather vaguely defined categories of ascriptive statuses (Himmelstrand, 1966).

2. Brutal dictatorships.

3. Societies strongly stratified according to social class or social rank. In such societies lower-class individuals are hindered by class barriers to indulge in social exchange. Inequalities of an economic nature, thus, are subsumed under factors which make for a strong pressure toward uniformity. Economic factors relate to our model in two ways. The overall economic output is one aspect of the division of labor whereas the distributive process is accounted for by the pressure toward uniformity.

4. Societies in which constraints are particularly imposed on groups that earlier have had a good social position. There may be, for instance, middle-class groups that are losing in status and rank because other groups have become more powerful. They are likely to experience constraints imposed on them, and they will tend to develop aggressive political attitudes. As in case 3, however, the pressure toward uniformity is strong only for a part of the population.

1. It has been indicated by Heiskanen (1967) that pressure toward uniformity always has to be specified according to the substantive system under investigation.

An empirical illustration: industrial and backwoods radicalism

Finnish political life, and particularly the strength of the Communist movement in Finland, provides a good case for testing the propositions derived from the basic paradigm. The Finnish Communist movement has had a rather heavy mass support. During the period after the Second World War, the Communists have received between 20·0 and 23·5 per cent of the total vote in national elections. Furthermore the Finnish working-class vote has been almost equally divided between the Communists and the Social Democrats.

Although caution is necessary, it is reasonable to say that the Communist vote during the 1950s more strongly indicated a protest against the system than the votes for other parties. It is, however, hardly so that the Finnish Communist voters regard the whole Finnish sociopolitical system as illegitimate (Torgerson, 1967). Rather they are apt to accept the political system, whereas some aspects of the economic system as well as certain administrative bodies are foci of protest and discontent. Survey studies indicate that a much greater proportion of the Communists than, for instance, the Social Democrats express discontent of an economic nature. Likewise, a greater proportion of the Communists than of the Social Democratic voters also express discontent with the administrative leadership in Finnish society, with the courts, with the Armed Forces, and so forth. This is particularly true for 1950s, the period covered by the findings used in this paper (Allardt, 1964). In any case, the Communist vote reflects a certain type of protest, which may be formulated so that the Communist voters more often than others are questioning the legitimacy of the Finnish sociopolitical system. When studying conditions of societal solidarity it is therefore fruitful to study the social sources of Communist support and to compare it with the support of other parties having a large lower-class vote.

In popular Finnish political terminology, Communist support is often described in terms that are clearly related to one of our independent variables, namely to division of labor. The Communism in the southern and western parts of Finland is often labeled *Industrial Communism* whereas the Communism in the north and the east is known as *Backwoods Communism*. As the names suggest, Industrial Communism exists in regions which are industrialized and developed whereas Backwoods Communism is concentrated in less developed, rural regions. The problem here is to specify under what conditions Industrial and Backwoods Communism are strong. Their background is, of course, different as regards the degree of industrialization in the communities in which these two forms of Communism exist but the question is whether there are also other differences.

The social background of these two kinds of radicalism have been studied both through survey studies and ecological research. The data units in the ecological analyses have been the 550 communes in the country. The communes, both the rural and urban ones, are the smallest administrative units in Finland, and they have a certain amount of self-government. Primarily because of the long historical tradition of local self-government, the communes form natural areas in the sense that the communes are important for people's identification of themselves. The communes are also the territorial units for which statistical data are easiest to obtain. In the analyses a file of seventy quantitative ecological variables referring to conditions in communes in the 1950s were used as a starting point (Allardt and Riihinen, 1966).

In analysing the data, factor analysis was used primarily, although the correlation matrices reveal from the start many consistent patterns. Because a single factor analysis is not always interesting – it gives just a structure or a conceptual framework – the communes were divided into five groups. For each of the five groups of communes (called communities) in what follows, separate correlational and factor analyses were done. Of the five groups, three represented the more developed regions in southern and western Finland, and two the more backward regions in northern and eastern Finland:

Groups of developed communities

1. Cities and towns.

2. Rural communities with a Swedish speaking population along the southern and western coast of Finland.

3. Rural communities in southern and western Finland.

4. Rural communes in eastern Finland.

5. Rural communes in northern Finland.

The intention of making separate analyses for the five different regions was to inquire whether Communist voting strength is explained by different or similar background factors in different regions (Allardt, 1964).

The comparisons of the findings for the five regions reveal some quite consistent patterns. The background factors of Communist strength in the three developed regions are very similar, and so are the background factors in the two less-developed regions. However, the background factors in Communist strength in the developed regions, on the one hand, and in the backward regions, on the other, seem to be very different.

In the developed regions the Communists are strong in communities in which

1. *Political traditions* are strong. This is indicated mainly by the fact that the Communists tend to get a heavy vote in those communities in which there are stable voting patterns.

2. *Economic change* is comparatively slow. This is mainly indicated by the fact that communities with a strong Communist support have had a rather slow rise in per capita income during the 1950s. These communities were modernized and industrialized in an earlier period.

3. *Social security* is comparatively high. The communities with a heavy Communist vote are those in which there is no or very little unemployment and those in which the standard of housing is high.

4. *Migration both into and out of the communities is small.* The communities with a heavy Communist vote have a very stable population.

The foregoing are the conditions prevailing in those developed communities in which the Communists get a heavy vote. When focusing on the background factors of Communist strength in the less developed and more backward communities, a very different pattern is revealed. In the more backward communities the Communist vote is heavy when:

1. *Traditional values* such as the religious ones, have recently declined in importance.

2. *Economic change is rapid.* In the backward regions the Communists are strong in those communities which have had a considerable rise in the per capita income during the 1950s and weak in those communities in which the income rise has been small.

3. *Social insecurity prevails.* Communities with Communist strength are those in which unemployment has been common. It may be said that unemployment in Finland is mainly a question of agrarian underemployment. Unemployment strikes those who are both small farmers and lumberjacks.

4. *Migration is heavy.* There is heavy migration both into and out of the communities.

While the Communist strength in the developed regions, the so-called Industrial Communism, seems to be associated with background factors reflecting stability, almost the contrary is true for Backwoods Communism. It is strong under conditions of instability and change.

Observations of particular strongholds in the developed and in the backward communities strongly support the results of the statistical analysis. The strongest Communist centers in the developed regions are towns that industrialized comparatively early. They are often towns in which one or a few shops completely dominate the community. Some of the communities voting most heavily Communist in rural Finland are located in Finland's northernmost province of Lapland. These communities are usually those in which there are many indications of a rapid modernization process.

In order to correctly assess the social background of Industrial and Backwoods Communism, it is important to observe also the background factors of the voting strength of the main competitors of the Communists. The Social Democrats are the competitors for the working-class vote in the more developed regions in southern and western Finland. In the backwoods of the north and the east, however, the Agrarians are the ones who compete with the Communists for the lower-class vote. The data and the finding clearly indicate that the Social Democrats in the south and in the west, on the one hand, and that the Agrarians in the north and the east, are strong in clearly different communities than the Communists. In the developed regions the Social Democrats are strong in towns and industrial centers undergoing rapid change and having a high amount of migration. In fact, workers who move from the countryside to the cities much more often vote Social Democratic than Communist. As has been shown, the Communists have their strength in communities with little migration. In the backward regions the Agrarians are strong in the most stable, the most traditional and the most backward communities. There are strong indications that a Communist vote in the more backward regions is a symptom of modernization. A switch of the vote from the Agrarians to the Communists is also a switch from traditional, particularistic loyalties to a more universalistic form of political thinking. In northern and eastern Finland the breakdown of regional barriers and loyalties is clearly associated with a tendency to vote Communist.

The results can be summarized in terms of our simple theoretical model. The conditions associated with Communist support in the developed regions reflect hindrances of movement, strong group ties and strong social pressures. Most of the crucial conditions related to Industrial Communism reflect, directly or indirectly, some kind of hindrances to people in using their resources and abilities. Strong political traditions, slow economic change and a small amount of migration can all be taken as indicators for strong pressures toward uniformity. In the backward regions the contrary is true. Radicalism is strong in those communities in which the social constraints are weak. The decline in traditional values, rapid economic change, social insecurity and a high amount of migration can all be interpreted as indicators of a low pressure toward uniformity. Accordingly, the findings fit very well into the fourfold table (see Figure 2).

Protests and reference groups:
institutionalized and diffuse deprivation

The theoretical model presented can be used for further explorations of the different kinds of protest displayed by Industrial and Backwoods Communism. According to the model, cells 2 and 3 describe situations in which people are apt to feel discontent and deprivation. There is also a likelihood for legitimacy conflicts in these situations. The political effects of the discontent will presumably depend very much on who the discontented compare themselves with. This leads to a consideration of the concept of reference group – a tricky concept

	division of labor	
	low	high
strong	1. mechanical solidarity: heavy agrarian vote	3. industrial communism
weak	2. backwoods communism	4. organic solidarity: heavy social democratic vote

pressure toward uniformity

Figure 2

because as we know, it has many denotations. Of these denotations, however, two seem to be crucial. On the one hand, a person's reference group is the group with which he identifies himself and from which he obtains his social norms and standards for social perception: this is his *normative reference group*. On the other hand, the term also refers to a group with which a person compares himself when he evaluates his status and his rewards: this is his *comparison reference group*. These two kinds of reference groups cannot always be empirically separated because the group for identification and the group for comparison often seem to be the same. In Festinger's theory of social comparisons it is assumed, for instance, that the two kinds of reference groups usually coincide because a person tries to be similar to those to whom he is comparing himself. It is obvious, however, that these two kinds of reference groups do not always coincide, and that we need a specification of the conditions under which the group for identification and the group for comparison are the same, different or altogether absent.

It goes without saying that there are many kinds of groups that may function as foci for identification and comparison. The groups relevant here are those related to a person's social status and the evaluation of his rewards. In modern industrialized societies social classes or strata are presumably most often used when a person either tries to justify the reward he gets or tries to evaluate whether his rewards are just or unjust. In any case, when speaking here of normative and comparison reference groups they denote groups identifiable in a total society, such as classes or strata.

It will be argued that the two major kinds of reference groups tend to coincide in situations of mechanical and organic solidarity, whereas this is not the case in the two situations of weak solidarity.

In a society of mechanical solidarity the satisfaction of individuals and their ability to predict the behavior of others is mainly produced through similarity and strong attachment to specific social norms. Outgroups and, accordingly also, alternative comparison groups are simply not available. As a result the groups for identification and for comparison tend to be the same. We may summarize:

5. The less developed the division of labor and the stronger the pressure toward uniformity (mechanical solidarity), the more the normative and the comparison reference groups tend to be the same.

In a society of organic solidarity, individual satisfaction and also ability to predict how other people behave is obtained mainly through intensive social exchange of items of many different kinds. People will be satisfied if they are hindered as little as possible in exchanging rewards. They compare their rewards and inputs with those with whom they are in exchange, and they tend to regard their exchange partners as norm-senders. In a summary form:

6. The more developed the division of labor and the weaker the pressure toward uniformity (organic solidarity), the more the normative and the comparison reference groups tend to be the same.

In a situation of high division of labor and strong pressure toward uniformity, there exists a rather high amount of social exchange but it is inhibited in many ways. The potentialities for a free exchange are hindered for instance by class and race barriers. Usually there will exist a very clear demarcation line between the rulers and the ruled. This is also the situation, described by Marx, in which the proletariat develops class-consciousness and clearly realizes its special position. Intraclass communication becomes strong, whereas interclass communication declines. In more general terms, people will tend to feel closely tied to their own group, whereas they compare themselves to members from other groups in evaluating their rewards. In summary form:

7. The more developed the division of labor and the stronger the pressure toward uniformity, the more people will tend to have distinct normative and comparison reference groups, and the more the normative and comparison reference groups will tend to be different.

If the situation described by proposition 7 prevails for a longer period of time, the deprivation felt because the rewards received are experienced as unjust will become institutionalized. Groups with a history of being deprived will tend to socialize their younger members to experience relative deprivation. The result can be labeled *institutionalized relative deprivation*.

The situation of low division of labor and weak pressure toward uniformity (cell 2) also leads to deprivation but of an entirely different kind. The division of labor is undifferentiated, and the individuals have few opportunities for the social exchange of rewards of different kinds. At the same time the social constraints are weak, and the individuals will experience difficulties in predicting the behavior of others. They have, so to speak, neither social norms nor the wishes to rely on. The result is that groups both f comparison tend to be lacking. In this situa feels deprived because he cannot find relevant The result can be labeled *diffuse deprivation*. A

8. The less developed the division of labor and pressure toward uniformity, the less the likelihoo ple have relevant normative and comparison reference ups.

Some specific behavior patterns are likely to be found in situations of institutionalized relative deprivation as well as in situations of diffuse deprivation. In situations of institutionalized relative deprivation, one can expect a high amount of social participation and organizational activities. The individuals are strongly tied to their communities and social classes but are isolated from the total national community. Social participation tends to be planned and instrumental.

In situations of diffuse deprivation, one may expect a low level of organizational activity. Political participation, if high, can be expected to be expressive and momentary. The individuals are isolated not only from the national community but also as individuals.

Backwoods and industrial radicalism as illustrations of diffuse and institutionalized deprivation

The relationship between the two forms of radicalism and the two types of deprivation can be substantiated by at least three independent observations of the Finnish Communist movement:

1. The Communists in the developed communities in the southern and western parts of the country have an efficient organizational network. According to the studies of some particular cities in the more developed parts of Finland, it appears that there is a network of Communist organizations that corresponds to the national network of all associations and voluntary organizations. The Communist network performs for its members the same social functions as the national network for citizens in general. There are women's clubs, sports associations, children's clubs and so on. The situation is on this count

in the north and the east. It is true that the population in the northern and eastern parts of the country has become politically alerted since the Second World War. This increase in the political consciousness is mainly displayed only during elections. It has not displayed itself as a general increase in social and intellectual participation. The Communist support in the north and the east is concentrated in groups in which the opportunities for social and intellectual participation are slight. A nation-wide study of youth activities shows that the young Communist voters in the north and the east belong to the most passive in the country as far as general social participation is concerned (Littunen, 1960).

2. Many observations of the Communist centers in the developed regions of the south and the west show how the Communist alternative in the elections is the conventional and respectable one. The Communist voters in these communities are well integrated in their communities and stable in their jobs. The population, and notably the Communist voters, in backward regions in the northern and eastern parts of Finland are in an entirely different position. This is already clear from the settlement patterns in the north and the east compared to the south and the west. Whereas life in the latter region has been always much more village-centered, the houses and farms in the north and the east have always been more isolated. Many of the Communist voters are small farmers who have to work as forestry workers in the winter. Unemployment in Finland has mainly the character of agrarian underemployment and this seasonal unemployment is particularly strong in those northern and eastern communities in which the Communists receive a heavy support. Today work for the unemployed is provided by the Government but it means that the unemployed have to leave their homes and communities for longer periods. In any case, whereas the Communist voters in the developed regions are strongly tied to their communities, the Communist supporters in the north and the east are much more migratory. This observation is also supported by the results from factor analysis in which a great amount of migration was characteristic for communities with a heavy Communist vote.

3. According to survey findings, the Communist voters in the more developed regions are the first to decide how to vote during election campaigns. Among the Communist voters in the north and the east, however, there is a very high proportion of voters who make their decision at the last minute. According to a national survey in 1958, as many as 82 per cent of the Communist voters in the south and the west have made their voting decisions at least two months before the elections while only 56 per cent of the Communist voters in the north and the east made their decision at that early moment. The latter was the lowest percentage in all groups established on the basis of party and geographical area.

The difference between Backwoods and Industrial Radicalism can be now summarized.

Backwoods radicalism	*Industrial radicalism*
Exists in communities of low division of labor and weak pressure toward uniformity	Exists in communities of high division of labor and strong pressure toward uniformity
Diffuse deprivation	Institutionalized deprivation
Low organizational and social participation	High organizational and social participation
High expressive political participation	High instrumental political participation
Loosely integrated into their communities	Strongly integrated into their local communities
Isolated as individuals from groups	Strongly tied to their social class but isolated from the total national community

Descriptions of the social background of radical movements on the Left resemble closely those given here as related to Backwoods Radicalism. In particular, this seems to be true for those findings and propositions usually subsumed under the label of the theory of mass society. According to this theory, the supporters of radical movements are usually described as uprooted and without ties to secondary groups which in turn would bind the individuals to the community or society at large (Kornhauser, 1959). This description goes for Backwoods Radicalism, but it does not offer an explanation of Industrial

Radicalism. Traditional Marxist theory, on the other hand, seems to render a good explanation of Industrial Radicalism. As stated before, Industrial Radicalism is characteristic for situations in which the proletariat already has developed a clear class-consciousness and in which intraclass communication is high but interclass communication low. The communities in which Industrial Radicalism is strong have polarized class conflicts, and very much of a two-class situation, as is assumed in traditional Marxist theory (Bottomore and Rubel, 1956).

References

ALLARDT, E. (1964), 'Patterns of class conflict and working-class consciousness in Finland', in E. Allardt and Y. Littunen (eds.), *Cleavages, Ideologies and Party Systems*, Westermarck Press.

ALLARDT, E., and RIIHINEN, O. (1966), 'Files for aggregate data by territorial units for Finland', in S. Rokkan (ed.), *Data Archives for Social Sciences*, Mouton.

BOTTOMORE, T. B., and RUBEL, M. (eds.) (1956), *Karl Marx: Selected Writings in Sociology and Social Philosophy*, Watts.

DAVIS, J. S. (1963), 'Structural balance, mechanical solidarity and interpersonal relations', *Amer. J. Soc.*, vol. 67, pp. 444–62.

DURKHEIM, E. (1960), *The Division of Labor*, trans. G. Simpson, Free Press.

FESTINGER, L. (1954), 'A theory of social comparison processes', *Hum. Rel.*, vol. 7, pp. 117–40.

HEISKANEN, V. S. (1967), *Social Structure, Family Patterns and Interpersonal Influence*, Transactions of the Westermarck Soc., vol. 14, p. 17.

HOMANS, G. C. (1961), *Social Behavior: Its Elementary Forms*, Harcourt, Brace & World.

HIMMELSTRAND, U. (1966), 'Conflict, conflict resolution and nation-building in the transition from tribal "mechanical" solidarities to the "organic" solidarity of modern (or future) multi-tribal societies', Sixth World Congress of Sociology.

KORNHAUSER, W. (1959), *The Politics of Mass Society*, Free Press.

LITTUNEN, Y. (1960), 'Activity and radicalism', *Politiikka*, vol. 2, no. 4, pp. 182–3.

LIPSET, S. M. (1959), 'Political sociology', in R. K. Merton, L. Broom and L. S. Cottrell Jr (eds.), *Sociology Today*, Basic Books.

LIPSET, S. M. (1960), 'Party systems and the representation of social groups', *European J. Soc.*, vol. 1, pp. 1–38.

TORGERSON, U. (1967), 'Samfunnsstruktur og politiska legitimitetskriser' *Tidskrift for samfunnsforskning*, vol. 8, pp. 65–77.

TURK, H., (1965), 'Social cohesion through variant values: evidence from medical role relations', *Amer. Soc. Rev.*, vol. 29, pp. 28–37.

21 Antonio Gramsci

Political Forces in 'Organic' Crises

Excerpt from Antonio Gramsci, *The Modern Prince and Other Writings*, translated by L. Marks, Lawrence & Wishart, 1968, pp. 168–76. First published in 1949.

An aspect of the same problem is the so-called question of the relations of forces. One often reads in historical narratives expressions like: 'favourable relations of forces, unfavourable to this or that tendency'. Thus, abstractly, this formulation explains nothing or almost nothing, since all it does is to repeat the fact which ought to be explained, presenting it once as a fact and once as an abstract law, as an explanation. The theoretical error consists therefore in giving a canon of research and interpretation as an 'historical cause'.

At the same time it is necessary to distinguish different stages and levels in the 'relation of forces', which fundamentally are the following:

1. A relation of social forces closely tied to the structure, objective, independent of men's will, which can be measured with the precision of the exact or physical sciences. On the basis of the level of development of the material forces of production we have social classes, each one of which represents a function and has a given position in production itself. This relation is what it is, stubborn reality: no one can change the number of factories and their workers, the number of cities with a given urban population, etc. This fundamental scheme enables us to study whether there exist in the society the necessary and sufficient conditions for its transformation, enables us, that is, to check the level of reality and attainability of the different ideologies which have come into existence on the same basis, on the basis of the contradictions which it has generated in the course of its development.

2. A late stage is the relation of political forces; that is to say, an

estimation of the degree of homogeneity, of self-consciousness and organization reached by the various social groups. This stage can be in its turn analysed and differentiated into various levels, corresponding to the different degrees of collective self-consciousness, as they have manifested themselves up to now in history. The first and most elementary is the economico-corporative stage: one trader feels that he *must* be solid with another trader, one manufacturer with another; in other words a homogeneous unity is felt, and the duty to organize it, by the professional group, but not yet by the wider social group. A second stage is that in which consciousness of the solidarity of interests among all the members of the social group is reached, but still in the purely economic field. Already at this stage the question of the state is posed, but only on the basis of reaching a politico-legal equality with the ruling group, since the right is proclaimed to share in legislation and administration and even to modify it, reform it, but inside the fundamental existing framework. A third stage is that in which consciousness is reached that one's own corporative interests, in their present and future development, transcend the corporative circle of the purely economic group, and can and must become the interests of other subordinate groups. This is the more strictly political phase, which marks the clear transition from the structure to the sphere of complex superstructures, it is the phase in which ideologies which were germinated earlier become 'party', come into opposition and enter the struggle until the point is reached where one of them or at least one combination of them, tends to predominate, to impose itself, to propagate itself throughout the whole social sphere, causing, in addition to singleness of economic and political purpose, an intellectual and moral unity as well, placing all questions around which the struggle rages not on a corporative, but a 'universal' plane and creating in this way the hegemony of a fundamental social group over a number of subordinate groups. The state is conceived, certainly, as an organism belonging to a group, destined to create the conditions favourable to the greatest expansion of that group; but this development and expansion are conceived and presented as the motive force of a universal expansion, of development of all the 'national' energies; that is to say, th ruling group is coordinated concretely with the general interests of the subordinate groups and state life is conceived as a continual formation and overcoming of unstable equilibriums (unstable within the ambit of the law), between the interests of the fundamental group and those of the subordinate groups, equilibriums in which the interests of the ruling group predominate but only up to a certain point, i.e. not as far as their mean economico-corporative interest would like.

In historical reality these stages are reciprocally mixed, horizontally and vertically so to speak – according to economic and social activities (horizontally) and according to territory (vertically), combining and splitting up differently: each one of these combinations may be represented by its own organized economic and political expression. It is also necessary to take account of the fact that international relations are interlaced with these internal relations of a nation-state, creating new, original and historically concrete combinations. An ideology, coming into existence in a more developed country, is diffused in less developed countries cutting across the local play of combinations.

This relationship between international and national forces is again complicated by the existence inside each state of several territorial sections with a different structure and a different relation of forces at all levels (thus *La Vendée* was allied with reactionary international forces and represented them inside the bosom of French territorial unity; similarly Lyons in the French Revolution represented a particular knot of relations, etc.).

3. The third stage is that of the relations of military forces, time and again immediately decisive. (Historical development oscillates continuously between the first and the third stage, with the mediation of the second.) But this also is not something indistinct and immediately identifiable in a schematic form; two levels can be distinguished: the military level in the strict or technico-military sense, and the level which can be called politico-military. In the development of history these two levels are presented in a great variety of combinations. A typical example which can serve as demonstration-limit, is that of the relation-

ship of military oppression of a state over a nation which is seeking to achieve its state independence. The relationship is not purely military, but politico-military; and, in fact, such a type of oppression would be inexplicable without a state of social disintegration among the oppressed people and the passivity of the majority; because of this, independence cannot be achieved with purely military forces, but with military and politico-military forces. If the oppressed nation, in fact, in order to begin the struggle for independence, had to wait for the hegemonic state to allow it to organize its own army in the strict and technical sense of the word, it would have to wait quite a while (it might happen that the aim of having its own army could be granted by the hegemonic nation, but this means that already a great part of the struggle has been fought and won on the politico-military plane). The oppressed nation will therefore oppose the hegemonic military force initially with a force which is only 'politico-military', that is, with a form of political action which has the virtue of causing repercussions of a military character in the sense (a) that it is effective in breaking up from the inside the war efficiency of the hegemonic nation; (b) that it obliges the hegemonic military force to dissolve and disperse itself over a large territory, nullifying the greater part of its war efficiency. In the Italian *Risorgimento* the disastrous absence of politico-military leadership can be noted, especially in the Party of Action (through congenital incapacity), but also in the Piedmontese moderate party, both before and after 1848, certainly not through incapacity, but through 'economic-political Malthusianism', or in other words because it was unwilling even to mention the possibility of agrarian reform and because it did not want the calling of a constituent national assembly, but only aimed at extending the Piedmontese monarchy, without limitations or conditions of popular origin, to the whole of Italy, solely with the sanction of regional plebiscites.

Another question connected with the preceding ones is that of seeing whether fundamental historical crises are directly caused by economic crises. The answer is contained implicitly in the preceding paragraphs, where we dealt with questions which are only another way of looking at the present one; nevertheless it is always necessary, for didactic reasons, given the particular public, to examine every way of presenting the same question as if it were an independent and new problem. It can be excluded that by themselves, economic crises directly produce fundamental events; they can only create a more favourable ground for the propagation of certain ways of thinking, of posing and solving questions which involve the whole future development of state life. For the rest, all assertions regarding periods of crisis or prosperity can give rise to one-sided judgements. Mathiez, in his review of the history of the French Revolution, opposing the popular traditional history, which 'found' *a priori* a crisis coinciding with the great breach in the social equilibrium, asserts that around 1789 the economic situation was, on the contrary, good in the short run, and that therefore one cannot say that the catastrophe of the absolute state was due to a crisis of impoverishment. It needs to be observed that the state was in the grip of a deadly financial crisis and the question arose of which of the three privileged social orders ought to bear the sacrifices and burdens in order to put the state and royal finances in order. Further: if the bourgeoisie was in a flourishing economic position, the popular classes of the cities and countryside were certainly not in a good situation, especially those who were racked by endemic poverty. In any case, the breach in the equilibrium of forces did not come about through the immediate mechanical cause of the impoverishment of the social group which had an interest in breaking the equilibrium and in fact did break it; it came about within the framework of conflicts above the immediate economic world, connected with the 'prestige' of classes (future economic interests), with an exasperation of the feeling of independence, autonomy and power. The particular question of economic malaise or health as a cause of new historical realities is a partial aspect of the question of the relations of forces in their various levels. Changes can be produced either because a situation of well-being is threatened by the selfish egotism of an opposed group, or because malaise has become intolerable and one cannot see in the old society any force which is capable of mitigating it and re-establishing normality by legal means. One can therefore say that all these elements are the concrete manifestations of the incidental fluctuations of the totality of social relations of force, on the basis of which occurs the transition of the latter, to political relations of force, culminating in the decisive military relationship.

If this process of development from one stage to the other is lacking, and it is essentially a process which has for its actors men and the will and capacity of men, the situation remains static. Contradictory conclusions can arise: the old society resists and is helped by a 'breathing space', physically exterminating the opposing elite and terrorizing the masses of reserves; or the reciprocal destruction of the conflicting forces takes place with the establishment of the peace of the graveyard, but under the watch of a foreign guard.

But the most important observation to be made about every concrete analysis of relations of forces is this: that such analyses cannot and must not be ends in themselves (unless one is writing a chapter of past history), and they only acquire significance if they serve to justify practical activity, an initiative of will. They show what are the points of least resistance where the force of will can be applied most fruitfully; they suggest immediate tactical operations; they indicate how a campaign of political agitation can best be presented, what language will be best understood by the multitudes, etc. The decisive element in every situation is the force, permanently organized and pre-ordered over a long period, which can be advanced when one judges that the situation is favourable (and it is favourable only to the extent to which such a force exists and is full of fighting ardour); therefore the essential task is that of paying systematic and patient attention to forming and developing this force, rendering it ever more homogeneous, compact, conscious of itself One sees this in military history and in the care with which at al times armies have been predisposed to begin a war at any moment. The great states have been great precisely because they were at all times prepared to enter effectively into favour able international situations, and these situations were favour able because there was the concrete possibility of effectivel entering them.

Observations on some aspects of the structure of political parties in periods of organic crisis

At a certain point in their historical life social groups detach themselves from their traditional parties; i.e. the political parties, in that given organizational form, with the particular men who constitute, represent and lead them, are no longer recognized as the proper expression of their class or fraction of a class. When these crises occur, the immediate situation becomes delicate and dangerous, since the field is open to solutions of force, to the activity of obscure powers represented by 'men of destiny' or 'divine' men.

How are these situations of opposition between 'represented and representatives' formed, situations which from the field of the parties (party organizations in the strict sense of the parliamentary-electoral field, newspaper organization), are reflected throughout the whole state organism, strengthening the relative position of power of the bureaucracy (civil and military), of high finance, of the Church, and in general of all the organisms which are relatively independent of the fluctuations of public opinion? In every country the process is different, although the content is the same. And the content is a crisis of hegemony of the ruling class, which comes about either because the ruling class has failed in some big political undertaking for which it asked, or imposed by force, the consent of the broad masses (like war), or because vast masses (especially of peasants and petty-bourgeois intellectuals) have passed suddenly from political passivity to a certain activity and put forward aims which in their disorganic complex constitute a revolution. One speaks of a 'crisis of authority' and this in fact is the crisis of hegemony, or crisis of the state in all spheres.

The crisis creates immediately dangerous situations, because the different strata of the population do not possess the same capacity for rapid reorientation or for reorganizing themselves with the same rhythm. The traditional ruling class, which has a numerous trained personnel, changes men and programmes and reabsorbs the control which was escaping it with a greater speed than occurs in the subordinate classes; it makes sacrifices, exposes itself to an uncertain future by making demagogical promises, but it maintains power, strengthens it for the moment and makes use of it in order to crush its opponent and disperse its leading personnel, which cannot be very numerous or well-trained. The transference of the effectives of many parties under the banner of a single party which better represents and embodies the needs of the entire class, is an organic and normal phenomenon, even if its rhythm is very rapid and almost like a thunderbolt in comparison with calm times: it represents the fusion of a whole social group under a single leadership which is alone considered capable of solving an existing, predominant problem and removing a mortal danger. When the crisis does not find this organic solution, but the solution of a divine leader, it means that there exists a static equilibrium (whose factors may be unequal, but in which the immaturity of the progressive forces is decisive); that no group, either conservative or progressive, has the force for victory and that even the conservative group needs a master (see *The Eighteenth Brumaire of Louis Bonaparte*).

This order of phenomena is connected with one of the most important questions relating to the political party; that is, to the capacity of the party for reacting against the spirit of habit, against the tendency to become mummified and anachronistic. Parties come into existence and are constituted organizationally in order to lead the situation in historically vital moments for their classes; but they are not always able to adapt themselves to new tasks and new periods, they are not always able to develop according to the development of the complex relations of force (and hence relative position of their classes) in the particular country or in the international field. In analysing this party development it is necessary to distinguish: the social group; the mass of the party; the bureaucracy and High Command of the party. The bureaucracy is the most dangerously habitual and conservative force; if it ends up by constituting a solid body, standing by itself and feeling independent from the masses, the party ends by becoming anachronistic, and in moments of acute crisis becomes emptied of all its social content, like an empty shell. One can see what happened to a number of German parties with the expansion of Hitlerism. The French parties are a rich field for this research: they are all mummified and anachronistic, historico-political documents of different phases of past French history, whose outworn terminology they repeat; their crisis might become even more catastrophic than that of the German parties.

Those who examine this kind of event usually forget to give a correct place to the bureaucratic, civil and military, element, and in addition, do not keep in mind the fact, that such an analysis must not only include active military and bureaucratic elements, but also the social strata from which, in the given state complex, the bureaucracy is traditionally recruited. A political movement can be of a military character even if the army as such does not openly participate in it; a government can be of a military character even if the army as such does not openly participate in it. In certain situations it can happen that it is convenient not to 'reveal' the army, not to make it step outside constitutionalism, not to bring politics among the soldiers, as it is said, in order to maintain homogeneity between officers and soldiers on a basis of apparent neutrality and superiority over factions; still it is the army, i.e. the general staff and the officers, which determines the new situation and dominates it. On the other hand, it is not true that the army, according to the constitutions, must never be political; the army must in fact defend the constitution, i.e. the legal form of the state, together with its connected institutions; therefore the so-called neutrality means only support for the reactionary side; but it is necessary, in these situations, to pose the question in this way in order to prevent the army reproducing the dissent of the country which would lead to the disappearance of the determining power of the High Command through the disintegration of the military instrument. All these observations are certainly not absolute; at different historical moments and in various countries they have very different import.

22 Frantz Fanon

Spontaneity: Its Strength and Weakness

Excerpt from Frantz Fanon, *The Wretched of the Earth*, translated by
Constance Farrington, Penguin 1967, pp. 85–94. First published in
French in 1963.

This consideration of violence has led us to take account of the
frequent existence of a time-lag, or a difference of rhythm, between the leaders of a nationalist party and the mass of the
people. In every political or trade-union organization there is a
traditional gap between the rank-and-file, who demand the total
and immediate bettering of their lot, and the leaders, who, since
they are aware of the difficulties which may be made by the
employers, seek to limit and restrain the workers' demands.
This is why you often are aware of a dogged discontentment
among the rank-and-file as regards their leaders. After a day
spent in demonstrating for their demands, the leaders celebrate
the victory, whereas the rank-and-file have a strong suspicion
that they have been cheated. It is through a multiplicity of
demonstrations in support of their claims and through an increase in trade-union demands that the rank-and-file achieve
their political education. A politically informed trade-union
member is a man who knows that a local conflict is not a decisive settlement between himself and the employers. The native
intellectuals; who have studied in their respective 'mother countries' the working of political parties, carefully organize similar
institutions in order to mobilize the masses and bring pressure
to bear on the colonial administration. The birth of nationalist
parties in the colonized countries is contemporary with the
formation of an intellectual elite engaged in trade. The elite will
attach a fundamental importance to organization, so much so
that the fetish of organization will often take precedence over a
reasoned study of colonial society. The notion of the party is a
notion imported from the mother country. This instrument of
modern political warfare is thrown down just as it is, without

the slightest modification, upon real life with all its infinite variations and lack of balance, where slavery, serfdom, barter, a skilled working class and high finance exist side by side.

The weakness of political parties does not only lie in the mechanical application of an organization which was created to carry on the struggle of the working class inside a highly industrialized, capitalist society. If we limit ourselves to the *type* of organization, it is clear that innovations and adaptations ought to have been made. The great mistake, the inherent defect in the majority of political parties in under-developed regions has been, following traditional lines, to approach in the first place those elements which are the most politically conscious: the working classes in the towns, the skilled workers and the civil servants – that is to say, a tiny portion of the population, which hardly represents more than one per cent.

But although this proletariat has read the party publications and understood its propaganda, it is much less ready to obey in the event of orders being given which set in motion the fierce struggle for national liberation. It cannot be too strongly stressed that in the colonial territories the proletariat is the nucleus of the colonized population which has been most pampered by the colonial regime. The embryonic proletariat of the towns is in a comparatively privileged position. In capitalist countries, the working class has nothing to lose; it is they who in the long run have everything to gain. In the colonial countries the working class has everything to lose; in reality it represents that fraction of the colonized nation which is necessary and irreplaceable if the colonial machine is to run smoothly: it includes tram conductors, taxi-drivers, miners, dockers, interpreters, nurses and so on. It is these elements which constitute the most faithful followers of the nationalist parties, and who because of the privileged place which they hold in the colonial system constitute also the 'bourgeois' fraction of the colonized people.

So we understand that the followers of the nationalist political parties are above all town-dwellers – shop-stewards, industrial workers, intellectuals and shopkeepers all living for the most part in the towns. Their way of thinking is already marked in many points by the comparatively well-to-do class, distinguished by technical advances, that they spring from. Here 'modern ideas' reign. It is these classes that will struggle against obscurantist traditions, that will change old customs, and that will thus enter into open conflict with the old granite block upon which the nation rests.

The overwhelming majority of nationalist parties show a deep distrust towards the people of the rural areas. The fact is that as a body these people appear to them to be bogged down in fruitless inertia. The members of the nationalist parties (town workers and intellectuals) pass the same unfavourable judgement on country districts as the settlers. But if we try to understand the reasons for this mistrust on the part of the political parties with regard to the rural areas, we must remember that colonialism has often strengthened or established its domination by organizing the petrification of the country districts. Ringed round by marabouts, witch-doctors and customary chieftains, the majority of country-dwellers are still living in the feudal manner, and the full power of this medieval structure of society is maintained by the settlers' military and administrative officials.

So now the young nationalist middle class, which is above all a class interested in trade, is going to compete with these feudal lords in many and various fields. There are marabouts and medicine-men who bar the way to sick people who otherwise could consult the doctor, oracles which pass judgement and thus render lawyers useless, *caids* who make use of their political and administrative powers to set up in trade or to start a transport service, customary chiefs who oppose, in the names of religion and tradition, the setting up of businesses and the introduction of new goods. The rising class of native traders and wholesalers needs the disappearance of these prohibitions and barriers in order to develop. The native customers, the preserve of feudal lords, who now become aware that they are more or less forbidden to buy the new products, therefore become a market to be contended for.

The feudal leaders form a screen between the young westernized nationalists and the bulk of the people. Each time the elite tries to get through to the country people, the tribal chieftains, leaders of confraternities and traditional authorities intensify their warnings, their threats and their ex-communications. These traditional authorities who have been upheld by the occupying power view with disfavour the attempts made by the elite to penetrate the country districts. They know very well that the ideas which are likely to be introduced by these influences coming from the towns call in question the very nature of unchanging, everlasting feudalism. Thus their enemy is not at all the occupying power with which they get along on the whole very well, but these people with modern ideas who mean to dislocate the aboriginal society, and who in doing so will take the bread out of their mouths.

The westernized elements experience feelings with regard to the bulk of the peasantry which are reminiscent of those found among the town workers of industrialized countries. The history of middle-class and working-class revolutions has shown that the bulk of the peasants often constitute a brake on the revolution. Generally in industrialized countries the peasantry as a whole are the least aware, the worst organized and at the same time the most anarchical element. They show a whole range of characteristics – individualism, lack of discipline, liking for money and propensities towards waves of uncontrollable rage and deep discouragement which define a line of behaviour that is objectively reactionary.

We have seen that the nationalist parties copy their methods from those of the western political parties; and also, for the most part, that they do not direct their propaganda towards the rural masses. In fact, if a reasoned analysis of colonized society had been made, it would have shown them that the native peasantry lives against a background of tradition, where the traditional structure of society has remained intact, whereas in the industrialized countries it is just this traditional setting which has been broken up by the progress of industrialization. In the colonies, it is at the very core of the embryonic working class that you find individual behaviour. The landless peasants, who make up the *lumpen-proletariat*, leave the country districts, where vital statistics are just so many insoluble problems, push towards the towns, crowd into tin-shack settlements, and try to make their way into the ports and cities founded by colonial domination. The bulk of the country people for their part continue to live within a rigid framework, and the extra mouths to feed have no other alternative than to emigrate towards the centres of population. The peasant who stays put defends his traditions stubbornly, and in a colonized society stands for the disciplined element whose interests lie in maintaining the social structure. It is true that this unchanging way of life, which hangs on like grim death to rigid social structures, may occasionally give birth to movements which are based on religious fanaticism or tribal wars. But in their spontaneous movements the country people as a whole remain disciplined and altruistic. The individual stands aside in favour of the community.

The country people are suspicious of the townsman. The latter dresses like a European; he speaks the European's language, works with him, sometimes even lives in the same district; so he is considered by the peasants as a turncoat who has betrayed everything that goes to make up the national heritage. The townspeople are 'traitors and knaves' who seem to get on well with the occupying powers, and do their best to get on within the framework of the colonial system. This is why you often hear the country people say of town-dwellers that they have no morals. Here, we are not dealing with the old antagonism between town and country; it is the antagonism which exists between the native who is excluded from the advantages of colonialism and his counterpart who manages to turn colonial exploitation to his account.

What is more, the colonialists make use of this antagonism in their struggle against the nationalist parties. They mobilize the people of the mountains and the up-country-dwellers against the townsfolk. They pitch the hinterland against the seaboard, they rouse up the tribespeople, and we need not be surprised to see Kalondji crowned king of Kasai, just as it was not surprising to see, some years ago, the assembly of the chiefs of Ghana making N'kruma dance to their tune.

The political parties do not manage to organize the country districts. Instead of using existing structures and giving them a nationalist or progressive character, they mean to try and destroy living tradition in the colonial framework. They believe it lies in their power to give the initial impulse to the nation whereas in reality the chains forged by the colonial system still weigh it down heavily. They do not go out to find the mass of the people. They do not put their theoretical knowledge to the service of the people; they only try to erect a framework around the people which follows an *a priori* schedule. Thus from the capital city they will 'parachute' organizers into the villages who are either unknown or too young, and who, armed with instructions from the central authority, mean to treat the *douar* or village like a factory cell.

The traditional chiefs are ignored, sometimes even persecuted. The makers of the future nation's history trample unconcernedly over small local disputes, that is to say the only existing national events, whereas they ought to make of village history – the history of traditional conflicts between clans and tribes – a harmonious whole, at one with the decisive action to which they call on the people to contribute. The old men, surrounded by respect in all traditional societies and usually invested with unquestionable moral authority, are publicly held up to ridicule. The occupying power's local authorities do not fail to use the resentment thus engendered, and keep in touch with the slightest decisions adopted by this caricature of authority. Police repression, well-informed because it is based on precise information, strikes. The parachuted leaders and the consequential members of the new assembly are arrested.

Such setbacks confirm the 'theoretical analysis' of the nationalist parties. The disastrous experience of trying to enrol the country people as a whole reinforces their distrust and crystallizes their aggressiveness towards that section of the people. Even after the struggle for national freedom has succeeded, the same mistakes are made and such mistakes make for the maintenance of decentralizing and autonomist tendencies. Tribalism in the colonial phase gives way to regionalism in the national phase, and finds its expression as far as institutions are concerned in federalism.

But it may happen that the country people, in spite of the slight hold that the nationalist parties have over them, play a decisive part either in the process of the maturing of the national consciousness, or through working in with the action of nationalist parties, or, less frequently, by substituting themselves purely and simply for the sterility of these parties. For the propaganda of nationalist parties always finds an echo in the hearts of the peasantry. The memory of the anti-colonial period is very much alive in the villages, where women still croon in their children's ears songs to which the warriors marched when they went out to fight the conquerors. At twelve or thirteen years of age the village children know the names of the old men who were in the last rising, and the dreams they dream in the *douars* or in the villages are not those of money or of getting through their exams like the children of the towns, but dreams of identification with some rebel or another, the story of whose heroic death still today moves them to tears.

Just when the nationalist parties are trying to organize the embryonic working class in the towns, we notice certain seemingly completely inexplicable explosions in the country districts. Take for example the famous rebellion of 1947 in Madagascar. The colonial authorities were categorical: it was a peasant rising. In fact we now know that as usual things were much more complicated than that. During the Second World War the big colonial companies greatly increased their power and became the possessors of all the land that up to then was still free. At the same time there was talk of planting the island eventually with Jewish, Kabylian and West Indian refugees. Another rumour was equally rife – that the whites of South Africa were soon going to invade the island with the collusion of the settlers. Thus, after the war the candidates on the nationalist list were triumphantly elected. Immediately after, organized repression began of the cells of the *Mouvement Democratique de la Rénovation Malgache* (Democratic Movement for Madagascan Restoration). Colonialism, in order to reach its ends, used the usual traditional methods: frequent arrests, racist propaganda between tribes, and the creation of a party out of the unorganized elements of the *lumpen-pro-letariat*. This party, with the name of the Disinherited Madagascans, gave the colonial authorities by its distinctly provocative actions the legal excuse to maintain order. It happened that this very frequent operation of liquidating a party which had been set up in advance took on in this context gigantic proportions. The rural masses, on the defensive for the last three or four years, suddenly felt themselves in deadly peril and decided to oppose colonialist forces savagely. Armed with spears, or more often simply with sticks and stones, the people flung themselves into the general revolt for national liberty. We know the end of the story.

Such armed rebellions only represent one of the means used by the country-dwellers to join in the national struggle. Sometimes when the nationalist party in the towns is tracked down by police repression the peasants carry on the tradition of urban agitation. News of the repression comes to the country districts in a grossly exaggerated form; the tale runs that the leaders are arrested, that machine-gunning is rife, that the town is running red with the blood of Negroes, or that the small settlers are bathing in Arab blood. Thereupon the accumulated, exacerbated hate explodes. The neighbouring police barracks is captured, the policemen are hacked to pieces, the local schoolmaster is murdered, the doctor only gets away with his life because he was not at home, etc. Pacifying forces are hurried to the spot and the air-force bombards it. Then the banner of revolt is unfurled, the old warrior-like traditions spring up again, the women cheer, the men organize and take up positions in the mountains, and guerrilla war begins. The peasantry spontaneously gives concrete form to the general insecurity; and colonialism takes fright and either continues the war or negotiates.

What is the reaction of the nationalist parties to this eruption of the peasant masses into the national struggle? We have seen that the majority of nationalist parties have not written into their propaganda the necessity for armed intervention. They do not oppose the continuing of the rebellion, but they content themselves with leaving it to the spontaneous action of the country people. As a whole they treat this new element as a sort of manna fallen from heaven, and pray to goodness that it'll go on falling. They make the most of the manna, but do not attempt to organize the rebellion. They don't send leaders into the countryside to educate the people politically, or to increase their awareness or put the struggle on to a higher level. All they do is to hope that, carried onwards by its own momentum, the action of the people will not come to a standstill. There is no contamination of the rural movement by the urban movement; each develops according to its own dialectic.

The nationalist parties do not attempt to give definite orders to the country people, although the latter are perfectly ready to listen to them. They offer them no objective; they simply hope that this new movement will go on indefinitely and that the bombardments will not put an end to it. Thus we see that even when such an occasion offers, the nationalist parties make no use at all of the opportunity which is offered to them to integrate the people of the countryside, to educate them politically and to raise the level of their struggle. The old attitude of mistrust towards the countryside is criminally evident.

The political leaders go underground in the towns, give the impression to the colonialists that they have no connection with the rebels, or seek refuge abroad. It very seldom happens that they join the people in the hills. In Kenya, for example, during the Mau-Mau rebellion, not a single well-known nationalist declared his affiliation with the movement, or even tried to defend the men involved in it.

The different strata of the nation never have it out with each other to any advantage; there is no settling of accounts between them. Thus, when independence is achieved, after the repression practised on the country people, after the *entente* between colonialism and the national parties, it is no wonder that you find this incomprehension to an even greater degree. The country-dwellers are slow to take up the structural reforms proposed by the government; and equally slow in following their social reforms, even though they may be very progressive if viewed objectively, precisely because the people now at the head of affairs did not explain to the people as a whole during the colonial period what were the aims of the party, the national trends, or the problems of international politics.

The mistrust which country-dwellers and those still living within the feudal system feel towards nationalist parties during the colonial period is followed by a similarly strong hostility during the national period. The colonial secret services which were not disbanded after independence keep up the discontentment and still manage to make serious difficulties for the young governments. All in all, the government is only being made to pay for its laziness during the period of liberation, and its unfailing mistrust of the country people. The nation may well have a reasonable, even progressive, head to it; its body will remain weak, stubborn and non-cooperative.

The temptation therefore will be to break up this body by centralizing the administration and surrounding the people by a firm administrative framework. This is one of the reasons why you often hear it said that in under-developed countries a small dose of dictatorship is needed. The men at the head of things distrust the people of the countryside; moreover this distrust takes on serious proportions. This is the case for example of certain governments which, long after national independence is declared, continue to consider the interior of the country as a non-pacified area where the chief of state or his ministers only go when the national army is carrying out manoeuvres there. For all practical purposes, the interior ranks with the unknown. Paradoxically, the national government in its dealings with the country people as a whole is reminiscent of certain features of the former colonial power. 'We don't quite know how the mass of these people will react' is the cry; and the young ruling class does not hesitate to assert that 'they need the thick end of the stick if this country is to get out of the Middle Ages'. But as we have seen, the off-hand way in which the political parties treated the rural population during the colonial phase could only prejudice national unity at the very moment when the young nation needs to get off to a good start.

Sometimes colonialism attempts to dislocate or create diversions around the upward thrust of nationalism. Instead of organizing the sheiks and the chiefs against the 'revolutionaries' in the towns, native committees organize the tribes and confraternities into parties. Confronted with the urban party which was beginning to 'embody the national will' and to constitute a danger for the colonial regime, splinter groups are born, and tendencies and parties which have their origin in ethnical or regional differences spring up.

23 Alain Touraine

The French Student Movement of May 1968

Excerpt from Alain Touraine, *The May Movement*, translated by
Leonard Mayhew, Random House, 1971, pp. 347–57. First published in
French in 1968.

The worldwide unity of the student movement is not due to a
common political orientation in Japan, Brazil, Poland and the
United States, for example, but arises from the symptoms of
post-war confusion. It is not a programmatic unity but a unity
of attitudes and methods. Universal and powerful institutionalization and re-enforcement of structures made the
conflict wild, disorganized, and non-negotiable, a force aimed
at the dismemberment of institutions, political criticism, scan-
dal and cultural Utopia. This general unity must not, nevertheless, conceal the differences that are due to the varied nature
of established power in different countries. In Latin America,
the end of populism and the strengthening of dualism – the
opposition between a sector increasingly devoid of resources
and urban centers of growth largely dominated by foreign
interests – provoked the students to speak of national independence and development for the benefit of all the people. The
intelligentsia fights against economic domination and the destruction of the national collectivity.

In the more industrialized countries, on the other hand, the
new fact, as we have already said, is that power is no longer an
instrument of economic exploitation for the benefit of a minority but rather a structure of management, control and manipulation of all social life. Whether it takes the form of
authoritarian state control of education, propaganda and investments, or whether it is a nebulous unity of big businesses
more or less closely bound to each other, it exerts a growing
influence over what was before the domain of private life, over
local and professional organizations and even over class heritage. In this situation, the students do not intervene as an avant-

garde intelligentsia but because their activity and professional situation confront them directly with the dominating and manipulating action of those in power. Education and research are such important determinants of growth that they must be planned by those in power and, hence, be subject to political decisions. In Czechoslovakia, the students' desire for intellectual liberty quite naturally joined the anti-bureaucratic efforts of the economists led by Ota Sik. In the United States, the conflicts began with the denunciation of the direct or indirect aid given by some universities to the Vietnam War. In France, the problem of student selection posed political choices. Like teachers and researchers, students are no longer the spokesmen for a people reduced to silence by wretchedness and oppression; they are workers directly concerned with the economic and social choices imposed in one form or another by politico-economic power.

Among the industrialized nations, the French situation was the least favorable to the formation of a student movement that would be the forerunner and revealer of new conflicts: because it had long been entangled in the liquidation of its colonial empire; because, as a semi-industrial country, it possessed a labor movement that remained partly revolutionary, fanning the flames of past conflicts without enkindling new ones; and finally political and cultural criticism was actively led by 'leftwing intellectuals' whose protests expressed opposition but did not achieve political power. Why then did the Paris movement, a latecomer, shake up French society more profoundly than the Berkeley or Berlin movements shook up the United States or Germany?

Its importance was not due to its original orientations which most often resembled those of other student movements but to the condition of French society. In the East, political repression is too strong; in the West, the universities are too independent for their crises to affect the state. France, both liberal and rigid, centralized and disorganized, modernist and archaic, grandiose and mean, exacerbated tensions within a university world that was in rapid expansion and absolute crisis.

These observations, made a hundred times, not only explain the extent of the crisis; they also explain the formation, in

France more than elsewhere, of a new class struggle and especially the partial and limited, but real, alliance between students and other groups close to them because of their social situation: researchers, professional experts, technicians. The struggle had a broader and more clearly defined front in France than elsewhere. The student revolt that faced the state in the East and the culture in the West faced the whole of society in France.

The principal cause of this is assuredly the role of the state in French society: not the legendary Napoleonic State which is more often evoked than precisely analysed, but the Gaullist State which insured unity between the old and new ruling classes, the bourgeoisie and the technocracy. Thanks to it, the student revolt combined rejection of the exhausted old liberal university with the struggle against the new centers of economic power. While its influence on French society was profound, the Gaullist State is the very opposite of a national and popular state. It mobilized no sentiment in its own favor, neither for the construction of the nation (something long since accomplished) nor for the voluntary transformation of society. It was driven by the idea of national *grandeur*, which has no meaning except on the international scene and has almost no effect on the attitudes of Frenchmen toward the workings of their own society. It brought about social and political changes for which it took the principal responsibility and at the same time it made them meaningless for those who lived through them. It was too liberal to use totalitarian propaganda or repression; it was too authoritarian to allow decisions and conflicts in any particular sector of national activity to be worked out independently. Therefore, the May Movement unloosed not only a profound crisis within the state but it also presented grievances against the state in the name of society, the people and the meaning of change.

In Germany, the student movement was closed in on itself and was creative of more ideas. In France, it transformed the situation of society. Against the state, it succeeded in uniting political opposition and cultural revolt within a social movement. In a country that is practically outside the great international rivalries, imperialism or foreign domination could no mobilize collective action. But in a country where the state dominates economic life and the functioning of society, the cultural revolt became a struggle against power. The result was that the conflict, slower to appear in France than elsewhere, took on greater importance there.

Social conflicts and the university

What enflamed some and scandalized others for those few weeks in May – was the realization that anything could happen, given the profound disruption of a society that had thought itself peaceful, rich and set on a course of modernization that seemed to relegate to the past the great conflicts and visions that had accompanied a century of industrialization. Society revealed its opposite side. The ease and suddenness with which the crisis burst forth, the university was occupied, the strike movement was spread, and the political regime was shaken up aroused either hopes or fears. It rearoused passion in a purportedly rational world. But there is a real danger that this situation will not be analysed accurately. The event is both so extraordinary and so important that there is a tendency to explain it either by very particular reasons – the sclerosis of the university system or the blindness of the government – or by the overly general reasons – generation gap or a crisis of civilization. Both cases ignore equally the essential consideration that historically situates and explains this social, political and cultural crisis: the revelation of the conflicts and forces at work in a type of society still too new to be conscious of its own nature and problems. A new class struggle between the dominant politico-economic structures and the people who must go through great change lent the May Movement importance. It is not the central moment of one crisis, but the beginning of many new conflicts that will be as fundamental and as enduring, as the worker movement was in the period of capitalist industrialization.

As at the birth of every major social movement, the most specific demands and the most Utopian visions were juxtaposed or mixed, without being joined in the kind of political action and organization. This can only come about gradually, through long struggles as political relationships are disentangled from older problems and rearranged to cope with new problems and new conflicts. University reform and the recognition of union negotiation, if they are singled out, are only elements of a more general social change that, in many other countries, was accomplished without such a storm. On the other hand, the cultural revolt proclaimed by what Edgar Morin called the 'Student Commune', advocated a drive for immediate gains to the tension and constraints that are imposed by a longer-term investment that allows growth (Lefort, Morin and Coudray, 1968). In isolation, this revolt had no lasting political importance.

The importance of the May Movement lies in neither of these alternatives, nor in the reforms that it will probably make possible, nor in the cultural revolt that gave it its passionate character, but in the social rupture that it created at the heart of a society dominated by the Utopianism of the ruling class. In the name of rational modernization and of technical progress that is supposed to bring social progress about naturally – a larger pie makes the problem of how it is cut secondary – this ruling class identified itself with the future. It did not speak in the name of special interests and made no political choices. It wanted only what was rational and did only what was reasonable. Certainly, obstacles to progress and resistance to change must be eliminated but more information, clearer thinking and greater decisiveness would be enough to take care of that.

Now French society knows once again that its decisions are political choices, even when they rest on the best technical studies and when they take account of the demands of economic coherence. Behind the ideology of rationality, the power of special interests has been laid bare; not so much those of speculators or even private capital as of the massive structures that control production and consumption. Social conflict reappeared. Those who reduce all social activity to adaptation, to necessary, rational change were opposed by those who demand a democratic power capable of regulating the massive structures that both ensure economic growth and manipulate society.

The movement simply revealed this conflict rather than solved the crises or contradictions and could not be considered 'constructive'. Those who, in their search for its virtues, marvel over the movement's positive results should be reminded first of this. Isn't an entirely new university system going to emerge from the May–June debates? Aren't reforms that were long judged impossible now going to be easy? Yes, certainly, but this is a weak justification that can be answered easily by saying that the prize was not worth the game. Other European countries have raised salaries in a less brutal manner and the reform of the faculties of letters or even of the whole university system did not merit a general social crisis. If the May Movement is to be judged on the basis of its modernizing effects, it must be condemned because the means were incommensurate with the limited and uncertain results.

Must we then say just the opposite? If there was a revolutionary movement, it was because France was already in a revolutionary situation, and that only betrayal or the decadence of the political structures had kept society from moving into a new socialism, equally distant from both capitalist society and Soviet bureaucracy? This isn't true either. The regime was certainly shaken but, even if it had succumbed, the social revolution would not have triumphed. If a government directed by either the Communist or non-Communist left had been formed, the measures that it would have taken would have been very different from the inspiration of the movement.

We have experienced an impossible revolution, a revolutionary movement without revolution. We must not confuse revolutionary self-expression in an extra-territorialized Sorbonne with political preparation for a real social revolution. Revolutionary consciousness cannot take the place of revolution. The more it was expressed, the less it nourished the forces that are committed to a new social conflict, and the more it revealed the crisis and disorganization of the university system in which it was rooted.

Therefore, it seems to me that the importance of the May Movement is best represented by the 22 March Movement, which kept its distance both from university reform and from the rhetoric of the Sorbonne and the Odéon. Its strength lay in confrontation and combat rather than in proclamation and reform. While its passionate and naïve activity attracted some students who were simply rebellious and had broken with a life-condition they found absurd and limiting, this activity alone had deep political significance. It helped create a new consciousness and new class action by joining students with other groups of workers. It accomplished this by clashing with the unions and those political organizations that were the leaders of past social struggles but today are reduced to institutionalizing old conflicts – not that this is such a negligible task.

It is no longer possible to accept the image of our industrial society as one enormous organization concentrating on its own growth and discarding a new class of poor or unfit individuals around its edges. The May Movement made clear what certain industrial conflicts of a new type had already indicated: the struggle is not at the periphery but at the center of this programmed society. It also demonstrated that revolutionary action in France cannot be reduced to support for the Vietnam struggle or the Che Guevara-type guerrillas through proclamations, meetings or violent gestures. Solidarity among revolutionaries has meaning only if each individual contributes in some practical way to the social struggle. This is what happened in France during May. The rebellion turned back toward French society and the other advanced industrial societies. It spoke to these societies, not that the non-integrated elements which protest from the outskirts are important but that the producers themselves oppose the power system to which they are subjected.

This movement is important because its transcends any particular institution. Those who judge the movement only from the point of view of the university system can only find it frantic, excessive, costly and ineffective. In the same way, general strikes always appeared costly and excessive to those who wished to see the labor movement only as an instrument of liberalization to promote participation within firms. Like the worker movement, the May Movement indicated an entire system of social power above and beyond a national political system. For that reason, the movement was internationalist and expressed solidarity with all who struggle against techno-bureaucratic power, whether they are part of capitalism or are degraded within the worker parties.

What differentiates this student revolutionary movement in industrial countries from those in developing and colonialized countries is that this is the first time that education in the economically advanced countries has become a factor of production and decisive growth, not merely the transmission of a cultural heritage. No one dreams of saying that now the students are the dominated class or even that they alone are the militant avantgarde of the oppressed. But students are more than the spokesmen for unaware or inarticulate groups. They are the representatives of all those who suffer more from social integration and cultural manipulation directed by the economic structures than from economic exploitation and material misery.

Because the movement was revolutionary force rather than the instrument of an actual revolution, its role as spokesman and advocate of a new class struggle is inseparable from its other aspects; conflict behavior was constantly accompanied by crisis behavior. Since rejection of the present society was not transformed into an organized struggle to form a new society, the revolt confused itself with revolution. Begun in rebellion and ending by rejecting society, the students' spring was marked by the increasing, then decreasing hope to affect the cultural crisis in some meaningful way. Without the first rebellion, revolutionary intent would have always remained enclosed in the 'little groups'; by June, revolutionary intentions were diluted into reform of university institutions. The May Movement was not launched by a 'new working class' or by the students in the most modern and best organized sections of the university. It was born in the crumbling faculties of letters in reaction to pointlessness and crisis. If this reaction did not give the movement its complete meaning, at least it gave it the initial strength to break with a system that fulfilled no real function and was, to that very degree, determined to perpetuate itself and to reject all debate over its purpose and means. The Week of the Barricades was the central moment of the events of May, the moment of maximum possible action; it was much more than a rebellion, much less than a revolution, and certainly not an insurrection. For a few days, words were joined to action and individual spontaneity became part of a collective struggle. After that, revolutionary intent wore itself out in the illusion of creating a worker revolution, which, however, led the movement to make its greatest progress, for it called forth the social groups outside the university which constitute, with the students, the new opposition. The cultural revolt became absorbed in self-expression, and university reorganization transformed the possibility of revolution into institutional reform.

Here, as we draw our conclusions, we rediscover the propositions presented at the beginning of this book, but each of the themes we sought to isolate has been substantiated with concrete images. We see clearly that within the movement there were three types of attitudes and preoccupations and almost three different types of individuals.

On one side were those committed to the precipitation of social and political conflicts. In common they held that university and student issues were secondary considerations. Some aimed directly at the downfall of capitalist society; others wished more immediately for the fall of Gaullism. There were many major differences among them, as marked as those that separated the Week of the Barricades from the week of 27 May–1 June; or those that separated Daniel Cohn-Bendit and Jacques Sauvageot. But whether the accent is put on the social movement or on political action, it was always a question of revealing and exploding the contradictions of society.

On the other extreme, the university and professional rebellion remained close to the situation in which it was formed and the crisis that it expressed, but from which it wished to free itself. Whether it took the form of university reformism, a struggle against governmental control of television, or a rejection of traditional professional organizations, it was a matter of affirming absolute, undefined, force against constraints and repression. It was Man and the People against barriers and control.

Between the two were the Utopians whose central theme was self-direction. While the first group involved itself in conflicts and the second affirmed itself against society, these wished to take possession of the social organization and to discover a way to fuse their individual spontaneity with collective life. Because, as I have said, the function of Utopianism was to create unity beyond the opposition between the social conflict and the cultural crisis, the Utopians affirmed the movement most vigorously and defined its objectives, while the first group worked out its action and the second group gave it its climate. The May Movement was Utopian communism.

Reference

LEFORT, C., MORIN, L., and COUDRAY, J. M. (1968), *La Brèche*, Fayard.

24 Michael Walzer

The Revolution of the Saints

Excerpts from Michael Walzer, *The Revolution of the Saints*, Athenaeum, 1969, pp. 1–4, 257–63 and 317–20.

A politics of conflict and competition for power, of faction, intrigue and open war is probably universal in human history. Not so a politics of party organization and methodical activity, opposition and reform, radical ideology and revolution. The history of reform and revolution is relatively short compared, for example, with that of the political order itself or of the power struggle. The detached appraisal of a going system, the programmatic expression of discontent and aspiration, the organization of zealous men for sustained political activity: it is surely fair to say that these three together are aspects only of the modern, that is, the postmedieval political world.

The study of modern politics might begin at many points in the sixteenth century: with Machiavelli and the new political realism, with Luther and the German princes and their attack upon Roman internationalism, with Bodin and the sovereignty of the new monarchs. The concern of this essay, however, is not with reason of state, the national church or the idea of sovereignty. It lies instead with another of those startling innovations of sixteenth-century political history: the appearance of revolutionary organization and radical ideology (Koenigsburger, 1955). Revolution as a political phenomenon and ideology as a kind of mental and moral discipline are both, of course, closely related to the rise of the modern state. Yet the idea that specially designated and organized bands of men might play a creative part in the political world, destroying the established order and reconstructing society according to the Word of God or the plans of their fellows – this idea did not enter at all into the thought of Machiavelli, Luther or Bodin. In establishing the state, these three writers relied exclusively upon the prince, whether they imagined him as an adventurer, a

Christian magistrate or a hereditary bureaucrat. All other men remained subjects, condemned to political passivity. But this was an incomplete vision, for in fact the revolutionary activity of saints and citizens played as important a part in the formation of the modern state as did the sovereign power of princes. In Switzerland, the Dutch Netherlands, Scotland and most importantly in England and later in France, the old order was finally overthrown not by absolutist kings or in the name of reason of state but by groups of political radicals, themselves moved by new and revolutionary ideologies.

It will be argued below that it was the Calvinists who first switched the emphasis of political thought from the prince to the saint (or the band of saints) and then constructed a theoretical justification for independent political action. What Calvinists said of the saint, other men would later say of the citizen: the same sense of civic virtue, of discipline and duty, lies behind the two names. Saint and citizen together suggest a new integration of private men (or rather, of *chosen* groups of private men, of proven holiness and virtue) into the political order, an integration based upon a novel view of politics as a kind of conscientious and continuous labor. This is surely the most significant outcome of the Calvinist theory of worldly activity, preceding in time any infusion of religious worldliness into the economic order (Friedrich, 1957). The diligent activism of the saints – Genevan, Huguenot, Dutch, Scottish and Puritan – marked the transformation of politics into work and revealed for the first time the extraordinary conscience that directed the work.

Conscience and work entered the political world together; they formed the basis for the new politics of revolution and shaped the character of the revolutionary. They also provided, it should be said, an internal rationale for the diligent efficiency of the modern official and the pious political concern of the modern bourgeois. But both these eminent men were revolutionaries in their time; they had first of all to construct a world in which their efficiency and concern would be respectable – and to attack an older world that had made them both objects of mockery or disdain.[1] In politics as in religion the

1. Brinton argues that the Jacobin clubs, all unknowingly, played an

saints were oppositional men and their primary task was the destruction of traditional order. But they were committed after that to the literal reforming of human society, to the creation of a Holy Commonwealth in which conscientious activity would be encouraged and even required. The saints saw themselves as divine *instruments* and theirs was the politics of wreckers, architects and builders – hard at work upon the political world. They refused to recognize any inherent or natural resistance to their labors. They treated every obstacle as another example of the devil's resourcefulness and they summoned all their energy, imagination and craft to overcome it. Because their work required cooperation, they organized to carry it through successfully and they joined forces with any man who might help them without regard to the older bonds of family and neighborhood. They sought 'brethren' and turned away if necessary from their relatives; they sought zeal and not affection. Thus there arose the leagues and covenants, the conferences and congregations which are the prototypes of revolutionary discipline. In these the good work was carried forward; at the same time, new saints were trained and hardened for their unremitting labor. The results of that labor can best be seen in the English Revolution of 1640.

In Elizabethan and Jacobean drama the Calvinist saints who later played such a crucial part in that revolution were described as men of hypocritical zeal, meddlesome, continually on the move, nervously and ostentatiously searching for godly things to do – thus Ben Jonson's Puritan, Zeal-of-the-Land Busy (Holden, 1954). Zeal-of-the-Land was a comic figure, but he was also a new man, especially susceptible to caricature. The saint's personality was his own most radical innovation. It was marked above all by an uncompromising and sustained commitment to a political ideal (which other men called hypocrisy), and by a pattern of rigorous and systematic labor in pursuit of that ideal (which other men called meddlesomeness). The origins and consequences of this godly commitment and this

important part in training the bureaucrats and petty officials of the Napoleonic era (1930, pp. 230–31). A similar argument, connecting Puritanism with the rise of parliamentary power and the training of parliamentarians, will be made below.

godly business will be examined below. It is necessary first to suggest how new both were in the sixteenth century, with what incomprehension the contemporaries of Calvin and then of Cromwell approached the savage struggles into which godly zeal and business plunged them, how frequently they doubted the 'sincerity' of the saint – long after he had, one would have thought, sufficiently demonstrated it. In discussing rebellion and sedition, for example, both Bodin and Francis Bacon still thought in terms of the ragged plebeians of the classical cities and the 'overmighty subjects' of bastard feudalism. Bacon, perhaps, had some foreboding of what was to come in England when he wrote a warning against unemployed scholars; such men would indeed become, though not merely because they were unemployed, the alienated intellectuals who fed the minds of the lay saints. But King James's Lord Chancellor had no sense of what this intellectual food would be like or of its consequences in human behavior. Even the great Clarendon, writing after the event, still saw the English Revolution as a conspiracy of discontented noblemen. He barely noticed the Puritans and examined their faith only as a species of hypocrisy and an excuse for 'turbulence'. Clarendon was very wrong; yet his opinions surely reflected the wisdom of the ages. The active, ideologically committed political radical had never before been known in Europe. Medieval society was, to use the word of a modern theorist, a society largely composed of *non-participants*, inactive men (Lerner, 1958). A brief glance at the history of that society will suggest the novelty of Calvinist politics. [. . .]

But opposition in practice required something else, some more special preparation – a peculiar certainty, a willfulness, almost a fanaticism. This was exclusively a Puritan product, the result of an intense, disciplined response to deeply felt anxieties, to some secular form of the ministers' 'unsettledness'. When the gentleman's nervous self-esteem took the form of sainthood, when he saw himself an instrument of God, then his pious willfulness set him free from traditional political controls. So the ministers had been set free in the 1580s and had laid the foundations of radical politics. 'In pursuit of their aims,' writes J. E. Neale, 'they taught the House of Commons methods of

concerted action and propaganda. Indeed, the art of opposition
. . . was largely learnt from them or inspired by them' (1953).
By the 1640s, this art had been widely diffused through lay
society and the philosophical or theological principles that
might have limited its use had been worn away. More than this,
a large number of laymen had been trained in the Puritan congregations who saw in the art of opposition an inescapable
duty.

'If we have the honour to be God's instruments,' Edward
Corbett told the Commons in 1642, 'we must do the office of
instruments and be active . . . we must go along with Providence.' But the 'office of instruments' included many duties
which the office of a member of Parliament did not traditionally include. The persistent invasions of the royal prerogative
by Puritan parliamentarians were probably the acts of instruments more often than of members – though for many men
the two identities fused, each strengthening the other. Thus
Peter Wentworth, a country gentleman from Northamptonshire
imprisoned in 1591 for his attacks upon the Queen's prerogative, asked the privy councilors how else he could have
behaved – 'the Lord opening a clear view thereof to mine eyes,
and I being a Parliament man?' (Neale, 1953, p. 261). They had
no choice, thought the Puritan member Dalton; they must 'proceed orderly to the discharge of their own consciences in
making law'. And 'let them care for the rest whom it behooveth'
(Neale, 1957, p. 213). Without some such attitude, radical politics is probably inconceivable. Oliver Cromwell at least would
never have acted as he did – so he told the First Protectorate
Parliament in September 1654 – had God not again opened a
'clear view'. Not as a Cambridgeshire gentleman but only as a
saint could he rule England. 'I called not myself to this place.'
But the Lord had 'most clearly by His Providence' put power
into Oliver's hands and not until the providences were clear
again could he yield it up (Paul, 1955, pp. 148, 271–2, 386–9).

This extraordinary sense of religious vocation, reinforcing
secular reasons for opposition to the crown, can be seen at work
in three different aspects of parliamentary life: in elections, in
political organization, and in the religious 'exercises' that were
so crucial to revolutionary activity in the 1640s. These can only

be outlined here; they deserve to be examined much more carefully – perhaps through a number of biographical studies of the political saints in which the delicate task of weighing the impact of religious zeal might be undertaken. For the moment, it can only be suggested that in the sixteenth and seventeenth centuries radical innovation in politics (especially when this involved the cooperation of numbers of men) was inconceivable without the moral support of religion – and that religion probably provided the major incentive for innovation.

1. *Elections.* Since the divine instruments (except for Oliver) were in fact elected by men, Puritan preachers tended to infuse the election process with a religious purpose. They appealed to the seriousness of the electors: the 'holy choice' was to be made with 'religious care', preached Thomas Adams, and only after a period of 'public devotion'. Adams's intention was to overcome or at least call into doubt the old ties of family and patronage. He could hardly have been successful in 1625; what is important is that the intention was present, working its way into the consciousness of the voters. The preacher warned against the casual assumption of office by the son of the previous incumbent: 'Nature is regular in the brute creatures; eagles do not produce cravens. ... But in man she fails. ... Children do often resemble their parents in face and feature, not in heart and qualities. ...' Similarly, John Preston insisted that 'it is an error to think that in the election of burgesses ... [they] may pleasure their friends or themselves. ...' Preston described the way instruments might be chosen who would be free, under God and the discipline of conscience, to act for the public good. The electors, he wrote, 'ought to keep their minds single and free from all respects; so that when they come to choose, they might choose him whom in their own consciences and in the sight of God, they think fittest for the place. ...' Had he lived, the Puritan leader would undoubtedly have been pleased with the report that Isaac Pennington was elected to Parliament by the London Common Hall in 1640 because of his 'known zeal, by his keeping a fasting Sabbath. ...' This was an election, presumably, in the godly manner – and it also suggests the nature of Puritan campaigning.

To insure such a choice as Preston described it was necessary to make the election a public proceeding and godliness a political issue. The Elizabethan Puritan Job Throckmorton told his constituents that he 'would not have this matter [the parliamentary election] huddled up in a corner, as most of your matters be' (Neale, 1949). He would not, in other words, have elections settled through old-fashioned familial negotiation. In the seventeenth century the spread of political consciousness made it increasingly difficult to 'huddle up' the choice of MPs. Elections became instead occasions for the assertion by the gentry of their new public spiritedness and their new godliness. When John Pym rode through England in 1640 promoting the election of 'puritanical brethren' he was acting out a conception of political activity that had had a long development. That same year the 'ripe statesmen' whom Ben Jonson once satirized were vividly present at the London elections. The result of all this activity, a Puritan preacher suggested, was that the members of the Long Parliament represented 'laconically and by way of abridgement, the piety and holiness . . . of a kingdom' and not the leading subjects merely or the dominant interests.

2. *Political organization.* As familial and personal loyalties were not to influence elections, so hierarchy was not to limit the zeal of elected representatives. Only action, the ministers taught, 'makes us instruments of God's glory'. In order that action might be free, the parity of ministers found its political parallel in the equality of magistrates. 'The conscience of the monarch and the conscience of the inferior judges are equally under subjection to the King of Kings,' wrote Samuel Rutherford, 'for there is here a coordination of consciences, and no subordination . . . it is not in the power of the inferior judge to judge . . . as the king commandeth him. . . .' This is another example of the leveling power of the Calvinist God. At the same time, it was exaltation indeed for rural JPs, city aldermen and members of Parliament and it made possible new sorts of organization among them. Like the ministerial conferences and the Puritan congregations, these new organizations were based upon the mutual recognition of equality and dignity. They committed men to coordinated activity and generated new patterns

of trust and loyalty appropriate to the difficult and dangerous work of the lay saints.

Among the parliamentary Puritans of the seventeenth century there already existed a complex system of matrimonial alliances. In part, this system was the outcome of Puritan separatism: the saints would have nothing to do, and would permit their children to have as little as possible to do, with the ungodly. But, of course, the Puritan 'party' was also, quite simply, an association of relatives and it was undoubtedly strengthened by familial loyalty. What was new about the Puritan parliamentarians, however, was that they were strengthened also in a very different way. Alongside the old-fashioned matrimonial alliances they developed associations more like those with which the ministers had experimented in the 1580s – just as, alongside the traditional parliamentary ritual, they produced new 'exercises' of commitment which resembled the religious exercises of the Puritan congregation. The Solemn Oath and Covenant was typical of the new associations; it was conceived as a parallel to the Old Testament covenants that had been explicated in great detail by Puritan writers and preachers. Pym had actually proposed a version of such an association as early as 1621 (Brett, 1940, p. 42). In 1628 the minister Alexander Leighton published an *Appeal to Parliament* in which he anticipated the coming revolution by suggesting a parliamentary covenant for 'the breaking down of Babel', to last 'til God give the victory'. Leighton would have required a commitment not to dissolve even at the king's command, an English Tennis Court oath: 'No sure . . . except you keep the ship . . . neither king, you nor we can be saved.' The covenants urged by Pym and Leighton were paralleled by associations outside Parliament (like the Feoffees of Impropriation) and undoubtedly by many less formal alliances similarly rooted in religious zeal.

3. *The 'exercises'*. The public fast was the most important of the religious 'exercises' that Puritans turned into a kind of political propaganda. Pym moved a day of national fast at the opening of Parliament in 1626, but the members voted the celebration only for themselves. Even so, it was a significant act, a deliberate effort to arouse emotion and already a feature of oppo-

sitional politics. Stephen Marshall in 1648 complained that before the revolution 'sometimes a dozen, sometimes more years passed in this land and kingdom without any public fasts. . . .' Throughout the revolutionary period fasts were held monthly and were accompanied by sermons and prayer meetings.

Days of 'solemn prayer' were also the occasions for public and private 'exercises' designed to stimulate religious zeal and political activity. Before going to London for the meeting of the Short Parliament in 1640, Sir Robert Harley 'kept a day' with his family, praying for guidance. A short time later his wife reported again: 'We at Brompton kept the day . . . to our God for his direction of the Parliament. I believe that hierarchy must down and I hope now.' Years later, in 1649, when monarchy went down as well, the remaining parliamentarians (Harley not among them), the army officers and the king's judges were stimulated and sustained by days of 'public humiliation', fasts and frequent prayer meetings. All this obviously tended to reinforce devotion to the cause, to calm the consciences of men doing terrible and dangerous deeds. The Long Parliament carried on its business in an atmosphere frequently marked by religious excitement and its accomplishments are hardly to be explained without taking that excitement into account.

Puritan electioneering, the equality of magistrates, parliamentary association, and the religious 'exercises' – these derived from the conception of the official as an instrument of God. They illustrate the role of Puritan piety in the education of the parliamentary gentleman. Taken together, given their maximum impact, however, they clearly reach beyond the gentleman, for all his serious ambition and his conscientious self-esteem. They suggest one of the most fundamental doctrines of radical politics: that men unwilling to be instruments have no right – whatever their social status – to be magistrates. Pym's Association of 1621 would have excluded from office anyone who refused the prescribed oath. The parliamentary purges of the 1640s were undertaken in the same spirit: it was necessary, preached George Hughes to the Commons in 164?

'to honour God's kingdom so much as to make gross sin un-capable of membership among you'. Even in Elizabeth's Eng-land, a daring Puritan preacher, the Welsh evangelist John Penry, had argued a similar doctrine. Addressing himself to the Queen's Lord President of Wales, Penry wrote: 'If it lie not in you to bring Wales unto the knowledge of God, or if your leisure will not serve thereto, then be not the Lord President thereof.' It belonged to the 'essence' of his calling, Penry went on, to see the true religion preached. Men 'have no allowance to be rulers where the Lord is not served . . . .' This was surely no more than a logical development of the Puritan doctrine of vocation; yet, just as obviously, it called the identity of gentleman and saint into question.

The Commons, after all, was a class organization; the Chris-tian gentleman might expect to behave with all due piety when he was a member and thus vindicate his gentility. He did not expect, however he behaved, to be excluded from membership. The purge of the Long Parliament and the dissolution of the Rump were thus revolutionary acts; yet they were also acts of godly gentlemen – functioning as instruments rather than as members. At this point, however, the two identities could no longer be joined and men had to choose. Those who were, in Cromwell's words, 'gentlemen, and nothing more' went home. The places left vacant had then to be filled with other men, saints without breeding. When Lazarus Seaman told the members of the House of Commons in 1644 that 'the supply of our king's failings are expected at your hands', he was stating a principle obviously capable of extension. So the supply of the aristocracy's failings would be filled from among other social groups. [. . .]

It is now possible to suggest a model of radical politics based on the history of the English Puritans and developed, at least in part, in their own terms. Such a model may serve to reveal the crucial features of radicalism as a general historical phenome-on and to make possible a more systematic comparison of Puritans, Jacobins and Bolsheviks (and perhaps other groups as well) than has been attempted here.

At a certain point in the transition from one or another form of traditional society (feudal, hierarchical, patriarchal, corporate) to one or another form of modern society, there appears a band of 'strangers' who view themselves as chosen men, saints, and who seek a new order and an impersonal, ideological discipline.

2. These men are marked off from their fellows by an extraordinary self-assurance and daring. The saints not only repudiate the routine procedures and customary beliefs of the older order, but they also cut themselves off from the various kinds of 'freedom' (individual mobility, personal extravagance, self-realization, despair, nervousness, vacillation) experienced amidst the decay of tradition. The band of the chosen seeks and wins certainty and self-confidence by rigidly disciplining its members and teaching them to discipline themselves. The saints interpret their ability to endure this discipline as a sign of their virtue and their virtue as a sign of God's grace. Amidst the confusion of the transitional period, they discover in themselves a predestination, a firm and undeviating sense of purpose, an assurance of eventual triumph.

3. The band of the chosen confronts the existing world as if in war. Its members interpret the strains and tensions of social change in terms of conflict and contention. The saints sense enmity all about them and they train and prepare themselves accordingly. They keep watch and continually calculate their chances.

4. The organization of the chosen suggests the nature of the new order they seek, but also reflects the necessities of the present struggle.

(a) Men join the band by subscribing to a covenant which testifies to their faith. Their new commitment is formal, impersonal and ideological; it requires that they abandon older loyalties not founded upon opinion and will – loyalties to family, guild, locality, and also to lord and king.

(b) This commitment is voluntary, based upon an act of the will for which men can be trained, but not born. It is not possible to take one's place in the chosen band through any sort of patronage. To be chosen, one must choose.

(c) The commitment and zeal of prospective saints must be

tested and proven. Hence it is not easy to choose sainthood and the band of the chosen remains exclusive and small, each of its members highly 'talented' in virtue and self-discipline. Even after men have been accepted as saints, they must still demonstrate their godliness on every possible occasion. They are subject to examination and as they could once have been rejected so they can always be purged. The godly tension which the saints maintain is thus in vivid contrast to the apathy of worldlings, secure and at their ease with their customs and traditions.

(d) Within the band of the chosen, all men are equal. Status counts for little. Members are measured by their godliness and by the contributions they can make to the work at hand.

5. The acting out of sainthood produces a new kind of politics.

(a) The activity of the chosen band is purposive, programmatic and progressive in the sense that it continually approaches or seeks to approach its goals. This activity may be defined as an organized effort to universalize sainthood, to reconstruct or reform the political or religious worlds according to objective criteria (revealed, predetermined, written), without any regard for the established forms.

(b) The activity of the saints is methodical and systematic. Politics is made into a kind of work, to which the chosen are required to commit themselves for long periods of time. At work they must suppress all purely personal feelings and behave in a disciplined fashion. They must learn to be patient and to concern themselves with detail. Above all, they must work regularly and hard.

(c) The violent attack upon customary procedures sets the saints free to experiment politically. Such experimentation is controlled by its overriding purposes and the right to engage in it is limited to the chosen few who have previously accepted the discipline of the band. It is not a grant of political free-play, but it does open the way to new kinds of activity, both public and secret. The saints are entrepreneurs in politics.

. The historical role of the chosen band is twofold. Externally, s it were, the band of the saints is a political movement aiming at social reconstruction. It is the saints who lead the final attack upon the old order and their destructiveness is all the more total because they have a total view of the new world. Internally, godliness and predestination are creative responses to the pains of social change. Discipline is the cure for freedom and 'unsettledness'. As romantic love strengthens the bonds of the conjugal family, so ideological zeal establishes the unity of the nonfamilial brethren and makes it possible for men to feel secure outside the traditional system of connections.

One day, however, that security becomes a habit and zeal is no longer a worldly necessity. Then the time of God's people is over. In this world, the last word always belongs to the worldlings and not to the saints. It is a complacent word and it comes when salvation, in all its meanings, is no longer a problem. But the saints have what is more interesting: the first word. They set the stage of history for the new order.

Once that order is established, ordinary men are eager enough to desert the warfare of the Lord for some more moderate pursuit of virtue. Once they feel sufficiently secure as gentlemen and merchants, as country justices and members of Parliament, they happily forgo the further privilege of being 'instruments'. Hardly a moment after their triumph, the saints find themselves alone; they can no longer exploit the common forms of ambition, egotism and nervousness; they can no longer convince their fellow men that ascetic work and intense repression are necessary. The experience of other revolutionaries has been similar: the history of their success is brief. An enthusiastic poet of the Bolshevik Revolution, for example, wrote as early as 1924 that his verse was no longer needed (Esenin, 1961). The vanguard, he suggested (not quite accurately) had settled down to a new routine:

I see before me
Villagers in Sunday best
Transact a meeting as if attending church.

Wrinkling his reminiscent forehead,
A lame Red Army man with drowsy face
Grandly expatiates upon Budyonny
And the Reds who captured Perekop by storm.

What a misfit I've become
. . . I feel a foreigner in my land.

So too the Puritan saint was a stranger before his revolution, and after. There was a difference, of course, for the new routine embodied many aspects of his radical faith. But the enthusiasm, the battle-readiness, the confident enmity, the polemical eagerness, the sense of unity among the brethren, the first pride of self-control – all these were gone. Something of the tension, vigilance and excitement they suggest might have been maintained in the holy commonwealth, but not in the world of the Restoration or the Whigs. They had helped carry men through a time of change; they had no place in a time of stability. They had been elements of strength in an age of moral confusion and of cruel vigor in an age of vacillation. Now it was suggested that saintly vigor had its own pathology and conventionalism its own health; peace had its virtues as well as godly warfare.

References

BRETT, S. R. (1940), *John Pym, 1583–1643: The Statesman of the Puritan Revolution*, London.

BRINTON, C. (1930), *The Jacobins: An Essay in the New History*, Russell.

ESENIN, S. (1961), 'Soviet Russia', *Partisan Rev.*, vol. 28, pp. 379–82.

FRIEDRICH, C. J. (1957), *Constitutional Reason of State: The Survival of Constitutional Order*, Blaisden.

HOLDEN, W. P. (1954), *Anti-Puritan Satire, 1572–1642*, Yale University Press.

KOENIGSBURGER, H. G. (1955), 'The organization of revolutionary parties in France and the Netherlands during the sixteenth century', *J. mod. Hist.*, vol. 27, pp. 335–51.

LERNER, D. (1958), *The Passing of the Traditional Society*, Free Press.

NEALE, J. E. (1949), *The Elizabethan House of Commons*, Cape.

NEALE, J. E. (1953), *Elizabeth I and her Parliaments*, Cape.

PAUL, R. S. (1955), *The Lord Protector: Religion and Politics in the Life of Oliver Cromwell*, Erdmans.

Further Reading

General

D. Bell, *The End of Ideology: On the Exhaustion of Political Ideas in the Fifties*, Free Press, 1960.

R. Bendix and S. M. Lipset, 'Political sociology', *Current Sociology*, vol. 6, no. 2, pp. 79–98.

A. F. Bentley, *The Process of Government*, Chicago, 1908.

J. M. Buchanan and G. Tullock, *The Calculus of Consent*, Michigan University Press, 1962.

D. E. Butler, *The Study of Political Behaviour*, Hutchinson University Library, 1958.

C. E. G. Catlin, *Systematic Politics*, Allen & Unwin, 1962.

J. C. Charlesworth (ed.), *Contemporary Political Analysis*, Macmillan, 1967.

B. Crick, *In Defence of Politics*, Weidenfeld & Nicolson, 1962.

R. A. Dahl and C. E. Lindblom, *Politics, Economics and Welfare*, Harper & Row, 1953.

R. A. Dahl, *A Preface to Democratic Theory*, University of Chicago Press, 1956.

R. A. Dahl, 'The behavioural approach in political science: epitaph for a monument to a successful protest', *American Political Science Review*, vol. 55, 1961.

R. A. Dahl, *Modern Political Analysis*, Prentice Hall, 1963.

B. Dejouvenel, *The Pure Theory of Politics*, Cambridge University Press, 1963.

K. W. Deutsch, *The Nerves of Government: Models of Political Communication and Control*, Free Press, 1963.

R. E. Dowling, M. Q. Hale and R. T. Golembiewski, 'Bentley revisited', *American Political Science Review*, vol. 54, 1960.

A. Downs, *An Economic Theory of Democracy*, Harper & Row, 1957.

D. Easton, *The Political System*, Knopf, 1953.

D. Easton, *A System Analysis of Political Life*, Wiley, 1965.

. N. Eisenstadt, *The Political Systems of Empires*, Free Press, 1963.

A. Etzioni, *The Active Society: A Theory of Societal and Political Processes*, Free Press, 1968.

J. Freund, *L'Essence du Politique*, Sirey, 1965.

A. Grabowsky, *Politik im Grundriss*, Dixreiter, 1952.

H. H. Hyman, *Political Socialization. A Study in the Psychology of Political Behavior*, Free Press, 1959.

T. P. Jenkin, *The Study of Political Theory*, Random House, 1967.

R. E. Jones, *The Functional Analysis of Politics. An Introductory Discussion*, Routledge & Kegan Paul, 1967.

W. Kornhauser, *The Politics of Mass Society*, Free Press, 1959.

R. E. Lane, *Political Life: Why People Get Involved in Politics*, Free Press, 1959.

R. E. Lane, 'The politics of consensus in an age of affluence', *American Political Science Review*, vol. 59, pp. 874–95, 1965.

H. D. Lasswell, *The Analysis of Political Behaviour*, Routledge & Kegan Paul, 1948.

H. D. Lasswell, *Politics: Who Gets What, When, How?*, 1936 (republished by Free Press, 1951).

H. D. Lasswell, *The Future of Political Science*, Prentice Hall, 1964.

B. Leoni, 'The meaning of "political" in political decisions', *Political Studies*, vol. 5, 1957.

Ch. E. Lindblom, 'The science of "muddling through"', *Public Administration Review*, vol. 19, pp. 78–88, 1959.

Ch. E. Lindblom, *The Intelligence of Democracy: Decision-Making through Mutual Adjustment*, Free Press, 1965.

S. M. Lipset, *Political Man: The Social Basis of Politics*, Doubleday, 1960.

W. J. Mackenzie, *Politics and Social Science*, Penguin, 1967.

R. M. MacIver, *The Web of Government*, Macmillan, 1947.

C. B. Macpherson, *The Political Theory of Possessive Individualism*, Oxford University Press, 1962.

Ch. Merriam, *Systematic Politics*, Chicago, 1945.

J. M. Mitchell and W. C. Mitchell, *Political Analysis and Public Policy: An Introduction to Political Science*, Rand McNally, 1969.

F. Oppenheimer, *Der Staat*, Gustav Fischer Verlag, 1954.

T. Parsons, 'The political aspects of social structure and process', in D. Easton (ed.), *Varieties of Political Theory*, Prentice Hall, 1966.

N. Poulantzas, *Pouvoir Politique et Classes Sociales*, François Maspero, 1968.

W. H. Riker, *The Theory of Political Coalitions*, Yale University Press, 1962.

W. G. Runciman, *Social Science and Political Theory*, Cambridge University Press, 1963.

C. Schmitt, *Der Begriff des Politischen*, Dunker und Humblot, 1963.

D. B. Truman, *The Governmental Process*, Knopf, 1951.

G. Tullock, *A General Theory of Politics*, published privately by Virginia University Press, 1958.

G. Wallas, *Human Nature in Politics*, Constable, 1908.

T. D. Weldon, *The Vocabulary of Politics*, Penguin, 1953.

H. V. Wiseman, *Political Systems*, Routledge & Kegan Paul, 1966.

S. Wolin, *Politics and Vision*, Allen & Unwin, 1961.

The Concept of Power

P. Bachrach and S. Baratz Morton, 'Two faces of power', *American Political Science Review*, vol. 56, 1962.

F. Bourricaud, *Esquisse d'une Théorie de l'Autorité*, Plon, 1961.

Z. Brzezinski and S. P. Huntington, *Political Power: USA/USSR*, Viking Press, 1964.

R. A. Dahl, 'The concept of power', *Behavioral Science*, no. 2, 1957.

A. Hacker, 'Power to do what', I. L. Horowitz (ed.), *The New Sociology*, pp. 134–46, 1964.

H. D. Lasswell and A. Kaplan, *Power and Society. A Framework for Political Inquiry*, London, 1952.

N. Long, 'Power and administration', *Public Administration Review*, vol. 9, p. 257, 1949.

C. E. Merriam, *Political Power*, McGraw Hill, 1934.

T. Parsons, 'On the concept of political power', reprinted from *Proceedings of the American Philosophical Society*, vol. 107, no. 3, June 1963.

T. Parsons, 'The distribution of power in American society', *World Politics*, vol. 10, pp. 123–43, 1957.

T. Parsons, 'On the concept of influence', reprinted from *Public Opinion Quarterly*, 1963.

T. Parsons, 'Some reflections on the place of force in social process', in Harry Eckstein (ed.), *Internal War: Basic Problems and Approaches*, Free Press, 1964.

P. H. Partridge, 'Some notes on concept of power', *Political Studies*, vol. 11, 1963.

B. Russel, *Power*, Norton, 1938.

Studies on Elites

R. Aron, 'Social structure and the ruling class', *British Journal of Sociology*, vol. 1, no. 1, pp. 1–17, March 1950; vol. 1, no. 2, pp. 126–44, June 1950.

P. Bachrach, *The Theory of Democratic Elitism: A Critique*, Little, Brown, 1967.

B. R. Berelson, P. F. Lazarsfeld and W. N. McPhee, *Voting*, University of Chicago Press, 1954.

T. B. Bottomore, 'The administrative elite', in I. L. Horowitz (ed.) *The New Sociology*, pp. 357–69.

T. B. Bottomore, *Elites and Society*, Watts, 1964; Penguin, 1966.

E. Burdik and A. J. Brodbeck, *American Voting Behavior*, Macmillan, chs. 12–13, 1959.

A. Campbell *et al.*, *The American Voter*, Wiley, 1960.

A. Campbell, G. Gurin and W. E. Miller, *The Voter Decides*, Row Peterson, 1954.

H. P. Dreitzel, *Elitebegriff und Sozialstruktur*, Ferdinand Erike Verlag, 1962.

E. Frank (ed.), *Lawmakers in a Changing World*, Prentice Hall, 1960.

W. L. Guttsman, *The British Political Elite*, MacGibbon & Kee, 1963.

S. Keller, *Beyond the Ruling Class: Strategic Elites in Modern Society*, Random House, 1963.

W. Kornhauser, 'Power elite or veto groups', in S. M. Lipset and L. Lowenthal (eds.), *Culture and Social Character*, Free Press, 1961.

P. F. Lazarsfeld, B. Berelson and H. Gaudet, *The People's Choice*, 2nd edn, Columbia University Press, 1948.

D. R. Matthews, *The Social Background of Political Decision-Makers*, Doubleday, 1954.

J. Meisel, *The Myth of the Ruling Class: Gaetano Mosca and the Elite*, Michigan University Press, 1958.

C. W. Mills, *The Power Elite*, Oxford University Press, 1956.

K. J. Ratnam, 'Charisma and political leadership', *Political Studies*, vol. 12, 1964.

A. Rogow and H. Lasswell, *Power, Corruption and Rectitude*, Prentice Hall, 1963.

R. Sereno, *The Rulers: The Theory of the Ruling Class*, Harper & Row, rev. edn, 1968.

Community Power

R. E. Agger, D. Goldrich and B. E. Swanson, *The Rulers and the Ruled*, Wiley, 1964.

E. C. Banfield, *Political Influence*, Free Press, 1960.

E. C. Banfield and J. Q. Wilson, *City Politics*, Harvard University Press and the MIT Press, 1963.

E. C. Banfield, *Big City Politics*, Random House, 1966.

A. H. Birch, *Small Town Politics: A Study of Political Life in Glossop*, Oxford University Press, 1959.

T. N. Clark, *Community Structure and Decision Making: Comparative Analysis*, Chandler, 1968.

R. L. Crain *et al.*, *The Politics of Community Conflict*, Bobbs-Merrill, 1969.

R. Dahl, *Who Governs?*, Yale University Press, 1961.

L. C. Freeman, *Patterns of Local Community Leadership*, Bobbs-Merrill, 1968.

H. F. Gosnell, *Machine Politics: Chicago Model*, Chicago University Press, 1937.

S. Greer, 'The social structure and political process of suburbia', *American Sociological Review*, pp. 514–26, August 1960.

F. Hunter, *Community Power Structure*, North Carolina University Press, 1953.

G. W. Jones, *Borough Politics*, Macmillan, 1969.

H. Kaplan, *Urban Political Systems*, Columbia University Press, 1967.

N. E. Long, 'The local community as an ecology of games', *American Journal of Sociology*, vol. 64, no. 3, pp. 251–61, 1958.

W. J. M. Mackenzie, *Theories of Local Government*, LSE, 1961.

D. C. Miller, *International Community Power Structure: Comparative Studies of Four World Cities*, Indiana University Press, 1970.

N. W. Polsby, *Community Power and Political Theory*, Yale University Press, 1963.

R. V. Presthus, *Men at the Top: A Study in Community Power*, Oxford University Press, 1964.

P. H. Rossi, 'Power and community structure', *Midwest Journal of Political Science*, vol. 4, no. 4, pp. 390–401, 1960.

J. Q. Wilson, 'Politics and reform in American city', *American Government Annual, 1962–1963*, Holt, Rinehart & Winston, pp. 37–52, 1962.

R. C. Wood, *Suburbia: Its People and their Politics*, Houghton Mifflin, 1958.

R. C. Wood, *1400 Governments*, Harvard University Press, 1961.

Interest Groups

E. G. Banfield and M. Meyerson, *Politics, Planning and the Public Interest*, Free Press, 1955.

H. Eckstein, *Pressure Group Politics (The British Medical Association)*, Allen & Unwin, 1960.

H. W. Ehrmann, *Organized Business in France*, Princeton University Press, 1957.

H. W. Ehrmann, *Interest Groups on Four Continents*, University of Pittsburgh Press, 1958.

S. E. Finer, *Anonymous Empire*, Pall Mall, 1958.

S. E. Finer, *The Man on Horseback; The Role of the Military in Politics*, Pall Mall, 1962.

J. H. Kaiser, *Die Repraesentation Organisierten Interessen*, Duncker und Humblot, 1956.

J. G. La Palombara, *Interest Groups in Italian Politics*, Princeton University Press, 1964.

E. Latham, 'The group basis of politics: notes for a theory', *American Political Science Review*, vol. 46, no. 2, pp. 376–97, June 1952.

J. Meynaud, *Nouvelles Etudes sur les Groupes de Pression en France*, Librairie Armand Colin, 1962.

A. Potter, *Organized Groups in British National Politics*, Faber & Faber, 1961.

G. Skilling, 'Interest groups and communist politics', *World Politics*, April 1966.

J. D. Stewart, *British Pressure Groups*, Oxford University Press, 1958.

Political Parties

R. Alford, *Party and Society*, Rand McNally, 1963.

E. Allardt and Y. Littunen, *Cleavages, Ideologies and Party Systems*, Westermark Society, 1964.

S. H. Barnes, *Party Democracy: Politics in an Italian Socialist Federation*, Yale University Press, 1967.

J. Blondel, *Voters, Parties and Leaders: The Social Fabric of British Politics*, Penguin, 1965.

J. G. Bulpitt, *Party Politics in English Local Government*, Longman, 1967.

M. Duverger, *Political Parties*, Methuen, 1954.

S. J. Eldersveld, *Political Parties: A Behavioral Analysis*, Rand McNally, 1964.

L. D. Epstein, *Political Parties in Western Democracies*, Praeger, 1967.

F. I. Greenstein, *The American Party System and the American People*, Prentice Hall, 1963.

V. O. Key, *Politics, Parties and Pressure Groups*, Crowell, 1958.

G. E. Lavau, *Partis Politiques et Réalités Sociales: Contribution à une Etude Réaliste des Partis Politiques*, Librairie Armand Colin, 1953.

S. M. Lipset and S. Rokkan (eds.), *Party Systems and Voter Alignments*, Free Press, 1967.

D. MacRae, *Parliament, Parties and Society in France, 1946–1958*, Macmillan, 1967.

R. T. Mackenzie, *British Political Parties*, Heinemann, 1955.

R. Michels, *Political Parties: A Sociological Study of the Oligarchical Tendencies of Modern Democracy*, New York, 1959.
(First published as *Zur Soziologie des Parteiwesens in der Modern Demokratie*, 1911.)

R. Miliband, *Parliamentary Socialism*, Allen & Unwin, 1961.

W. E. Miller, 'Party Identification and Partisan Attitudes', in R. E. Wolfinger (ed.), *Readings in American Political Behavior*, Prentice Hall, 1966.

S. Neumann (ed.), *Modern Political Parties*, Chicago University Press, 1956.

A. Ranney and W. Kendall, *Democracy and the American Party System*, Harcourt Brace & World, 1956.

R. Rose, 'Complexities of party leadership', *Parliamentary Affairs*, Summer 1963.

C. Rossiter, *Parties and Politics in America*, Cornell University Press, 1960.

G. Roth, *The Social Democrats in Imperial Germany*, The Bedminster Press, 1963.

G. Sartori, 'The typology of party system: proposals for improvement', in E. Allardt and S. Rokkan (eds.), *Mass Politics, Studies in Political Sociology*, Free Press, 1970.

E. E. Schattschneider, *Party Government*, Holt, Rinehart & Winston, 1942.

E. E. Schattschneider, Committee on Political Parties of the American Political Science Association, *Toward a More Responsible Two-Party System*, Holt, Rinehart & Winston, 1950.

F. J. Sorave, *Political Parties in the American System*, Little, Brown, 1964.

D. E. Stokes and W. E. Miller, 'Party government and the saliency of congress', in R. E. Wolfinger (ed.), *Readings in American Political Behavior*, Prentice Hall, 1966.

S. Tarrow, *Peasant Communism in Southern Italy*, Yale University Press, 1967.

J. J. Wiatr, 'The hegemony party system in Poland', in E. Allardt and S. Rokkan (eds.), *Mass Politics, Studies in Political Sociology*, Free Press, 1970.

A. B. Wildavsky, 'A methodological critique of Duverger's political parties', *Journal of Politics*, vol. 21, pp. 304–18, May 1959.

Political Participation and Militancy

F. Alberoni *et al.*, *L'Attivista di Partito*, Il Mulino, 1967.

E. Allardt and P. Pesonen, 'Citizen participation in political life in Finland', *International Sociol. Science Journal*, vol. 12, no. 1, pp. 27–39.

G. Almond and S. Verda, *The Civic Culture*, Princeton University Press, 1963.

G. Di Palma, *Apathy and Participation. Mass Politics in Western Societies*, Free Press, 1970.

U. Himmelstrand, 'Depoliticization and political involvement: a theoretical and empirical approach', in E. Allardt and S. Rokkan (eds.), *Mass Politics, Studies in Political Sociology*, Free Press, 1970.

T. H. Marshall, 'Citizenship and social class', in *Class, Citizenship and Social Development*, Doubleday, 1964.

L. W. Milbrath, *Political Participation*, Rand McNally, 1955.

A. Pizzorno, 'An introduction to the theory of political participation', in *Social Science Information,* vol. 9, no. 5, pp. 29–61.

S. Rokkan, 'Mass suffrage, secret voting and political participation', *European Journal of Sociology*, vol. 2, pp. 132–52, 1961.

S. Rokkan (ed.), *Approaches to the Study of Political Participation*, Christian Michelsen Institute, 1962.

S. Rokkan, 'The comparative study of political participation: notes towards a perspective on current research', in A. Ranney (ed.), *Essays on the Behavioral Study of Politics*, University of Illinois Press, 1962.

M. Rosenberg, 'Some determinants of political apathy', *Public Opinion Quarterly*, vol. 18, pp. 349–66, 1959.

G. Vedel (ed.), *La Dépolitisation: Mythe ou Réalité?*, Librairie Armand Colin, 1962.

Electoral Analyses

M. Abrams, 'Social class and British politics', *Public Opinion Quarterly*, vol. 20, no. 3, pp. 342–50, 1961.

A. J. Allen, *The English Voter*, English Universities Press, 1964.

F. Bealey, J. Blondel and W. P. McCann, *Constituency Politics: A Study of Newcastle-under-Lyme*, Faber & Faber, 1965.

B. Berelson, P. F. Lazarsfeld and W. N. McPhee, *Voting*, University of Chicago Press, 1954.

J. Blondel, 'Towards a general theory of change in voting behaviour', in *Political Studies*, vol. 13, pp. 93–5, 1965.

E. Burdick and A. Brodbeck (eds.), *American Voting Behavior*, Macmillan, 1959.

A. Campbell *et al.*, *The Voter Decides*, Harper & Row, 1954.

A. Campbell *et al.*, *The American Voter*, Wiley, 1961.

A. Campbell *et al.*, *Elections and the Political Order*, Wiley, 1966.

V. Capecchi *et al.*, *Il Comportamento elettorale in Italia*, Il Mulino, 1968.

Ph. E. Converse and G. Dupeux, 'Politicization of the electorate in France and the United States', *Public Opinion Quarterly*, vol. 26, no. 1, pp. 1–23, 1962.

J. de Sola Pool, R. P. Abelson and S. L. Popkin, *Candidates, Issues and Strategies; A Computer Simulation of the 1960 and 1964 Presidential Elections*, MIT Press, 1965.

F. Goguel, 'La sociologie electorale en France', in G. Gurvitch (ed.), *Traité de Sociologie*, Presses Universitaires de France, pp. 46–63, 1958.

V. O. Key Jr, *The Responsible Electorate; Rationality in Presidential Voting 1936–1960*, Belknap Press, pp. 21–158, 1966.

P. F. Lazarsfeld, B. Berelson and H. Gaudet, *The People's Choice*, 2nd edn, Columbia University Press, 1948.

D. W. Rae, *The Political Consequences of Electoral Laws*, Yale University Press, 1967.

H. Tingsten, *Political Behavior, Studies in Election Statistics*, London, 1937.

Change and Revolution

H. Arendt, *On Revolution*, Viking Press, 1963.

C. Brinton, *Anatomy of Revolution*, Prentice Hall, 1952.

J. C. Davies, 'Toward a theory of revolution', *American Sociological Review*, pp. 5–19, 1962.

H. Eckstein, *The Problem of Internal War*, Princeton University Press, 1963.

L. P. Edwards, *The Natural History of Revolution*, University of Chicago Press, 1927.

M. Janowitz, *Political Conflict*, Quadrangle Books, 1970.

C. Johnson, *Revolutionary Change*, Little, Brown, 1966.

B. Moore Jr, *Social Origins of Dictatorships and Democracy; Lord and Peasant in the Making of the Modern World*, Beacon Press, 1966.

J. Skolnick, *The Politics of Protest*, Ballantine, 1969.

Acknowledgements

Permission to reproduce the Readings in this volume is acknowledged to the following sources:

1 Harper & Row Inc. and Fontana Paperbacks
2 Doubleday & Co. Inc. and Fontana Paperbacks
3 Oxford University Press
4 Princeton University Press
5 Free Press
6 Suhrkamp Verlag, Beacon Press and Heinemann Educational Books Ltd
8 Guis. Laterza & Figli
9 *British Journal of Sociology*
10 American Political Science Association
11 Harvard University Press
12 Harvard University Press
13 *Government and Opposition*, Jerzy J. Wiatr and Adam Przeworski
14 University of California Press
15 American Academy of Political and Social Science and Samuel H. Beer
16 Free Press
17 Methuen & Co. Ltd
18 UNESCO
19 Doubleday & Co. Inc. and Heinemann Educational Books Ltd
20 Free Press
21 International Publishers and Lawrence & Wishart Ltd
22 Grove Press Inc. and Granada Publishing Ltd
23 Seuil and Random House Inc.
24 Harvard University Press, Weidenfeld & Nicolson Ltd and Michael Walzer

Author Index

Subject Index

Unemployment, 281, 282, 288
Uniformity, 273, 274, 275–6, 277
United Party of the Cuban
    Socialist Revolution (Cuba), 178
United Peasants' Party (Poland),
    173
URAS (France), 256, 257
United States of America
  class basis of parties in 240–42,
      244, 252–3, 258, 263–5, 266
  collectivist market in, 192
  elections in, 119, 218–19, 242
  electoral participation in, 230
  nineteenth-century economy in,
      113–14, 117
  organizational activity in, 242, 246
  organizational participation in,
      229–31, 234–7, 244, 250
  parties' development in, 15, 22,
      193, 202, 212, 218
  political order in, 114–15, 116–17,
      118
  power of party leaders in, 194
  power structure in, 111, 114–25
  pressure groups in, 191, 194, 197,
      199, 200–205
  professional politicians in, 38, 115
  scientization of politics in, 67,
      72–4
  student movement in, 310, 311
  wealth and politics in, 67, 72–4,
      104, 105 see also Corporations,
      Military
United States Chamber of
    Commerce, 201

Universities, 125, 174, 221, 311, 312,
    313, 314, 315, 316, 318

Veto groups, 117
Veterans, 202
Vietnam War, 311, 315
Violence, 12, 17–18, 28–9, 31,
    112–13, 300–309
Voting
  absention from, 156
  party origins and, 215
  pressure groups and, 196
  public opinion and, 194
  social conditions and, 263–7 see
      also Elections, Political parties

Wealth, 36, 37, 103–5, 255–6
Welfare state, 192
Wentworth, Peter, 324
Westendhal (Germany), 214
Whig Party (Britain), 252, 333
Workers' Self-Government, 172
Works Councils (Italy), 265
Working class
  in capitalist countries, 301
  revolutionary movements and, 17
  student movement and, 316 see
      also Political parties, class basis
      of, Trade unions

Yugoslav Communist Party, 169
Yugoslavia, 170, 175
Young Christian Farmers, 222
Young Christian Students, 222
Young Christian Workers, 222

Leisure, Sport and
Working-Class Cultures:
Theory and History

Hart Cantelon and Robert Hollands,
editors

Garamond Press
Toronto, Ontario

A publication of Garamond Press

Garamond Press
67A Portland Street
Toronto, Ontario M5V 2M9

Cover design: Peter McArthur
Typesetting: PageCraft in Halifax, N. S.

Printed and bound in Canada

This book was published with the support and cooperation of:
The Centre for Sport and Leisure Studies
School of Physical and Health Education
Queen's University
Kingston, Ontario K7L 1P8

Canadian Cataloguing in Publication Data

Cantelon, Hart and Hollands, Robert (Eds.)
Leisure, sport and working-class cultures

ISBN 0-920059-58-9

1. Labor and laboring classes - Recreation - Political aspects - History. 2. Leisure - Political aspects - History. 3. Sports and state - History. 4. Capitalism. I. Cantelon, Hart, 1944-

HD7395.R4L44 1988   306'.48'0880623   C88-093472-7

Contents

Contributors

HART CANTELON teaches sociology, history and comparative studies in the School of Physical and Health Education, Queen's University. He also serves as the Director of the Centre for Sport and Leisure Studies. His research interests encompass sport and leisure in state-socialist societies, the workers' sports movement and children in high-performance sport.

ROBERT HOLLANDS was a Research Fellow at the Centre for Sport and Leisure Studies at Queen's University. He is currently working at the Trade Union Resource Centre, Newcastle, England. His major areas of interest include youth and leisure, sport and working-class culture, and Marxist theories of cultural production.

ALAN METCALFE is a professor in the Faculty of Human Kinetics, University of Windsor. He is widely recognized as one of Canada's foremost sport historians. In addition to his numerous articles and books on Canadian sport, Alan edits the prestigious *Canadian Journal of the History of Sport and Physical Education*.

ALAN TOMLINSON teaches sociology and cultural studies on Sports Science and Physical Education degrees in the Faculty of Social and Cultural Studies, Brighton Polytechnic. His research interests in the sociology of culture embrace popular culture, leisure and art/literature.

Preface

This book is based on presentations originally given at a workshop on "Leisure, Sport, and Working-Class Cultures," hosted by the Queen's University Centre for Sport and Leisure Studies in March, 1983. A preliminary compilation of workshop presentations was circulated in 1985 as part of the Centre's *Working Papers* series. However, there has been considerable demand for Centre publications in recent years, and Garamond Press has generously undertaken to make selected volumes available to a broader audience. The volume at hand is the first of several planned volumes in a Garamond/Centre series on "Leisure, Sport and Popular Culture."

The Centre for Sport and Leisure Studies first took shape in the late 1970s as a loosely organized work group located in the School of Physical and Health Education (PHE) and the Department of Sociology at Queen's University. The purpose of the working group was to promote and co-ordinate interdisciplinary research on leisure, sport and popular culture in both capitalist and state-socialist countries. A *Working Papers* series under the editorship of Rick Gruneau was initiated in 1978 in conjunction with a series of seminars and workshops. A grant from the Principal's Development Fund at Queen's provided space and resources, for the creation, in 1982, of a more formalized Centre for Sport and Leisure Studies within the School of PHE.

One research area that we considered underdeveloped was the relationship between leisure, sport and working-class cultures. Alan Tomlinson's stint as the Centre's first Visiting Scholar initiated a broad-ranging debate about theory, history and the analysis of sports and leisure in working-class cultures. Out of these discussions, a workshop was planned to bring together a number of scholars (some working in virtual isolation) from diverse backgrounds (sociology, history, anthropology, leisure studies, physical education, political studies) to present and discuss their developing theories and research interests on the subject. We wanted to create a true workshop environment—one in which there were no star guest speakers lecturing to a stuporous, passive and wide-eyed audience. In this respect, the workshop succeeded. A high level of discussion and solidarity among the participants was very evident.

No printed selection of papers can capture the atmosphere of a successful workshop. Furthermore, because of the emphasis on informality and on discussion of work in progress, only some of the material presented at the workshop could be compiled for publication. John Alt, Bruce Kidd, Frank Manning, Wally Seccombe, and Ian Taylor also made presentations at the workshop and greatly contributed to the overall discussion. We are grateful to them all.

Other acknowledgements are also in order. Rick Gruneau played a central role in bringing the Centre's work to the attention of Garamond Press. Peter Saunders and Errol Sharpe of Garamond Press have been both patient and supportive. Finally, the School of Physical and Health Education and the School of Graduate Studies and Research at Queen's have provided much-needed financial support for many of the Centre's scholarly activities.

Hart Cantelon
Robert Hollands
June 1988

Leisure, History and Theory:
Some Preliminary Points of Departure for Studies of Working-Class Cultures

Hart Cantelon
Robert Hollands

The papers in this collection all pertain to a set of themes focused on relationships between leisure and work, class and culture; they are organized around the tensions between history and theory. The theoretical focus in the papers is deliberate. If there has been only a smattering of theoretical work of any consequence on leisure, there has been even less on the role of leisure in working-class cultures. Historical studies of working-class leisure have been equally scarce. This is not to say that one cannot find histories of working-class cultures that take account of "leisure," but rather to make two key points.

First, the majority of studies on working-class cultures that have actively and consciously emphasized the cultural experiences of working men and women are relatively recent products of the traditions of oral and social history. Second, the issue of leisure and its relationship to the basic elements of working-class cultures in various periods of history is only now beginning to be adequately theorized. Let us take up the first point and examine it in greater detail, before we come back to the issue of leisure.

Labour History, Cultural and Leisure Studies:
Toward a Unified Perspective
It is impossible to overemphasize the degree to which labour history remained cultureless until the 1950s. Richard Johnson's 1979 article "Culture and the Historians"[1] serves as a constant reminder that "the new kind of history," particular British labour history, should emphasize the breaks and progressions

that occurred. Grounded in the theoretical approaches taken by the Marxist scholars Maurice Dobb and Dona Torr, the "new history" that developed in Britain during the 1970s included the early works of Christopher Hill, J.F.C. Harrison and E.P. Thompson, along with the literary/cultural influences of Richard Hoggart and Raymond Williams. Such histories attempted to articulate specific social, cultural and economic experiences and determinations among various fragments of the working classes. Other developments in oral and social history, not to mention studies concerned with popular religion, nationalism, the family, feminism and (lo and behold) popular culture and leisure, also sprang up in the 1970s and have further contributed to our understanding of working-class cultures.[2] Yet these developments did not signal the complete alliance of labour history and cultural studies. Alan Tomlinson's anecdote in the introduction to his paper in this collection provides a personal example of the difficulty of marrying up such seemingly disparate subjects as "Working-Class Movements" and "Education and the Idea of Culture," two courses he took as a British undergraduate.

Developments in Canadian and American labour history have followed similar patterns, each having its own particular nuances and specific sets of conjunctures. With a few notable exceptions, serious studies of working-class life and cultural experience did not become a force to be reckoned with until the 1970s. In the Canadian context, the work of Bryan Palmer and Gregory Kealey, among others, has had a substantial impact on the form of historical research on working-class organization and expression.[3] Informed by the Marxist debates of the sixties and seventies and the historiography of E.P. Thompson, Kealey and Warrian have noted that "Canadian historical writing has left little room for the inclusion of ordinary working people".[4] Similar comments could be made about American scholarship. While research on working-class culture in the U.S.A. is slightly more complicated in its evolution, it has, on the whole, underplayed the cultural experiences of the working class. Notable exceptions to this during the 1970s could be found in the works of Herbert Gutman and Stanley Aronowitz, both of whom have played a pivotal role in the recent expansion of work in this area.[5]

These broad-ranging studies of working-class culture included, but did not always highlight, the importance of leisure pursuits in working-class life.[6] More important was the fact that leisure was not seriously theorized, primarily because it was not seen to be serious. In Britain and Canada, alongside (but rarely informed by) the general working-class culture studies, there grew up a substantial body of sport history. Again with a few notable exceptions,[7] much of this work, while emphasizing the importance of sport and leisure, failed to connect these activities with the economic, political and ideological realms of social life. In Canada, the pioneering works of Alan Metcalfe, Bruce Kidd and Richard Gruneau have attempted to link class structure and leisure/culture practices with the broader processes of social and historical development.[8] In "A Culture in

Conflict," Bryan Palmer also takes such leisure activities as baseball, picnics, outings and parades seriously as cultural forms of solidarity for Hamilton's skilled workers, as they lived through the onslaught of industrial capitalism in the late 19th century. While much more work needs to be conducted in this area, these writers have ploughed the first furrows in the study of leisure and sport in working-class cultures. We must follow them into the field.

Central Themes and Key Assumptions

The papers contained in this volume collectively demonstrate four major themes in the study of leisure and working-class cultures: (a) the need to radically reconceptualize and struggle over the important categories of leisure, work and culture; (b) the central importance of cultural experience and local structures in mediating the broader influence of capital accumulation and the policing of particular leisure activities; (c) the notion that leisure and sport as forms of cultural experience are neither free-floating idealist entities nor mechanically determined reflections of an economic base, but rather are the active lived-out expressions of particular historical social relations; and (d) the necessity of theoretically informed, concrete historical studies for further understanding the changing conditions and fragmentation of working-class life in contemporary capitalist and state-socialist societies. We deal briefly with each of these themes in this collection of papers.

The first section of Robert Hollands' paper concerns transforming the conventional definitions and relationships between the concepts of leisure and work. It would be unrealistic to suggest that we simply stop using these concepts, but Hollands's main thrust is to shift the whole problematic of the leisure/work dichotomy. He argues that, in order to do this, we must examine the historical specificity of work and leisure as they have developed under capitalism. He goes on to provide an alternative to the mainstream leisure literature by considering relationships between leisure-taking, the labour process, and shop-floor culture. Alan Metcalfe also struggles to come to terms with the class meanings of leisure and culture and the social relations underlying these processes and experiences. Both authors seek to locate their analyses of leisure practices at the intersections of cultural studies, history and social theory.

Although all four papers in this collection make reference to the central importance of lived experience and localized structures, Alan Tomlinson's British case study on Colne, and Alan Metcalfe's discussion of working-class leisure in Montreal and North-East England are particularly sensitive on this point. Tomlinson's historical ethnography emphasizes the role that such inter-mediate factors as leisure, sport and locality had in blurring class divisions and blunting the economic tensions of the 1930s. In the spirit of E.P. Thompson's well-known remark about the English working classes, "... their aspirations were valid in terms of their own experience ..."[9] Tomlinson argues that it was through the experience of community and the active making of good times that the working classes of Colne "contributed to the reproduction of bad times." Metcalfe also hints at how the experiences of work, locality and (in the case of Montreal) ethnicity were manifest in contributing to both the homogeneous and the heterogeneous elements of these working-class cultures.

A concern with the cultural experience of working-class men and women need not imply that human meaning and subjectivity (or indeed activity) within the realm of leisure and community are somehow cut off from broader social and material circumstances. Again, what is common to all these papers is the key notion that leisure and cultural experience are actually embedded in particular social relations of power, between classes, between genders, or—in the case of Hart Cantelon's paper—between the working-class and the state. Tomlinson makes this point quite clear when he suggests that we must "develop an adequate notion of what social bonds are, both within working-class life and between the working-class and other classes." Although humans must always be seen as the makers of history, we do not always make it as we choose.[10] Metcalfe and Tomlinson, respectively, make reference to the inhumane and sometimes brutal policing of leisure pursuits and the actual physical removal of "rough" sections of a working-class community. Perhaps more to the point is Cantelon's discussion, in a much different context, of the dislocation between the official regulations and policies of the Communist Party on rationalized leisure and the varied responses of sections of the Russian working-class and peasantry—a dislocation that he argues, continues to prevail. Additional theorizing on leisure as an active, constitutive component of social relations is necessary in order to understand working-class cultures in their entirety.

Finally, these papers address some of the problems of historical research and its intersection with theory and method. This is a particularly difficult area and the papers only begin to elaborate the questions and tensions that came out of the workshop, at which original drafts of these papers were presented. There is always, for example, tension between traditional methods of historical scholarship and the ethnographic approaches to historical enquiry. Even more problematic is the debate over history as a collection of "facts" that stand on their own or of the necessity of theories to constitute historical data as facts in the first place. The problem of conducting ethnographic and oral histories of periods from which neither people nor adequate unofficial sources (diaries, log books, records of songs, local games, etc.) now exist was also raised in workshop discussions. Not all such questions were answered during the workshop. However, the papers included in this volume presuppose two main points. First, all histories are conducted within certain frameworks and dominant assumptions and it is necessary to strive for the most comprehensive and explanatory theories and methods possible. Second, ethnographic histories can work to buttress and modify broader historical theories by showing how groups and classes actively lived out, made, remade, negotiated, handled, transformed and reproduced the conditions of their dominance and freedom. Hegemony of one social group over another can never be simply asserted; it must continually be made and re-made, often in the face of considerable opposition.

In conclusion, we want to emphasize that the papers published here were written more to raise questions and open up issues for study than to attempt any definitive conclusions. Our goal has been to stimulate debate and to draw attention to the study of leisure in working-class cultures. Our coverage has necessarily been selective.[11] Clearly, there is a great deal more work to be done.

Notes

1. Richard Johnson, "Culture and the Historians", in John Clarke, Chas Critcher and Richard Johnson (eds.), *Working Class Culture: Studies in Theory and History* (London: Hutchinson, 1979), pp. 57-8.

2. Ibid., p.61.

3. See Bryan Palmer, *A Culture in Conflict: Skilled Workers and Industrial Capitalism in Hamilton, Ontario 1860-1914* (Montreal: McGill-Queen's University Press, 1979). Also see Palmer's *Working-Class Experience: The Rise and Reconstruction of Canadian Labour, 1800-1980* (Toronto: Butterworth, 1983), and Gregory Kealey, "Labour and Working Class History in Canada: Prospects for the 1980s," *Labour/Le Travailleur*, 7 (Spring, 1981).

4. Gregory Kealey and Peter Warrian (eds.), *Essays in Working Class History* (Toronto: McClelland and Stewart, 1976), p.7.

5. Herbert Gutman, *Work, Culture and Society in Industrializing America* (New York: Knopf, 1976); Stanley Aronowitz, *False Promises: The Shaping of American Working Class Consciousness* (New York: McGraw Hill, 1973).

6. Aronowitz's discussion of "Colonialized Leisure/Trivialized Work" in *False Promises: The Shaping of American Working Class Consciousness*; Roy Rosenzweig, "Middle-Class Parks and Working-Class Play: The Struggle Over Recreational Space in Worcester, Massachusetts, 1870-1910," *Radical History Review*, 21 (1979); Stephen Hardy and Alan Ingham, "Games, Structures and Agency: Historians on the American Play Movement," *Journal of Social History*, 17 (2, Winter, 1983).

7. See Peter Bailey, *Leisure and Class in Victorian England*, (London: Routledge and Kegan Paul, 1978) and Hugh Cunningham, *Leisure in the Industrial Revolution, 1780-1880*, (New York: St. Martin's Press, 1980). It should be noted that unlike his or her British counterpart, the Canadian social historian had little chronological descriptive sport material that could be referred to. Thus, although we would not classify it as part of the cultural historical

tradition, the work of Maxwell Howell (and that of his graduate students) has been invaluable in the development of such a tradition. See M. Howell and N. Howell, *Sports and Games in Canadian Life*, (Toronto: Macmillan, 1969).

8. See Alan Metcalfe, *Canada Learns to Play*, (Toronto: McClelland and Stewart, 1987); Bruce Kidd, *The Political Economy of Sport* (Ottawa: CAHPER, 1979); Richard Gruneau, *Class, Sports, and Social Development* (Amherst: University of Massachusetts Press, 1983).

9. E.P. Thompson, *The Making of the English Working Class*, (Harmondsworth: Penguin, 1968), p.13.

10. Of course, this is a paraphrase of Karl Marx's famous comment in *The Eighteenth Brumaire of Louis Bonaparte*, (New York: International Publishers, 1969), p.15.

11. There was, for example, considerable discussion of gender issues during the original workshop, most notably in conjunction with Wally Seccombe's interrogation of the concept of "leisure" from the perspective of women's role in the traditional working-class household. This presentation, however, was conducted extremely informally and was never developed into a paper for publication. For a feminist critique of the leisure literature see Christine Griffin, Dorothy Hobson, Sue MacIntosh and Trisha McCabe, "Women and Leisure," in Jennifer Hargreaves (ed.), *Sport, Culture and Ideology*, (London: Routledge, 1982).

Leisure, Work and Working-Class Cultures:
The Case of Leisure on the Shop Floor

Robert G. Hollands

Introduction

The subject matter of this essay strikes directly at what may be called the conventional wisdom of leisure research, and hints at its fundamental "problematic." In the first part of this paper, I argue that conventional approaches to leisure are flawed in two central respects. First, it is often the case that leisure is viewed as separate from work on the basis of its location along an arbitrary freedom and constraint scale. In other words, researchers have usually imbued the concept of leisure with such qualities as freedom, joy and expression, and then have gone on to proclaim it as the obverse of work. Second, the conventional leisure research concerning the work/leisure relationship often glosses over the historical specificity of these spheres as they are shaped under capitalist production. A critique of idealist theories of the work/leisure relationship is combined with a brief introduction to the materialist categories of social labour and cultural production.

While mainstream literature on work and leisure can be confronted on its own terms, it can also be reconceptualized by dealing with a body of literature on leisure, the labour process and shop-floor culture. In the second part of the paper, I argue that the concept of "leisure in work" can provide both an active critique of conventional definitions and hints at an alternative theoretical framework. The term "leisure in work," rather than "leisure at work," is used to convey the impression that these are really indissoluable processes. In fact, in this case, I argue that "leisure in work" and the playing of work-games—what I would call cultural forms—occupy precisely the same spaces as activities that aid in the production and accumulation of capital. An extension of this idea is that leisure must be understood as an element in the production and reproduction of social life as a whole. The purposes of my analysis of "leisure in work," then, are: (a) to question the validity and applicability of conventional notions of leisure; (b) to capture the historical specificity and determinate conditions affecting the labour/leisure dialectic in the context of lived cultures and the broader political economy; and (c) to provide a starting point for the analysis of work, leisure and working-class cultures.

Leisure and Work: Conventional Approaches

Uncovering the real relationship between work and leisure is absolutely essential if we are to understand what is meant by working-class cultures. If we see their apparent separation as ahistorical and natural, then it is unlikely that we will pursue this relationship in much depth. From a materialist standpoint, however, work and leisure do not exist in a vacuum; rather, they are interrelated products of human activity that have been created and struggled over in particular socio-historical, economic and cultural contexts. So-called "modern leisure" was made possible not only with the rise of market societies, the development of adequate technology and the cultural acceptance of mechanical time, but also with the struggle over these historical processes. In other words, leisure is historically and socially constituted. Similarly, while humans have always had to interact with nature to feed, cloth, shelter and reproduce themselves—a process known commonly as work, or, more correctly, as labour[1]—it is clear that this general activity is qualitatively different in primitive, communal societies, than in monopoly, capitalist social formations. The manner in which these processes have been struggled over and transformed, particularly from the Industrial Revolution to the present, relates to changing patterns of working-class organization and expression in both the productive and cultural spheres.

I have used the term "uncover" here to imply that the real relations between the leisure and work spheres have been mystified or distorted. In order to reconceptualize this relationship—which I would call the labour/leisure dialectic—it is necessary to make reference to the "conventional wisdom" in leisure research.[2] By conventional wisdom I do not mean that there is in any straightforward sense a consensus in leisure studies, but rather that the concept of leisure itself can be located within a limiting ideological and methodological framework.

I want to start by "problematizing" conventional notions of work and leisure and of the relationships between them. This is not the same as saying that work and leisure are social problems, a common presupposition among policy-makers and bureaucrats bent on providing band-aid solutions through "integration," "cooperation" and "tension-management."[3] By problematic I mean (to quote Richard Johnson) "a field of concepts, which organizes a particular science or individual text by making it possible to ask some kinds of questions and by surppressing others."[4] For example, I want to argue here that conventional notions of leisure and work, and the foundations upon which they ultimately rest, are soaked in selective meanings and dominant assumptions that both preclude and exclude alternative conceptions of labour, economy and social relations. By exposing some of these underlying assumptions and dealing with the paradoxical nature of leisure on the shop floor, I am in a sense calling for a radical reconstruction of the whole problematic.

The conventional wisdom of leisure research can be, and has been, attacked from a number of fronts.[5] Due to the broad-ranging character of leisure studies, I want to focus on a number of general points derived largely from two particular authors. The following comments and criticism will be limited to two interrelated aspects of the work/leisure relationship: (a) leisure as "freedom from constraint," and (b) the historical specificity of work and leisure under capitalism. I have chosen to concentrate on the work of Stanley Parker—primarily his *The Future of Work and Leisure*—and Ken Roberts's recent book, *Contemporary Society and the Growth of Leisure*.[6] Both of these theorists are well respected in the leisure studies field and their work is widely cited in the literature. However different their findings and analysis may be, I want to argue that they both make some underlying assumptions that are completely at odds with a materialist perspective and with the historical record.

Leisure as 'Freedom from Constraint'

To preface a discussion of leisure and liberation, we must return once again to the notion of a problematic. In other words, what is it about definitions of leisure that lead us to ask some questions and prevent us from asking others? Parker,[7] in his second chapter ("Problems of Definition") expresses this very point when he argues that differing definitions of leisure are grounded in particular philosophical and political arguments about what "it ought to be" (p.20). So, for example, he notes that Josef Pieper, a Catholic theologian, restricts his definition of leisure to simply a "mental and spiritual attitude."[8] Similarly, Sebastian De Grazia's elitist (and sexist) Aristotelian approach to leisure is ostensibly displayed in his statement that it is "a condition of man, which few desire and fewer achieve."[9] Parker's difficulty is that he hardly pursues this point in any evaluative sense; this becomes a problem when we get to his own attempt to define leisure.

Ken Roberts, in his most recent work on leisure,[10] makes the interesting point that sociological definitions in general cannot really be proven right or wrong; they are simply more or less useful. What he might have added here is that definitions are also ideological—that is, they sometimes allow us to ask some questions by suppressing others. One of the common assumptions underlying both Roberts's and Parker's conceptions of leisure is their potentially liberating capacity. The idea that leisure somehow fulfills "real" and timeless human needs is not just restricted to the conventional wisdom of leisure studies, which makes it all the more important to expose the ideological significance of such a claim.[11]

At first glance, it would appear that such a claim is incompatible with the overall thrust of Parker's *The Future of Work and Leisure*. Indeed, his "holist" philosophy is reflected in the opening comment of the book, which states quite clearly that leisure and work "are really part of the same problem" (p.11). It might be argued that under this scheme, leisure cannot possibly be viewed as liberating without corresponding changes in the work-place and in the economic structures of society. Yet there is a strong sense in which Parker conceptualizes leisure as fulfilling "real" human needs, and his definition of work is somewhat ahistorical and naive. For example, he states quite emphatically that "the need for better facilities for different types of leisure activities is widely recognized" (p.13). The questions he fails to pose here are where these needs have come from, who is pushing what kinds of activities, and what constitutes "widely recognized?"

Parker's underlying assumptions about the nature of leisure are most clearly revealed in his effort to provide a definition. In an attempt to construct a typology of human practices ranging from work to non-work to leisure, he makes a number of statements that hint at the voluntarist potential of the latter concept. Consider the following examples:

> Leisure is time free from obligations either to self or to others—time to do as one chooses (p.27).... there remains the point that leisure means choice (p.29) ... The position of leisure is rather special. It is clearly at the "freedom" end of the freedom-constraint scale... (p.28).

With respect to the subject at hand, he goes on to add that leisure "... need not be restricted to non-working time" and that "'work' and 'leisure in work' may consist of the same activity:," but he qualifies this by stating quite clearly that "the difference is that the latter is chosen for its own sake" (p.28). In other words, "work" and "leisure in work" are not the same, the difference being that one is "chosen for its own sake." By stating, "leisure as freedom from constraint can be a counter both to work and to non-work obligations" (p.135), Parker has practically conceded that the problems of work and leisure are, and can be, separated after all.

Now this is not Parker's overall position, and I do not want to distort his contribution. What I do want to argue is that any conceptual separation made on the basis of such problematic categories as freedom and constraint runs the risk of compartmentalizing work and leisure into two separate spheres by idealizing the latter's capacity to liberate. While this is exactly what Parker is trying not to do, Ken Roberts makes no pretence about separating the two concepts in terms of their inherent characteristics. In *Contemporary Society and the Growth of Leisure*, he states that to "understand leisure in modern societies it must be seen, in part at least, as the obverse of work" (p.3). And while he admits that there is no society that does not stamp its indelible print on the sphere of leisure, Roberts concludes that leisure must be understood as a "relatively self-determined activity" (p.5).

What evidence is there in Roberts's theory for his acceptance of the "leisure as liberation" thesis? His rhetoric about the "scope for choice" in modern leisure is carefully tempered by the paradoxical term "relatively self-determined." One might pose the important question, "relative to what?" Interestingly enough, Roberts comes closest to linking leisure with liberation within anomie theory. "Leisure" he says, "is intrinsically anomic" (p.89). That is, inherent in leisure are situations in which individuals are left without any meaningful values or moral guidelines. On the one hand, Roberts emphasizes the negative consequences of anomie. On the other hand, he sees meaninglessness and the lack of guidance as the necessary conditions for freedom. For example, he writes the following passage about the capacity of leisure:

> It is certainly possible for individuals to miss their way and descend to the vaccuum where they can only cling to whatever friends and pastimes surface. But the enormous freedom makes it possible as never before for individuals to shape their lives with the imprint of their own identities. Uncertainty, unpredictability and diversity are not necessarily pathological. (p.91)

I want to make two related points here. First, I fail to see, even within the logic of anomie theory, how meaninglessness and alienation could ever be construed as freedom in any sense of the term. Second, this idealized conception of leisure is completely undermined by a wealth of social and cultural theory that asserts that action and consciousness presuppose meaning.[12] Taken to the extreme, anomie theory is not only pre-sociological, it is the worst form of abstract individualism.[13]

Roberts attempts to provide a contemporary example of how liberal democracies have created the conditions for relatively self-determined leisure, by drawing a parallel between sports and games in pre and post-industrial societies. He notes that a central feature of industrial society is the loosening of social ties and moral constraints. He goes on to say, "Individuals' duties to relatives and neighbours, for example, are no longer clearly defined by law, custom or religion. Nor are the sports and games in which individuals participate so stipulated" (p.7). This comment neglects two very powerful economic and cultural forces: the rise of market societies and the structuring influence of capital on all human practices; and the process of rationalization. The importance and impact of these interrelated processes have been widely debated and documented with respect to 20th-century sports and games[14] and I think Roberts has ushered in an overly idealistic portrayal of sport as it exists in industrial societies. In fact, many writers have convincingly argued that rationalized sports have actually decreased the possibilities for freedom, by squeezing out alternative forms of bodily practices.

What is wrong with placing leisure and work at opposite ends of a freedom and constraint scale, and extolling the former as potentially liberating? Those of us familiar with Johan Huizinga's *Homo Ludens,* not to mention a series of debates within the sociology of sport, can draw a parallel between idealist theories of play and conventional definitions of leisure.[15] One of the difficulties incurred by viewing leisure as freedom from constraint is the related assumption that it fulfills some ahistorical, biological, or "real" human need. Theories of human needs often tend to raise certain features of mediate activity to the status of eternal "species needs," which transcend history.[16] Adherence to such a position can only move us backward into the depths of idealist aesthetics, rather than forward into the realm of social analysis. Perspectives that continually "confuse history with nature" act to deflect attention away from the production and reproduction of human activities and cultural forms and how they are constituted in a particular historical period. As I will later argue, both Roberts and Parker are somewhat negligent about expressing the historical specificity of work and leisure as they have developed within capitalism. We need to look at how certain leisure activities have been structured, transformed, incorporated or simply pushed aside in the struggle over dominant values and human practices. As Rob Beamish argues, questioning the "transformative potential of the play component of sport [or of leisure practices—R.H.] leads us to these questions but it does not confront the *particularity* of change under *specific historical conditions*" [his emphasis].[17] Theories of freedom through play or leisure make no mention of broader political freedoms, problems of economic scarcity, or cultural representation. It is also important to remember that the "promise of play [and leisure—R.H.] in terms of freedom and constraint is actually quite different from what these activities 'actually deliver' in the context of existing social conditions,"[18] which brings us back to the determinate conditions and historical specificity of work and leisure under capitalist production.

The Historical Specificity of Work and Leisure Under Capitalism
I have argued that an underlying problematic of conventional leisure research is the conceptualization of leisure as separate from work, based on its position along an arbitrary freedom and constraint scale. In doing so, I have perhaps strayed somewhat from Parker's main thesis. Despite his definitional difficulties, his basic theory is that work and the experience of work produce particular relationships to the types of leisure in which members of various social groupings engage. He is in fact promoting the centrality of work. On the other hand, Roberts's discussion of this relationship is quite distinct from, if not in opposition to, Parker's findings. His main argument is that there are other variables, such as family, the life-cycle and social networks, which are much better predictors of how much and what type of leisure humans pursue (see Chapter 7). Despite their differences in both methodology and results, I want to suggest that Roberts and Parker share common deficiencies with respect to the historical specificity of work and leisure in capitalist societies. I should also add that a historical materialist analysis is far more concerned with the production and maintenance of styles of leisure—especially as they relate to working-class

cultures[19]—than with predicting participation rates. In other words, while questions of representation are important, they must be viewed in the broader context of ideology and cultural production.

One of the difficulties in determining the position of "work" relative to that of leisure is that the particular nature of "social labour"[20] under capitalism is glossed over, both in class terms and in the organization of production. Parker is well aware of the historical development of work and leisure, and of how this has created and influenced the existing relationship between them (see Chapter 3). Roberts is also cognizant of this development, but as he is more concerned with contemporary leisure, his book contains only a short discussion of this historical transformation (pp.3-4). His problem is that he sees this development through the well-known, but ill-understood concept of industrialism. E.P. Thompson has carefully reminded us that this transition was not to "industrialism *tout court* but to industrial capitalism."[21] Parker, on the other hand, looks at this development primarily, from a history-of-ideas perspective. Because of these oversights, neither of these theorists says much about the impact of class conflicts and how the actual forms of work and leisure have been struggled over through the historical process. How does this affect their definition and understanding of the term work, or, more correctly, labour? When Parker asserts that work "... is independent of *any* [my emphasis] particular form of society ..." (p.33), he is completely ignoring how different social formations specifically shape both the form and content of social labour. Roberts's discussion of work and leisure is even more crippled by his lack of sensitivity to history and struggle, as is evidenced by his treatment of work and class as variables rather than as social relations.

If the changing nature of social labour is not understood and incorporated into one's analysis, then it is unlikely that the historical development of leisure will be viewed in the context of struggle and working-class culture. Although both Parker and Roberts see leisure as a product of modern civilization resulting from industrialization, a decreased work-week and the rise of market societies, they say little about the driving forces behind these processes. So, for Roberts, industrialism appears to have just happened, resulting in work being "undertaken in particular places," the boss having authority at work but not outside the factory gates, and the creation of a new type of leisure (p.4). But how did this happen, and why? What individuals, classes and historical processes were at work in this transformation? What exactly was this force, conveniently called industrialism, and what did it entail? It is ironic that both writers talk of the declining work-week without mentioning the fact that the struggle for nine- and ten-hour work-days was, in a sense, also a struggle for leisure. Perhaps this point is too obvious or trivial to make, but it reminds us that leisure was struggled for and made in the context of working-class life and culture, rather than being endemic to capitalism. Seen in this light, both work and leisure can be interpreted as sites of lived experience, culture and protracted historical struggle.

Roberts has recently attempted to deflect the criticism that his approach to leisure study lacks an adequate historical base, by suggesting that this type of history is only now being written. In response to this lack of historical information, one might, for instance point to E.P. Thompson's early essay on "Time, Work-Discipline, and Industrial Capitalism." Thompson provides a piece of history that attempts to assess the impact of mechanical time and factory discipline on the cultural habits of craftsmen/craftswomen and farm labourers in 19th-century England. It is absolutely essential reading for contemporary researchers and theorists concerned with the "problem of leisure," for, in Thompson's own words, "a part of the problem is: how did it come to be a problem?" (p.95). His other work, varied as it may be, also contains many valuable insights into the importance of cultural traditions and customs in resisting the economic onslaught of industrial capitalism.[22] There is also a growing body of historical literature in the U.S.A. dealing with worker control and technology, working-class culture and workers' communities.[23] In Canadian history, Bryan Palmer has documented the importance of what he calls "cultural continuities" (which includes leisure pursuits) in the stabilization of working-class life during the consolidation of industrial capitalism in Hamilton in the late 19th century.[24] Those who are not prepared to engage in historical work, or gloss over the important work that has already begun, are not likely to contribute anything new to our understanding of work, leisure and working-class culture.

I want to argue that these difficulties stem from a lack of concern with changes in the labour process and the cultural responses of workers living under monopoly capitalist development. Parker's optimistic statement that the time will come when automation and technological progress "will mean that the choice between more work and more leisure need no longer be dictated by economic necessity" (p.11) may have been justified in the early 1960s, but can only be rejected by the economic situation of the 1980s. This whole position is based on the assumption that wealth will be shared and leisure will be chosen, not enforced. Furthermore, his feeling that employees, either "individually or through their unions" (p.13) can demand more interesting work and a greater say in how it is organized completely ignores numerous changes in the labour process that have militated against any effective worker control. In short, workers toiling under capitalist production have never had the prerogative to formally re-organize production.[25] Indeed, many scholars have argued that the logic of capitalist accumulation manifest in the rise of "scientific management" and the detailed division of labour has worked in exactly the opposite direction. The suggestion that work under capitalism can somehow be made more interesting is negated by changes in the labour process instituted by management for the benefit of capital.

Situating social labour in a historical context makes one far less optimistic about the future of creative work. However, I cannot attribute Ken Roberts's pessimism to his attention to the specificity of the labour process or to a thorough understanding of broader historical developments. His stance is clearly one of liberal piecemeal reform, and I believe it would be fair to say that he is at least partially resigned to a "degrading work/creative leisure" dichotomy.[26] The essential question Roberts fails to ask are why work is organized in this fashion, who benefits, and what structures maintain the organization of work. To say that "Work could be made more fulfilling if that was what people valued above all"(p.143) ignores who benefits from work as it is presently constituted and the ways in which the power structure is maintained. By asserting that leisure and work are not part of a sum-zero equation, Roberts misses the equally important point that the diversification of leisure practices has taken place in the context of: (a) the homogenization of the labour process; and (b) the development of the universal market.[27]

I would like to make one final comment regarding the failure of conventional leisure research to grasp the historical specificity of the labour/leisure dialectic. To be blunt, this position does not come to terms with the notion of class as a social relationship. For Roberts, this is surprising, considering his previous research on the working class.[28] Yet , there is little evidence in *Contemporary Society and the Growth of Leisure* to suggest that class structure must be linked with the dominant forms of social labour and cultural practices. Instead of viewing class in a relational sense, Roberts prefers to treat it as but one variable in his analysis. His comment that "the influence of work is much less powerful than the familiar variables examined in the last chapter" (p.109) negates the way in which the modern nuclear family is structured by and through the wage-labour relationship.[29] Roberts's attempt to provide data refuting the centrality of work in structuring leisure simply does not deal with the "relational" nature of classes in a capitalist economy. In evaluating the contributions of what he calls "class domination theory" (see Chapter 5), Roberts is more concerned with the way in which social class is a useful predictor of leisure behaviour (p.85). Both his evaluation and refutation of this body of work take place on the terrain of a scientific model that largely ignores historical and cultural processes. As I have stated earlier, a materialist analysis is far less concerned with prediction and representation than with the processes of struggle, ideology and cultural production. Parker's discussion is more "conceptual" than "variable" in this regard, which results in his oppositional argument for the centrality of work in leisure studies. Yet, I have strongly criticized his ahistorical and idealist conception of "work," by contrasting it with the historical and materialist concept of social labour. In a similar way, Parker has overextended his emphasis on work to the detriment of fully developing the relationship between class and leisure. And while he has recently argued that a concern with the centrality of work is a way into a discussion of class, the counterargument has been to understand the manner in which class structures both education and the work experience.[30]

Despite their valuable contributions, both Parker and Roberts make a number of questionable assumptions about the nature and historical development of the relationship between work and leisure. I have argued that conventional notions of the work/leisure couplet are fundamentally deficient in two central respects: (a) they make the separation of work and leisure on the basis of their location along an arbitrary freedom and constraint scale; and (b) they fail to grasp the historical specificity of work and leisure under capitalist production. The acuteness of these flaws becomes increasingly apparent when one confronts the paradoxical character of "leisure in work,"[31] to which I now turn.

Leisure in Work: Gameplaying, Shop Floor Culture and the Labour Process

One of the difficulties conventional leisure research has in dealing with "leisure in work" is that it often mistakes the nature of culture itself. As Paul Willis states, "Culture is not artifice and manners, the preserve of Sunday best, rainy afternoons and concert halls. It is the material of our daily lives, the brick and mortar of our most commonplace understanding, feelings and responses."[32] Because culture in this sense is not only those "special, heightened" moments but all experiences—"especially as they lie around central life activities and struggles" (p.186)—the labour/leisure dialectic must occupy a central place in our understanding of working-class cultures. In order to comprehend the expansion and diversification of human activities in capitalist society (and hence the fragmentation of working-class cultures), we must also come to grips with the homogeneous character of the labour process and the effect of the universal market.

There is a body of work on labour, leisure and shop-floor culture that challenges many of the assumptions of conventional leisure study and simultaneously attempts to deal with some of the above concerns. Literature from industrial sociology has very rarely been incorporated into mainstream leisure research, due to the simple fact that it does not fit the conventional definition of what leisure is supposed to be. This is unfortunate for a number of reasons. In the first place, this material tends to remind us that leisure is not simply a "special, heightened" moment of consciousness, but part of a totality of human life experience and struggle. To quote Willis again, the question becomes, "What degree of frenzy, activity, boredom and suffering have been objectified into a thousand articles on glamorous display in the department store?" (p.185). In other words, this material tells us, as Marx himself theorized,[33] that the productive and consumptive sectors of capitalist society are nothing but two sides of the same coin. Second, this literature points to an essential site of working-class culture often overlooked by theorists who point to the fragmentation of "the working class" as evidence of the triumph of liberal democracies, rather than seeing it as being due to the changing face of monopoly capitalism. Studies of the shop floor are one way (and one way only) into understanding the contradictory nature of class culture in contemporary society; fragmented and divided in some spheres, yet linked in very fundamental ways to the wage-labour relationship and the demands of capital.

The material on "leisure in work" can only be comprehended in the context of two interrelated processes: (a) the changing nature of the labour process under monopoly capitalism, and (b) the creation of a meaningful work-place culture that simultaneously rejects, handles, transmits and reproduces these changes and their corresponding relations. Throughout my discussion, I will be returning again and again to these two central processes.

The relationship between "leisure in work," shop floor culture and changes in the labour process becomes clearer when situated in a historical perspective. Historians have suggested that prior to the institutionalization of mechanical time and factory discipline, workers combined social intercourse and labour in what has been described as "task-orientation." Task-orientation was characterized by irregularity of the working-week, an attendance to what was immediately necessary, and a lack of distinction between "life" and "work."[34] Malcolmson, in his discussion of popular recreations in pre-industrial England, has suggested that "sometimes work and recreation were so closely related that they were almost indistinguishable."[35] He cites singing weavers, spinners who passed the time story-telling and workers "spelling" each other off so one could read aloud as examples of the combination of leisure and labour.

Even during the transition from mercantile to early industrial capitalism, workers still maintained the right of "leisure in work" based upon their informal control of the work-place through craft unions and specialized knowledge of the production process. Bryan Palmer notes that in 19th-century Canada, it was standard fare for iron workers and heaters to punctuate their day with a smoke and a glass of beer. Highly organized craft unions such as that of the glass workers controlled their trades to the extent that they could shut the plant down over the hot summer months for a well-deserved rest.[36] As Braverman argues, these factors plus the inefficiency of the sub-contracting system proved inadequate to the demands of capital accumulation—not only because of loss of materials and lack of uniformity in the products, but also because the work culture of the people militated against the stable usurpation of surplus value.[37] The factors leading to the demise of this way of life are diverse, complex and uneven—the division of labour, the rise of scientific management, the creation of public schools, the suppression of popular recreations, etc.—but it is clear that the second and third generation of factory workers in Britain began to fight "not against time, but about it."[38] The main point I want to make here is that my historical framework for understanding the separation of work and leisure is grounded in the struggle between cultural traditions and the changing nature of industrial capitalism.

It is interesting, then, to begin my discussion of "leisure in work" with a study of the occupational culture of shipbuilders—still a relatively skilled trade.[39] Due to the unevenness of capitalist technology and the relative strength of craft unions, shipbuilders have been able to retain their knowledge of the production process and resist some of the more obvious features of managerial control. Richard

Brown et al. argue that this lack of control by management allows workers to labour at their own pace and facilitates their movement around the shipyard to receive special tools and parts. These two factors create the conditions for skilled labourers to engage in conversation and other activities that Brown et al. label "leisure-taking." The form of this occupational culture is varied, but it revolves around such practical activities as story-telling, joking, card games, and being perceived as sociable—in Willis's terms, being one of the "lads."[40] Brown et al. go on to suggest that this major element of shop-floor culture—that is, being a "character"—is an intrinsic work satisfaction for many workers (p.107). The effect of this satisfaction, or what some might call "relative satisfaction," as a basis for either the transcendence or reproduction of the underlying social relations of production is not really addressed in this study. What is clear is that shipbuilders have carved out a meaningful space within the work-place on the basis of their retention of craft knowledge about the production process.

In any event, the potential of cultural forms on the shop floor to challenge the basis of capitalist production need not be restricted to the domain of skilled labour. It may very well be that the opportunity and illusion of worker control through "new working arrangements" and the piece-rate system, can simultaneously obscure the fundamental relations of production and generate consent to the rules originating from those relations.[41] Bill Watson's "Counterplanning on the Shop Floor"[42] and John Lippert's "Shopfloor Politics at Fleetwood"[43] both provide illustrations of how semi-skilled and unskilled automobile workers in the U.S.A. informally attempt to control the speed and manning of production, in addition to creating spaces for their own enjoyment. In both cases, most of the jobs were highly automated and organized on an assembly-line basis, with the exception of Watson's motor-testing group and Lippert's semi-skilled Kotan section workers.[44] Interestingly enough, it was here that many of the cultural forms, including leisure activities, were initiated—not to mention numerous acts of sabotage and strike action.

Lippert, in his analysis of the types of workers at Cadillac, suggests that the occupational culture promoted by the "vanguard" was enhanced by the creation of "games." In his own words:

> The big thing last fall was pitching quarters. It was initiated by some of the white vanguards and pretty soon the games grew into big events—people would gather around and cheer and so on. ... Pretty soon people all over the department were playing, partly for the fun of it and partly for the joy of outfoxing the foreman. (p.57)

Another game that caught on was basketball. Again, Lippert explains how this activity was made possible during working time:

> People would carve hoops out of packing material and shape balls out of tape and cardboard. And then they'd have really dynamite games of two on two or three on

three. This lasted for a couple of weeks, and then the foreman started tearing down the hoops. (p.57)

In much the same way, it was a specific group—the motor-testing gang in Watson's shop—that initiated and engaged in numerous diversions and games. Like Lippert's Kotan workers, this group was aided by its position in the production process and capacity to create "free time" through acts of sabotage. Watson mentions that, at times, simple water-fights escalated and "squirt guns, nozzles and buckets were soon brought in, and the game took on the proportions of a brawl for hours on end" (p.81). Sabotage was seen as a "means for controlling one's working time." Projecting from his own experience, Watson states that:

> The seizing of quantities of time for getting together with friends and the amusement of activities ranging from card games to reading or walking around the plant to see what other areas are doing is an important achievement for laborers. (p.80)

It is not only the seizure of time, but the creation of "space" that was seen to be of importance on Watson's shop floor. He mentions the off-limits character of a room in the plant, which was informally occupied by workers and subsequently filled up with lawn chairs and cots. His anecdote about an inexperienced foreman being knocked out the door and down the stairs upon entering is moving testimony to the importance of privacy and "collective" space. To draw from a personal example, I found that general labourers in an ironworks plant would sacrifice doing a dirty, unpleasant job for the sanctity of a location where management would fear to tread.[45]

These latter examples would seem to suggest that skill level is not necessarily a barrier for workers wanting to create pockets of time and space on the shop floor. Even those factory jobs in which operators must respond to technological forms of control (i.e., highly organized assembly-line production) can be and have been, subverted. Lippert's own job on the line provides a good example of this phenomenon. By working double-time, he was able to create 15-to-20-second breaks, in which he either read or talked to his workmates. Watson, among others,[46] has also mentioned the creation of an alternative break system whereby workers create chunks of free time for each other on a regular basis. "This plan" he says, "involves a voluntary rotation of alternatively working long stretches and taking off long stretches" (p.82).

It is necessary to stop here and reassert two fundamental principles. The first point is that these various activities, ranging from the outwardly subversive (sabotage) to the superficially benign, are the exception rather than the rule in shop-floor culture. To trivialize them would be to err too much in the other direction, but we should be reminded that Lippert optimistically estimates that his "vanguard workers" make up only 20 percent of the plant's population, while Nichols's and Armstrong's "politicals" at Chemco are a very definite minority.[47]

Although this point is tremendously difficult to explain due to its sheer complexity, two obvious barriers to the creation of real cultural alternatives lie within the scientific approach to management and the day-to-day drudgery of physical production.

The second principle acts as a necessary corrective to the first, and brings us back to the "rootedness" of shop-floor culture and its intimate relationship with the labour process. The bottom line here is that both alienated labour and meaningful work cultures ultimately arise out of a particular "determinate" and historical mode of production. We need to historicize rather than naturalize the structures of capitalist production and the way in which workers create, struggle, transform and reproduce this raw material of human experience. Workers have no natural propensity to disrupt production and create "leisure in work," but, rather, do so only in the context of their particular position and experience in the current social relations of production. They are also not naturally acquiescent with respect to capitalist work arrangements. Nor are they simply "naturally" lazy. All that is gained by the naturalizing human phenomena, whether it comes from the left or the right, is the explaining away of the complex and contradictory historical process. Shop-floor culture must be understood in terms of the specific, historical, determinate conditions that provide the raw materials of human action. Again, I draw on the work of Paul Willis to illustrate this interaction:

> Work is where the demands of capital must be met but from the resources not simply of potential abstract labour but from concrete, cultural forms of labour power. Whatever "free play" there is in cultural forms articulates always around this most central point of reference. Non-work supplies many of the categories and meanings of work but it can only be understood in relation to work and is finally shaped by it (p.187).

An approach anchored to these principles also prevents us from trivializing various elements of the shop-floor culture. Workers are not just "bearers" of the logic of capital, but are very real agents in its construction and reconstruction. "Merely because capital would like to treat workers as robots does not mean they are robots."[48] Shop-floor culture is but one example of the active process of handling, transmitting and even distorting life experience in both formal and informal, but always meaningful ways.[49] "Leisure in work" as a cultural form is always meaningful and potentially subversive. Yet, because it is constituted out of specific and historical conditions, it may continue to reproduce those conditions even while it resists them. Leisure-taking as a form of practical human activity (praxis) arises from the site of production, and provides "the conditions for capitalist relations and also partially penetrate[s] and variably challenges those relations."[50] So, for example, while the practice of "doubling up" may be seen as a meaningful way of controlling one's worktime, it simultaneously reproduces the necessary conditions for the extraction of surplus value.

I have argued that leisure-taking on the shop floor occupies precisely the same spaces as work activities that aid in the process of capital accumulation. I have also mentioned that the creation of leisure in work and various other acts designed to lead to "free time" is rare. The question, then, is what historical processes are present in monopoly capitalism that convince workers, for the most part, to physically and ideologically acquiesce to the demands of production? In short, "why do workers work as hard as they do?"[51] Asking why workers work as hard as they do is the mirror image of the question of why they do not participate in more leisure-taking at the workplace.

Michael Burawoy, in his recent book *Manufacturing Consent,* attempts to come to terms with some of these questions by developing a reconstituted theory of the capitalist labour process. His approach is especially interesting with regard to "leisure in work" because, in a sense, he fuses the concepts of labour and leisure by constructing the labour process as a form of "game-playing." Exactly how does this process work, and how is it connected to the organization of shop-floor culture and the social relations of production?

By positing the labour process as a game, Burawoy is outwardly rejecting both crude determinist models of social behaviour and the equally one-sided assertion that workers naturally erect their own autonomous cultural systems of opposition to management. In essence, the game metaphor takes us beyond either of these positions. The work-games engaged in by operators are not abstract creations of human nature, nor are they developed outside of management strategies.[52] Instead they "emerge historically out of struggle and bargaining" (p.80). Work-games arise out of a meaningful shop-floor culture concerned with the confrontation of the task, masculinity and physical skill, which is then shaped and twisted to meet the demands of capitalist production.[53] This paradoxical and contradictory statement is best expressed in terms of a game:

> The very activity of playing a game generates consent with respect to its rules. The point is more than the obvious, but important assertion that one cannot both play the game and at the same time question the rules. (p.81)

On the other hand, it is only by playing a game (human agency) that one can change it. Burawoy later admits that the playing of a game can in fact "undermine the rules that define it" (p.86). The conundrum for him is as follows: what are the necessary conditions for the continued reproduction of work-games?

Burawoy presents two major structures[54] that help to constitute the labour process as a game. The first structure is an aspect of shop-floor culture he labels "making out."[55] Making out essentially involves the engagement and successful completion of a work-game. These work-games obviously take on different forms depending on the type of shop and the organization of production. In Burawoy's piece-work machine shop, making out involved the skillful engagement and completion of tasks over and above the quota rates. The initiative for making out was not motivated by economic factors or coercive pressure from management, but from the successful completion of the task. As Burawoy explains it:

> "Making out" called for the exercise of skill and stamina, it offered opportunities for "self-expression". The element of uncertainty of outcome provided by the ever-present possibilities of "bad breaks" made "quota" attainment an "exciting game" played against the clock on the wall. (p.84)

The impact of making out on the organization of shop-floor culture is seen as highly significant by Burawoy. In fact, he argues that it has been the dominant element of shop-floor interaction at Allied for the past 30 years. Burawoy found himself being sucked into the game, which, on the one hand, absorbed his attention and, on the other hand, spontaneously led him to cooperate with management in the creation of surplus value (p.64). Because the culture of the shop floor revolved around making out, Burawoy found that his status was contingent on his capacity for, and skill in, winning the game. In his own words: "Until I was able to strut around the floor like an experienced operator, as if I had all the time in the world and could still make out, few but the greenest would condescend to engage me in conversation" (p.64). The concept of making out need not be limited to a piece-work machine shop. The general phenomenon of physical confrontation with a task and its link to masculinity and the wage-form have also been documented and discussed by Willis. Bureaucratic and technical modes of control may also lead to different forms of making out.[56]

The second structure Burawoy develops has to do with management's facilitation of making out. It also has implications for contemporary theories of the labour process.[57] Burawoy argues that work-games have actually been enhanced by management and changes in the labour process. He cites such examples as increasing worker autonomy, promoting individualism on the shop floor, relaxing the inspection of pieces, participating in output restriction, promoting an internal labour market and allowing workers to create newer, informal ways of making out. In other words, by facilitating workers' capacities to succeed and by giving the impression that game-playing is entered into "freely," making out acts (a) to obscure the relations of production under which the game is ultimately constructed, and (b) to generate consent to the social relations of production that define the rules (p.82). It may very well be that leisure-taking on the shop floor is a tacit rejection of the rules of the game, but in the context of making out, it may only represent a moment in the continued reproduction of capitalist relations.

Conclusions

What conclusions can we draw from a discussion of "leisure in work" and shop-floor culture? I think there are three. First, I think it is obvious that conventional notions of leisure are inadequate in dealing with the "leisure in work" literature. In defining leisure by its position along an arbitrary freedom and constraint scale, and dehistoricizing its relationship with social labour, leisure research has moved outside of the realm of lived cultures and material circumstances.

Second, the material on "leisure in work" reminds us that human experience cannot be easily compartmentalized into convenient sectors of leisure and work and evaluated in terms of such loaded concepts as freedom and constraint. We have to start re-thinking conventional definitions and asking ourselves such difficult questions as just what this thing we call leisure is, what its properties and determinations are, and how it articulates with other spheres of production and reproduction. This involves locating leisure historically, relationally, and politically. If the concept of "leisure in work" does anything at all, it provides us with the historical properties and conditions that ultimately shape and determine leisure. In Richard Johnson's terms, it provides us with one aspect of leisure's "social site." [58] I would argue that any theory of contemporary leisure remains inadequate and incomplete unless one situates it in the specific, historical conditions of the society in which it is constructed.

Finally, I want to suggest that increased attention to the work-place may be a relevant starting point for the revival of concrete, historical and contemporary studies of working-class cultures. I have concentrated on just one aspect of the modern work-force (and a strictly male one at that)—the industrial shop-floor culture. Any comprehensive theory of working-class cultures must also look closely at workers in the growing service occupations (who are primarily women),[59] the working-class household,[60] working-class communities, youth cultures,[61] the urban poor and the unemployed,[62] and the ethnic and racial dimension of working-class experience. There is also a growing body of scholarship in the U.S.A., Britain and Canada[63] that deals with the cultural dimensions of working-class history. Researchers dealing with modern societies will have to struggle against those who assert that there is no working class and hence no working-class culture. Our task is not simply to assert but, rather, to explain, the changing structure of wage-labour and the fragmentation of cultural traditions under capitalism.

Notes

1. I want to use the term "labour" to refer to both the productive and reproductive spheres—conventionally known as "social" and "domestic" labour respectively. For a discussion of their interconnections, see Wally Seccombe, "The Expanded Reproduction Cycle of Labour Power in Twentieth Century Capitalism," in

Bonnie Fox (ed.), *Hidden in the Household* (Toronto: The Women's Press, 1980). The amount of material written on the concept of labour is simply staggering. My own work has primarily benefited from the following sources: Harry Braverman, *Labor and Monopoly Capital: The Degradation of Work in the Twentieth Century* (New York: Monthly Review Press, 1974); Karl Marx, *Capital* Vol. I (Moscow: Progress Publishers, 1977); David McLellan, *The Thought of Karl Marx: An Introduction* (London: MacMillan, 1971); Rob Beamish, "Sport and the Logic of Capitalism," in Hart Cantelon and Richard Gruneau (eds.), *Sport, Culture and the Modern State* (Toronto: University of Toronto Press, 1982); Lawrence Krader, *A Treatise on Social Labour* (Assen: Van Gorcum Press, 1979).

2. This notion of the convential wisdom of leisure studies comes from Chas Critcher and John Clarke, "The Sociology of Leisure: Review of the Conventional Wisdom," in Alan Tomlinson (ed.), *Leisure and Social Control* (Brighton Polytechnic, Chelsea School of Human Movement, August, 1981).

3. It would be interesting in this regard to trace the concomitant rise of the "human relations" school in both industry and leisure.

4. Richard Johnson, "Three Problematics: Elements of a Theory of Working-class Culture," in John Clarke, Chas Critcher and Richard Johnson (eds.), *Working Class Culture* (London: Hutchinson, 1979), p.201.

5. Perhaps the strongest condemnation of conventional leisure research can be made from a radical feminist perspective. For a lively critique and debate on this issue see the Work Group, Centre for Contemporary Cultural Studies, "Women and Leisure," in Alan Tomlinson (ed.), *Leisure and Social Control*, pp. 93-160.

6. See Stanley Parker, *The Future of Work and Leisure* (London: Paladin, 1972), and Ken Roberts, *Contemporary Society and the Growth of Leisure* (London: Longman, 1978). I have concentrated on Parker's earlier work for two reasons: (a) *The Future of Work and Leisure* is perhaps his most sustained discussion of the work/leisure relationship; and (b) much of his later work is based on his earlier theoretical framework and findings. For some of Parker's other work, see *The Sociology of Leisure* (London: Allan and Unwin, 1976); "Work and Leisure: Theory and Fact," in J.T. Haworth and M.A. Smith (eds.), *Work and Leisure* (London: Lepus Books, 1975); M.A. Smith, Stanley Parker and Cyril Smith , *Leisure and Society in Britain* (London: Allan Lane, 1973). Ken Roberts's other work includes *Leisure* (London: Longmans, 1970), and *The Working Class* (London: Longmans, 1979). This paper was written before the re-publication of Stanley Parker's *The Future of Work and Leisure* and Ken Roberts's new book *Youth and Leisure*. The author has decided not to incorporate this work into this essay.

7. Stanley Parker, *The Future of Work and Leisure.*

8. Josef Pieper, *Leisure, The Basis of Culture* (London: Faber, 1952).

9. Sebastian De Grazia, *Of Time, Work and Leisure* (New York: Twentieth Century Fund, 1952), pp. 7-8.

10. Ken Roberts, *Contemporary Society and the Growth of Leisure*, p. 2.

11. It has been suggested that the notion of leisure as the fulfillment of "real" needs has also characterized some elements of the Frankfurt School's work. For an elaboration on this point, see Richard Johnson's comments in Alan Tomlinson (ed.), *Leisure and Social Control*, p. 167.

12. See Roland Barthes, *Mythologies* (London: Paladin, 1972); John Berger, *Ways of Seeing* (London: British Broadcasting Company and Penguin Books, 1972); Anthony Giddens, *New Rules in Sociological Method* (New York: Basic Books, 1976); *Studies in Social and Political Theory* (New York: Basic Books, 1977).

13. Steven Lukes, *Individualism* (Oxford: Basil Blackwell, 1973).

14. Allan Guttmann, *From Ritual to Record* (New York: Columbia University Press, 1978); Bero Rigauer, *Sport and Work* (New York: Columbia University Press, 1981); Richard Gruneau, "Sport, Social Differentiation, and Social Inequality," in Don Ball and John Loy (eds.), *Sport and Social Order* (Reading: Addison-Wesley, 1975), pp. 117-184; Alan Ingham, "Occupational Subcultures in the Work World of Sport," in Don Ball and John Loy (eds.) *Sport and Social Order* (Reading: Addison-Wesley, 1975), pp. 333-389; John Marie Brohm, *Sport—A Prison of Measured Time* (London: Ink Links, 1978); Rob Beamish, "Sport and the Logic of Capitalism."

15. Johan Huizinga, *Homo Ludens: A Study of the Play Element in Culture* (Boston: Beacon Press, 1968). For an ongoing debate within the sociology of sport, see, Richard Gruneau, "Power and Play in Canadian Social Development," *Working Papers in the Sociological Study of Sports and Leisure* Vol. 2, No. 4 (Kingston: Sport Studies Research Group, 1979); Rob Beamish, "Sport and the Logic of Capitalism,"; Alan Ingham, "Sport, Heroes, and Society: Issues of Transformation and Reproduction," in *Working Papers in the Sociological Study of Sports and Leisure* Vol. 2, No. 4 (Kingston: Sport Studies Research Group, 1979).

16. For a Marxist analysis of nature see Alfred Schmidt, *The Concept of Nature in Marx* (London: New Left Books, 1971).

17. Rob Beamish, "Sport and the Logic of Capitalism," p. 171.

18. Richard Gruneau, "Power and Play in Canadian Social Development," p. 2.

19. Stuart Hall and Tony Jefferson (eds.), *Resistance Through Rituals* (London: Hutchinson, 1976).

20. The concept of social labour is tremendously complex, and is best understood in a comparative fashion. In general terms, it refers to the specific social characteristics of labour peculiar to any "given historical phase." So, for example, the socially specific forms of human labour in primitive, communal types of societies are characterized by (a) a unity of production and consumption; (b) the concrete production of use-values (goods for the immediate consumption of all members); (c) a low division of labour; and (d) an adherence to task-orientation rather than to mechanical time.

   The social labour of capitalist production is typified by the wage-labour relation, and can be characterized by the following specific forms: (a) the worker has the formal legal freedom to sell his labour; (b) the worker has simultaneously lost access to the means of production; and (c) labour power becomes a unique commodity, in that it can be purchased for use over a specified period of time to create surplus-value. I have drawn heavily on the insights of Rob Beamish here and would like to thank him for his many contributions. Besides his "Sport and the Logic of Capitalism," pp. 151-166, see Karl Marx, *Capital* Vol. 1, p. 290, and Lawrence Krader, *The Dialectic of Civil Society* (The Netherlands: Van Gorcum Press, 1976).

21. E.P. Thompson, "Time, Work-Discipline, and Industrial Capitalism," *Past and Present*, 38 (December, 1967), p. 80.

22. See especially E.P. Thompson, *The Making of the English Working Class* (Harmondsworth: Penguin Books, 1968), and "Patrician Society, Plebian Culture", *Journal of Social History*, 7 (Summer, 1974).

23. This literature is growing tremendously. For starters, see, Jeremy Brecher, "Uncovering the Hidden History of the American Workplace," *Review of Radical Political Economy*, 10 (4, Winter 1978); John Cumbler, *Working Class Culture and Communities in America* (Connecticut: Greenwood Press, 1979); David Montgomery, "The Past and Future of Workers' Control," *Radical America*, 13 (November-December, 1979).

24. Bryan Palmer, *A Culture in Conflict: Skilled Workers and Industrial Capitalism in Hamilton, Ontario, 1860-1914* (Montreal: McGill/Queen's University Press, 1979).

25. Harry Braverman, *Labour and Monopoly Capital*; Wally Clement, *Hardrock Mining* (Toronto: McClelland and Stewart Ltd., 1981), p. 26. Richard Edwards, *Contested Terrain* (London: Heinemann, 1979); Theo Nichols and Huw Beynon, *Living With Capitalism: Class Relations in the Modern Factory* (London: Routledge and Kegan Paul, 1977). This of course does not mean that workers have not informally attempted to control the work-place.

26. In this regard also see J. Dumazedier, *Sociology of Leisure* (Amsterdam: Elsevier, 1974), p. 240.

27. The phrase "universal market" comes from Harry Braverman, *Labour and Monopoly Capital*, ch. 13 and refers to the incorporation of all goods and services into the commodities market.

28. See Ken Roberts, *The Working Class*.

29. Meg Luxton, *More Than a Labour of Love* (Toronto: The Women's Press, 1980); Wally Seccombe, "The Expanded Reproduction Cycle of Labour Power in Twentieth-Century Capitalism"; Annette Kuhn and Ann Marie Wolpe, *Feminism and Materialism* (London: Routledge and Kegan Paul, 1978).

30. Stanley Parker in Alan Tomlinson (ed.), *Leisure and Social Control*, p. 58. For a graphic negation of Parker's assertion see Paul Willis, *Learning to Labour* (Westmead: Saxon House, 1977).

31. I have used the term "leisure in work" as opposed to "leisure at work" to connote that the creation of work-games and "free time" occupy precisely the

same spaces as does social labour itself. I want to convey the notion that leisure and labour are not two separate concepts, but rather, human activities that take place in the production and reproduction of a particular political economy. In other words, I am pursuing a dialectical understanding of social life rather than a static, segmented one. I should also say that the following analysis is solely confined to principally male forms of labour.

32. Paul Willis, "Shop-floor culture, masculinity and the wage form," in John Clarke, Chas Critcher and Richard Johnson (eds.), *Working Class Culture* (London: Hutchinson, 1979), pp. 185-186.

33. Karl Marx, *Grundrisse* (Harmondsworth: Penguin Books in association with New Left Review, 1973), pp. 87-96.

34. E.P. Thompson, "Time, Work-Discipline, and Industrial Capitalism," p. 60.

35. Robert Malcolmson, *Popular Recreations in English Society, 1700-1850* (Cambridge: Cambridge University Press, 1973), p. 16.

36. Bryan Palmer, *A Culture in Conflict*, pp. 75-76, 91.

37. Harry Braverman, *Labour and Monopoly Capital*, pp. 135-136.

38. E.P. Thompson, "Time, Work-Discipline and Industrial Capitalism," p. 85.

39. Richard Brown, et al., "Leisure in work: the 'occupational culture' of shipbuilding workers," in M.A. Smith, Stanley Parker and Cyril Smith (eds.), *Leisure and Society in Britain* (London: Allan Lane) 1973.

40. See Paul Willis, *Learning to Labour*, p. 11.

41. Theo Nichols and Peter Armstrong, *Workers Divided: A Study of Shopfloor Politics* (London: Fontana, 1976); Theo Nichols and Huw Beynon, *Living With Capitalism*; Michael Burawoy, *Manufacturing Consent* (Chicago: University of Chicago Press, 1979).

42. Bill Watson, "Counterplanning on the Shop Floor," *Radical America*, 5 (May-June, 1971).

43. John Lippert, "Shopfloor Politics at Fleetwood," *Radical America*, 12 (July-August, 1978). Lippert attempted to classify workers in terms of the level of their political consciousness. The 'vanguard' was considered the most political faction at Fleetwood. For a similar classification, referred to as the "politicals," see Theo Nichols and Peter Armstrong, *Workers Divided*, p. 61.

44. The Kotan section workers were semi-skilled workers responsible for installing the vinyl tops on the car. Because this material had to be cut to measure by hand, this section of the plant possessed additional bargaining power with the company.

45. Although this particular job was the dirtiest in the plant, day labourers could escape from the watchful eye of management by effectively controlling an appraisal of the amount of work left to do. When asked about progress, they were able to respond by saying that there was probably 3-4 days' work remaining. By working extra hard and producing some external measure of job output, they were also able to create "free time" for drinking and smoking.

46. Theo Nichols and Huw Beynon, *Living with Capitalism*, 135; *New York Times*, September 9, 1973, Section III, p. 1; Paul Willis-personal conversation.

47. John Lippert, "Shopfloor Politics at Fleetwood," p. 55; Theo Nichols and Huw Beynon, *Living with Capitalism*, p. 61.

48 Paul Willis, "Shop-floor culture, masculinity and the wage form," p. 187.

49. My expression of culture here is strongly influenced by the work of E.P. Thompson. See his "The Long Revolution I," *New Left Review*, 9 (May-June, 1961), p. 33.

50. Paul Willis, "Shop-floor culture, masculinity and the wage form," p. 187.

51. This question was posed by the Lynds in 1929 and is taken up by Michael Burawoy, *Manufacturing Consent*, p. xi.

52. The work-games Burawoy is talking about here are not the same as the games discussed by Watson and Lippert. He is referring to the labour process itself being constructed as a game.

53. Paul Willis, "Shop-floor culture, masculinity and the wage form."

54. I am using the term structure here to mean the capacity to define rules in the context of differential resources. See Anthony Giddens, *New Rules in Sociological Method*.

55. Also see Donald Roy, "Banana Time: Job Satisfaction and Informal Interaction," *Human Organizations*, 18 (1958).

56. Richard Edwards, *Contested Terrain*.

57. Burawoy mentions in the preface to *Manufacturing Consent*, pp. xiii-xiv, that this approach is developed largely in opposition to many of the dominant themes in Harry Braverman's *Labour and Monopoly Capital*. However, I believe it is possible to maintain Braverman's general "deskilling" thesis even in the face of Burawoy's findings at Allied, which suggest that there has been increased worker autonomy and a greater scope for choice. As even Burawoy admits, the expansion of choices within narrower limits in the work place need not be seen as an outright rejection of the separation between the execution and conception components of the labour process (p. 94). For a demonstration of Braverman's thesis within the Canadian mining industry, see Wally Clement, *Hardrock Mining*, Toronto: McClelland and Stewart Ltd., 1981

58. Richard Johnson, in Alan Tomlinson (ed.), *Leisure and Social Control* pp. 63, 66.

59. Richard Edwards, Michael Reich, and David Gordon (eds.) *Labor Market Segmentation* (Lexington, Mass.: D.C. Heath, 1975).

60. Meg Luxton, *More Than a Labour of Love*; Wally Seccombe, "Domestic Labour and the Working-Class Household," in Bonnie Fox (ed.), *Hidden in the Household* (Toronto: The Women's Press, 1980).

61. Paul Willis, *Profane Culture* (London: Routledge and Kegan Paul, 1978); Stuart Hall and Tony Jefferson (eds.), *Resistance Through Rituals*.

62. David Gordon, *Theories of Poverty and Underemployment* (Lexington, Mass: D.C. Heath and Lexington Books, 1972); Richard Edwards, *Contested Terrain*, Chapter 10.

63. The literature on Britain is too prevalent to mention here. With respect to Canada, I would point to the following sources to begin: Bryan Palmer, *A Culture in Conflict*; Steven Langdon, *The Emergence of the Canadian Working Class Movement* (Toronto: New Hogtown Press, 1975); Gregory S. Kealey and Peter Warrian (eds.), *Essay in Canadian Working Class History* (Toronto: McClelland and Stewart, 1976); and the spirited debate between Gregory Kealey, in "Labour and Working Class History in Canada: Prospects in the 1980's," and David Bercuson, in "Through the Looking Glass of Culture," *Labour/Le Travailleur*, 7 (Spring, 1981). For a discussion of recent work in the U.S.A. see Bryan Palmer, "Classifying Culture," *Labour/Le Travailleur*, 8/9 (Autumn-Spring, 1981/82).

Good Times, Bad Times and the Politics of Leisure:
Working-Class Culture in the 1930s in a Small Northern English Working-Class Community

Alan Tomlinson

I

At many academic gatherings, it is said that the conference to which the participants have been attracted is "at the forefront of things," or is "extending the frontiers" of the discipline or subject involved. These sorts of claims are made for different reasons. They may be genuinely subscribed to by innovative thinkers—or, they may be rolled out as a way of legitimating expensive gatherings, in the eyes of either employing institutions or funding agencies. Often, of course, these claims are either utterly without foundation or greatly exaggerated. Most of us are not usually "at the forefront" or at a new frontier. We usually find ourselves working where other intellectual explorers have worked. It then becomes necessary to pool our common experiences of the different routes that we may have taken toward the same frontier. This, I believe, is the value of talking to each other about our work on working-class leisure, in which we see leisure as a central aspect of working-class culture generally. A lot of work has been done on working-class culture in the last decade or two. It is perhaps time to see whether or not this does indeed constitute a recognition of a new frontier in the trek toward an adequate understanding of leisure in the modern period.

I will begin this paper with a little bit of intellectual biography. As an undergraduate fifteen years ago, I took two courses that I realize, on reflection, I have been retaking, and then offering myself, ever since. These were interdisciplinary courses on "Working-Class Movements" and "Education and the Idea of Culture."

The first course comprised the study of the rise of the trade union movement in Britian, an analysis of the political movements of the emergent industrial working class, and the consideration of selected aspects of the everyday life and work experience of the industrial worker. Representations of the working class—in fiction and in popular cultural forms such as the cartoon and the illustration—were also covered in the course. In the course on "Education and the Idea of Culture," I studied the rise of influential educational philosophies, the view of education built into the work of novelists and poets such as Dickens and Wordsworth, and views of culture and debates about culture that dominated much thinking about education in the late 19th and the early 20th centuries. Not surprisingly, certain works of T.S. Eliot, F.R. Leavis and Raymond Williams featured quite prominently at certain points in the course. Although the two courses ran together—they were two options of half a dozen or so that an undergraduate could select in his or her first year—they were not seen as sharing much common ground. They stood alone, autonomous and self-contained.

I am making the point—in rather a roundabout and anecdotally self-indulgent way, for which I apologize, but which is justifiable, I hope, on the basis of the clarity with which the point will then be made—that the of study working-class culture is a relatively recent project. Studies of particular aspects of working-class culture, such as religion or the unions, have gone on for a long time, but not always in the context of a concern about what is culturally specific to working-class life. It might be true to say that working-class historiography was dominated for a long time by a Fabian view of history, which saw the development of industrial capitalism as a struggle over political power between an entrenched bourgeoisie and a politically embryonic working class. Every milestone in the development of trade-union rights could then be seen as a progressive and critical statement mounted against the employing, bourgeois, capitalist class. Now, one problem with working-class historiography of this sort is that other aspects of working-class life are relegated to the sidelines—are seen as peripheral or merely incidental to the "real stuff" of historical development, which becomes defined as the "political" and can then become polarized and set apart from the "cultural."

All sorts of theoretical challenges to this view of working-class history have been mounted in the last decade or so, from within social history itself and, perhaps most tellingly, from within neo-Marxist debates, drawing particularly upon the ideas of the Italian Marxist Antonio Gramsci. The outcome of this is that when we speak of working-class culture we can no longer treat "culture" as some peripheral music-making or worship marked off from the more influential spheres of the "political" or the "economic." Rather, to speak of working-class culture is to speak of the relation between these spheres, and of the ways in which these spheres are joined together to make a distinctive way of life.

It is interesting, then, to think back to the two undergraduate courses that I have instanced. Looking closely at the titles—"Education and the Idea of Culture" and "Working-Class Movements"—one sees how important the move toward talking about "working-class culture" has been. What I came to realize—some time after taking the courses—was that, though they were separate options, they were connected in very important ways. In "Education and the Idea of Culture," the debates about culture that were studied were promoted by established intellectual and social elites whose main concern was with stemming the tide of democracy, or, at best, controlling the tide—rather than thinking, in the manner of King Canute, that it could be turned back. Members of certain elites really did believe that to enfranchise the working class would be to undermine the foundations of British culture. Matthew Arnold believed that the question could be simply put: culture was under threat from anarchy. This idea of rampant masses stampeding wildly all over established cultural territory resurfaced in the literary/cultural criticism of F.R. Leavis, whose self-imposed task in the face of what he saw as an increasingly influential *mass*-culture was to identify and preserve some "great tradition" in British literary and cultural life. The idea of culture that we studied in this course was a notion subscribed to by an elite that had privileged access to a repository of worthwhile values. Although Raymond Williams's work featured in the course, it was there as illustrative of another idea of culture, rather than as an analytical cornerstone (which it could very easily have been).

In the course on "Working-Class Movements," as already noted, the main emphasis was on, say, politics rather than the pub. Now, once we start to work with a notion of working-class culture, the terms of reference must be widened, and the two courses must be seen as interconnected in an absolutely basic way. I did not fully grasp, when I took the courses, just what these interconnections were. I will now make the point with reference to the analytical terms employed more and more clearly by Raymond Williams during his own period of theoretical retrospection in the 1970s (Williams, 1977a; and Williams, 1977b, pp. 121-127). In the course on "Education and the Idea of Culture," I was studying aspects of a dominant culture on the defence. In "Working-Class Movements" I was studying aspects of an emergent culture, looking in particular at a projective vision, within the working class, of how the world might be differently structured around notions of equality and collective modes of social organization.

There were several debates from within the New Left in Britain that simply did not feature in these two courses. Perhaps if they had, I would have seen more clearly, more fully, and much earlier the vital relation between the two courses. But as it was, I did feel that I was studying ways in which an elite viewed the challenge from below to its authority. In retrospect, I think that something was missing from the course on working-class movements; this was a concern with the nature of working-class culture generally, not just in its industrial and political manifestations, but in its various and diverse forms—what was life like in the new industrial towns? What cultural practices developed in such settings? What was the relation of the new industrial working class to other class groupings? How are the cultural practices of the working class related to new developments in the consumer market and to the increasing significance of state intervention in everyday life? These questions, given the developments in oral history, socialist history and some aspects of social history generally, can now be posed and explored. With such questions in mind, the connections between the two courses of my undergraduate days are not difficult to make. What I was studying, 15 years ago, was a process of contestation in which two different views of the world were staking their claims to the territory of the future.

This is why it is so important not just to look at working-class institutions one by one (the family, the club, work and so on) and to reproduce a sociological-variables emphasis in looking at the one class, but also to look at the nature of working-class culture as a *whole*; to see precisely how it is made, remade, consolidated or undermined. It is also important, in doing this, to look at elements in working-class culture that are not explicitly progressive (or emergently challenging)—which is what Richard Hoggart did in Part One of his study of working-class life (Hoggart, 1958)—but which might constitute a conservative (I say conservative, and not reactionary or residual) core at the centre of working-class culture. I will say more about this conservative core in the final section of this essay, when I discuss the way in which aspects of working-class leisure show how social actors might recognize injustices and reject dominant values, but choose to retreat into their own familiar social world.

Perhaps Matthew Arnold would have joined the Labour Party in post-war Britain under Harold Wilson. "Culture" has not given way to anarchy and, despite extreme tensions in the social structure—sometimes framed in terms of youth, industrial struggle and, now, the issue of peace—we still have, in Britain, a parasitical monarchy and a Tory fundamentalist who is already anticipating yet another term of office in which to roll back the frontiers of welfare capitalism.

In this context, a working-class culture that is now characterized by a mixture of privatized social life, industrial/political struggle, and a stress upon locality-cum-community and hedonism is a much more complicated phenomenon than a master-servant view of history would imply. To understand the complexity of working-class culture therefore, I think we need to consider how individuals and groups are positioned in relation to the labour-process and the labour-market—something upon which theoretical ethnographies of past and present working and everyday life are very much needed. And to come anywhere close to grasping what working-class culture is and has been, we need to take the task of historical reconstruction very seriously indeed. In other words, past and present ethnographies are required—ethnographies on how the general social processes that we know to be at work in modern industrial capitalism are actually *lived through* and experienced by the working-class in specific places and at particular times. I want, therefore, in this essay, to report and speculate on a small project on which I am currently engaged—a study of working-class sports/leisure in Colne, a small industrial community in North-East Lancashire, in the current century (particularly concentrating upon the inter-war years).

In doing this, I want to feature very prominently the voices of the working-class respondents to whom I have talked. The question "How is Colne, as an entity, possible in a period of massive social divisiveness?" will be at the heart of the enquiry.

II

My own work on the 1930s developed out of a dissatisfaction with what was available in the field of sports history. We have no shortage of histories of sports (results, personalities and so on) but some years ago there were few *social* histories of sports. Also, I wanted to find out just what kind of significance sports had in working-class culture. And so, when I encountered some references to a sport called knur-and-spel in some Northern towns in England, I wanted (a) to reconstruct this sport's history in truly social, rather than "quaintly archaic," historical ways (see Tomlinson, 1982), and (b) to consider in some detail the nature of and influences upon working-class sport and leisure in one small town in the inter-war years. As has been commented about this period: "we probably know more about Victorian pubs, coffee rooms and clubs than we do about those of the 1920s and 1930s" (Howkins and Lowerson, 1979:57). So a general aim in my two tasks was simply to reconstruct the sports/leisure activities within the cultural life of a working-class community.

Of course the 1930s is a fascinating period, too, for comparison with the 1970s and 1980s. As Howkins and Lowerson noted, "interwar Britain presents a mixed picture ... in the first place we see an enormous growth of leisure both in terms of time and expenditure ... the second area of importance is ... enforced leisure created by unemployment" (Howkins and Lowerson, 1979:55). And perhaps one of the most important questions about both periods is this—how are massively significant creases in the social fabric smoothed out? How is it that working-class males continue to gather together in tens of thousands to watch a game of football, rather than to demand bread or social justice? I am not alone in commenting upon the lack of work on this. In fact, I am in rather elevated company in pointing this out. Listen to what Stuart Hall has to say (his "us" refers to a gathering he was addressing at a History Workshop conference):

> It isn't by chance that very few of us are working in popular culture in the 1930s. I suspect there is something peculiarly awkward, especially for socialists, in the non-appearance of a militant, radical, mature culture of the working-class in the 1930s when to tell you the truth—most of us would have expected it to appear. From the viewpoint of a purely "heroic" or "autonomous" popular culture, the 1930s is a pretty barren period. This "barreness"—like the earlier unexpected richness and diversity—cannot be explained from *within* popular culture alone. (Hall, 1981:230)

So we must look at the underlying social relations embodied in the popular cultural forms of Hall's "barren" period. What Hall implies here is that popular culture must be autonomous, set apart from the dominant culture and pitted against it.

The questions that really need to be put, though, are (a) what are the social consequences of the emergence of non-heroic yet autonomous popular cultural forms? (I address this question in preliminary fashion elsewhere (Tomlinson, 1982); and (b) what kind of social relations are bound up with non-heroic, non-autonomous popular cultural forms such as sport? It is the latter question that I address in this paper.

III

Colne is a small, North-East Lancashire cotton town at the end of a line of four townships that runs through a valley typical of the kind of townships that grew up in the early industrial revolution. Beyond this line lies the pretty wild area of the Yorkshire moors famous for producing the Brontë family. The town rises up the foothills of the Pennine hills and is surrounded on all sides by hills and moorlands that are immediately accessible. Closed in by hills it has the *feel* of a self-contained, if not isolated, community. Only a few miles away lies one of Northern England's biggest wool towns, Bradford. But that is in a different county—Yorkshire—and Colne retains a strong sense of its Lancashire affiliation. Although Colne surrendered its independence as a separate borough in 1974—to be absorbed into the new Borough of Pendle (total population 85,600), which incorporates half a dozen other towns and villages—it has retained, among its smallish population, a fiercely partisan sense of its own local identity.

The population of the town is now under 20,000 and within a couple of miles of it lie several industrial villages that were seen, in the inter-war years, as separate and distinct "communities," and whose culture was based very much on the chapel. A tradition of political support for the Labour Party was rudely interrupted in the 1970s, when a swing to Conservatism reflected the crisis of British Labour Politics. That is the context, then. What I want to do now is to describe the range of activities that characterized working-class culture; to say something about the range of lived cultures *within* the working-class generally; and to consider some of the influences upon and meanings of particular cultural practices.

There was a range of male-dominated cultural forms still thriving in the 1930s (many of which are still thriving half a century later). The working-men's club; the brass band; the pigeon-fanciers' club—these are some of the voluntaristic or self-provided and self-organized types of activities. There was also a strong commercial base to leisure experience: the cinema; boxing and wrestling three nights a week; dancing; and the pub. Local amateur football and cricket were extensively played. So too were games of various kinds (ranging from stick games to whippets/pigeons) clustered around betting/gambling. One of the main characteristics of such activities is the dominance of the male. Outlets for leisure activities for women were severely restricted. For most married, working-class women away from the church, the chapel, the women's institute, or the cinema, patterns of leisure were a matter of creating forms of sociability within the work place of the home or the communal washing-house (see, for an example of this in the culture of the South Wales working-class, Crook, 1982)—in much the same way as that in which male shop floor culture can include attempts to usurp industrial labour-time for non-work purposes (see the paper by Hollands in this collection). It is really the rise of the commercial sector on a new large scale in, for instance, the cinema and dance-hall, which created spaces where women could go, and be accepted. Mrs. Baxter recalls her "courting" days in the early years after World War I:

> We used to go to the pictures and I was only allowed out on Wednesday night and Saturday and Sunday and I used to have to be in at nine o'clock at 21 years of age ... ooh, pub, no, never 'eard of ... .

This is quite a change from her own mother's social life, which had revolved exclusively around the chapel, and which had been an early influence in Mrs. Baxter's own life:

> I used to be in concerts ... oh, yes, and especially when the talking pictures came, yes, we used to go to the pictures Christmas eve—operatics, we've seen quite a lot and I still go to operatics now.

Mrs. Baxter's patterns of leisure changed after marriage, coming closer to how she recalls her own mother's routinized week—"Oh, routine, Mother used to wash Monday ... and ironin' on Tuesday. ... Bakin' days, oh they *were* bakin' days." And so, "after marriage," Mrs. Baxter no longer went "dancin';" instead she "went to plays—that were my pleasure." Dancing, then, was a space for the un-attached or courting woman, not for the married one. After marriage, the domestic site and its responsibilities put constraints upon the social life of the woman. And we should not imagine that popping in and out of houses was a firmly entrenched activity within the working class. Mr. Billy Baxter is emphatic in recalling that, though support was always available in a crisis, neighbours were not there to be imposed upon:

> As soon as yer start tea-partyin' yer start fallin' out.

And so, within the commercial sector, the cinema offered a potentially liberating space for women's leisure—a space in which the surroundings of everyday life could be temporarily escaped. In the words of Andrew Faulds:

> It could open up a new world ... standard of living ... if your own rotten, miserable life were spent in a stinkin', dirty cotton mill [or the home: A.T.] you wanted to get away from that and be transferred ... call it what you like ... and then you could see there were somethin' else in life beside work.

It is not coincidental that one of the biggest stars in British cinema in the 1930s was Gracie Fields, the "lass from Rochdale" who so easily found a responsive audience among the working-class cinema audiences of the times (Aldgate,

1981). It is in what one writer has called the "growth of the industries of entertainment" (Wild, 1979:59) that working-class women find the possibility of experiencing newer forms of leisure away from the spheres of male-dominated leisure that are so central to Colne's working-class culture. Bingo, for instance, is an example of this in the past quarter century (Dixey, 1983). We have, then, to see gender—male dominance within the sites of leisure, if not in the home—as an absolutely central dimension of working-class culture. Although women might not be actually debarred from certain kinds of activities, and could, as they did in the bigger working-class town of Bolton, attend wrestling matches, this was not approved of by other elements within the culture. Evidence on audiences at wrestling matches in Bolton indicates that the women who attended did so in order to see specimens of male virility ("real men") the like of which were not available, claimed some respondents, at home (Mass Observation, 1939). But such activities met with double disapproval: they were seen as non-female activities, and they were also seen as lacking in any moral dimension. So the first, general point that I want to make about working-class culture in Colne at this time is that it is gender-distinctive.

My second point refers to the elements within the working-class itself. For in Colne at this time there was no single, easily identifiable, homogeneous working-class culture. There was a range of lived cultures within the working-class itself. Hugh Cunningham has illustrated this sort of point beautifully with reference to the 19th century (Cunningham, 1980); Anthony Delves has empha-sized how popular culture can be influenced by the outcome of intra- and inter-class relations (Delves, 1981). And it is always worth remembering that when Karl Marx got round, in the *18th Brumaire*, (Marx, 1973), to talking about *class* in given moments, at particular points, he proposed long lists of factions across and within class lines. So we must beware of any simple notion of a pure working class. All elements within working-class culture might share a common situation in terms of, say, their relation to capital (though things are complicated here by the persistence in the inter-war years of transient, casual labour as a means of supporting oneself), but there are other mediating influences that partially structure the experience of particular groups—such as the church, the kind of worker-employer relation characteristic of the work place, and a sense of neighbourhood or extreme locality.

There was, then, no single working class within Colne. It is worth breaking down some of the separate elements, first according to location/place; second, according to what I will call the local social structure.

At the bottom of the town's really quite steep high street was the station area, described to me by one respondent (Norman Atkinson) as a separate, self-contained area with its own shops, its own services, and even its own hawking system; in the middle of the town, into the 1930s, there was the notorious Windy Bank, a kind of centre for the "rough" working-class, where "Irishmen" might also come in as casual immigrant labour for the haymaking season; there was "Water-Side," another self-contained, respectable working-class area around the town's river valley; and there were the surrounding villages, which often clustered around the chapel as a major influence. There is no single, united view of the world to which these different cultural worlds subscribed. They need to be explored separately, and yet in the context of the processes prevailing in the time of which they are all a part.

These areas, then, had distinctive class cultures. In Windy Bank, before it was redeveloped out of existence in the mid-1930s, a "rough" working-class culture prevailed. It was a culture that in the inter-war years, was subjected to a systematic attack by decision-making bodies in the local community. Perceiving Windy Bank as a threat to "respectable" elements in the town, the town's Council drew up, in 1931, a ten-year plan that included the demolition and redevelopment of the Windy Bank area and of two other areas, Waterside and Nineveh. Windy Bank's seven streets had 315 residents (when not swollen, presumably, by Irish labour)—a mere 1.3 percent of the town's population of 23,791 in 1931. But it was in a central position in the town, running down one side of the high street, a sore sight for respectable eyes. In this sense, it never stood a chance when the image of the town began to be worked upon systematically. Waterside was the next "clearance area" in 1934, when 516 people in 12 streets with three pubs were redeveloped out of their own culture. (My figures on these processes are culled from the work of a local amateur historian (see Crombie, 1978). What, then, in this inter-war period, was so distinctive about the culture that it was undermined so effectively by "respectable" citizens of the town?

One local historian has said that "off the main streets of Colne were many courts and alleys where closely knit communities had to make do with the most meagre living standards ... The warren of buildings behind the Robin Hood in Waterside survived until the early 1930s ..." (Spencer, 1972:27). But there has been little investigation of what the life of such "closely knit" communities was.

A pictorial representation of Colne refers to a number of the characters of Windy Bank, but says little about the area itself (Crombie, 1978:12-13). I have spoken in depth to one of the cited characters, Jim Hird, and to Jimmy Hines, the brother of another. There seems little doubt that life could be quite rough in the area. This is what Jimmy Hines told me:

> Fighting was popular among the locals themselves ... street fighting ... it was a rough area you know was Windy Bank ... the Heaps and the Leonards, they was the main culprits, it was like a vendetta with 'em, it were a rough quarter you know, but they'd be the best of pals next day. People never held grudges against one another ... they were good people ... them days down Windy Bank policemen didn't go down there singlehanded, there were two or three at a time ... I've no idea what it [the fight] was about, but they were always at it.

A.T.: What happened with all the other people in the neighbourhood? Did they gather round?

Jimmy H.: Oh aye they all watched ... they all loved a good fight ... it'd take sometimes half an 'our.

A.T.: What was it ... just fists?

Jimmy H.: Oh it were the lot, the boot and the lot went in, then it nearly always was a free-for-all, and the police 'ud come down an' break it up ... it were, like, telegraph.

A.T.: Were women ever involved in this?

Jimmy H.: Oh, they were at it anole ... What do they call 'er? Big Maggie, Maggie Mackenzie ... un Big Willie 'ud fight over nothing.

Unsurprisingly, Windy Bank bred fighters. Jimmy Hines himself was an experienced local boxer and his brother Laddie, who died at 21, had already won 81 of his 90 fights. The Hines were involved with a few gyms in the area, and boxing booths came to town with the local fair and then were set up on a more regular basis in the town. Windy Bank, then, was a "rough" area where toughness was respected. Toughness as a trait of working-class culture has lacked serious investigation, apart from one detailed exploration of a London boxer at the turn of the century (Shipley, 1983). Life in Windy Bank may also have been less routinized or structured than in other parts of town, for work-discipline may not have been so rigorously formalized. Joseph Hird, for instance, was born in 1908 to a gypsy family in Windy Bank, and raised in the area. Joseph's motto was "I'd 'awk owt for a bob", which means, to the non-Yorkshire person, "I'd sell anything for a few pennies or a shilling." Joseph Hird lived in Colne all his life, though he farmed for 33 years on the edge of town:

Joseph H.: I never worked for nobody in mi life. I've bin on mi own since I left school ... used to 'awk when I were young, used to 'awk fruit you know ... earn a bob where we could ... an' when we earned a bob in them days it were yer own, an' we used to mek thi' own sports.

Married at 21, Joseph Hird lived in Puddling Pond in one of a row of six houses. His rent was six shillings and four pence per week, and included two bags of coal. He lived there throughout the 1930s, in a small "two-up-two-down terraced house", before taking up his farming:

There were no baths them days ... there were nowt like that ... outside toilets.

Joseph's brother also lived in Windy Bank; he ran a rag-shop there for most of his working life. Windy Bank had more than just a "rough" everyday culture to worry the local authorities. It also had a local informal or "black" economy. These combined to create a specific culture of the casual labouring class. In such parts of the town as the Station area and Waterside, more "respectable" working-class cultures made their contribution to the entity known as Colne. Further divisions could operate within these categories, and it is important to recognize religion politics as sources of such divisions. Two major cultural categories within the working class, then, could be seen as the non-conformist religious working-class and the secular culture of the working-class. It is with elements that contribute to the latter that I have been most concerned so far. In the 1920s, the local authorities had banned the sport of bowling stones and, in a legendary 1920s' police raid on the moors around the town, the gambling networks had been broken.

So what I have been looking at in talking about Windy Bank and in instancing forms of street culture is a predominantly hedonistic element in secular working-class culture, which was under attack from the "respectable" local society. It is worth noting that most of my respondents, with whom I made contact on the basis of networks of sport and leisure, had little and often absolutely nothing to do with political associations. In other sections of the working-class, popular culture revolved around the chapel, which could be an all-embracing influence upon social life, particularly in the small industrial villages around the immediate countryside. Victor Bertwhistle talked to me about life in tiny Trawden, a mere mile or two outside Colne. As a boy, he would play any of a wide range of games available, all of them based upon the street and items of everyday life. "Nick-nacking" involved a thread and a drawing pin. "Tin In't Ring," "Billet and Stick," "Wooden and Iron," "Hoops," "Whip and Top," "Devil up Pipe," and "Statues" were all street games, several of which were of an obviously irritating type to the adults in the community. Yet, from his boyhood, it was the chapel that constituted the major influence upon his non-work life. Leisure-time, for both men and women, became increasingly defined and structured by the chapel. Victor Bertwhistle recalls the early 1920s:

> In the evenings at winter time well the churches would have events ... socials, concerts, at-homes, pantomimes and what have you ... there was the Church of England, the Primitive Methodist, the Trawden Wesleyan, the Zion Independent and then the Inghamites ... there were five churches ... and organized by the Sunday School scholars you'd 'ave the annual outing and you'd go to Ilkley or something like that which was a great event.... in 1920-21 we went to Ilkley from our Sunday School on what was a converted coal wagon and thought it was absolutely marvellous to go to Ilkley ... that was like going abroad.

Ilkley is only a few miles from Trawden. It is difficult to over-emphasize the significance of locality in working-class culture of the time. Colne and the area around it was defined by the hills and the landscape as well as by place names and boundaries. The area, and areas within it, are physically enclosed communities. This had the effect, in the pre-motor age, of solidifying the local culture. Around the church or the chapel, in places like Trawden (where the places of worship outnumbered by more than two to one the places of drinking) and certainly in areas within Colne itself, Victor Bertwhistle and people like him could structure their social and family lives almost completely around the church or the chapel; and many of the activities in this setting were self-generated and self-organized, and contributed to an energetic and dynamic participatory culture.

I have spent most time, then, describing the "rough" variant within secular working-class culture, and the respectable religious working-class culture.

There were, within working-class culture, all sorts of shaded areas between these somewhat polarized extremes. Mrs. Baxter, quoted earlier, went to dancing as well as to chapel. But proponents of the latter generally retained a strong sense of disapproval of the former, and so the tension between the religious and the secular in working-class culture produced many different types of cultural experience at and between the two extremes. My point is a simple one in the end. It is that we must be aware of the diversity *within* the working-class if we are to develop an adequate sense of the local social structure of the time. Beside these various working-class cultures, the other elements in the local social structure were the middle classes (traders, professionals, teachers, and "public administrators"), and the local squirearchy, made up of "significant" families that had, through ownership of land or factories, or through trade, assumed the position of the local "leaders."

The single most significant fact about this local social structure in the inter-war period is that it survived intact—apart from the rough working-class culture, which was "redeveloped" away. This survival took place during two decades of almost uninterrupted crisis in the local cotton industry, intensified by the Great Crash and the Depression years in the 1930s. The Great Crash did not plummet a secure world into an unanticipated crisis. As one specialist has put it, "in the 1920s and the 1930s the threat of unemployment hung over most workers in Britain irrespective of where they lived" (Constantine, 1980:17). Cotton, coal, shipbuilding and the iron and steel industries (the great boom industries of early industrialization) were in permanent decline at the beginning of the inter-war period. Constantine refers to the gross "inefficiency" of an industry that "had been slow to convert to ring-pinning, automatic looms and electric power before the war," and therefore became increasingly uncompetitive in the world market between the wars (Constantine, 1980:12). The slump intensified a crisis already well-entrenched, particularly in towns dependent upon single industries. As yet, I have been unable to work on the raw data to acquire figures on Colne, but for a bigger cotton town—Blackburn, some 20 miles away—the figures illustrate this well. In Blackburn, where 60 percent of the work-force was employed in the cotton industry, the 1931 slump "left 46.8 per cent of workers unemployed" (Constantine, 1980:19). Here, "the dawn of affluence" and the expansion in the "range of entertainment" (Stevensons and Cook, 1979) were clearly far from the general experience.

The question I really want to raise is how, in times (long-term times, not simply occasional moments) like these, times of obvious tension in the social fabric, the diverse elements in the social structure of Colne could constitute Colne as an entity. In answer to that question it is important, I believe, to point to the experiences of the people in the community that show how Colne could be experienced as a common point of reference, despite the potential tensions built into the social relations of the time. The example that I take to illustrate this is the game of cricket.

In the 1920s and the 1930s, Lancashire League cricket drew big crowds to watch teams representative of small towns or areas within larger towns play each other. To play for the team, residence or employment within the town or area was a qualification, though each club was allowed one full-time professional. The Lancashire League still operates in the 1980s, along much the same principles but with nowhere near the same crowds. I want to look at how the social relations of the time (or at least a central aspect of them) became manifested in a prominent local cultural form. This can be usefully explored by considering how individuals of diverse types came to construct a common subjectivity around the popular cultural form of cricket. This is most dramatically exemplified in the reception given to Indian and West Indian cricketers who came to the towns of North-East Lancashire as club professionals in the Lancashire League. The game of cricket, therefore, introduced black people into the local culture long before the waves of post-World War II immigration from the Commonwealth territories. From 1935 to 1938, for instance, Lalah Amar Singh played as a professional for Colne, and entered the local mythology through his sporting feats. An Indian, he scored 2,700 runs as a batsman and took 336 wickets as a bowler in his three seasons with Colne, and once, it was recorded, hit a score of 110 not out in only 20 minutes. Singh died, tragically, on the way home to India in 1939, aged only 29.

Perhaps the most famous black person to play Lancashire League cricket was Learie Constantine, who played for neighbouring Nelson. It is recorded that the largest ever crowd for a Colne vs. Nelson match gathered in 1929, when Constantine was playing (Crombie, 1978). And a 1935 match, with Singh the professional for Colne, drew a "gate" (a total income from admission fees) of 367 pounds 13 shillings and seven pence, at sixpence each for admission. Now, this makes a gate of between 14,000 and 15,000, in a town with a population of just under 24,000. I asked Ellis Dickinson, a former Colne player, how the black players were perceived by the local people:

> Well, there weren't a lot of black 'uns about in them days yer see ... a black chap it didn't matter ... 'e were an attraction as a cricketer if 'e were a good 'un.

There was, in fact, more to Constantine than that he was a "good 'un" at cricket." The West Indian Marxist C.L.R. James has related to an English writer a tale that shows that Constantine was more than a mere sportsman: it was he who urged James to "'come over here' to Nelson, if you want to get published" (Ward, 1983:475). James took Constantine's advice and got his manuscript published by a small publisher in Nelson, Colne's neighbouring town, which was known as one of Lancashire's "Little Moscows." Yet it was exclusively for the cricket, that Constantine was recognized as "a good 'un" and welcomed by the local populations. In this sense, then, the sporting experience has the capacity to supercede differences. And if you were "a good 'un," a lot of privileges might come your way. This was as true of working-class sportsmen as of the black club professionals.

By concentrating in detail on the career of Ellis Dickinson, I want to show how the bonding of community can be experienced, lived out and, perhaps, partially achieved in the sphere of sports. Ellis Dickinson was born in 1906 in the nearby village of Earby. At the age of 15, he started working in the mill—"you've got to go into t' mill, that's all there were knockin' about 'ere in those days ... I worked in a small mill and I were determined to get out as quickly as ever I could." Cricket became Ellis' escape route from unrelenting work in the cotton mill. At one point, he was asked to practice with the Yorkshire County Cricket Club, which paid travelling expenses and ten shillings a day, and 13 for an appearance in a second team match. Another county, in the West Midlands, also approached Ellis, asking him to join them as a wicket-keeper.

Ellis resisted the approach from Worcestershire in the Midlands and, in the end, the approach from the Yorkshire club. Pulled in one direction by the club—to play for its second team—and in another by his uncle—to join the local police force—he chose the latter. At the age of 19, Ellis saw this as offering a secure future, and he recalls that "I never valued sport as a career for the simple reason you're only as good as what you are." But Ellis was not happy in the police force, and only lasted 14 months—"I didn't like it a bit an' I soon chucked out of that." Having left the police force he went back to the mill as a weaver, and it was now that his sporting prowess began to affect the direction his life was taking. Colne Cricket Club wanted him to play for them but, living and working in Earby, he did not fulfill the residential or the employment qualifications. Nelson Cricket Club moved for him, and this prompted the Colne Club to act with more urgency. Ellis was offered work in Colne itself:

> Things were pretty bad in t' local village in Earby you see an' they offered mi' work in t'town. Well chairman of Colne Cricket Club, thi' called 'im Scase. ... he belonged to cricket club as a lot of influential men in t'town were in them days. ... And they sort of offered you talent money and all sorts of things to mak sure you 'ad a good income like ... back 'ander shall we say and all sorts of things and then Harry Scase he offered me a job there an' I worked there and played wi' Colne.

So Ellis moved to Colne:

> They found me a house in Colne, so I worked there and then 'ad a working qualification and living qualification ...

A.T.: Did you pay rent?

Ellis D.: No I didn't really. They paid it like ... a man on t' Committee let mi' 'ave it for next to nothing.

Ellis worked for more than 20 years at the engineering firm that had offered him the job. I asked him what his view of influential local men such as his first club chairman was:

Yes, very interested, different to what they are today. ... If you did well, shall we say ... suposin'... I used to get talent money, I used to get seven and six for everyone I caught and stumped ... well that were a guinea ... and then there were fellers that ran mills or ... same as I'd tell yer my boss ... he'd er ... and various people that had money them days who were interested in t' club who'd think nothin' about comin' and stickin' a ten bob note in yer 'and and say 'Here you are ... you've 'ad a good day today', and sometimes you might pick a couple of quid up ... as much as yer wage were for workin' for a week in them days—well you never turned yer nose up at things like that and if yer were lucky to get a 50 or anythin' like that ... well you'd get a collection of 20 ... well that were big money in them days.

Benefiting from the patronage of local businessmen, Ellis nevertheless still retained a strong sense of his class position. It is interesting to consider Ellis' response to my question "What about the team? You were a working man. Were the rest of the team working men?" Ellis held a team photograph from the mid-1930s in his hand and went through the line-up:

Well this were team about when I cum ... This feller were what thi' call a warp dresser ... that were Freddie Harrison. That's Norman Spence, he were a weaver— this feller were a warp dresser connected wi' t'mill ... this feller worked in t'mill ... this feller worked in t'mill ... it were Stan Wright ... this chap here, Jim Gough ... he were a florist, his father 'ad a florist shop. Now this were Ernest Dyson, you've 'eard of Dyson 'appen and Bracewells ... 'e's just retired now ... 'e were apprentice tailor ... that's Armagh Singh ... that's Jack Hardacre, 'e were t'manager of Stanroyd Mill, down Cottontree ... it were Courtauld ... 'e were a good cricketer Jack Hardacre, one of t'best all round cricketers in league, were Jack ... 'e could bat, 'e could bowl, 'e could field. Now that's miself of course ... This lad, they called 'm Jim Pollard ... 'is father 'ad what they called an oatcake business ... They were working men ... when I came to Colne at first thi' were a little bit o' school tie attached to it but it faded away when I cum to Colne and round about then for the simple reason that ... were sort o' wouldn't wear it ... you know what I mean ... I were one o' them I din't care ... an' I always thought like it didn't mak no difference to me whether they were solicitors or schoolteachers or whatever they were ... if they were good cricketers they were alright ... it din't matter to me whether they were well off or they weren't ... if they could play cricket it were just O.K. wi' me.

A.T.: What about the committee ... Did you get on well with the committee?

Ellis D.: Well aye ... we 'ad difference of opinion ... differences of opinion of course but generally speaking we voiced us opinion ... but yes ... I think we did... .

This, then, is how cricket (as one popular cultural form) can constitute community. Ellis is fully aware of his class position, but all differences are irrelevant when the team co-operates to represent the locality. Colne transcends class as the structuring influence. Despite the differences between the committee (of local dignitaries) and the team (predominantly made up of working-men in the area), the ultimate affiliation is to Colne, to the locality. Local identity and community as experienced through sport contribute to the perpetuation of a local set of social relations in which bourgeois hegemony—the position of the local plutocracy and squirearchy as the apparently "natural" leaders of the community—is successfully reproduced, despite the tensions of the time. Look at some of Ellis' phrases—"if they were good cricketers they were alright ... if they could play cricket it were just O.K. wi' me." Ellis also experienced the material advantages of the patronage system (not unlike some of the "pedestrians" or runners in the early days of working-class athleticism)[2]—and he also played cricket on Tuesday afternoons, but this was no economic deprivation. As Ellis recalls:

> I used to get mi' wages just same 'cos chairman of club were boss of this firm and he let me off and I got "loss of work" off cricket club, well that were a good do.

There are forms, therefore, in which class conciliation is achieved. Lancashire League cricket was neither primarily a middle-class cultural form nor a working-class cultural form; it was a form in which the vertical relations of class and status were central, but in which such relations were often superceded by the sense of shared community. To be a Colner, as player, or spectator, could be more important than to be a member of this or that class. If you were "a good 'un," or in terms of spectatorship a "keen 'un" or a "knowledgeable 'un," then whether you were black, bourgeois or proletarian was in a sense immaterial. You were part of a united community; you were a Colner. John Clarke has argued that "locality" as an element of working-class culture "continues to act as a focus in a number of forms ... to act as a focus for some working-class cultural identifications, often among those who are in some senses marginal to production and to the collective solidarities generated there" (Clarke, 1977:251). Locality, for Clarke, becomes a base for a "magical" or "imaginary" reconstitution of community (as in, say, Skinhead groups), and operates as a form of limited oppositional consciousness that, ultimately, has little effect upon things. Clarke is talking about the meaning that locality can have in a period of what Ian Taylor emphasizes as one of dis-location rather than one of ideological reproduction.[3] Locality, though, can be the source of major reaffirmative and conservative aspects of working-class culture. And "community" in inter-class relations can be more than merely imaginary. It might serve one group's interests rather than another's, but that does not make the shared experience any less real. Within processes of ideological reproduction, community is lived through and experienced consciously as a major influence. In a very real everyday sense it is the actual experience of community that makes the reproduction of the status quo possible. In Colne, in the 1930s, it was a very real way of making sense of your place in the world. There could, though, be tensions *within* the community that could be literally "played" out. I will go back to the cricket field to try and illustrate this in one way at least. Listen to Hyndeman Snell, a loom-maker born in 1906, who was a fast bowler for the Colne cricket team—also recruited by "the boss where I worked, he was on the committee at Colne." Hyndeman started playing for the Colne First Eleven regularly in 1943, but had played occasionally for them, and quite regularly for the second team, in the 1930s. He had, he recollects, not got right into the first team in the late 1920s and 1930s because his father was "... Labour man". So community was not always achieved smoothly: Hyndeman displays a strong sense of class differentiation in his recollection that when he took the wicket of some opponent, he would be especially pleased if his victim was a local toff. He also took much pride from being a "better" or more effective player than other, "posher" or more middle-class members of his own team. Community prevailed, though, and Hyndeman, after playing at a lower level in his fifties, returned to the Colne club to run a fourth team for two years, before becoming a member of the committee himself. He was excluded from the club as a young man—he claimed for his family Labour connection—then asked in a few years later, when the power of "the old school tie" seemed to fade, and eventually finished up as a club committee member himself. Hyndeman's life history in cricket captures the underlying social relations in which a community identity prevails over a class identity. Throughout all this, community is rooted (as in the case of "enlightened" factory owners such as the Quaker chocolate manufacturers)—unequal social relations: the local middle class, the dignitaries, ran the club and so controlled an activity watched and played, on the whole, by "working men." Within this process, new recruits like Hyndeman Snell himself might be incorporated into the established power structure. But community was still experienced—it was not imaginary. To be from Colne and not from some other Lancashire township was what gave people a large part of their collective social identity. To be a "Colner" was a way of making sense of an otherwise "difficult to situate" wider world.

Community was also "achieved" in other, more coercive ways, as I have already indicated with reference to urban redevelopment and police action against street sports and gambling. The latter two phenomena are worth looking at in more detail. Gaming and gambling were "policed" out of existence as, in the early 1920s, a raid was made on gambling in the local hills. As Andrew Faulds has told me (drawing upon the gossip of the time rather than direct experience), in 1923 uniformed police in a furniture van raided the main organized gambling area around a pub on the moors outside Colne, where 300-400 gamblers gathered regularly. Faulds sees this event as:

> the result of so many complaints going into the police station about men working in the mill, drawing their wages and going straight up to Coldwell and the wives never saw the wages .... the wives made the complaint.

Wives, the churches, the police, the local judiciary; this was a powerful cross-sectional alliance indeed, which formed to attack a major cultural form of the "rough," or at least not-so-respectable, working-class. Andrew Faulds recalls that gambling carried on on street corners, but this was no more than "little lads' stuff" and was policed more mildly.

Also, in the 1920s, a local sport of "bowling stones" was policed and legislated out of existence in the town. In 1928, for instance, police started motor-car patrols to stop the sport. This game involved throwing a fist-sized round stone from Point A to Point B—both "points" usually being drinking places. The thrower to reach Point B in the least number of throws was the winner. As streets were built, as transport emerged on these streets, bowling stones began to be seen as an undesirable and "rough" activity, incompatible with a developing sense of petty-bourgeois civic pride. So it had to go. The conditions for "community" were certainly not purely organic; they were in the making, the social construction of particular class groups with power and influence, but also of the social relationships that were forged across and within classes in everyday life.

And sometimes, if community was threatened—or seen, even remotely, to be threatened—then more coercive steps would be taken to reinstate the sense of common community. My last example of this comes from a Colne man recollecting an incident in the early 1930s in the next town down the valley, Nelson—also known as "Little Moscow" because of a strong political element in local working-class life. I asked Andrew Faulds whether forms of policing were directed against forms of working-class political life in the inter-war period. He recalled direct policing of, for instance, the National Unemployed Union's collective action. A police charge of "absolute brutality" was mounted against a demonstration, in the early 1930s, in Nelson:

> Battleship Potemkin showed at the Regent in Nelson and the damn silly idiotic authorities ... the police surrounded the cinema ... because they thought people were goin' to get ideas into their 'ead about revolution ... the silly idiots ... Oh, they surrounded the cinema, dear me, it were idiotic.

Such measures, particularly in Colne, were not always necessary. The powerful pull of locality—with cricket matches played between teams of striking workers and teams of employers/manufacturers—was often sufficient to serve as a foundation for the reconstitution of community.

IV

In this concluding section, I will suggest some answers that might be given to a central question raised in some remarks in the second section of this paper. I will then make some comments about how case-studies of working-class culture in the past might be most adequately theorized.[4]

The question posed earlier in the paper, about the inter-war period, was "how are creases in the social fabric ironed out?" There is a threefold answer to this. First, new class conciliations are constantly in the making. There is no single, unitary working-class ready to condemn the inadequacies and injustices of the capitalist system. Second, as a consequence of some new class alliances, "undesirable" elements of the working-class are redeveloped or policed out of existence in ways meant to suggest that things were "improving," environmentally and morally, despite the social problems. And third, social relations are often lived out around the principle of community, through experiences like sport, in spite of the objective membership of different individuals and groups to particular social classes.

It is easier to live with the world as it is than to change it. Working-class culture has, in many of its elements, a strong traditional and conservative core that has as a major characteristic an inveterate hedonism. It is not adequate to talk just about whether or not hegemony is achieved. Bourgeois hegemony certainly was achieved—or, more accurately, sustained—in Colne in the inter-war years, but some sort of hegemony is always achieved wherever the social fabric remains intact. In Colne, it was achieved or reproduced through the real, lived experience of locality and community. But it is not an explanation of a social process to point to the existence or non-existence of hegemony. The processes through which hegemony is negotiated are what must always be given detailed consideration. To say that hegemony is achieved is a starting point in a more revealing general enquiry into how and why it is achieved at all. So my first major point is that the notion of hegemony must be seen as a starting point rather than a conclusion in the exploration of working-class cultural forms.

Second, we should be careful not to read into cultural practices meanings that were not there. If we have a chance to hear the voices of the social agents whose practices we are examining, the chance should be taken. It would be easy to take a cultural practice like sport and to read off a meaning from it that might fit a particular view of the world. But this can lead to extremist readings of, say, sport as repression or as an opiate (Hoch, 1972, and Brohm, 1978); or of sport or play as some kind of utopian category in which images of a new future society can be glimpsed (Hearns, 1978). But to plunder and pillage the past for meat to put on the bones of a skeletal model of history is to ignore the complex mediations through which experiences are actually lived. Forms of sport and leisure arise in specific sets of social conditions. Forms of domination may well be potentially resisted by play forms, but there is no inherent characteristic within sport that makes of it a utopian or a subversive category with regard to structures of domination. Close study of the nature of the play form in the particular social setting has to take place. There can be no substitute for this sort of detailed ethnographic work.

My third point is that forms of sport and leisure are often essentially conservative simply because of the good sense they make to human agents in terms of how the social world can be comprehended and accommodated. By this, I mean that the hedonistic element in working-class culture often operates to produce collective modes of social closure (Parkin, 1974 and 1979).[5] This is a complicated process, but it has developed alongside new forms of inter- and intra-class relations in ways that often contribute to the reproduction of the status quo—of existing relations of domination. In sport and leisure, too, strategies of social closure have often exhibited the same male-dominated traits that are characteristic of forms of social closure in the workplace and in politics. The point to emphasize here is that forms of social closure can often seem to be initially disruptive of the established order, but are usually incorporated into that order, or at least ultimately unthreatening to it.

As a final point, I want to emphasize how important it is, in the study of working-class culture, to develop an adequate notion of what social bonds are both within working-class life and between the working-class and other classes. Social actors do not simply mouth words written by some omnipotent script-writer. They often write, with great self-consciousness, their own scripts. But such scripts are often permeated by a realistic view of the world that recognizes the odds against changing things as they are. Social actors recognize the nature of their bonds in everyday life. Too much work on the working-class has underemphasized this. Sports can, in some circumstances, be experienced as a realm of apparent freedom or collective bliss (in, say, open competition, or through team effort), but the sport and leisure forms within working-class culture are bound up with what Ralf Dahrendorf has recently called ligatures (or bonds, constraints) rather than options (Dahrendorf, 1979). Ellis Dickinson, in Colne, could get a job, a house and local fame as a cricketer. But his real options were a gamble, or illusory, and he knew it. The advantages that did become available to him had as a premise his experience of community as a ligature, as an ultimately constraining "allegiance, bond or linkage" (Dahrendorf, 1979) that limits the ways in which Ellis could move out of or beyond his position in the local social structure. Fully aware of the nature of these bonds—of the balance between ligature and option—Ellis Dickinson, Hyndeman Snell and others could nevertheless manage to have some good times in the bad times of the 1930s.

The points raised in this final section suggest that the study of working-class culture in the inter-war years has yet to be developed in ways that might point toward some form of explanation, rather than mere description. We might live under capitalism, but we are also members of communities. We might be British, but we are also "Colners," people of particular places. There is a rich vein of work on working-class culture in the period of its emergence, in its making and remaking (to quote the classical terms derived from Thompson, 1963, and Stedman-Jones, 1974). There is also much work on the experience within working-class culture of the period after World War II, when various influences have been said to have altered fundamentally the social and economic basis of everyday working-class life.

But what was the nature of that culture that was made, once it was actually made, in the phase of its consolidation? This is what work on the inter-war period can help us understand. In this essay, by stressing the diversity of working-class culture—pointing to the different elements within the working class itself—and by considering two major ways in which cross-class relations were achieved (the one coercive, the other more subtly based upon the experience of community),

I hope to have shown that the 1920s and the 1930s must be explored in depth if evolving patterns of working-class culture are to be understood. We might mourn the lack of a "mature culture of the working class," to use Stuart Hall's term again. But by "mature culture" Hall means political practice—he is using the word in a highly specific developmental sense, rather than in the sense of a general process. There were plenty of "matured" popular cultural forms in working-class life in the inter-war period. They reminded women of their allocated position in working-class culture. And some of them, in the spheres of sport and leisure, showed that elements within the working-class were perfectly aware of their objective position as exploited worker, but nevertheless chose not to sacrifice the good times of the here-and-now on the altar of a vision of the good (or at least a better) society.

Many chose to reconstitute themselves as "Colners," rather than to mount an offensive against the social order; and to carry on "having a good time" rather than to seek to transform the structures that gave them a sense of their own subordinate place in the world, but a more "equal" place in Colne. The politics of working-class leisure and sport in the period considered were essentially conservative—through good times, they contributed to the reproduction of bad times.

Notes

1. The data reported on in this essay were gathered mostly on the basis of funding provided by the British Academy. I would therefore like to acknowledge the Academy's support for this project.

2. There is a biographical obituary, for instance, of a 73-year old athlete, in the 1929 *Craven Herald* (August 16). This man, from Cowling, a few miles outside Colne, was a professional athlete from the age of 19 to his 40th year. He lived on this, and had sports trophies worth £250. His first handicap, at the age of 19, was set up by a sporting entrepreneur (Alec Whipp, from a town 20 to 25 miles away); there were seven heats, four in each heat, over 120 yards. At the age of 25 (1881) he jumped across the canal. At one Lakes Sports he won all field events, getting an extra 10 shillings and a week's royal hospitality from a local gentleman. So patrons supported him. Factory work on pill boxes; drumming in a theatre band; jumping over galloping horses in a circus—these are some of the jobs he took in between his athletic action. Hustling was important. He would wear an old cap, a worn-out coat, thin trousers and laced-up clogs, and would then challenge some local jumping champion, for £25 a match, and usually win easily.

3. This refers to a point made by Ian Taylor at the workshop.

4. At the Workshop at which this paper was presented, Alan Metcalfe reminded the participants that, just because some speakers were dealing with the past, talking about the past, this didn't necessarily make their work "historical." Just to talk about the past, he went on, is not enough to comply with the canons of historical scholarship. I have rarely used the word "historical" anywhere in my paper; I have certainly not described my own work as the work of a historian. If I were German, I would perhaps call myself a cultural scientist of past and present time, but that sounds awfully pompous. I am perfectly aware of the dangers involved in using oral historical sources, and in some cases I have gone to other sources (records of factories, newspaper accounts) to "check out" the recollection that I have collected. But if I did this in every case, it would denigrate the oral historical source as a method in itself. The popular memory often gets dates wrong in the retrospective haze, but why should the popularly memorized account not be quite as much an authentic piece of raw historical data as is, say, the contemporaneous newspaper account? If the popular memory of the past distorts a little, who is to say that it distorts any more than the mass media or the institutions of social control? So, in this piece, I have let many of the voices come through unchecked. If this is historically inadequate, then so be it. I will one day attempt to find a less pompous sounding version of the term cultural scientist to stick on my badge at conferences.

5. Although some of the cultural forms I have discussed in this paper can be understood as forms of closure, this point really refers to gender-based associations or clubs within working-class culture, the like of which I mentioned early on in my third section, but to which I have not given any detailed consideration.

References

Aldgate, Tony. "British Cinema in the 1930s," Unit 7, Block 2 (The historical development of popular culture in Britain, 2), Course U203 Popular Culture, Open University, 1981.

Brohm Jean-Marie. *Sport—A Prison of Measured Time*. Ink Links,1978.

Clarke, John. "Capital and Culture: The Post-war Working-class Revisited." in John Clarke, Chas Critcher and Richard Johnson (eds.). *Working Class Culture— Studies in History and Theory*, Hutchinson, 1979, pp.238-253.

Constantine, Stephen. *Unemployment in Britain Between the Wars*. Longman, 1980.

Crombie, Geoff, R. *1926-1951 A Colne Festival*. M.M. Publishing Corporation, 1978.

Crook, Rosemary. "'Tidy Women': Women in the Rhondda Between the Wars." *Oral History*, 10 (2, 1983), pp.40-46.

Cunningham, Hugh. *Leisure in the Industrial Revolution c. 1780—c. 1880*. Croom Helm, 1980.

Dahrendorf, Ralf. *Life Chances—Approaches to Social and Political Theory*. University of Chicago Press, 1979.

Delves, Anthony. "Popular Recreation and Social Control in Derby,1880-1850." in Eileen and Stephen Yeo (eds.), *Popular Culture and Class Conflict 1590-1914: Explorations in the History of Labour and Leisure.* Harvester Press, 1981, pp.87-127.

Dixey, Rachael. "The Playing of Bingo: Industry, Market and Working-class Culture." in Alan Tomlinson (ed.), *Leisure and Popular Cultural Forms.* Brighton Polytechnic, 1983, pp.52-67.

Hall, Stuart. "Notes on deconstructing 'the popular'," in Raphael Samuel (ed.), *People's History and Socialist Theory.* Routledge and Kegan Paul, 1981, pp.227-240.

Hearns, Francis. *Domination, Legitimation and Resistance—the Incorporation of the Nineteenth-Century English Working Class.* Greenwood Press, 1978.

Hoch, Paul. *Rip Off the Big Game—the Exploitation of Sports by the Power Elite.* Doubleday Anchor, 1972.

Hoggart, Richard. *The Uses of Literacy.* Penguin, 1958.

Howkins, Alan and J, Lowerson. *Trends in Leisure, 1919-1939.* Sports Council/Social Science Research Council, 1979.

Jones, G. Stedman. "Working-Class Culture and Working-Class Politics in London, 1870-1900: Notes on the Remaking of a Working-class." *Journal of Social History,* 7 (1974), pp.460-508.

Marx, Karl. "The Eighteenth Brumaire of Louis Bonaparte." in *Surveys from Exile, Political Writings, Volume 2.* Edited by David Fernback, Penguin, 1973.

Mass Observation. "All-In, All-Out." in Britain by Mass-Observation. Penguin, pp.114-138, 1939.

Parkin, Frank. "Strategies of Social Closure in Class Formation." in F. Parkin (ed.), *The Social Analysis of Class Structure.* Tavistock, pp.1-18, 1974.

Parkin, Frank. *Marxism and Class Theory: a Bourgeois Critique.* Tavistock, 1979.

Shipley, Stan. "Tom Causer of Bermondsey: a Boxer Hero of the 1980s." in *History Workshop—A Journal of Socialist and Feminist Historians.* 15, (Spring, 1983), pp. 28-59.

Spencer, Wilfred. *Colne As It Was—Photographs Selected and Introduced by Wilfred Spencer.* Hendon Publishing Company, 1971.

Stevenson, John and C. Cook. *The Slump.* Quartet Books, 1979.

Thompson, Edward P. *The Making of the English Working Class.* Gollancz, 1963.

Tomlinson, Alan. "It Puts a Spel on You: 'Knur and Spel' in Colne in the Twentieth Century." Unpublished paper delivered at Graduate Student Seminar, Queen's University, 1982.

Ward, Colin. "We Are All Historians Now." *New Society,* 64, (1075, 23 June,1983), pp. 475-476.

Williams, Raymond. "Literature in Society," in Hilda Schiff (ed.), *Contemporary Approaches to English Studies*. Heinemann, 1977a.

Williams, Raymond. "Dominant, Residual, Emergent," Chapter 6 of *Marxism and Literature*. Oxford University Press, 1977b.

Leisure, Sport and Working-Class Culture:
Some Insights from Montreal and the Northeast Coalfields of England

Alan Metcalfe

The difficulty in approaching a topic of this nature is where to begin. The starting point is predicated upon one's theoretical background and actual concrete database, and the background and knowledge of the readers. Thus this paper may be theoretically immature for some, lack in depth analysis for others and provide inadequate practical data for the rest. This, in many respects, is a reflection of the state of the art in the field of working-class studies. The essential ingredients of the area of study are a number of weighty and contradictory theoretical approaches, some brilliantly insightful case-studies of selected elements, and a lack of agreement over what working-class culture is.

Many studies of working-class culture serve more to obscure than to illuminate. In other words, it is difficult to find a starting point upon which even a minority can agree. In fact, any study works from sets of assumptions that define the boundaries and accentuate certain attributes whilst ignoring others. Unless these assumptions are clearly stated, it is often difficult to separate the wheat from the chaff. Thus, I feel it is important to identify, as clearly as possible, my own theoretical leanings and that database from which my examples are selected. My personal, individual development is a cumulative experience that has created my own approach to the study of the working class. As is the case with so many others, my foundations lie in inadequate and incomplete readings in the works of Karl Marx. These were given some shape by my professor of 19-century English history, J.F.C. Harrison. It was he who introduced me to the works that have been most influential, including those of E.P. Thompson and Raymond

Williams.[1] In a Canadian context, the works of G. Kealey, B. Palmer and R. Gruneau have had the greatest influence upon my views of the Canadian working class. More recently, I have been particularly influenced by two sets of writings, and it is these that provide the theoretical focus for this paper. The first is Ian McKay's article "History, Anthropology, and the Concept of Culture".[2] More pertinent still has been "Working-Class Culture: Studies in History and Theory".[3] Most influential of all were two of Richard Johnson's contributions: "Culture and the Historians," and "Three Problematics: Elements of a Theory of Working-Class Culture." It is this latter work, and in particular, its conclusions, that provide the framework for my examination of sport, leisure and working-class culture.[4]

The database from which concrete examples have been drawn is contained in two of my own articles and the research that accompanied them. These articles are "Working Class Physical Recreation in Montreal, 1860-1895," and "Organized Sport in the Mining Communities of South Northumberland, 1800-1889."[5] Thus the data are taken from two distinctive and strictly limited working-class environments. The mining communities of the North-East consisted of approximately 44 mining villages contained within an area 17 miles by 12 miles, and inhabited almost exclusively by miners. Montreal, on the other hand, was a more complex society, containing a variety of working groups in close proximity to other societal groups. Together they provide ideal case-studies of working-class culture at a critical period in its history.

Richard Johnson's "Three Problematics: Elements of a Theory of Working Class Culture" serves to pinpoint basic issues that face any student of working-class culture. I will use ideas gleaned from this essay as a springboard for an examination of sport, leisure and working-class culture. This presentation, therefore, will consist not of a coherent, structured analysis but rather of a number of views that, I hope, provide new insights into sport, leisure and culture.

First, if one works within the definitions used by Johnson, history once again moves to centre stage. Any examination of culture in the tradition of Thompson, Williams, and Johnson makes it mandatory to use a historical methodology. The concepts of reproduction, ideology, and culture are rooted in history. At the same time this is an acceptance not of all histories, but rather of those that address certain aspects of society and culture. It is not a history that addresses "the whole way of life" but rather one that examines not only people "but the whole complex set of relations in which they stand, within which, indeed, they are made as social beings".[6] Thus a history of sport per se provides little information as to the nature of the relationships between individuals, groups, and society. Histories of sport must, therefore, address the relationship of sport to those conditions that determine the nature of social relationships.

While extensive debate and discussion have focused upon the relationship between the means of production and working-class culture, less attention has been paid to the actual physical boundaries within which the workers played and the constraints these placed upon the choices available to various groups. In both areas, sport was played within severely circumscribed boundaries, which were imposed from the outside by local government in the case of Montreal and by the mine owners in the mining villages. In each instance, indigenous working-class games bore the brunt of the full force of the law. It would appear that the authorities were trying to force the worker into acceptable activities, in particular organized team games. The police actions, the city bylaws, and the lack of facilities are documented. However, this provides only a partial picture. The case of the mining communities provides more subtle shades to the picture. To the casual observer, playing-space would not appear to be a problem, since the majority of villages were relatively small and located in open country. In fact, the villages were, in some respects, prisons surrounded by private estates and farms. The miners, in their search for space, were forced to public land—the Town Moor at Newcastle and the links at Newbiggin in particular—or to public houses or commercial grounds. What the history of facilities for the miners reflects is complete disinterest by those outside the area with regard to the plight of the miners. In fact, they made little effort to change them but rather left them alone as long as they remained invisible. However as soon as they became visible— by travelling to Newcastle and the commercial grounds—there was immediate and often brutal reaction. For example, in 1875, just after the miners had gained "free time", the authorities successfully closed all the commercial sporting grounds that catered to the working class. What I am trying to suggest is that, in both cases, sport was pursued within increasingly constrained boundaries. At the same time, there were differences in the nature and intensity of these constraints. It would appear that the miners were, in some respects, freer to forge their own identities than was the working class of Montreal. The intrusion of alternative institutions—and thus the probability of a greater fragmentation of the working class—was greater in the larger cities.

More central to sport and its relationship to culture is the concept of leisure. Johnson deliberately identifies leisure pursuits with "partial or trivializing conceptions of culture" (p.230). Basically, he suggests that they are not relevant to a real understanding of culture. This obviously is a central question that we must be able to answer. In part, he answers it himself, first by using a particular definition of leisure: "freedom or spare time provided by the cessation of activities." This, of course, is a purely quantitative definition, which denies a qualitative element in which meaning would be embedded. At the same time, this question serves as a point of departure that leads to new insights. I suggest that leisure entails more than "free time"; it requires time that is truly "free"; free from the constraints imposed by factory owners, mine owners, and survival itself. Thus, leisure was not a meaningful concept until the second half of the 19th century. The miners themselves recognized this differentiation in their attitude to idle time—that time free from work—that was forced upon them by the owners. This time was recognized as completely unproductive and, in fact, destructive. Perhaps for activities to be symbolic beyond their mere performance it is necessary for working-class groups to acquire leisure. If this is the case, sport did not attain symbolic meaning, until the second half of the century.[7] For the miners, this occurred in 1872, with the final abolition of the bond, and the acquisition of a five-day week. In Montreal, different groups attained it at different times, and thus it is impossible to talk about a homogeneous working class. Throughout the 19th century it was restricted to the industrial workers in Point St. Charles and the East end of Montreal, and was never real for the carpenters, labourers and other people engaged in traditional trades, whose lives were lived within the context of pre-industrial patterns of living. Thus, while it will be possible to examine the symbolic meaning of sport for the miners, it is virtually impossible, at this juncture, to talk about the leisure of the Montreal working class in any meaningful way.

There is yet another answer to Johnson's attack upon leisure pursuits and, in fact, he provides it himself:

> The relation between economic conditions of existence of a particular class and its culture is a problematic one. Yet is it absurd to believe that there is no relation between ideological and political forms of economic classes.[8]

One could quite easily transpose leisure in the quotation. It is ridiculous to suggest that culture is associated with all aspects of life except those activities undertaken during their non-work time. In fact, it appears logical to argue that it would be during these periods that individuals and groups would be most likely to reveal their true social beings. At the same time, Johnson's concern serves to focus upon the fact that the sporting activities in and for themselves hold no cultural meaning; they are to be seen as symbolizing deeper relationships and meanings. Thus, much of what passes for sport history is irrelevant to our understanding of culture.

Johnson's essay focuses on three problematics that lie at the heart of the debate over working-class culture. Central to the debate is the concept of culture itself. Johnson successfully attempts to add greater depth to our understanding of this concept. Central to his approach is the concept of the cultural ideological:

> The characteristic feature of the ideological-cultural instance, then, is the production of forms of consciousness—ideas, feeling, desires, moral preferences, forms of subjectivity.[9]

He then suggests that there is no separate or institutional area of social life in which forms of consciousness arise. Thus, various areas of social life will affect each other to create particular forms of consciousness. Underlying sport in both Montreal and the mining villages were certain outward signs that symbolized certain relationships.

Central to all indigenous working-class sports was money and gambling. In over 3,000 individual challenge matches involving miners between 1872 and

1889, not one did not involve a money stake. I suggest that the predominance of money prizes and gambling reflects some fundamental attributes of working-class culture. Sport was not a vehicle for the demonstration of social qualities; it was for victory itself. In some respects, sport was symbolic of the continuing struggle to survive, but it was a struggle in which one could achieve a momentary victory. Perhaps more illuminating was the pervasiveness of gambling. The clearest illustrations of its importance can be observed in the mining villages of South Northumberland. The evidence suggests that, until the advent of organized soccer in the late 1880s, every contest was accompanied by gambling. Life was a gamble; nothing existed beyond the present. The miners, more than most other working groups, faced a daily confrontation with death, and their attitudes to sport reflected this. Conditions of existence both at home and at work made it necessary for the miners to snatch whatever moments of joy they could.

Even deeper insights can be obtained by examining their attitude to money. Although money was not irrelevant, it was not considered by the working class as it was by the middle classes; rather, it was something to be used for the fulfillment of life. Thus it was the process of gambling that was important, and not the prize per se. This is reflected in the game of bowling, in which bets were made upon each throw as well as on the outcome of the game. There are many references to the miners' relative indifference to money and their ready acceptance of defeat. The question, of course, is what does this mean, especially in relation to the cultural ideological instance? Sport reflected the real conditions of work and life—there was no future. Life was a continual struggle against mine owners and the conditions of existence. Any victory was temporary, having no ultimate bearing on the quality of life. So too was the struggle against the mine owners; there was no ultimate victory, simply a temporary and often illusory success in the ongoing battle. The conditions of life and work would not change, the owners would remain owners and the miners, miners. Thus, any victory must be savoured immediately, whether it be on the playing field or against the owners; ultimate reality would not change. If there is any merit in this argument, it is critical to an understanding of working-class consciousness.

Central to nearly all discussions of the working class is the concept of culture. There has been increasing dissatisfaction with the "whole way of life" definition because it fails to discriminate between different elements. Johnson, while rejecting this definition, does not reject the importance of culture as a category. His definition provides a point of departure somewhat different from that of the advocates of the "whole way of life" definition. He defines culture as:

> the common sense or way of life of a particular class, group, or social category, the complex of ideologies that are actually adopted as moral preferences or principles of life.[10]

Thus, culture can be seen as an essential element of the cultural ideological— as the ground within which consciousness is rooted. However, again, it is not to be equated with leisure pursuits per se, but rather with the underlying relationships that they exemplify.

Perhaps the most interesting insights into culture come at that moment when leisure becomes a meaningful term for the working class. The two case-studies provided completely different insights. In Montreal "free time" was acquired by different groups at different times and thus never embraced all working groups during the 19th century. Thus, the ongoing reproduction of culture was specific to the individual groups as they acquired "free time." It first occurred among the workers in the factories along the Lachine Canal and in the East end of Montreal. This working class was further fragmented by race, religion, and a continuing influx of new immigrants. What can be observed is some attempt to institutionalize the practices of the past with their attached values. The French identified with strength; hence the importance of the French Canadian strongman tradition. Scotsmen, on the other hand, perpetuated the Highland Games. In each instance, the emphasis was upon individual contests and not team sports. Also there is evidence that ethnic background was more important than class. If anything new emerged within Montreal, it was the working-class entry into the arena of team sports—sports that were created and run by the middle class and which, in an organizational sense, were modeled on the bureaucratic structures of capitalist society. These threatened the traditional values of working-class culture and created ideological boundaries beyond which it is nearly impossible to go.

Once again the miners of the North-East provide a clearer example of the relationship. The two decades following the acquisition of "free time" in 1872, witnessed the creation of a thriving sport culture based upon the traditional mining games and the intrusion of middle-class team games into the community. The 1870s and 1880s witnessed an explosion of interest in a variety of mining sports, and the concomitant development of structures to organize and promote the sports. All the sports were individual contests that placed miner against miner. These sports—bowling, handball, quoits, dog racing, pigeon racing, and rabbit coursing—had long traditions in mining life. What is most important is that they were highly individualistic and that, in each case, chance played a major role. At this level, it was not community that was important, but the individual. Contemporary observers and indigenous literature all recognized the extreme individualism of the miners, who continually drew attention to themselves by their exploits, dress, and manner. Perhaps within their extreme individualism the miners recapitulated the underlying values of the mining community as a whole.

It was with the introduction of team sports that the miners and the Montrealers demonstrated similar patterns of development. In each instance, team games were introduced from the outside. These games exemplified values and relationships that were different from those underlying the workers' society; cooperation instead of confrontation. While the miners resisted outside domination, their entrance onto the soccer playing fields inevitably brought them into contact with a new and, in many senses, destructive ideology.

One of the central questions concerning culture is whether it is homogeneous or heterogeneous. I suggest that it can be either—depending upon the level of discourse, the questions being asked and the particular historical moment. Montreal provides examples of both homogeneity and heterogeneity. It appears that the process of industrialization served to intensify differences. This certainly appears to be the case with organized sport. During the 1870s and 1880s, clubs were clearly organized according to occupation, in both the formation of teams and the teams they competed against: machinists played machinists; railway workers played railway workers. If there was any degree of working-class homogeneity, it lay at a level deeper than that of the day-to-day interactions of individuals and groups. Even in the case of team sports, the purity of a team's composition was often contaminated by ethnicity and religion. Only amongst the French Canadians is there evidence of significant numbers of teams that were based on criteria other than occupation, and this was limited to the baseball teams that proliferated after 1890. In this instance, the criteria for membership was locality or street, rather than occupation. Thus there was a possibility of teams based on class. There was, however, some evidence that these teams did espouse values different from those of the middle class. The persistent references to violence and unsportsmanlike conduct suggest that the games meant something different to the workers as a group, and it is at this level that homogeneity may have some meaning.

The heterogeneity of the industrial working class, as reflected in team sport, is highlighted by the homogeneity of a culture that has roots in the past. Such was the case with the popular Sunday athletic entertainments and periodic cockfighting, held without exception in the working-class areas of the city. The fragmentary evidence suggests that the spectators at these events, while undisputably working-class, were not divided along occupational lines. All the pursuits involved individual activities, all involved gambling, and all involved behaviour that lay outside the boundaries of what the middle class termed acceptable. Perhaps industrialization, by creating widely differing situations for different segments of the working class, served to destroy any degree of homogeneity there was.

The sometime paradoxical relationships that existed within the working class are illustrated in a clearer form in the case of the miners. During the period after 1872, when there was a significant increase of competition between the miners, inter-colliery rivalry reflected deep-seated divisions within the community. These conflicts frequently spilled over into physical violence. The differences between the collieries were perceived by the miners to be real and important. The question is, were these differences in fact real? In reality, the miners were exhibiting characteristics that allowed them to survive as individuals and as members of communities within the oppressive physical conditions of work and home. Visible demonstrations of homogeneity, on the other hand, only occurred when they ventured out of the colliery districts either to play sport, to shop in town, or to engage in collective action. Sport became a focal point for uniting collieries and the coalfield, and it was when sports champions challenged the outside world that the expression of community solidarity became most visible. Two examples will suffice to illustrate the point. In 1846, when the great rowing champion Harry Clasper was beaten by a Londoner in a race on the River Tyne, before "a vaste concourse of peoples the race terminated without even a solitary cheer. The banks of coaly Tyne were dumb." The pride of the community had been destroyed. Twenty-four years later, in 1870, on the death of the same Harry Clasper—a pitman turned professional rower—more than 100,000 working men turned out to witness the largest funeral yet held in Newcastle. The authorities, realizing the significance of the occasion, held the funeral on a Sunday "to meet the convenience of numerous bodies of working men." It was only during these significant events—the professional rowing races on the Tyne, the championship bowling matches on the Town Moor, and later the soccer exploits of Newcastle United—that the miners became visible as a collectivity through leisure. It is possible that, for the collective consciousness to reveal itself, it is necessary to place the working class in a conflict situation with the outside world; a situation in which both sides recognize the threat to their own integrity. In a more general sense, it would be at times like this that any real victories would be won. More often than not, however, the working class retreats without victory; collective consciousness collapses, and intra-working-class differences take over once again.

In a final section, Johnson addresses one of the central questions of any examination of working-class culture: "The relation between the economic condition of existence of a particular class and its culture." He further suggests two main ways of understanding this relationship as it pertains to working-class culture.

> The first concerns the material conditions of the class itself and the sense that is made of these. The second concerns the particular relation to capital and capital's need continuously to transform the cultural conditions of labour.[12]

Both in Montreal and in South Northumberland, new forms of leisure activities emerged at the time new work relationships were established. In fact, a new culture emerged. In Montreal, the new sport forms emerged first amongst the industrial workers of Point St. Charles and St. Anne, who were the first to gain real "free time." At first, the sport forms contained residual elements of pre-industrial society, but these were soon overtaken by the acceptance of team sports that reflected the forms used by the middle classes: bureaucratic organizations with a clearly delineated authority structure, and rules of fair play determined by the middle classes. Only in baseball, a game not popular with the Canadian middle class, do we find any evidence of alternative systems. In the mining districts, the pre-industrial sports, in particular bowling, maintained a foothold well into the 20th century before it disappeared. By 1889, however, organized team sport had gained a foothold although, in this instance, the miners deliberately rejected the middle-class leadership of Newcastle by forming their own organization. At the same time, there was increasing contact with the outside world and the inevitable introduction of new ideas.

It would appear reasonable that, with its increasing popularity amongst the working class, organized team sport would be seen as a vehicle for the replication of labour power and the transformation of the working class. This is illustrated in the gradual acceptance of sport by the schools and the churches. In each instance, it was used to propagate basic values. Increasingly, leisure was recognized as an important site for the establishment of the hegemony of the middle class. Like so many of the interactions between the two groups, the process was complex, uneven, and the site of conflict.

Perhaps the most visible and informative of these interactions is reflected in the years immediately after the miners and other working men on Tyneside gained "free time" and became consumers of leisure. The first commercial sporting grounds were opened in Newcastle in the mid-1850s. From that time, there were always at least two grounds in the vicinity of Newcastle. While they were not universally popular, no overt actions were taken to close them. During the period 1873-1876, three commercial grounds were opened in the heart of the coalfield. The reaction was immediate and ruthless. Within a period of one year, all the grounds on Tyneside were closed. In each instance, the method of closing was the same; two individuals were charged with gambling, prosecuted and found guilty. It is interesting that gambling had been practised on these grounds since 1858 but that only now, when there was a significant increase in working-class involvement, was action taken. Only when the workers became visible and posed a threat to Victorian morality was action taken. The basic antipathy between the two groups and the blatant hypocrisy of the middle classes was illustrated even more clearly four years later. For more than a hundred years, the miners had used the Town Moor in Newcastle for their bowling matches. The early 1870s witnessed a significant increase in the number of matches. By 1876, on the great match days, crowds of ten to twenty thousand—composed of colliers and their wives and families—were descending upon Newcastle. This sudden influx was of great concern to the authorities and led, in 1880, to the Newcastle Town Council prohibiting bowling on the Moor. Within two weeks, the Moor was devoid of activity. This, however, was not the end of the affair. Exactly one year later, a crowded public meeting was held to protest the prohibition. What was the cause of this sudden interest? Very simply, money. The meeting had been organized by the tradespeople of Newcastle, who brought with them a petition signed by 1,200 of their peers. Great pains were taken to explain that they had waited for one year to see if the fall in trade was due to bad times or the stoppage of bowling. The conclusion was that it was the stoppage of bowling. Subsequently, they were successful in getting the ban lifted. These examples are classic because of their overt nature. The middle class soon learned their lesson and devised more appropriate methods of exerting force to change the working class; in particular through the schools and the churches. What this suggests is that it was only when the working class became visible and were perceived as posing an actual threat that action was taken. By the 1880s, this process could no longer be ignored, but the actions of the middle class became more complex and subtle.

Conclusions

Rather than attempting to summarize my presentation, I will address the issues in the light of insights gained from the other papers presented at the workshop. In keeping with my presentation, this will not be a coherent analysis but, rather, a set of observations on certain issues—in particular, the idea of leisure, the importance of history and the complexity of culture, relationships, and historical moments.

One of the central terms is "leisure." As Robert Hollands (see his paper in this collection) suggests, there is a need to radically reconceptualize the term. The concept and definition of leisure that has been used as a starting point for all discussion is one that was defined by the dominant class and thus reflected its ideology. Additionally, the tendency to define leisure in terms of discrete, well-defined entities of time has served to obscure the degree to which it penetrates other aspects of life. In other words, leisure is seen to equal "free time." Certainly in pre-industrial society the whole concept of time, and thus of leisure, was different. Another aspect that served to further separate leisure from work was the assumption that leisure presupposed meaning. However, meaning was defined in class terms. Thus, since the activities of the miners and the industrial workers were unacceptable to the middle class, the workers had no leisure (or at least an attempt was made to control their leisure). If, on the other hand, one accepts a definition of meaning that is predicated upon the culture of which it is a part, it is apparent that the miners did indeed have leisure, albeit a leisure significantly different from that of the dominant class. Thus, it appears that it is necessary to reconceptualize and contextualize the term "leisure."

A second major concern is the centrality of history—or should I say "the past"—to an understanding of culture. While the studies of the English working class are solidly rooted in history, the Canadian work is far less solidly based. This, perhaps, arises from the relative newness of Canadian working-class culture to use facts from the past that have been abstracted from their historical context. In some respects, there is a somewhat cavalier approach to the canons of historical methodology. What is needed are some more solidly based historical works along the lines of those contained in *Working Class Culture: Studies in History and Theory*. In other words, a little more care is needed in tackling the history component.

Related to the last point is the importance of particular historical moments or eras—times when the very nature of class stands at a crossroads. For example, for much of the 19th century, mining culture and life remained unchanged. The year 1872 was a critical historical moment that changed mining culture; the acquisition of the five-day week and the elimination of the bond changed the material conditions of life and culture. It is important, therefore, that crucial historical moments be identified within Canada as a whole or, within particular localities. I suggest, for example, that, in terms of working-class sport in Montreal, the early 1890s were one such moment. At that time, the workers and the middle classes were precipitated into new relationships on the playing fields that changed some of the attributes of working-class culture.

This leads us into the next area—that of "social relationships." While this term is used with great frequency in working-class literature, it is extremely difficult to operationally define what it means in a sporting context. Social relationships are the foundation stone upon which culture is built. Therefore, it is important that we explore this basic element.

Finally, this brings us to the question of culture itself. Central to any understanding of culture is its extreme complexity. Any attempt to oversimplify leads to a distorted view of reality. It is the complexity of the relationships between individuals, groups, and classes that lies at the heart of culture. At the same time, it is necessary to discern similarities and differences, and to generalize and simplify, in order to understand culture more fully. However, these abstractions often serve to obscure social reality. Thus, our struggle to understand culture must continually fluctuate between a recognition of complex relations and an attempt to determine the basic elements of cultural formations. At times, there is indeed a degree of homogeneity to working-class culture, while at other historical moments it is more accurate to describe such culture as heterogeneous. Thus, we must continually advance and retreat within the web of culture, and try and unravel its underlying complexities.

Notes

1. Their initial works are still fundamental to studies in this area, even though both have changed positions significantly. E.P. Thompson, *The Making of the English Working Class*, 1968; Raymond Williams, *Culture and Society*, 1958.

2. Ian McKay, "Historians, Anthropology, and the Concept of Culture," *Labour/ Le Travailleur*, 8/9 (Autumn-Spring, 1981) pp. 185-241.

3. J. Clarke, C. Critcher and R. Johnson, *Working-Class Culture: Studies in History and Theory* (St. Martin's Press Edition, 1980).

4. Richard Johnson, "Culture and the Historians", pp.41-74, and "Three Problematics: Elements of a Theory of Working-Class Culture," in Clarke, et al., *Studies in History and Theory*, pp.201-237.

5.   Alan Metcalfe, "Working Class Physical Recreation in Montreal, 1860-1895," in *Working Papers in the Sociological Study of Sports and Leisure.* Sports Studies Research Group, Queen's University, Kingston. Vol. 1, No. 2, 1978, p.48; "Organized Sport in the Mining Communities of South Northumberland, 1800-1889," *Victorian Studies,* 25 (4, Summer, 1982), pp.469-495.

6.   Johnson, "Culture and the Historians," p.70.

7.   It is necessary to make the distinction between pre-industrial and industrial forms of working-class culture. In this paper, we are talking about the industrial working-class culture.

8.   Johnson, "Three Problematics," p.236.

9.   Ibid., p.232.

10.   Ibid., p.234.

11.   Metcalfe, "Organized Sport in the Mining Communities," p.49.

12.   Johnson, "Three Problematics," p.236.

The Leninist/Proletkul'tist Cultural Debates:
Implications for Sport Among the Soviet Working Class

Hart Cantelon

Introduction

The first attempt to create a workers' state grounded on Marxist principles came about with the Russian Revolution of 1917. By 1920, the political revolution in Russia had been stablized and Lenin and the Bolsheviks turned their attention to the revitalization of the national economy and the construction of the Marxist society they envisaged.

The decade 1920 to 1929 is a most exciting period in which to explore working-class culture, and how it was perceived and constructed. The Bolshevik preoccupation with improving Party discipline and eradicating the inertia that plagued the economy meant that "the rest of society was left free from direct political control, thus producing an explosion of experiment and creative energy" (Nettle, 1967:114). This was, as Carmen Claudin-Urondo suggests, "a world in a state of creative ferment, in constant motion, to which Lenin's thought contributed its share of leaven along with many others" (1977:35). One of the more influential movements concerned with the form and direction that socialist culture should take was that of the *Proletkul'tists*. The imprint of the *Proletkul't* was found in art, literature, music and sport.

Given the importance of this group, it is fruitful to ascertain the arguments that it put forward regarding culture and to suggest how its philosophy influenced the *proletkul't*-dominated sports clubs. But in spite of the influence of the proletarian culture movement in many areas of social life and its support among Lenin's closest colleagues (the Commissar of Education, Anatoli Vasilifevich

Lunacharsky, for example, had been a keen supporter of the *proletkul'tists* since 1912—Plekanov, V:1981), Lenin himself was uneasy with its particular view of culture. Therefore, following the discussion of the former, I will introduce Lenin's conception of culture and his criticisms of the *proletkul' t* movement, and some of the sporting alternatives that resulted from this debate.

The first section of the paper will conclude with the sports model that, I argue, represents the dominant form of sport in the USSR today: the Stakhanovite athlete.

In Section Two, I want to consider the lived experience of Soviet workers and peasants in light of the Lenin/*Proletkul' t* cultural debates; to bring into question many of the offical accounts of participation in leisure activities among the contemporary Soviet working class.

I. The Proletarian Culture of the *Proletkul'tists*

Proletarian culture was a term that the philsopher Alexander Bogdanov used to describe life in a future socialist society.[1] Bogdanov was most interested in examining the relationship that existed between ideology and social structure— an interest that alienated him from Lenin. The disagreements between the two men were such that Bogdanov refused to join the Bolshevik party, although he was considered one of the outstanding Marxist scholars in tsarist Russia. Despite Bogdanov's refusal to apply for Party membership and the tension that existed between him and Lenin, Bogdanov profoundly influenced some important Party figures (Claudin-Urondo, 1977:39). Nicholai Bukharin, the foremost Party theoretician during the 1920s and early 1930s, was one such notable. So too, as noted above, was Lunacharsky. In his *Recollections of Lenin*, Lunacharsky notes that he and Lenin "disagreed rather sharply about the *Proletkul' t*" and that Lenin particularly disapproved of the sway that Bogdanov held in the organization (Lenin, 1966:245-246).

For Bogdanov, the socialist state would incorporate four aspects of the labour process: the political form, the economic, the administrative and the cultural (Vucinich, 1976). It was the fourth form, the cultural, which particularly interested him, since here the creative role of the working class could be liberated to transform culture and ideology. As early as 1912, Bogdanov began to work out his theories, most clearly summarized in the pamphlet *Proletarian Culture*. Proletarian culture would include those forms of artistic, literary and social life that would dramatize the workers' state. This new culture could flourish only because the old authority patterns had been destroyed. As Bogdanov put it:

> All implements of the new society were already prepared in the framework of the old; only, the life activity of the new forms was chained by the dominance of the old and could not freely unfold until this dominance was removed (Cited in Utechin, 1962:123).

The successful Russian Revolution broke the chains of tsarist domination and ushered in an utterly new pattern of authority—worker control of the state apparatus. A unique proletarian culture could now blossom forth. And, following Bogdanov's argument to its logical conclusion, this culture should dramatize socialist society.

Proletkul't is the Russian acronym for the Proletarian Culture and Educational Organization, which was offically organized in February 1917 and remained a politically independent body for two years. It was during this autonomous period that Bogdanov was most influential in directing *Proletkul't*. As noted above, Bogdanov, in his four forms, recognized the intimate connection between the political, the economic, the administrative and the cultural. However, he resisted any notion that considered the cultural as a determinate of the economic. The cultural had a degree of relative direct autonomy from the other three forms. In fact, it was in the realm of the cultural that the most intense struggle for domination of the workers' state would be carried out, for here the bourgeois influence was most firmly entrenched and most uncontested. The idealist notion of culture as something separate from life, from the "real world," Bogdanov argued, suggested that it was *the form* most likely to be ignored and forgotten in the excitement of building the workers' state. But in the very act of ignoring the cultural, the workers would be losing the moment to consolidate their new authority. A flourishing, unchallenged culture from the old society would ultimately result in the collapse of the new one. Not surprisingly, then, Bogdanov viewed the cultural form "as the last bastion and last refuge of the bourgeoisie in retreat" (Claudin-Urondo, 1977:39), and the area in which the class struggle would continue even more intensely than before the political revolution took place.

Opponents of the movement, particularly Lenin, accused the *Proletkul'tists* of advocating the total destruction of all culture and values merely because they were bourgeois. *Proletkul't* countered:

> Our task is not to destroy the material values of the old culture, but to destroy the ideology, the foundation in which these values have developed. (Pravda, 27. September, 1922).

The Marxian dialectic pointed the way for the undoing of this bourgeois ideology. Bourgeois culture was dominant (the thesis). The antithesis of this was the proletarian class culture. The synthesis, as the *Proletkul't* saw it, was universal human culture, and could only be realized under socialism. But it was not an evolutionary process. Experimentation and debate had to be encouraged and, to cite a phrase from the Chinese Cultural Revolution, for which *Proletkul't* has been compared (Claudin-Urondo, 1977), "a thousand flowers should be allowed to bloom."

It is not surprising, therefore, that the First All-Russia Conference of *Proletkul't* (1918) passed a declaration that emphasized the autonomy of the organization:

"The First All-Russia Conference of Proletarian Culture Organizations, considering:
1) That the cultural movement among the proletariat should have an independent place alongside the political and economic movement,
2) That its task consists in elaborating a proletarian culture which, with the destruction of society's division into classes, will become common to all mankind,
3) That the organization of this new culture must be based upon social labour and comradely collaboration.
Resolves:
1) The proletariat, in order to carry out the task assigned to it, must assimilate everything in previously-existing culture that bears the imprint of common humanity.
2) It must undertake this assimilation in a critical way, and recast the material in the crucible of its own class-consciousness.
3) Proletarian culture must be revolutionary-socialist in character, so that the proletariat may be able to equip itself with fresh knowledge, organize its feelings by means of the new art, and transform its way of life in a new, truly proletarian, that is, collective spirit.
4) In its work in creating the new culture the proletariat must show the greatest class energy and independence, while using, so far as this is possible, the help of revolutionary-socialist individuals.
5) In laying the foundations of this new form of the working class-movement, *Proletkul' t*, and defending its independence from the standpoint of organization, so that proletarian creativity of a strictly class character may develop to the fullest extent, the Conference considers that the institutions of government, both central and local, ought to promote the movement by every means available, so as to consolidate the conquests of the literary revolution, to vanquish the bourgeoisie not only materially but also spiritually, and to build all the sooner the new edifice of the socialist society of the future" (Proletarskaya Kultura No. 5, November, 1918: 31).

It is noteworthy that the cultural movement was to be independent of the political and the economic. Moreover, all cultural forms were to be critically examined as to their propriety under socialism. Hence, *Proletkul' t* was cognizant of the need to re-examine bourgeois culture and not simply sweep it away as reactionary. Finally, the government organ of worker authority—the soviet— was to ensure that *Proletkul' t* was promoted. And promoted it was, not only by members of the Party or the "revolutionary-socialist" fellow travellers, but also by those members of the *intelligentsia* who simply took advantage of the freedom of the decade to experiment in art, literature, sculpture, and drama.

New cultural forms were developed on the basis of two fundamental premises: that, in a workers' state, cultural forms should dramatize the collectivism that proletarian democracy would usher in, and that culture should glorify the labour process and the new economic order being built by the working class.

For example, the 1920s saw the emergence of the artistic talents of the futurist painter Iunni Annekov, the entirely new techniques of wood engraving developed by N.F. Favorski and the proletarian ceramic art of S.V. Chekhonin. *Proletkul' t* nurtured the "technical architectural" school, which insisted that proletarian architecture should be both aesthetic and functional, i.e., not only should a building house offices or provide living accommodation, it should also serve as an artistic monument. Moreover, the materials for producing artistic works were to be the "revolutionary building materials"—metal, concrete and glass. Stone and wood were rejected as counter-revolutionary symbols of bourgeois society (Fulop-Miller, 1927:100).[2]

The decade propagated both the ridiculous and the sublime in literature. Alongside the works of Boris Pasternak, Maxim Gorky and Evgeny Zamyatin were the sterile offerings of the "word chemists," This supra-nationalist school, heavily influenced by Dadaism,[3] was convinced that all poetry could be reduced to scientific formulae, just as chemisty could. Once these formulae were uncovered and understood, it was possible to train "writers, poets, translators and critics of the highest quality in a three-year course" (Fulop-Miller, 1927:155).

The ridiculous and the sublime were also evident in the theatre. Vistors to Soviet Russia could not help but marvel at the theatrical innovations of V.E. Meyerhold in his revolutionary October Theatre and admire the film techniques demonstrated by Sergei Eisenstein and his *Proletkul' t* Company. But foreigners also could not help but notice the absurd in the form of noise symphonies,[4] described by one visitor in the following way:

> The first public divine service of these "machine worshippers" began with a noise orchestra composed of a crowd of motors, turbines, sirens, hooters and similar instruments of din; the choir master stood on a balustrade and "conducted" the din with the aid of a complicated signalling apparatus (Fulop-Miller, 1927:183).

The noise symphonies, supposedly in the spirit of "social labour and comradely collaboration," also moved out of the confines of the music hall to the working-class districts of Petersburg, Baku and Nizhni-Novgorod. The inhabitants of these cities were "treated" to the *Symphony For Factory Whistles*, in which naval fog horns, factory sirens, artillery batteries, infantry regiments and choirs of spectators joined together to create a new proletarian symphony. All the "musicians" were led by a conductor, who was using semaphore flags and standing on the roof of the tallest building in the district.

In sport, or physical culture,[5] as it was called from 1918, there were similar experiments taking place. And as in other cultural forms, anarchy broke out among different groups, "in which now one group, now another seemed to gain the upper hand" (Fulop-Miller, 1927:166). The influence of *Proletkul' t* was considerable, predictably among its affiliate, the *Proletkul' tists*, but also among the hygienists and the pedagogues.[6]

Despite differences as to the actual form that physical culture should take, all groups agreed upon the necessity of viewing physical culture from a materialist perspective, and the role that physical culture could play in addressing the problems of the new Soviet state. The *Proletkul'tists* felt that the emphasis of any physical culture movement in a workers' state should be on the glorification of the labour process. Such an emphasis suggested to some of the *proletkul'tists* that choreographic gymnastics would be the form that the activity should take. Not only would these gymnastics improve the individual health of workers, but they would also decrease absenteeism from work. Hence, they would create greater productivity of the work force. Vyacheslav Meyerhold was invited to adapt his October Theatre experiences to the work place and, in 1921, was appointed director of the newly-organized *Tefizkul't* Commission.[7] Meyerhold's efforts in the Commission resulted in the "Artistic Design of the Labour Process," a group of theatrical-type gymnastic stations in various factories. Here workers were to learn to be more productive members of socialist society. They performed exercises that coordinated the movement of hands and feet, initiated labour skills on specially-constructed apparatus, practised dexterity and efficiency in fulfilling labour objectives, and dramatized the labour process through rhythmic and artistic movements.

Away from the work place, the *proletkul'tists* were experimenting with equally futuristic physical culture forms. "Collective proletarian sport," wrote Ippolit Sokolov, a leading *Proletkul'tist*, must take the place of individual competition; one must only have group competition (Sokolov, 1922:6). The collective activity involved several thousand individuals and ranged from socialist morality plays culminating with the triumph of the working class (cf. Riordan, 1977 and Berkman, 1925) to mass calisthenic displays synchronously performed with the noise orchestras.

The hygienists also eschewed bourgeois sports and competition, not on ideological grounds, as the *Proletkul'tists* had done, but because of the physiological underdevelopment of the peasant and working classes. The hygienists argued that the cruel exploitation of generations of the common people had left them with weakened physical constitutions. Only through the careful and exclusive application of rehabilitative gymnastics could this physiological weakening be eradicated. Rather than the pursuit of sport, the hygienists advocated "normal lessons" that included the choreographic exercises of *Tefizkul't* and the natural movements of running and jumping (Samoukov et al, 1967:50).

For their part, the pedagogues were much more careful in the criticisms they leveled at bourgeois sports. Led by Professor A.A. Zigmund, the Director of the State Central Institute of Physical Culture (CTSIFK), the pedagogues developed a system based upon the study of the social/biological principles of humankind. Marx's dialectical materialist philosophy[8] underpinned all their work and, as such, followed the the *Proletkul't* resolution to critically examine all previous cultural forms (in this case physical education and sport) and to "recast the material in the the crucible of its own class-consciousness" (Proletarskaya Kultura—No. 5, November, 1918:31). Zigmund's Soviet System of Physical

Culture, as it was called, attempted to create a rational system that would incorporate all the positive features of diverse physical culture approaches, both within the USSR and abroad. His system was an attempt to provide participants with a comprehensive education (moral, physical, psychological) in order to prepare them for labour and defence; equally important, the Soviet System of Physical Culture was to stimulate the creation of a truly proletarian physical culture.

In 1932, *Proletkul' t* was abolished, with the more influential figures in the movement standing accused of being "wreckers" of the Stalinist image of Soviet socialism. Those who were not physically caught up in the purges of the 1930s were easily dismissed—as was Bogdanov himself—as "idealist," "subjectivist," or "objectively counter-revolutionary" (Claudin-Urondo, 1977:30).

Lenin's very different interpretation of culture, and the debates he had with *Proletkul' tists*, played no small part in the rapid demise of the organization. It is appropriate, therefore, to look at Lenin's position on culture.

Lenin's Conception of Culture

Lenin's opposition to *Proletkul' t* is also the best vehicle for illustrating his conception of culture. In the "Rough Draft Of A Resolution On Proletarian Culture" (written in 1920), one readily notes the difference between Leninist culture and the declaration adopted by the *Proletkul' t* Conference in 1918. Lenin had written:

1. Not special ideas, but Marxism.
2. Not the "invention" of a new proletarian culture, but the "development" of the best models, traditions and results of the "existing" culture, "from the point of view" of the Marxist world outlook and the conditions of life and struggle of the proletariat in the period of its dictatorship.
3. Not apart from the People's Commissariat for Education, but as part of it, since the R.C.P. (Russian Communist Party) + Commissariat for Education = Proletkul't.
4. Proletkul't's close link with and subordination to the Commissariat for Education (Lenin, 1966:149).

Lenin's entire political career personified his commitment to debate. This commitment, and his personal confession that he did not truly understand all the *Proletkul' t* objectives, allowed the *Proltetkul' t* to flourish while he was alive. The best example of Lenin's liberal attitude comes from his wife Krupskaya in her *Reminiscences of Lenin*. In 1921, Lenin was invited to a commune for art students. There he met a group of young people, living in the most primitive of conditions, but enthusiastically debating the role of art in the new socialist society. Krupskaya continues:

> They (the young people) showed him their naive drawings, explained their meaning and bombarded him with questions. And he, smiling, evaded answering

and parried by asking questions of his own: "What do you read? Do you read Pushkin?" "Oh no", said someone, "after all he was a bourgeois; We read Mayakovsky." Ilyich smiled. "I think," he said, "that Pushkin is better."(Lenin, 1966:226).

This preference for Pushkin is indicative of Lenin's opinions of the free experimentation that characterized the arts in the 1920s. Not only did he not understand much of Mayakovsky's verse; he resolutely abhorred most of the sculpture, describing one piece as "a futuristic monstrosity" (Lenin, 1966:240, 231). But his major fear of *Proletkul't* was its insistence on autonomy (Notes 3 and 4 in his Resolution, cited above). Proletarian culture, like politics and economics, was to be nurtured under the vanguardism of the Party;[9] and any debates about culture should take place *within* the structure of the Communist Party, and not in autonomous "arms length" organizations.

Carmen Claudin-Urondo, in her book *Lenin and the Cultural Revolution*, has assiduously studied Lenin's works to ascertain his particular concept of culture. She presents a well-documented argument (and one to which I would concur) that suggests that culture, for Lenin, had three main connotations: culture as civilization, culture as ideology and culture as knowledge (Claudin-Urondo, 1977:13). All three connotations are juxtaposed to the political revolution that the Bolsheviks had brought about. "What is most important," Claudin-Urondo rhetorically asks:

> ... Lenin's reply is categorical: the gravest danger threatening our revolution is the lack of culture-as-knowledge, and consequently, the lack of civilization. Solve that problem, and the revolution will be irreversible (Claudin-Urondo, 1977:14).

Claudin-Urondo then goes on to suggest how Lenin perceived his cultural connotations merging. Russia must learn, learn, and learn again, all there is about bourgeois culture. This education will result in a Russian civilization in which the ideological alliance with the masses will be achieved.

Unlike *Proletkul't*, which put its faith in the peasantry and working classes to hew a culture out of the specifics of the revolutionary experience and the particular history and social circumstances of Russia, Lenin's culture as civilization is precisely and exclusively that of the industrial societies of Western Europe; and although he spoke with pride about the concerts, ballets and operas performed in Petersburg and Moscow, he also lamented, "we are a poverty-stricken people, completely beggared" (Lenin, 1966:232). Consequently, above all else, the new Soviet state was to acquire Western culture. Lenin assumed that socialism was "synonomous with accession to the ranks of the civilized countries, which are recognized .... by their highly-developed productive forces,the superiority of their science and technology and the high degree of rationality in their organizations of labour, with a set of patterns of behavior which are expressions of this" (Claudin-Urondo, 1977:17).

Such a conception is diametrically opposed to that of *Proletkul't* in that there is little suggestion of *critically* examining Western culture. Lenin automatically assumes that Russia must acquire Western civilization, but on *its own terms*, namely those of a socialist state. In short, Russia must gain the civilization without the capitalist dressing. Now there is a fundamental flaw in this argument, which Lenin does not appear to consider—that is, the organic connections between European civilization and a capitalist mode of production. It is doubtful that the former is separable from the latter. Nonetheless, Lenin thought this possible, (a specific example of his thinking on the subject is his arguments concerning Taylorization of Soviet industry. Taylorism without alienation of the workforce was entirely realistic in the USSR, he argued).[10]

Culture as Ideology
As noted above, Bogdanov and *Proletkul't* placed vital importance on the struggle with the bourgeoisie on the ideological level. For Lenin, culture as ideology was not crucial in Russia. The extreme backwardness of the Russian peasantry, he argued, made it much easier to carry out a revolution than would have been possible in the highly industrialized European states (Lenin's weakest-link-of-imperialism theory) (Lenin, 1939). In Europe, the existence of a long history of bourgeois, reactionary and clerical cultural forms meant that the accompanying ideology underscoring the *dominance* of these forms was well established. Consequently, the revolutionary movement in Europe must take the form of ideological battle. Conversely, the cultural backwardness of Russia (the resulting ideological backwardness) suggested that a revolution could be successful.

The stability of the revolution was what concerned Lenin. In Europe, which was culturally strong (in terms of ideology), a successful revolution would have relatively clear sailing, since civilization and socialist ideology were fused. In Russia, the revolution was on fragile grounds, precisely because of a lack of civilization. Lenin made this clear in conversation with the German communist Clara Zetkin. Zetkin, reiterating an argument reminiscent of Trotsky's advantage-of-backwardness theory, (Trotsky, 1971) suggests that the Bolsheviks are in an advantageous position. When Lenin asks how this is so, Zetkin points out that the Bolshevik socialist agitation and propaganda are being planted in "virgin soil" and that the Party does not have to clear a "primeval forest" of bourgeois ideology. Lenin concurs, but then goes on

> However, only within certain limits or, to be more exact, for a certain period of our struggle. We could stand illiteracy during the fight for power, while it was necessary to destroy the old state machinery (Lenin, 1966:233).

But to maintain the revolution, civilization was required. And this could only be achieved through culture as knowledge, the most important of Lenin's three connotations.

Culture as Knowledge

There could be no culture as civilization until the Soviet population gained knowledge. Again, Lenin is very specific about culture as knowledge. It amounts to the reorganization of industry, utilizing modern science and technology (technological rationality). Culture as knowledge is best summarized by Lenin's famous edict, "electrification plus Soviet power equals socialism." But there was a major difficulty with this pursuit of modern bourgeois science and technology, and that was the degree of illiteracy in the new state. The Bolsheviks could only reach socialism with the introduction of a massive literacy campaign. The figures from 1917 are almost unimaginable: Aamong the non-Russian nationalities, 99.5 percent of the Tajiks, 99.4 percent of the Kirghiz, 99.3 percent of the Yakuts, 99.3 percent of the Turkmen and 98.4 percent of the Uzbeks were illiterate. The situation was so bad that the tsarist publication *The Educational Herald* estimated in 1906 that if the current rate of development was maintained, it would take 180 years to reach universal literacy among men and 280 years among women (History of the USSR II, 1977:273). Such incredible backwardness plagued Lenin until his death and significantly coloured his perception of *Proletkul't*. He could see little use in spending time promoting the new *avant garde* experimentation in the Arts when, as he put it:

> ... millions of people are striving to learn how to spell their names and count, are trying to attain enough culture to know that the earth is round, not flat, and that the world is not governed by witches and sorcerers and a "heavenly father" but by natural laws (Lenin, 1966:233).

However, as I mentioned above, Lenin was most opposed to *Proletkul't* because of its insistence on remaining autonomous from the Party. As Lunacharsky remembered it, Lenin was concerned with the attempts to create proletarian science and culture when the workers needed to assimilate the bourgeois equivalents, but he was most afraid "that some political deviation would ensconce itself in the Proletcult". (Lenin, 1966:246). Claudin-Urondo aptly summarizes Lenin's conception of culture:

> Knowledge and Civilization are the perogative of industrial society, and present themselves as a sort of purely objective entity, something aseptic which is "already there" and which *may*, when placed in certain historical circumstances, bear with it certain ideological values, the bourgeois or proletarian nature of which is not, on the whole, inherent but added to it (Claudin-Urondo, 1977:102, Emphasis in original).

The Development of the Bourgeois Games Among
Party-affiliated Groups

Lenin's advocacy of bourgeois culture had a direct influence on groups that were involved with sport but did not concur with either the *proletkul'tist* nor hygienist philosophies. Zigmund's Soviet System of Physical Culture was a weak attempt at compromise, but did not satisfy those most closely aligned with the Party: the Red Army, the State Security Forces (CHEKA, NKVD, KGB) and the *Komsomol*.

The *Komsomol*, as the youth wing of the Party, was in the most difficult position. On the one hand, young workers, both inside and outside the *Komsomol*, were naturally caught up in the excitement of creating proletarian culture. On the other hand, they were reluctant to give up the "bourgeois sports," particularly in exchange for the *proletkul'tist* theatrical gymnastics, which excessively rationalized the labour process and viewed humankind as machines.[11] Consequently, the *Komsomol* created its Spartak system of games, gymnastics and hiking, all more popular among the urban working youth.[12] As for the Red Army (TSSKA) and Security Forces (Dinamo), they appeared to simply follow the official Party line and, as the coercive arm of the Party, implement any and all activities that would maintain political control. Thus, when *proletkul'tists* and hygienists, working through the trade unions, abolished many sports competitions, the military/para-military carried on. Sports competition and skill-improvement were secondary to the discipline that could accrue from participation in these activities. It is not surprising, therefore, that TSSKA and *Dinamo* have always fielded the strongest sports team in the USSR.[13]

As strongly as the debate between the Leninists and the *Proletkul't* raged during the 1920s, by 1932, it was over. Stalin, with his mechanistic Marxist-Leninist philosophy, had purged *Proletkul't* and effectively removed all sport forms except the officially sanctioned one: that of the technically-rational Stakhanovite athlete/worker. Having dealt more fully with the Stakhanovite movement elsewhere (Cantelon, 1979), I will limit my remarks to a brief argument on how the Stakhanovite athlete/worker evolved, and what the movement entailed.

Stalin was never considered a Party intellectual and invariably his policies were supported by reference to Lenin (usually taken out of context). This was true of his smashing of *Proletkul't*. In 1920, Lenin had advocated not the invention of new proletarian culture, but the adaptation of all previous culture from a Marxist perspective. In 1932, as offically-recognized Soviet sources put it, "*Proletkul't* finally ceased to exist."

Similarly, Lenin had suggested that Soviet industry must aspire to the productivity and efficiency of the Americans and that the best aspects of Taylor's scientific management system should be introduced. For Stalin, this amounted to suppressing the egalitarian policies of the early Bolsheviks, the introduction of piecework and the monetary incentives for the Stakhanovites. These were the workers, (usually young, recent migrants from rural areas, trained in the Bolshevik trade schools) who epitomized Lenin's synthesis of science and technology in human labour. They were technically trained and committed to accuracy in their work. They counted not only the minutes but the seconds, as Stalin was fond of noting (Stalin, 1954:666-667). They were individuals "who had completely mastered the technique of their trades, were able to make the most efficient use of their tools and equipment, work rationally and without waste and regularly exceeded the prescribed standards of output" (Markus, 1936:11). And, whereas the Stakhanovite worker pursued the unique Soviet labour norms for coal hewed, shoes made, thread spun, etc., his/her athletic counterpart pursued the sports record.

The Stakhanovite was also encouraged to be productive and efficient away from the work place. "The more gifted Stakhanovites buy musical instruments, engage tutors, and find time after a working day of 6 or 7 hours for the ardent cultivation of the arts" (Markus, 1936:23). Their inflated salaries allowed them to purchase imported suits, shoes and bicycles (Trotsky, 1972:124). Lenin would, no doubt, have been pleased at how readily the workers took to the rationality and efficiency of bourgeois work patterns—the mechanical time of the factory replacing the task-oriented time of the countryside and the pursuit of "proper" cultural activities.[14] (It is estimated that, by 1938, 41.4 percent of all industrial workers were members of the Stakhanovite movement) (Baykov, 1946:350).

It is this technical rationality (Stakhanovism) that continues to define official policy on the most appropriate work patterns and how one should pursue leisure. Thus Vladimir Bogatikov, Secretary of the All-Union Central Council of Trade Unions, outlines the objectives of the trade union movement (Bogatikov, 1980):

> ...the trade unions play a part in moulding communist consciousness, Soviet patriotism and a communist attitude to work and socialist property in the mass of the working people, instilling in them high moral principles (p.27).

> The activites of trade-union sport organizations are indissolubly linked with nationwide efforts to fulfill the economic and social development plans of the USSR. (p.31).

> The aim (of the T.U.) is to improve the worker's health, working capacity and creative activities and help organize national holidays for them. (p.32).

> At present a good deal is being done to ensure that leisure-time is more fully utilized and that sport and health-improvement work.

Quite clearly, all the "official" debates I have discussed thus far are problematic. They all ignore the dialectical relationship that must exist between the official pronouncements and the lived experience of the workers and peasants. As Willis remarks, "Culture is not simply a response to imposition that blinds or blunts a 'proper' understanding, nor is it merely a compensation, or adjustment to defeat—these are essentially mechanized, reactive models ... Merely because capital would like to treat workers as robots does not mean they are robots." (Willis, 1979:186-187). Similarly, neither the suggestion of Bogdanov and the *Proletkul't* intelligentsia that new cultural forms are to result from a socialist revolution, nor Lenin's view of forms are to result as a backward savage lacking in culture, nor the contemporary official pronouncements stressing the rational pursuit of work/leisure has necessarily been universally accepted. Thus, Claudin-Urondo, speaking of the Soviet factory worker notes:

> For the factory is not merely, as Lenin seems to "forget", the place where footwear and tractors are made, but also and above all the place where a certain structure of social relations between men is created and reproduced, a structure the mechanisms of which are necessarily based on the division of labour and, consequently, on the division of the producers into those who direct and those who execute, those who give orders and those who obey, those who "know" what has to be done and those who "wait to be told" what they have to do. The dialectic of history is not such that blind obedience engenders a spirit of initiative, that unconditional subordination fosters a critical and personalized attitude, or that treating men as tools results in creative activity on their part. It is not possible to "disalienate" by alienating means. (Claudin-Urondo, 1977: 98-99).

What Claudin-Urondo is forcefully asserting is that, very quickly, the "backward savage"—illiterate though he or she was—realized that the Soviet collective farm, the Soviet industrial work-place, was not the "theatre of happiness," and that Lenin's ideas ultimately meant that there was to be little change from the tsarist authority relationships: and he or she did not have to be literate to understand this—he or she experienced it in his or her everyday life. Now, I do not wish to present a picture of the Soviet peasant or worker as a mindless dupe, compensating for or adjusting to defeat. The peasant and working classes, I want to argue in the second half of this paper, have "carved" and are "carving out" their own cultural existence from that prescribed by the official CPSU pronouncements.

The Contested Terrain of Peasant and Working-Class Cultures

Elsewhere, I have argued that much of everyday life remains in a state of "settled orientation," to use a term widely used by Max Weber (Cantelon, 1981) and also that, despite the violent re-structuring of Russia in 1917, the day-to-day activity remained remarkably stable. Thus, reports of peasant-workers, employed in small rural factories in the 1880s, sleeping in the premises where they worked, had not drastically changed 50 years later (Zagladin,II-1976:92). This settled orientation to the traditional way of life has been carefully argued by American labour historian Peter Stearns, in his article "The Effort at Continuity in Working-Class Culture" (1980). Although Stearns is primarily concerned with the making of the industrial working class in Western Europe, his underlying argument does have relevance for my paper. He believes that any research concerned with working-class values in the 19th century (and also I would argue in the 20th century in the USSR) must address two interrelated questions:

1. Can working class cultures best be understood in terms of change or of continuity, a continuity best described as a preservation of tradition amid admittedly changing circumstances?

2. Was the working class basically in control of its own values, using them indeed as shields against changes in environment (whether the values themselves were new or old), or were values imposed by capitalist society— employers, schools, military authorities, ministers, even bourgeoisified labour leaders? (Here I would include revolutionary socialist intelligentsia and vanguard Bolsheviks) (Stearns, 1980:626).

Admittedly, these are complex questions to which no simple "yes or no" answer can be given. Specifically in the Soviet Union, I would argue, there are examples of traditional continuity (settled orientation), imposition of a new value structure and also the simple disgarding of the old with no evidence of resistance or imposition. What follows are illustrations of each.

1. Traditional continuity
Quite naturally, most evidence of traditional continuity occurred in the very decade in which the greatest experimentation with new forms of socialist physical culture was emerging. In the urban areas, despite the official pronouncements against sports like football and the massive propaganda campaigns to encourage "average achievement"[16] rather than excellence, the young worker continued to participate in the pre-Soviet football clubs and if athletically gifted. to pursue individual excellence. Resistance to the new forms was even more pronounced in the countryside. Response among peasants expected to organize themselves into choreographic groups, swinging their scythes to music, was less than enthusiastic, particularly after a long and arduous day in the fields. And it is not surprising that contemporary Soviet sports historians, identify the groups that had the most success in encouraging physical culture among the peasants, as those that encouraged it by promoting the traditional rural activities—tug-of-war, lapta, gorodki (See Demeter, 1969; Samoukov et al, 1967; Stolbov and Chudinov, 1970).[17]

Even when *Komsomol*-organized clubs initially experienced success in attracting peasants to the organization, the participant, once in the club, often redefined the activities to reproduce the traditional culture. Thus, sports clubs in the rural Ukraine abolished boxing in 1927, when it was discovered that scientific "English boxing," as it was called, was pursued, not for its science, regulation, or rational training methods, but because it allowed the participants to learn new strategies for the centuries-old, wall-to-wall village fist-fights (Vestnik, 1927:21).[18] Indeed, on more than one occasion, the training sessions resembled this rural pursuit.

But even in contemporary Soviet society, I would argue, there are examples of traditional continuity. However it is continuity within a distinctly modern, rationalized framework—what David Whitson has described as a "redefinition of the periphery to maintain the core" (Whitson, 1982). And I would also argue that the working class/peasantry has led in this regard, and the government and Party authorities have followed. Thus, for instance, traditional sport forms continue to flourish, not as tourist attractions but regular features of the sports calender. This has not been the case in many Western societies. Some of the top Soviet international wrestlers learn their skills, not in urban sports schools, but in rural festival competitions in which the sport has a distinctly traditional flavour—chidaoba (Georgia), koch (Armenia), gyulesh (Azerbaijan), kurash (Uzbekistan), kuresh (Kirghizia), kures (Kazakstan) huresh (Tuva) hapsagi (Yakutia), trynta (Moldavia). In fact, official sports publications admit that the pre-industrial activities of axe throwing, sledge jumping, and gorodki (skittles) are "jealously preserved and flourish today" (Lukashin, 1980:7-8).

What is distinctly new is that the core of all these folk activities has been maintained within a highly rationalized periphery. Thus, the Soviet gorodki player can gain a Master of Sport ranking in his centuries-old sport, the Master of Sport in axe-throwing must project his 350 gram missle over 120 metres, and the Yakutia sledge-jumper must clear 30 vehicles of specified height without pausing.

2. Imposition of a new value structure

It is obvious from the re-definition of the periphery of these traditional games that Lenin's insistence upon the technical rationality of bourgeois Europe has been introduced to the sports activities of contemporary Soviet society. Certainly it was evident in the 1930s that Stakhanovism was not universally accepted by the working class. Alongside the articles lauding the new labour-productivity record holders, one can read accounts of Stakhanovites being physically attacked, tools being sabotaged, etc. (Trotsky, 1972; Deutscher, 1952). Not all viewed their work in terms of the continual pursuit of the record, and that which could not be avoided at the factory, wherever possible, was rejected away from the workplace. However, the purges swept up wreckers, suspected wreckers and even non-wreckers so that, in many cases, the workers today have seemingly been co-opted into acceptance of the official urgings to pursue rationalized forms of leisure.[19] Or have they? This is a difficult question to answer. Certainly the countless time-budget studies of the Soviet leisure researchers would suggest that they have. The "acceptable" activities of attending concerts, visiting museums, participating in sports, reading, and furthering one's education are constantly reiterated.[20] But, as Rosemarie Rogers has indicated (1974) there is a significant difference between what the Soviet citizen indicates "ought" to be done and what actually "is" done. (The level of alcoholism is just one indicator of the variance).

Stearns provides a logical argument that would support the "imposition of values" thesis. He notes that, by the late 19th century, increasing numbers of workers had learned what the middle-class employer expected of them in behaviour and attitudes. They could provide public appearances of moderation and restraint and "express classic mobility expectations for their children if asked by a middle-class sociologist or reformer" (Stearns, 1980:653). Similarly, in the

USSR, when the velvet glove was removed from the iron fist in the 1930s, the workers quickly learned to separate the public from the private. And so, reading between the lines of official Soviet publications, one constantly confronts the public/private argument. Yovchuk, for instance, notes the necessity of organizing workers' councils to encourage young apprentices to study, and to arrange excursions for them, and then goes on to provide a particular example of the worker pursuing rationalized work and leisure (Yovchuk, 1966:178). But he finds it necessary to conclude his article on "Improvement of Standards of Workers" with the following comment:

> Workers actively oppose all manifestations of the old life and ideology that distract their fellows from the socialist way of life, from advanced methods of work, from education and culture. At their meetings and in the press, they criticize backward people who make no attempt to improve their qualifications, fail to study, or show idleness and laziness (Yovchuk, 1966:178).

Similarly, Bogatikov, the All-Union Central Council of Trade Union secretary, to whom I referred earlier, speaks with pride of the trade union societies bringing the rational sport and leisure form to working people's homes—another suggestion that the imposition of the public is resisted in the private sphere.

But there is also a trade-off here—a negotiation between official policy and lived experience. There is evidence not only of this possible imposition, but also of probable official resignation to the fact that certain cultural practices persist despite all efforts at suppression. This is most clearly indicated in the area of rituals, particularly the religious rituals of birth, marriage and death. The longstanding and massive atheism campaigns have never managed to eradicate the Russian Orthodox Church rituals surrounding the birth of a baby, the marriage of son or daughter, or the death of a loved one. But recently, as Christel Lane has clearly shown (1981), the Party has taken a different tack. Instead of continuing the crude atheistic arguments, the Party has *reintroduced* the ritual in a socialist context; and Soviet authorities believe that it has been effective. Figures are cited to indicate that religious funeral rites have dramatically fallen in the Baltic Republics. However, like the public/private utterances regarding leisure-time activity, there is almost no way of ascertaining whether the ritual is seen as socialist or simply as a more acceptable form of demonstrating a personal religious faith.

Finally, I would argue that many cultural activities have simply been given up with no sense of resistance or imposition. The dramatic increase in literacy alone (universal literacy is a reality in the USSR) would simply render many of the pre-literate superstitions and practices to the trash barrel of life.

In conclusion, it would be wrong to suggest that the official pronouncements concerning culture at any period of Soviet history were universally accepted. They must be viewed dialectically, as a marker of the terms upon which the Soviet citizen negotiates his/her individual life.

Notes

1. Bogdanov was the pseudonym that Alexander Malinovsky used to publish his philosophical treatises both in tsarist Russia and in the Soviet Union. Much of Bogdanov's writing remains untranslated, but Vucinich, 1976 and Utechin, 1962, provide concise treatments of his work.

2. Fulop-Miller (1927) provides an interesting foreign point of view of the cultural developments that took place in the USSR during the 1920s.

3. Dadaism was initiated in 1916 in Zurich, Switzerland. It was an international movement in poetry and painting, which rejected tradition, culture and reason.

4. The noise symphonies exemplified the experimentation that was carried on in the 1920s. Many of the experiments, including this one, had their basis in the artistic communities of Western Europe. Italian futurists were creating noise symphonies as early as 1916, and one particular individual saw himself as a "noise tuner" and the creator of "symphonies of the urban setting." (See Luigi Russolo,"L'arte dei rumori," *Alfaheta*, 43, (Milan: December, 1982).

5. The term "physical culture" included physical education of children and youth; development of sport among workers in cities, towns and the countryside; use of physical exercises for the preservation and improvement of health of the population (See Stolbov and Chudinov, 1970). Today, as in the first years of existence of the Soviet state, physical culture has three main objectives: "developing personal health of workers, preparation towards socialist labour, and defence of the motherland" (Kukushkin, 1962: II-226-227).

6. The discussion of the differing physical culture perspectives comes from Demeter, 1969; Fisher Jr., 1959; Kukushkin, 1962; Morton, 1963; Riordon, 1977; Riordon, n.d.; Samoukov et al, 1967; Shneidman, 1978; Stolbov and Chudinov, 1970.

7. Meyerhold's *Tefizkul't* program was part of the much larger *Nauchnaya Organizatsiya Truda* (NOT) plan to create more efficient work habits among the population. NOT had been developed to realize Lenin's edict "Learn to Work." For an interesting account of the total program, see Zenovia Sochor, 1981.

8. Mandel (1969:25) notes that, in Soviet Marxism and social science, materalism "signifies merely that the world really *is* and that ideas ultimately, however indirectly, derive from human observation and thought about a world that is a material reality. This is summed up in the notion that matter is primary while ideas are secondary—secondary not in the sense of being unimportant, but simply that they are derivative from actual reality." For Zigmund and the pedagogues, any concept of physical culture must be derived from the *actual* reality of the USSR, the first attempt to create a workers' state. Moreover, the *dialectical materialist* study of sport involves understanding that the philosophy and concrete forms that games take are part of a material reality (materialism), and that how these forms and ethos change is the result of innumerable material changes in the society under study. This follows from the definition of material-

ism cited above and from the fact that "dialectics is essentially the notion that everything in the world is interrelated, however remotely, that the waves set in motion by any single happening reach out to intersect others and yet still others, although ultimately their influence may be so eroded by this friction as to have no significant effect upon a single point. This point is defined partly by the significance of the force of the initial happening and partly by the force of those which it intersects" (Mandel, 1969:26).

9. There is ample historical evidence to support the contention that Lenin (and Trotsky) both believed that the Bolsheviks were to be the vanguard of the proletariat—that the Party was to guide the peasant and working classes toward future communism. In *State and Revolution,* Lenin asserts that those who were educated in Marxism were the vanguard, "capable of assuming power and of *leading the whole people* to Socialism, of directing and organizing the new order, of being the teacher, guide,and leader of all the toiling and exploited in the task of building up their social life without the bourgeoisie and aganist the bourgeoisie" (Lenin, 1969:24, Emphasis in original).

10. In his "Six Theses On the Immediate Tasks of the Soviet Government," Lenin pointed out the importance of adapting much of was was "scientific and progressive in the Taylor system" (Lenin, 1969:151). For my argument concerning the application of Taylorism to sport see Cantelon, 1979.

11. This tension is implied in the many debates that occurred in the *Komsomol* Congresses during this period. For a detailed account of these Congresses, see Fisher Jr., 1959.

12. This should not be confused with the Voluntary Sports Society "Spartak" established in 1935.

13. Cantelon,1981 has a detailed account of the military/paramilitary involvement during this period.

14. The classification of time and the increased dominance of mechanical time with the growth of industrial capitalism is developed in E.P. Thompson's classic essay "Time, Work-Discipline, and Industrial Capitalism," in *Past and Present,* 38 (December, 1967).

15. I am using the concept of "relationship of authority" as developed by Max Weber. For an analysis of this concept as it relates to sport, see Cantelon, 1981.

16. Average achievement was a basic principle of both Zigmund's "Soviet System of Physical Culture" and the *Komsomol* "Spartak" program. It suggested that the aim of all sports was to ensure that all participants reached the average norm, rather than highlighting the best performance. In this regard, average achievement was very similar to the German Turner approach to athletics.

17. Lapta is a traditional ball and bat game, gorodki a sophisticated skittles-type activity.

18. The wall-to-wall fist fight pitted different occupational groupings against each other. There are many examples of these class and occupational competitions in

pre-industrial societies. For example see Dunning, 1971; Dunning and Sheard, 1979; Malcolmson, 1973; Gosow, 1890).

19. This "iron-cage coercion" argument forms the basis of Marcuse's *Soviet Marxism: A Critical Analysis*, 1958.

20. There are countless examples of these time-budget studies published in Russian sources. The most complete treatment in English can be found in Riordan, 1977.

Bibliography

Baykov, Alexander. *The Development of the Soviet Economic System: An Essay on the Experience of Planning in the USSR*. Cambridge: Cambridge University Press, 1946.

Berkman, Alexander. *The Bolshevik Myth (Diary 1920-1922)*. New York: Boni and Liveright, 1925.

Bogatikov, Vladimir. "The Trade Unions and the Popular Sports Movement." *The USSR: Sport and Way of Life*. Moscow: USSR Academy of Sciences, 1980.

Cantelon, Hart. *The Social Reproduction of Sport*: A Weberian Analysis of the Rational Development of Ice Hockey Under Scientific Socialism in the Soviet Union. Unpublished doctoral dissertation. University of Birmingham, 1981.

Cantelon, Hart. *Stakhanovism and Sport in the USSR*. Working Papers in the Sociological Study of Sports and Leisure, II(2),Queen's University: Sports and Leisure Studies Research Group, 1979.

Claudin-Urondo, Carmen. *Lenin and the Cultural Revolution*. Sussex: The Harvester Press, 1977.

Demeter, G.C. *Lenin: Ob okhrane zdorov'ya trudyaschikhsya i fizicheskoi kul'ture*. Moscow: Fizkul'tura i Sport, 1969.

Deutscher, Issac. "Russia", in Walter Galenson, ed. *Comparative Labour Movements*. New York: Prentice-Hall, Inc., 1952.

Dunning, Eric (ed.). *The Sociology of Sport*. London: Frank Cass & Co. Ltd., 1971.

Dunning, Eric and Sheard, Kenneth. *Barbarians, Gentlemen and Players: A Sociological Study of the Development of Rugby Football*. Oxford: Martin Robertson & Co., 1079.

Fisher Jr., Ralph Talcott. *Pattern for Soviet Youth: A Study of the Congresses of the Komsomol, 1918-1954*. New York: Columbia University Press, 1959.

Fulop-Miller, Rene. *The Mind and Face of Bolshevism: An Examination of Cultural Life in Soviet Russia*. London: G.P. Putman's Sons, Ltd., 1927.

Gosow, Borys. "Sport in Russia." *The Overland Monthly* 16 (October), 1890.

History of the USSR (in Three Parts). Moscow: Progress Publishers, 1977.

Kukushkin, G.I., (ed.). *Entsiklopedicheskii slovan 'po fizicheskoi kul'tura i sportu.* (in Three Volumes). Moscow: Fizkul'tura i sport. Volume I, 1961; Volume II, 1962; Volume III, 1963.

Lane, Christel. *The Rites of Rulers: Rulers in Industrial Society: The Soviet Case.* Cambridge: Cambridge University Press, 1981.

Lenin, V.I. *Imperialism: The Highest Stage of Capitalism: A Popular Outline.* New York: International Publishers, 1939.

Lenin, V.I. *On Culture and Cultural Revolution.* Moscow: Progress Publishers, 1966.

Lenin, V.I. *On the Soviet State Apparatus.* Moscow: Progress Publishers, 1969.

Lenin, V.I. *State and Revolution.* New York: International Publishers, 1969.

Lukashin, Yuri (ed.). *National Folk Sports in the USSR.* Moscow: Progress Publishers, 1980.

Malcolmson, Robert W. *Popular Recreations in English Society 1700-1850.* Cambridge: Cambridge, University Press, 1973.

Mandel, William M. "Soviet Marxism and Social Science" in Alex Simirenko editor. *Social Thought in the Soviet Union.* Chicago: Quadrangle Books, 1969.

Marcuse, Herbert. *Soviet Marxism: A Critical Analysis.* London: Routledge & Kegan Paul, 1958.

Markus, B. L. "The Stakhanov Movement and the Increased Productivity of Labour in the USSR." *International Labour Review* 34 (July-December, 1936) pp.5-33.

Morton, Henry W. *Soviet Sport: Mirror of Soviet Society.* London: Collier Books, 1963.

Nettl, J.P. *The Soviet Achievement.* London: Thames and Hudson, 1967.

Plekanov, Georgi. *Selected Philosophical Works* (in Five Volumes). Moscow: Progress Publishers, 1981.

Pravda. (27.09.1922).

Proletarskaya Kultura (5), November, 1918.

"ProtivBoksa." *Vestnikfizicheskoikul'turi* (No.1),Yanvar 1927 p.21

Riordan, James. *Sport in Soviet Society: Development of Sport and Physical Education in Russia and the USSR.* Cambridge: Cambridge University Press, 1977.

Riordan, James. Why Sport Under Communism?: The "Physical Culture vs Sport" Debate After the Russian Revolution. University of Bradford, n.d. (Mimeographed).

Rogers, Rosemarie. "Normative Aspects of Leisure Time Behavior in the Soviet Union." *Sociology and Social Research* 58 (No.4) July, 1974, pp.369-379.

Samoukov, F.D., Stolbov, V.V., and Toropov, N.I. *Fizicheskaya kul'tura i sport v SSSR.* Moscow: Fizkul'tura i sport, 1967.

Shneidman, N. Norman. *The Soviet Road to Olympics: Theory and Practice of Soviet Physical Culture and Sport.* Toronto: The Ontario Institute For Studies in Education, 1978.

Sochor, Zenovia. "Soviet Taylorism Revisited." *Soviet Studies* 33(2), 1981, pp.246-264.

Sokolov, Ip. *Sistema trudovoi gimnastika* Moscow: Fizkul'tura i sport, 1922.

Stalin, Joseph. *Problems of Leninism.* Moscow: Foreign Languages Publishing House, 1954.

Stearns, Peter N. "The Effort at Continuity in Working-Class Culture." *Journal of Modern History* 52 (December, 1980) pp.626-655.

Stolbov, V.V. and Chudinov, I.G. *Istoriya fizicheskoi kul'turi.* Moscow: Fizkul'tura i sport, 1970.

Trotsky, Leon. *The Revolution Betrayed: What is the Soviet Union And Where Is It Going?* New York: Pathfinder Press, Inc., 1972.

Trotsky, Leon. *1905.* Harmondsworth: Penguin Books, 1971.

Utechin, S.V. "Philosophy and Society: Alexander Bogdanov", in Leopold Labedz, editor. *Revisionism: Essays on the History of Marxist Ideas.* New York: Frederick A. Praeger, 1962.

Vucinich, Alexander. *Social Thought in Tsarist Russia: The Quest for a General Science of Society, 1861-1917.* Chicago: The University of Chicago Press, 1976.

Whitson, David. "Factors in the survival of local games against the inroads of metropolitan culture: A Scottish case study", in Bruce Kidd. *Proceedings: 5th Canadian Symposium on the History of Sport and Physical Education.* Toronto: University of Toronto Press, 1982.

Williams, Raymond. *Marxism and Literature.* London: Oxford University Press, 1972.

Willis, Paul. "Shop-floor culture, masculinity and the wage form", in John Clarke, Chas. Critcher and Richard Johnson (eds.), *Working Class Culture.* London: Hutchinson, 1979.

Yovchuk, M.T. "Improvement of the cultural and technical standards of workers" in G.V. Osipov, ed., *Industry and Labour in the USSR..* London: Tavistock Publications, 1966.

Zagladin, V.V. *The International Working-Class Movement: Problems of History and Theory* (in Five Volumes) Moscow: Progress Publishers, 1981.

Bibliography

Aldgate, Tony. "British Cinema in the 1930s," Unit 7, Block 2 (The historical development of popular culture in Britain, 2), Course U203 Popular Culture, Open University, 1981.

Barthes, Roland. *Mythologies*. London: Paladin, 1972.

Baykov, Alexander. *The Development of the Soviet Economic System: An Essay on the Experience of Planning in the USSR*. Cambridge: Cambridge University Press, 1946.

Beamish, Rob. "Sport and the Logic of Capitalism." in Hart Cantelon and Richard Gruneau (eds.). *Sport, Culture and the Modern State*. Toronto: University of Toronto Press, 1982.

Bercuson, David. "Through the Looking Glass of Culture," *Labour/Le Travailleur* 7 (Spring, 1981).

Berger, John. *Ways of Seeing*. London: British Broadcasting Company and Penguin Books, 1972.

Berkman, Alexander. *The Bolshevik Myth (Diary 1920-1922)*. New York: Boni and Liveright, 1925.

Bogatikov, Vladimir. "The Trade Unions and the Popular Sports Movement." *The USSR: Sport and Way of Life*. Moscow: USSR Academy of Sciences, 1980.

Braverman, Harry. *Labor and Monopoly Capital: The Degradation of Work in the Twentieth Century*. New York: Monthly Review Press, 1974.

Brecher, Jeremy. "Uncovering the Hidden History of the American Workplace." *Review of Radical Political Economy* 10 (4, Winter 1978).

Brohm, Jean-Marie. *Sport—A Prison of Measured Time*. London: Ink Links, 1978.

Brown, Richard, et al. "Leisure in work: the 'occupational culture' of shipbuilding workers." in M.A. Smith, Stanley Parker and Cyril Smith (eds.). *Leisure and Society in Britain*. London: Allan Lane, 1973.

Burawoy, Michael. *Manufacturing Consent.* Chicago: University of Chicago Press, 1979.

Cantelon, Hart. *The Social Reproduction of Sport: A Weberian Analysis of the Rational Development of Ice Hockey Under Scientific Socialism in the Soviet Union.* Unpublished doctoral dissertation. University of Birmingham, 1981.

Cantelon, Hart. *Stakhanovism and Sport in the USSR.* Working Papers in the Sociological Study of Sports and Leisure II (2). Queen's University: Sports and Leisure Studies Research Group, 1979.

Clarke, John. "Capital and Culture: The Post-war Working-class Revisited." in John Clarke, Chas Critcher and Richard Johnson (eds.). *Working Class Culture— Studies in History and Theory.* Hutchinson, 1979, pp.238-253.

Clarke, J., Critcher, C., and Johnson, R. *Working-Class Culture: Studies in History and Theory.* London: St. Martin's Press, 1980.

Claudin-Urondo, Carmen. *Lenin and the Cultural Revolution.* Sussex: The Harvester Press, 1977.

Clement, Wally. *Hardrock Mining.* Toronto: McClelland and Stewart Ltd., 1981.

Constantine, Stephen. *Unemployment in Britain Between the Wars.* London: Longman, 1980.

Critcher, Chas. and Clarke, John. "The Sociology of Leisure: Review of the Conventional Wisdom," in Alan Tomlinson (ed.). *Leisure and Social Control.* Brighton Polytechnic, 1981.

Crombie, Geoff, R. *1926-1951 A Colne Festival.* Colne: M.M. Publishing Corporation, 1978.

Crook, Rosemary. "'Tidy Women': Women in the Rhondda Between the Wars." *Oral History* 10 (2, 1983), pp.40-46.

Cumbler, John. *Working Class Culture and Communities in America.* Connecticut: Greenwood Press, 1979.

Cunningham, Hugh. *Leisure in the Industrial Revolution c. 1780—c. 1880.* London: Croom Helm, 1980.

Dahrendorf, Ralf. *Life Chances—Approaches to Social and Political Theory.* Chicago: University of Chicago Press, 1979.

De Grazia, Sebastian. *Of Time, Work and Leisure.* New York: Twentieth Century Fund, 1952.

Delves, Anthony. "Popular Recreation and Social Control in Derby,1880-1850." in Eileen and Stephen Yeo (eds.), *Popular Culture and Class Conflict 1590-1914: Explorations in the History of Labour and Leisure.* Chicago: Harvester Press, 1981, pp.87-127.

Demeter, G.C. *Lenin: Ob okhrane zdorov'ya trudyaschikhsya i fizicheskoi kul'ture.* Moscow: Fizkul'tura i Sport, 1969.

Deutscher, Issac. "Russia." in Walter Galenson, ed. *Comparative Labour Movements*. New York: Prentice-Hall, Inc., 1952.

Dixey, Rachael. "The Playing of Bingo: Industry, Market and Working-class Culture." in Alan Tomlinson (ed.). *Leisure and Popular Cultural Forms*. Brighton Polytechnic, 1983, pp.52-67.

Dumazedier, J. *Sociology of Leisure*. Amsterdam: Elsevier, 1974.

Dunning, Eric (ed.). *The Sociology of Sport*. London: Frank Cass & Co. Ltd., 1971.

Dunning, Eric and Sheard, Kenneth. *Barbarians, Gentlemen and Players: A Sociological Study of the Development of Rugby Football*. Oxford: Martin Robertson & Co., 1079.

Edwards, Richard. *Contested Terrain*. London: Heinemann, 1979.

Edwards, Richard, Reich, Michael, and Gordon, David (eds.). *Labor Market Segmentation*. Lexington, Mass.: D.C. Heath, 1975.

Fisher Jr., Ralph Talcott. *Pattern for Soviet Youth: A Study of the Congresses of the Komsomol, 1918-1954*. New York: Columbia University Press, 1959.

Fulop-Miller, Rene. *The Mind and Face of Bolshevism: An Examination of Cultural Life in Soviet Russia*. London: G.P. Putman's Sons, Ltd., 1927.

Giddens, Anthony. *New Rules in Sociological Method*. New York: Basic Books, 1976.

Giddens, Anthony. *Studies in Social and Political Theory*. New York: Basic Books, 1977.

Gordon, David. *Theories of Poverty and Underemployment*. Lexington, Mass: D.C. Heath and LexingtonBooks, 1972.

Gosow, Borys. "Sport in Russia." *The Overland Monthly* 16 (October), 1890.

Gruneau, Richard. "Power and Play in Canadian Social Development." *Working Papers in the Sociological Study of Sports and Leisure* II (4). Queen's University: Sport Studies Research Group, 1979.

Gruneau, Richard. "Sport, Social Differentiation, and Social Inequality." in Don Ball and John Loy (eds.). *Sport and Social Order*. Reading: Addison-Wesley, 1975.

Guttmann, Allan. *From Ritual to Record*. New York: Columbia University Press, 1978.

Hall, Stuart. "Notes on deconstructing 'the popular'." in Raphael Samuel (ed.). *People's History and Socialist Theory*. London: Routledge and Kegan Paul, 1981, pp.227-240.

Hall, Stuart, and Jefferson, Tony, (eds.). *Resistance Through Rituals*. London: Hutchinson, 1976.

Hearns, Francis. *Domination, Legitimation and Resistance—the Incorporation of the Nineteenth-Century English Working Class*. Connecticut: Greenwood Press, 1978.

History of the USSR (in Three Parts). Moscow: Progress Publishers, 1977.

Hoch, Paul. *Rip Off the Big Game—the Exploitation of Sports by the Power Elite.* New York: Doubleday Anchor, 1972.

Hoggart, Richard. *The Uses of Literacy.* Harmondsworth: Penguin, 1958.

Howkins, Alan and J, Lowerson. *Trends in Leisure, 1919-1939.* London: Sports Council/Social Science Research Council, 1979.

Huizinga, Johan. *Homo Ludens: A Study of the Play Element in Culture.* Boston: Beacon Press, 1968.

Ingham, Alan. "Occupational Subcultures in the Work World of Sport." in Don Ball and John Loy (eds.). *Sport and Social Order.* Reading: Addison-Wesley, 1975.

Ingham, Alan. "Sport, Heroes, and Society: Issues of Transformation and Reproduction." in *Working Papers in the Sociological Study of Sports and Leisure* II (4). Queen's University: Sport Studies Research Group, 1979.

Johnson, Richard. "Culture and the Historians." in John Clarke, Chas. Critcher and Richard Johnson (eds.). *Working Class Culture.* London: Hutchinson, 1979.

Johnson, Richard. "Three Problematics: Elements of a Theory of Working-class Culture." in John Clarke, Chas Critcher and Richard Johnson (eds.). *Working Class Culture.* London: Hutchinson, 1979.

Jones, G. Stedman. "Working-Class Culture and Working-Class Politics in London, 1870-1900: Notes on the Remaking of a Working-class." *Journal of Social History* 7 (1974), pp.460-508.

Kealey, Gregory, S., and Warrian, Peter (eds.). *Essay in Canadian Working Class History.* Toronto: McClelland and Stewart, 1976.

Kealey, Gregory, in "Labour and Working Class History in Canada: Prospects in the 1980s." *Labour/Le Travailleur* 7 (Spring, 1981).

Krader, Lawrence. *The Dialectic of Civil Society.* Assen: Van Gorcum Press, 1976.

Krader, Lawrence. *A Treatise on Social Labour.* Assen: Van Gorcum Press, 1979.

Kuhn, Annette, and Wolpe, Anne Marie. *Feminism and Materialism* London: Routledge and Kegan Paul, 1978.

Kukushkin, G.I., (ed.). *Entsiklopedicheskii slovan 'po fizicheskoi kul'tura i sportu* (in Three Volumes). Moscow: Fizkul'tura i sport. Volume I, 1961; Volume II, 1962; Volume III, 1963.

Lane, Christel. *The Rites of Rulers: Rulers in Industrial Society: The Soviet Case.* Cambridge: Cambridge University Press, 1981.

Langdon, Steven. *The Emergence of the Canadian Working Class Movement.* Toronto: New Hogtown Press, 1975.

Lenin, V.I. *Imperialism: The Highest Stage of Capitalism: A Popular Outline.* New York: International Publishers, 1939.

Lenin, V.I. *On Culture and Cultural Revolution.* Moscow: Progress Publishers, 1966.

Lenin, V.I. *On the Soviet State Apparatus.* Moscow: Progress Publishers, 1969.

Lenin, V.I. *State and Revolution.* New York: International Publishers, 1969.

Lippert, John. "Shopfloor Politics at Fleetwood." *Radical America* 12 (July-August, 1978).

Lukashin, Yuri (ed.). *National Folk Sports in the USSR.* Moscow: Progress Publishers, 1980.

Lukes, Stephen. *Individualism.* Oxford: Basil Blackwell, 1973.

Luxton, Meg. *More Than a Labour of Love.* Toronto: The Women's Press, 1980.

Malcolmson, Robert W. *Popular Recreations in English Society: 1700-1850.* Cambridge: Cambridge, University Press, 1973.

Mandel, William M. "Soviet Marxism and Social Science." in Alex Simirenko editor. *Social Thought in the Soviet Union.* Chicago: Quadrangle Books, 1969.

Marcuse, Herbert. *Soviet Marxism: A Critical Analysis.* London: Routledge & Kegan Paul, 1958.

Markus, B. L. "The Stakhanov Movement and the Increased Productivity of Labour in the USSR." *International Labour Review* 34 (July-December, 1936) pp.5-33.

Marx, Karl. *Capital* I. Moscow: Progress Publishers, 1977.

Marx, Karl. "The Eighteenth Brumaire of Louis Bonaparte." in *Surveys from Exile, Political Writings, Volume 2.* Edited by David Fernback. Harmondsworth: Penguin, 1973.

Marx, Karl. *Grundrisse.* Harmondsworth: Penguin Books in association with New Left Review, 1973.

Mass Observation. "All-In, All-Out." in *Britain by Mass-Observation.* Harmondsworth: Penguin, 1939, pp.114-138.

McKay, Ian. "Historians, Anthropology, and the Concept of Culture." *Labour/Le Travailleur* 8/9 (Autumn-Spring, 1981) pp. 185-241.

McLellan, David. *The Thought of Karl Marx: An Introduction.* London: MacMillan, 1971.

Metcalfe, Alan. "Working Class Physical Recreation in Montreal, 1860-1895." in *Working Papers in the Sociological Study of Sports and Leisure* I (2). Queen's University: Sports Studies Research Group, 1978.

Metcalfe, Alan. "Organized Sport in the Mining Communities of South Northumberland, 1800-1889." *Victorian Studies* 25 (4, Summer, 1982), pp.469-495.

Montgomery, David. "The Past and Future of Workers' Control." *Radical America,* 13 (November-December, 1979).

Morton, Henry W. *Soviet Sport: Mirror of Soviet Society.* London: Collier Books, 1963.

Nettl, J.P. *The Soviet Achievement.* London: Thames and Hudson, 1967.

Nichols, Theo, and Beynon, Huw. *Living With Capitalism: Class Relations in the Modern Factory*. London: Routledge and Kegan Paul, 1977.

Nichols, Theo, and Armstrong, Peter. *Workers Divided: A Study of Shopfloor Politics*. London: Fontana, 1976.

Palmer, Bryan. "Classifying Culture." *Labour/Le Travailleur* 8/9 (Autumn-Spring, 1981/82).

Palmer, Bryan. *A Culture in Conflict: Skilled Workers and Industrial Capitalism in Hamilton, Ontario, 1860-1914*. Montreal: McGill/Queen's University Press, 1979.

Parker, Stanley. *The Future of Work and Leisure*. London: Paladin, 1972.

Parker, Stanley. *The Sociology of Leisure*. London: Allan and Unwin, 1976.

Parker, Stanley. "Work and Leisure: Theory and Fact." in J.T. Haworth and M.A. Smith (eds.). *Work and Leisure*. London: Lepus Books, 1975.

Parkin, Frank. "Strategies of Social Closure in Class Formation." in F. Parkin (ed.) *The Social Analysis of Class Structure*. London: Tavistock, 1974.

Parkin, Frank. *Marxism and Class Theory: a Bourgeois Critique*. London: Tavistock, 1979.

Pieper, Josef. *Leisure, The Basis of Culture*. London: Faber, 1952.

Plekanov, Georgi. *Selected Philosophical Works* (in Five Volumes). Moscow: Progress Publishers, 1981.

Pravda. (27.09.1922).

Proletarskaya Kultura (5), November, 1918.

"Protiv Boksa." *Vestnik fizicheskoi kul'turi* (No.1), Yanvar 1927 p.21

Rigauer, Bero. *Sport and Work*. New York: Columbia University Press, 1981.

Riordan, James. *Sport in Soviet Society: Development of Sport and Physical Education in Russia and the USSR*. Cambridge: Cambridge University Press, 1977.

Riordan, James. " Why Sport Under Communism?: The Physical Culture vs Sport Debate After the Russian Revolution." University of Bradford, n.d. (Mimeographed).

Roberts, Ken. *Contemporary Society and the Growth of Leisure*. London: Longman, 1978.

Roberts, Ken. *Leisure*. London: Longmans, 1970.

Roberts, Ken. *The Working Class*. London: Longmans, 1979.

Rogers, Rosemarie. "Normative Aspects of Leisure Time Behavior in the Soviet Union." *Sociology and Social Research* 58 (No.4 July, 1974), pp.369-379.

Roy, Donald. "Banana Time: Job Satisfaction and Informal Interaction." *Human Organizations*, 18 (1958).

Samoukov, F.D., Stolbov, V.V., and Toropov, N.I. *Fizicheskaya kul'tura i sport v SSSR*. Moscow: Fizkul'tura i sport, 1967.

Schmidt, Alfred. *The Concept of Nature in Marx*. London: New Left Books, 1971.

Seccombe, Wally. "Domestic Labour and the Working-Class Household." in Bonnie Fox (ed.), *Hidden in the Household*. Toronto: The Women's Press, 1980.

Seccombe, Wally. "The Expanded Reproduction Cycle of Labour Power in Twentieth Century Capitalism." in Bonnie Fox (ed.), *Hidden in the Household*. Toronto: The Women's Press, 1980.

Shipley, Stan. "Tom Causer of Bermondsey: a Boxer Hero of the 1980s." in *History Workshop—A Journal of Socialist and Feminist Historians* 15 (Spring, 1983), pp. 28-59.

Shneidman, N. Norman. *The Soviet Road to Olympics: Theory and Practice of Soviet Physical Culture and Sport*. Toronto: The Ontario Institute For Studies in Education, 1978.

Smith, M.A., Parker, Stanley, and Smith, Cyril. *Leisure and Society in Britain*. London: Allan Lane, 1973.

Sochor, Zenovia. "Soviet Taylorism Revisited." *Soviet Studies* 33(2), 1981, pp.246-264.

Sokolov, Ip. *Sistema trudovoi gimnastika* Moscow: Fizkul'tura i sport, 1922.

Spencer, Wilfred. *Colne As It Was—Photographs Selected and Introduced by Wilfred Spencer*. Colne: Hendon Publishing Company, 1971.

Stalin, Joseph. *Problems of Leninism*. Moscow: Foreign Languages Publishing House, 1954.

Stearns, Peter N. "The Effort at Continuity in Working-Class Culture." *Journal of Modern History* 52 (December, 1980) pp.626-655.

Stevenson, John and C. Cook. *The Slump*. London: Quartet Books, 1979.

Stolbov, V.V. and Chudinov, I.G. *Istoriya fizicheskoi kul'turi*. Moscow: Fizkul'tura i sport, 1970.

Thompson, E.P. "The Long Revolution I." *New Left Review* 9 (May-June, 1961).

Thompson, E.P. *The Making of the English Working Class*. 1968.

Thompson, E.P. "Patrician Society, Plebian Culture". *Journal of Social History* 7 (Summer, 1974).

Thompson, E.P. "Time, Work-Discipline, and Industrial Capitalism." *Past and Present* 38 (December, 1967).

Tomlinson, Alan. "It Puts a Spel on You: 'Knur and Spel' in Colne in the Twentieth Century." Unpublished paper delivered at Queen's University, 1982.

Trotsky, Leon. *The Revolution Betrayed: What is the Soviet Union And Where Is It Going?* New York: Pathfinder Press, Inc., 1972.

Trotsky, Leon. *1905*. Harmondsworth: Penguin Books, 1971.

Utechin, S.V. "Philosophy and Society: Alexander Bogdanov." in Leopold Labedz, editor. *Revisionism: Essays on the History of Marxist Ideas*. New York: Frederick A. Praeger, 1962.

Vucinich, Alexander. *Social Thought in Tsarist Russia: The Quest for a General Science of Society, 1861-1917*. Chicago: The University of Chicago Press, 1976.

Ward, Colin. "We Are All Historians Now." *New Society* 64 (1075, 23 June,1983), pp. 475-476.

Watson, Bill. "Counterplanning on the Shop Floor." *Radical America* 5 (May-June, 1971).

Whitson, David. "Factors in the survival of local games against the inroads of metropolitan culture: A Scottish case study." in Bruce Kidd. *Proceedings: 5th Canadian Symposium on the History of Sport and Physical Education*. Toronto: University of Toronto Press, 1982.

Williams, Raymond. *Culture and Society*. London: Heinemann, 1958.

Williams, Raymond. "Literature in Society," in Hilda Schiff (ed.). *Contemporary Approaches to English Studies*. London: Heinemann, 1977a.

Williams, Raymond. *Marxism and Literature*. London: Oxford University Press, 1972.

Willis, Paul. *Learning to Labour*. Westmead: Saxon House, 1977.

Willis, Paul. *Profane Culture*. London: Routledge and Kegan Paul, 1978.

Willis, Paul. "Shop-floor culture, masculinity and the wage form." in John Clarke, Chas. Critcher and Richard Johnson (eds.). *Working Class Culture*. London: Hutchinson, 1979.

Yovchuk, M.T. "Improvement of the cultural and technical standards of workers." in G.V. Osipov (ed.). *Industry and Labour in the USSR*. London: Tavistock Publications, 1966.

Zagladin, V.V. *The International Working-Class Movement: Problems of History and Theory* (in Five Volumes). Moscow: Progress Publishers, 1981.

Garamond Books:

- Argue, Gannagé, Livingstone: *Working People and Hard Times: Canadian Perspectives*
- Basran and Hay: *Political Economy of Agriculture in Western Canada*
- Bolaria and Li (eds): *Racial Oppression in Canada* (2nd. ed.)
- Brickey and Comack (eds): *The Social Basis of Law*
- Brym (ed): *The Structure of the Canadian Capitalist Class*
- Burrill and McKay: *People, Resources and Power*
- Cantelon and Hollands: *Leisure, Sport and Working Class Cultures*
- Centennial College English Faculty Association: *Writing for the Job*
- Dickinson and Russell: *Family, Economy and State*
- Gruneau: *Popular Cultures and Political Practices*
- Henderson: *The Future on the Table: From Liberalism to the Challenge of Feminism*
- Knuttila: *State Theories: From Liberalism to the Challenge of Feminism*
- Livingstone (ed): *Critical Pedagogy & Cultural Power*
- Moscovitch and Albert (eds): *The Benevolent State: Growth of Welfare in Canada*
- Niosi: *Canadian Multinationals*
- Olsen: *Industrial Change and Labour Adjustment in Sweden and Canada*
- Panitch & Swartz: *The Assault on Trade Union Freedoms* (2nd. ed.)
- Young (ed): *Breaking the Mosaic: Ethnic Identities in Canadian Schooling*

The Network Basic Series

- Acheson, Frank and Frost: *Industrialization and Underdevelopment in the Maritimes, 1880-1930*
- Armstrong and Armstrong: *Theorizing Women's Work*
- Armstrong et al: *Feminist Marxism or Marxist Feminism*
- Buchbinder et al: *Who's On Top: The Politics of Heterosexuality*
- Burstyn and Smith: *Women, Class, Family and the State*; Intro by Ng
- Cohen: *Free Trade and the Future of Women's Work*
- Duffy, Mandell and Pupo: *Few Choices: Women, Work and Home*
- Lacombe: *Ideology and Public Policy: The Case Against Pornography*
- Livingstone: *Social Crisis and Schooling*
- Lowe and Northcott: *Under Pressure: a Study of Job Stress*
- Luxton and Rosenberg: *Through the Kitchen Window: the Politics of Home and Family*
- Newson and Buchbinder: *The University Means Business*
- Ng: *The Politics of Community Services*
- Veltmeyer: *The Canadian Class Structure*
- Veltmeyer: *Canadian Corporate Power*
- White: *Law, Capitalism and the Right to Work*

Garamond Press, 67A Portland St., Toronto, Ont., M5V 2M9
(416) 597-0246